Prima Games
An Imprint of Random House, Inc.
3000 Lava Ridge Court, Suite 100
Roseville, CA 95661

WWW.PRIMAGAMES.COM

The Sims 3

PRIMA OFFICIAL GAME GUIDE

Written by Catherine Browne

Product Manager: Todd Manning

Associate Product Manager: Sean Scheuble

Copyeditor: Asha Johnson

Editorial Intern: Jenkey Hu

Design & Layout: In Color Design

Manufacturing: Stephanie Sanchez

Important:

Contents

Catherine Browne

Catherine grew up in a small town, loving the proverbial "great outdoors." While she still enjoys hiking, camping, and just getting out under the big sky, Catherine also appreciates the fine art of blasting the Covenant in *Halo* as well as arranging a perfect little village in *Animal Crossing*. (Seriously, you cannot just plant apple trees all willy-nilly. Neat rows, people!)

We want to hear from you! E-mail comments and feedback to

cbrowne@primagames.com

ISBN: 978-0-7615-6137-8

Library of Congress Catalog Card Number: 2008943293

Printed in the United States of America

09 10 11 12 GG 10 9 8 7 6 5 4 3 2 1

How to Use This Guide

The Sims™ 3 is a huge playground loaded with options, tools, and tricks for maximizing the happiness (or misery, if you have a touch of the dark side in you) of your Sims. Our guide will explain the essentials of moving into your new neighborhood such as furnishing a house, creating unique Sims, and developing skills or career. Here's how we've organized all of the information in this guide for easy reference:

Chapter 1: What's New explains all of the revolutionary and evolutionary features in *The Sims 3*. The newest chapter in *The Sims™* franchise offers improved tools for Sim creation, home building, and more.

Chapter 2: Creating a Sim helps you understand all of the new tools for fashioning Sims out of digital clay. Learn how to make physical changes to your new Sims and discover how assigning traits shapes their personalities.

Chapter 3: Creating a House digs into the building process. We show you how to use Build Mode and Buy Mode to erect your new house then build on to it when the Simoleons start rolling in. We also detail all of the existing lots you can move into if you want to jump into a pre-made life.

Chapter 4: A Day in the Life is all about the unfolding life of your new Sim. This chapter talks about getting settled in your house, meeting neighbors, and starting a job. Developing useful skills and exploring the town of Sunset Valley is also explained.

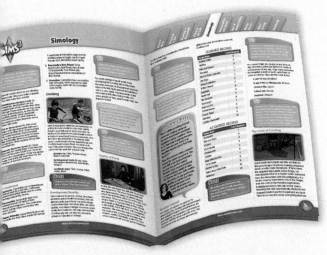

Chapter 5: Simology drills down into what makes your Sims tick. Every trait is detailed here and the effects they have not only on personality, but on jobs and relationships. Moods and moodlets are elaborated here, too, so you can keep your Sim happy. Goals and wishes are also detailed here.

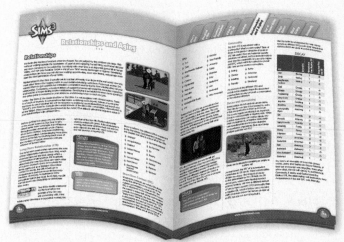

Chapter 6: Relationships and Aging talks about friends, romance, and families in Sunset Valley. Learn how social interactions affect your Sim's life. Plus, we offer tips for getting your groove on with a potential significant other.

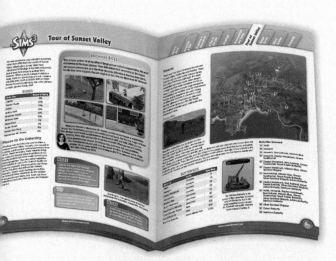

Chapter 7: Tour of Sunset Valley is where you'll find all of the necessary knowledge about Sunset Valley, such as store inventories, job sites, and communal locations.

Chapter 8: Design Corner highlights some professional lots created by Sims experts specifically for *The Sims 3*. Get your inspiration here!

How to Use This Guide

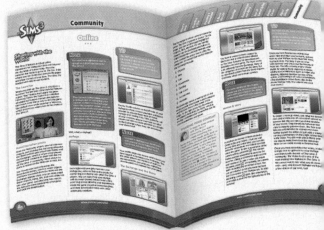

Chapter 9: The **Object Catalog** contains every single object you can buy for your Sims. Prices, effects, and depreciation are all detailed in here.

Chapter 10: **Community** details everything you can do wi the online world of *The Sims 3,* such as share screenshots and videos of your Sim stories.

What's New

● ● ●

The Sims franchise has inspired millions of people around the world to try out a second or third (or fourth) life on the other side of the computer screen. These alternate realities give players the chance to explore different personalities: whether it's an abundance of caution or an id gone wild. Thanks to the game's easy-to-use set of tools and a welcoming interface, fulfilling the dreams of Sims has become an engaging pastime. More than 100 million copies have been sold around the world, making The Sims the bestselling PC game of all time.

The Sims 3 is the next step in the continuing collective narrative. Each Sim has a story to tell and The Sims 3 provides the tools needed to explore that personal narrative and then let the entire world share in each unique story. No two Sims are ever alike, no matter how hard you attempt to adhere to the same decisions. Thanks to everything from a world of seemingly random opportunities, exciting careers, and individual evolving personality traits, each Sim is as unique as a child.

How will you explore the dreams and wishes of your Sims? Will you nurture them by making safe choices that always advance personal goals? Or will you follow the advice of authors across the centuries and "torture your darlings," presenting them with hardships that inspire true growth? These are the ultimate decisions that affect your experience with The Sims 3. And this guide will help you plan out every stage of your Sims' lives—although you know what they say about the best laid plans. Chance and happenstance—two of the greatest forces in this universe—can land in your lap at any moment and send you and your Sims on adventures you never imagined.

A World Without Limits

Create a Sim

Create a Sim returns in The Sims 3, but with a vastly expanded set of options and more possibilities than previous versions.

But there's more to a Sim than looks, of course. The Sims 3 uses a system of personality traits to define the behavior, wants, dislikes, and desires of your individual Sims. There are more than 60 different traits to assign your Sim and the number of possible traits per Sim changes with age—just as you would expect from any developing personality. For example, Child Sims have three traits, while toddlers and babies only have two.

Thanks to visual enhancements, Sims now look more real than ever, complete with softer curves and more features. You can now choose from more specific body details, like expanded skin tones options and body shapes. You can really zoom in on facial details, too, and change the shape of lips, cheekbones, noses, eyes, and more with a simple set of slider bars that instantly show you the results of your digital cosmetic surgery.

The traits are all based on actual real-life personality tics and tweaks, such as having a good sense of humor, being a vegetarian, or harboring just a touch of evil. When you assign these traits, you see the effect it has on your Sim right away, too. Assigning the Evil trait to a Sim results in a devious smirk and cackle. The Vegetarian trait makes your Sim triumphantly hoist an eggplant into the air as if it were manna from the heavens.

These specific traits not only define personality, but also shape the lifetime goals and wishes of your Sims. A Sim who is a natural cook, for example, will be more apt to want a culinary career and have a better developed Cooking skill. An athletic Sim will be happier pursuing an active lifestyle, such as running or playing sports.

> **NOTE**
>
> Some traits cannot be assigned to the same Sim at the same time, such as the Good and Evil traits. Creating a digital Sybil is a no-go.

Building Homes and Neighborhoods

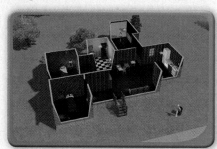

Your Sims are not the only means of expressing yourself and creating an exciting story—the place you hang your hat is a huge way to customize your Sims' lives. As in previous versions of *The Sims*, you can erect a home from scratch or move into an existing lot. There are hundreds of objects to buy and place inside your house as well as a host of landscaping options that let you truly make your home unique to your Sims. You must operate within your means, of course, and consider important financial ramifications before making big purchases. However, you need to also consider the needs and wants of your Sims. Specific items bring certain levels of happiness to Sims and help them develop skills.

> **TIP**
>
> Certain items are also absolutely essential for basic living, such as a tub or a toilet.

The Sims 3 is not a static world. Just outside your front door is a town that is alive with activity. There are dozens of Sims in your town, living their own lives, building careers, and running basic errands, such as going to the grocery store. Some Sims are friends you haven't met yet—others you may never share a laugh with, either. Over time, you will see relationships build and fall apart, families created, and neighbors age. So don't just

spend entire afternoons with your nose dee in a book. Get outside and mingle. Head to communal spots like the park and chat up th other Sims. Who knows what you'll find out there? Love has a strange way of coming ou of nowhere, after all.

Wishes, Skills, and Dreams

Life is a series of opportunities, and you are defined by the ones you pursue. In *The Sims 3*, hundreds of different opportunities slip in and out of reach depending on the personalities and goals of your Sims. Rarely will the same opportunity present itself to a similar Sim—or at least it w not happen in the same way or at the same time. The politically minded Sim may be aske to write his or her memoirs to bolster public opinion, while one with culinary inclinations may be asked to cater a special event at City Hall. Completing these opportunities results rewards, both financial and social.

> **NOTE**
>
> Most opportunities are time-sensitive. So keep an eye on the calendar when a new opportunity is dangled in front of you. Fortunately, failing to beat the clock does not result in any personal setbacks. You just don't earn whatever rewards were associated with the opportunity.

What's New

Creating a Sim

Creating a House

A Day in the Life

Simology

Relationships and Aging

Tour of Sunset Valley

Design Corner

Object Catalog

Community

opportunities are often related to the specific skills and careers of your Sims. Career choices are typically determined by the traits you assign your Sims, too. There are a variety of possible careers, such as cooking, writing, politics, and even a life of crime. You are not required to pursue a full-time career, though; 9-to-5 isn't for everybody. If you want to tackle other interests, just pick up a part-time job for income and then try out other activities like being an author or musician.

TIP

While on the job, you can also set your Sims' behaviors. While working at the local newspaper, for example, you can choose to brown-nose the boss in hopes of climbing the ladder faster. However, this risks affecting your relationships with your co-workers. You may inadvertently turn off the Sim of your dreams.

To make the most out of your career or personal pursuits, you must work on your Sims' skills. Every Sim has specific aptitudes depending on assigned traits, but you can also enhance your Sims' skills by performing activities such as reading educational books or practicing an instrument. Honing a specific skill is a good option instead of a career to give your Sim's life some drive and definition.

In addition to opportunities and skills, Sims are further defined by individual wishes. These wishes may be short-term goal or lifelong dreams. Your Sim will constantly come up with a series of wishes that you can choose to pursue or abandon. Simple goals may include getting a date or starting a book. By completing these wishes, you earn Lifetime Happiness points, the ultimate measure of a Sim's success. Lifetime Happiness points can be cashed in for special talents and skills. You can buy the ability to completely alter your

Sim's personality, for example. Try to maximize the Lifetime Happiness of all of your Sims so that when they get ready to shuffle off this digital coil, they go to that great beyond fulfilled and satisfied.

Moodlets

One of *The Sims 3*'s most interesting advancements is the introduction of the "moodlet," a real-time look at what your Sim is thinking and feeling right now. Moodlets will help you understand the needs and wants of your individual Sims in a variety of ways, such as letting you know when they are tired or need to use the restroom. Moodlets also serve as useful warnings, such as letting you know a Sim is getting unhappy about a messy house. Unless you clean up a bit, your Sim's overall mood will suffer. A happy Sim is a more productive and successful Sim, so let these moodlets guide you.

NOTE

Many moodlets are directly related to a Sim's traits. If your Sims is a loner, you are likely to see the "Too many people" moodlet while at a party. If you do not extricate your Sim from the party within a set amount of time, your Sim's overall mood drops.

Show the World

The Sims 3 is not meant to be a solitary experience. Every player will have unique Sims with individual narratives, so why not throw open the doors to your neighborhood and show the world what your Sims have been up to. *The Sims 3* includes easy tools for taking screenshots and video of your Sims and then uploading them right away to a central area for other Sims fans to see. The filming tools let you direct the story, enabling you to set up scenes as simple or complex as your imagination will allow. You can even add effects in post-production so your movies are

as unique as your Sims themselves. You can also share custom content with other players, such as fabric patterns.

BROWNIE BITES

As you might imagine, I've played quite a bit of *The Sims 3* to create this guide for you. I love that even after hours of playing, the game can still surprise me. Yes, I have complete control over the traits that make up my Sims' personalities, but they will occasionally do things or encounter situations I did not imagine. And when these new opportunities or wishes arise, it is then up to me to decide how the Sims will react to new information or experiences. Sometimes a new opportunity or desire will take your Sim in an unintended direction—which is pretty much how life works on this side of the computer screen, too.

But unlike the real world, *The Sims 3* does not punish you for trying out new things. There are no consequences for passing up opportunities or denying your Sims their little wishes. Because you're not threatened with the "wrong stick" at every step, you feel comfortable trying new things. My Sim wants to go on a date? Sorry, we need to concentrate on learning recipes tonight or else we'll never be a master chef. Right-click and shoo away such romantic distractions. And unlike something I would do when denied a wish, my Sim does not pout (or "malfunction," as my friends like to call my little...episodes). Life marches on as I nudge my Sim back toward the bookshelf to check out a newly acquired cookbook.

Creating a Sim

How long have you been *you*? Throughout your whole life, you've played one role, occupied one skin, and seen through one set of eyes. And while this life is indeed what you make of it, there is always an inherent human curiosity about what this world must look, taste, sound, and feel like to everybody else. In the simple town of Sunset Valley, you have the chance to indulge that curiosity. Actually, you have a million chances: to become a world-class chef, to build a magnificent home, to light up the stage as a pop singer, or just to finally bake the perfect batch of cookies. After all, dreams can come in any size. Sometimes the happiest moments in your life are the smallest victories.

But you cannot start on this alternate life without first creating a new Sim. Sims are the people that live inside this game; they are the vessels in which you live out a secondary life (or as many as you can successfully juggle). *The Sims 3* has a very powerful Create a Sim toolkit for developing and sculpting a variety of people of all shapes and sizes. You aren't just assigning hairstyles and shirts here, though. The Create a Sim process lets you really tinker with what makes your Sim tick by assigning traits. These different traits—and there are plenty to choose from—allow you to craft wonderfully unique personalities, all with their own life goals, wants, and needs. That's not to minimize the simple fun of picking out the right pair of shoes, though. Remember…the smallest victories are sometimes the best.

A New You

To some painters, a blank canvas is the most terrifying thing in the world. But to others, it represents nothing but opportunity and hope. Let's hope you approach the Create a Sim toolkit with the latter thinking. When you choose the Create a Sim tool, you are taken to a modest dressing room complete with a full-length mirror and a little sunlight.

The Create a Sim springboard. From here, you can create zillions of Sims to your own liking. All that limits you is your imagination.

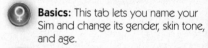

When you first dig into Create a Sim, you already have a Sim waiting for you, but this is just molding clay. You can accept this Sim if you like. You can also browse a collection of pre-made Sims by clicking on this button. You do not have to use these pre-made Sims as-is. You can drop one into the toolkit and then start shaping it to your liking. Maybe change those pajamas or put on a few pounds?

You can choose pre-made Sims of all ages, from toddler to elder, to create a bona fide insta-family.

To start tinkering with your soon-to-be-new Sim, use the five buttons on the left side of the screen to alter and adjust different facets of the Sim. Each button opens up a tab from which you can start making your changes. No change is permanent as long as you are inside the Create a Sim toolkit. Here are the five buttons/tabs and their functions:

- **Basics:** This tab lets you name your Sim and change its gender, skin tone, and age.

- **Hair:** Use this tab to change your Sim's hairstyle, which includes adding headgear.

- **Looks:** Go here to change the general appearance of your Sim's head and face, including making adjustments to chin, nose, eyes, and cheeks.

- **Clothes:** Select your Sim's basic wardrobe from this tab, including everyday wear, athletic garb, and formal clothes.

- **Personality:** This tab lets you assign specific traits to your Sim, choose personal favorites (food, music, and color), and select a Lifetime Wish.

NOTE

Why not test the fates and see what happens if you click on the little dice icon below the five tabs? This randomizes your Sim. Maybe you'll love what rolls onto the screen. And even if you don't, the randomized Sim may be a great launching pad for the tweaks needed to get your Sim "just right."

Basics

If you are going to fashion a Sim from the ground up, you always start at the first tab of the Create a Sim toolkit: Basics. This includes your Sim's name, age, and gender. From this tab, you can immediately name your Sim—but you can also wait to name your Sim until the end of the process. (Sometimes Liz just doesn't look like a Liz by the time you've selected hair, eyes, and whatnot.) Here, you also choose your Sim's gender and age. Gender has zero effect on your Sim's traits—just physical appearance and initial wardrobe. You can select your Sim's starting age from six different periods: toddler, child, teen, young adult, adult, and elder.

NOTE

Age does affect the number of traits you can give your Sim because longevity affects the development of a personality. A toddler gets only two traits, a child gets three traits, and a teen gets four.

You can also alter the general look of your Sim here, too. Skin tone is pretty self-explanatory. The body modifiers, however, let you change the overall shape of your Sim. The top slider bar controls weight. With just a swipe of your mouse, you can go from heavy in the drivers to lithe. Sliding the bottom bar adjusts muscle mass. If you move it to the right, you get some pretty impressive pythons. Sliding it to the left, though, turns the studly into the scrawny.

Hair

There are very few things we humans are more vain about than hair. In the Hair tab, you can select from a number of different hairstyles or opt for a hat. If you are creating a female Sim, you have a few extra options, such as working with long hair and different accessories like flowers or berets. After settling on a hairstyle, you select the color. *The Sims 3* comes fully loaded with lots of super-customizers, so if you aren't satisfied with normal hair colors, you can dive into a dye scheme and go wild. Give your Sim that purple dye job your folks told you would have you banished from the house when you were a freshman in high school.

After selecting a hairstyle, move on to the eyes—more specifically, eyebrows and eyelashes. There are a number of pre-created eyebrows that you can match to your hair. Using the slider at the bottom of the tab, you adjust the length of your eyelashes. The farther to the right you move the slider, the longer your lashes.

Looks

It's been said that the eyes are the windows into the soul. If that's true, then here's where you really do some soul-searching. The Looks tab is essentially a painless plastic surgery shop where you select eyes, noses, mouths, and everything else that makes up the human face. There are multiple sub-tabs inside the Looks tab. Each of these sub-tabs opens up a toolset for altering a specific part of the face: head shape, ears, eyes, nose, mouth, topical details (freckles, etc.), and make-up.

This tab is loaded with pre-made features to place on your Sim's digital mug, but you can also tweak many of these features via a series of slider bars. For example, after picking a set of lips for your Sim, you can adjust the widths and thickness of both the upper and lower lip.

TIP

Although this is just a quick start helper for getting you into the world of *The Sims 3*, take some time to tinker with all the different sliders that shape facial features. You'll be surprised at how closely you can create yourself or your friends.

Clothes

Do clothes truly make the (wo)man? If so, then you can make and remake your Sim five times over in the clothing tab of the Create a Sim toolset. Grown Sims get five different sets of clothes: everyday, formal, sleepwear, athletic, and swimwear. Depending on the gender and age of your Sim, your choices change in this tab. The everyday clothing is what your Sim will wear normally when just living life during normal waking hours. You can select individual tops and bottoms or zero in on a complete outfit.

The other clothing sets are used for specific occasions. Formal is good for dates or high society get-togethers. Sleepwear is what your Sim automatically switches into at bedtime. Athletic is good for lounge wear or when you are participating in a sporting activity. Swimwear is for, well, swimming. You set a default outfit for each of these categories from the available choices, but you can easily change the outfit colors.

NOTE

The "*" button toggles viewing custom content only. To customize clothing, click on the brush and palette.

Check out how you can dig down and really customize something like this bikini. You can select patterns, different colors, or even import your own textures.

Create a Style

Truly, there are few limits in *The Sims 3* save for your imagination, and the Create a Style tool is proof of that. You are not limited to just the fashions in the initial wardrobe, although it's easy just to pick from them and get right into the game. But if you click on the little paint palette after selecting an outfit, you can really turn on your inner fashion designer and stitch together an individual look for your Sim. You can apply various patterns to an article of clothing, from geometric shapes to different fabric textures like denim. And you can also change the colors, targeting sleeves, collars, and the main body of the piece of clothing.

Here's how the Create a Style tool breaks down:

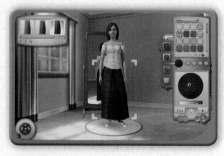

1. **Patterns:** Use the pull-down menu to select from different pattern categories, such as abstract and geometric.

2. **Elements of Pattern:** These color circles are individual parts of the pattern. Click a circle to change the color of that part of the pattern or texture.

3. **Colors:** Depending on how you choose to look at colors, they appear here. Clicking on the different colors changes the selected element.

4. **Color Palette:** View individual colors in small boxes.

5. **Color Wheel:** View colors on a wheel to see how they blend together.

6. **Color Numbers:** Use hex values to assign colors to elements of your outfits.

Let's turn this regular summer dress into a houndstooth classic.

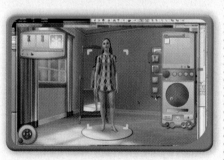

A plain nightie becomes a unique piece of sleepwear if you choose a pattern for the main body and then use the color wheel to make some matching trim.

> **TiP**
>
> There is zero cost to modify an article of clothing, so dig in and start mixing and matching colors and patterns to assemble your own special closet. You'll definitely be the only Sim in town with your duds!

Personality

Let's keep up this "old saw" motif: Never judge a book by its cover. No matter how beautifully (or beautifully bizarre) you made your Sim, it's what's on the inside that is truly going to shape his or her fortunes in Sunset Valley. You assign each Sim a handful of traits (the actual number is entirely dependant on the age of the Sim) from a considerable list of heralded behaviors, character flaws, quirks, and other idiosyncrasies. While you are always the puppeteer, pulling the strings on your Sim's activities, these traits create the basis for your Sim's personality and goals.

Traits

Traits affect your Sim's guiding desires and core personality. Your selections here stick with a Sim throughout life, so think about potential repercussions and choose wisely. Little things can have big consequences depending on how you manage your Sim's life. If you select the Flirt trait from the list, your Sim will naturally be on the prowl for romance. This could be helpful in either developing a bustling social life or landing a mate for starting a household. (However, marriage and kids does not end the Flirt trait. Maybe that will cause a little trouble later?) But there are also traits that affect the more mundane aspects of life. Selecting the Bookworm trait means the Sim is an avid reader and will gravitate toward books instead of the TV or the computer during free time.

Some traits also affect your Sim's mood. Mood is fully explained in the Simology chapter, but just understand that mood affects your performance in life, such as on the job. If your Sim is in a good mood, chances are strong your Sim will do better. One of the things that affects your mood is sleep. A lack of sleep means your Sim may make get cranky or excessively drowsy. The Light Sleeper trait means your Sim wakes up at the slightest noise. That threatens your Sim's mood. Sounds bad, right? Well, being Light Sleeper might not be so bad if a burglar breaks into your Sim's house.

You may choose from the following traits:

 Absent-Minded

 Ambitious

 Angler

 Artistic

 Athletic

 Bookworm

 Brave

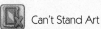 Can't Stand Art

 Charismatic

 Childish

 Clumsy

 Commitment Issues

 Computer Whiz

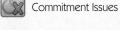 Couch Potato

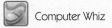 Coward

 Daredevil

 Dislikes Children

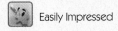 Easily Impressed

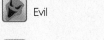 Evil

 Excitable

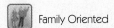 Family Oriented

 Flirty

 Friendly

 Frugal

 Genius

 Good

 Good Sense of Humor

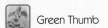 Great Kisser

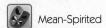 Green Thumb

 Grumpy

 Handy

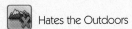 Hates the Outdoors

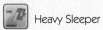 Heavy Sleeper

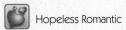 Hopeless Romantic

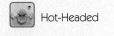 Hot-Headed

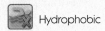 Hydrophobic

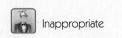 Inappropriate

 Insane

 Kleptomaniac

 Light Sleeper

 Loner

 Loser

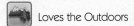 Loves the Outdoors

 Lucky

 Mean-Spirited

 Mooch

 Natural Cook

 Neat

 Neurotic

 Never-Nude

 No Sense of Humor

 Over-Emotional

 Party Animal

 Perfectionist

 Schmoozer

 Slob

 Snob

 Technophobe

 Unflirty

 Unlucky

 Vegetarian

Virtuoso

Workaholic

As you can see, not every trait on this list is positive—but that's only human. We are not wholly virtuous beings and so you should consider not making your Sim a total white knight. Drop one nasty or questionable trait in the mix. Not only will it keep you from being a goody-two-shoes, but it will also open up Lifetime Wish avenues that you may find more rewarding than something attainable only by a straight arrow. Be honest with yourself. You probably have a little Grumpy, Snob, or Mooch in there, don't you? So why not transfer these traits to a Sim and see how they play out in a world where you don't necessarily have to control them as much as you do in this one.

TIP

Your traits are not entirely permanent. In fact, you can change an entire set of traits if you buy the Mid-Life Crisis with the Lifetime Happiness points you accumulate by meeting your Sim's goals and fulfilling their small wishes.

The Natural Cook trait aids your Sim's ability to make food. Most Sims can cook to a certain degree—at least, they can make quick meals like cereal—but the Natural Cook trait means your Sim will pick up on culinary nuances at a quicker pace. Expect them to perfect cooking talents faster and never botch a recipe.

NOTE

Some traits cancel each other out, such as Artistic and Can't Stand Art. If you select one of these two, you cannot select the other. Some ages also eliminate possible traits. For example, a toddler cannot be Flirty.

For a full explanation of each trait and Lifetime Wish, please see the Simology chapter.

Lifetime Wishes

Traits also affect your Sim's Lifetime Wish. The Lifetime Wish is the overall goal for your Sim. There will be plenty of smaller goals along the way, but the Lifetime Goal is the over-arching goal of your Sim's virtual life. Lifetime Wishes can include reaching the top spot in a specific career or mastering a craft, such as gardening.

Depending on the traits you select, you have up to five Lifetime Wishes to choose from. Different combinations or specific single traits result in specific Lifetime Wishes. Install the Angler trait in your Sim and the Presenting the Perfect Private Aquarium wish becomes available. The requirement for this wish is to have at least 10 perfect fish in fishbowls. Because the Angler trait makes your Sim especially adept at the rod and reel, you have a much greater chance of achieving this Lifetime Wish before the inevitable conclusion of your Sim's life.

NOTE

Young Sims—toddlers, children, and teens—do not have Lifetime Wishes. Instead, they have a litany of short-term goals (like get a Play Table). When they grow into young adults, they can select Lifetime Wishes.

Favorites

In addition to selecting traits and a Lifetime Wish, you can assign your Sim personal favorites that become topics of conversation when socializing with other Sims. Having favorites in common with another Sim is a useful tool for connecting on a deeper level. You can assign your Sim a favorite food, favorite music, and favorite color. Here are some the possible favorite foods:

 Belgian Waffles

 French Toast

 Pancakes

 Fruit Parfait

 Autumn Salad

 Grilled Cheese

 Veggie Burger

 Tofu Dog

 Mac and Cheese

 Peanut Butter and Jelly

 Ratatouille

 Spaghetti with Veggie Sauce

 Stu Surprise

 Cobbler

 Cookies

 Key Lime Pie

There are seven possible favorite music style for your Sim:

 Electronica   Indie

 Pop   Classical

 Latin   Kids

 Custom Music (you pick!)

These are the available favorite colors for your Sim:

Blue	Spiceberry
Aqua	Violet
Turquoise	Lilac
Spice Brown	Pink
Green	Hot Pink
Irish Green	Red
Lime	White
Gray	Sea Foam
Orange	Yellow
Purple	Black

And, finally, you can adjust your Sim's voice. There are three choices for your Sim. Click on each to hear a sample of their Simlish. Once you make your selection, use the slider bar to alter the pitch and tenor of the voice to your personal liking

Family and Aging

ou can either start out completely single or nter the world of *The Sims 3* with a family nd friends. After creating a Sim, click on the dd a Sim button to start building a new m. You can work in any of the age groups, om toddler to elder to build anything from a assive clan to a young twosome just starting ut in life.

amily

he quickest way to grow your Sim family is o have a child. Once you have created two ms of adult age, one male and one female, ou can pair them up and automatically enerate a child. Basic laws of genetics ck in and some physical attributes from a arent Sim are passed along to the child. For xample, if one parent has blond hair, there a good chance the child will also have lond hair.

To create a child from two adult Sims, choose the "Make a Child" option. This brings up a window with your available adult Sims. After selecting two adult Sims, the child appears below. You can adjust the gender of the child and the age. Actually, you can do some pretty wild stuff here. You can create a child but then age the child into an elder right away and then place it in the household. The elder is not the couple's child anymore, but it's an interesting way to play with genetics.

> **NOTE**
>
> You do not need to "keep" the first child created by your couple. Keep pressing the button with the pacifier to roll the dice and create a new child. When you see the one you like, finalize it with the checkmark.

Once you have created a second Sim—or a variety of Sims—you can start assigning their relationships. The most basic relationship you can assign between two Sims is "housemates." Any of the Sims of any age can be housemates. If you do not assign this relationship between members of a household unit, it is ascribed by default. You can make two adult or young adult Sims spouses (different genders is not a requirement for spouses). Younger Sims like teens or children can be assigned as siblings.

Drag-and-drop Sims on top of each other in the family tree to assign relationships, such as spouses, siblings, or housemates.

> **CAUTION**
>
> As you might imagine, there are some limitations with relationships within the accepted social order. You cannot make a toddler the parent of an elder, nor may an elder be the spouse of an adult. (No May-December romances right off the bat. You can, however, make them housemates and go from there.)

Aging

Sims are not static creatures. They age just like you and I do, but certainly at an accelerated pace. As each day inside the game passes, your Sims age a little bit, inching ever closer to the next phase in life. Each life phase lasts for a specific number of days.

- ◆ **Toddler:** 7 days
- ◆ **Child:** 7 days
- ◆ **Teen:** 14 days
- ◆ **Young Adult:** 21 days
- ◆ **Adult:** 21 days
- ◆ **Elder:** 16 days minimum

When a toddler ages into a child, the Sim earns an extra trait. This continues with each phase until the young adult phase, which has five traits—the maximum for a Sim. Traits are carried over from the young adult through the elder unless a specific trait is incompatible with the age. The final phase in life, the elder phase, culminates with the inevitable: death. However, as long as there are children in a household of Sims, the household will continue to thrive.

> **NOTE**
>
> Take good care of your Sims, especially as they close in on age transitions. If a toddler is happy or a child/teenager is getting good grades, you get to choose the extra trait. If these Sims aren't doing so hot at the transition, you don't select the extra trait and you risk getting saddled with a negative trait.

Creating a Sim

Making Catherine Browne

Let's create a sample Sim together, Catherine Browne, whom you will see throughout the majority of this guide. Of course, you will create your own personalized Sims, but follow along here to see how you can recreate yourself—or the version of yourself you see inside your own head.

Physical Appearance

Okay, that is just not what Catherine Browne looks like. (For one thing, I wouldn't be caught dead in those capris.) But when you start creating your Sim, you get a completely random Sim standing in front of the mirror. That's your canvas. So, to start turning myself into a Sim, I first name myself. I then must choose my age. I choose "young adult" from the six possible categories. And since I get a sunburn if I even think about Arizona, I slide the skin tone pretty far to the left.

Okay, now it's time to practice what I preach as far as being honest with yourself if you're turning yourself into a Sim. Let's just slide that weight bar a little to the right. What can I say? I am good at baking and what's the fun of baking if you aren't going to try what you made?

I have a pretty basic hairdo—kinda short but kinda not, so I'm choosing this style from the Hair tab. And then I'll select black hair, making a slight color adjustment for purple highlights.

My brows aren't nearly that thick, so let's do some virtual plucking and get those down to size. Also, I like my long eyelashes, so I'll add those in, too.

Next, I'll sculpt my general head shape. I have a nice little pointy chin, so let's add that and make sure my ears don't stick out too far.

This randomized Sim had eyes uncannily similar to mine, so I'll leave those alone but change the eye color to green.

I like this set of lips. They're full, like mine.

Now it's time for a little make-up. I keep my eye shadow mildly conservative now (my sophomore year photo looks like a cosmetics ad), so I'll choose the first option here. I use earth tones, so I picked brown from the menu. I also gave my lips a little color. I don't use rouge, so I left that make-up choice alone.

Alright, that's me. Now, let's start picking out a wardrobe.

lothing

Everyday Wear: I like basics for just normal everyday stuff, so I'll select a simple black urtleneck and a pair of jeans I wish I could afford in the real world.

ormal: I like black dresses for formal occasions, so I'll pick this one and then hope I can one day ctually find this dress at the mall. I wear it well. Or, at least my Sim does.

Sleepwear: Nothing fancy for me. This basic nightie is perfect.

thletic: A simple hoodie and running pants works r me. And those pink low-tops and just too cute.

Swimwear: Thank goodness for boy shorts.

Accessories: And finally, some plastic-rimmed glasses that drive those librarian-lovin' boys wild. At least, that's what I tell myself.

Personality

Now it's time to assign five traits to my Sim. I chose Bookworm, Good Sense of Humor, Hopeless Romantic, Lucky, and Natural Cook. (Yes, I didn't choose any perceived negative traits, but I let you see me in a bikini so I think I'm entitled to let myself off the hook here, okay?) As a result of choosing these traits, my Sim is always on the lookout for romance, has a knack for making other Sims laugh, has good fortune, and is something of a wizard in the kitchen. These traits gave me the following five Lifetime Wishes to choose from:

Golden Tongue, Golden Fingers:
Master the Charisma and Guitar skills

Celebrated Five-Star Chef:
Reach level 10 of the Culinary career track

The Culinary Librarian:
Learn every recipe

Illustrious Author:
Master the Painting Skill or master the Writing Skill

Hit Movie Composer:
Reach level 10 in the Music career track (symphonic branch)

I chose the Illustrious Author since it fits me so well and works in tandem with the Bookworm trait. Now that I have my Sim all finished, I can choose my favorites (grilled cheese, pop music, and spiceberry) and finalize my Sim. Now I'm ready to move into my new digs and start an alternate life in Sunset Valley.

Oh, I suppose I ought to move in with my husband, Chris.

Creating a House

A Sim's home is his castle—and in the case of *The Sims 3*, that can be quite literal. You have unparalleled freedom to create a dream house for your Sim household out of brick or mortar, stone or wood and then fill it with the things your Sims need...and perhaps a few things they don't really need but that are cool to have anyway. As with sculpting an individual Sim in Create a Sim, you have very few limits when building a home, save for your initial bank account when you first move in. Once you start gathering Simoleons with a steady job or lucrative hobby (or maybe even luck into a major payday), you can add on to your house or move into a new one, working your way up to the proverbial castle.

(Seriously. You can build a castle in *The Sims 3*. With a moat.)

However, if you don't want to construct a house right away, or just prefer a lived-in home, you can choose from a vast number of pre-built lots to buy. Some of these lots might be a touch expensive from the get-go, though. And if you want to try out not just a pre-owned house, but a pre-owned *life*, you can assume control of a host of families and individuals. Each pre-set household has a different scenario that offers some structure to your narrative, as well as a pre-built house. Use these scenarios as inspiration for when you decide to build your new life from the ground up.

Moving Day

So, it's time to move into your new neighborhood and begin life in Sunset Valley. You have two options when it comes to housing your Sims: buy a furnished lot or build a brand new house on an empty lot. Buying a furnished lot is the quickest way to get started, and you can always move to your own digs after you've advanced your career and built up a bank account. But if you feel like getting your hands dirty by laying concrete and tacking up drywall, then read on. We'll take you through the essentials of building a house from scratch and filling it with the objects you will need for a contented Sim.

TIP

When you move into Sunset Valley, the amount of Simoleons afforded to you is based on the number of Sims in the household. A single Sim gets §16,000. Each additional adult adds §2,000. A teen adds §1,500 while a child adds §1,000. Toddlers add only §500 to the household.

Building Basics

Building a house is easy and intuitive with *The Sims 3* toolsets. With just two tool bars, you can construct a house. The first tool is Build Mode, selectable by clicking on this icon or pressing F3:

The other is Buy Mode. Click on this icon or press F2 to enter Buy Mode:

 Each of these icons expands a toolbar with a shared interactive menu of construction options and a specialized catalog of purchasable items, depending on which mode you selected. Build Mode grants access to the materials for assembling a house, such as laying a foundation and erecting walls. Build Mode also lets you select outdoor features, like trees and landscaping tools. Buy Mode is where you purchase objects to fill your house, such as bathtubs and couches.

A universal set of tools applies to both Build Mode and Buy Mode. Use these buttons to manipulate on-screen construction and purchases, as well as make interface adjustments that will help you with building and object placement. Here is the function of each button, as well as the keyboard shortcut for each:

Hand Tool H: The Hand tool is used to move objects around your house or property. To grab an object, left-click on it. To drop the object, left-click again. To rotate an object, click and hold the left mouse button on the object and move the mouse around. The object will spin to face the cursor as you drag the mouse.

NOTE

One major upgrade to *The Sims 3* is the ability to use freeform placement and rotation. Hold the Alt key while using the Hand tool, and objects won't stick to the grid as you move them, and they won't snap to specific rotation angles while you're rotating them. Instead, they will move smoothly during placement and rotate to any angle, allowing for extremely precise and natural-looking floor plans.

Create a Style R: This tool enters the Create a Style menu, which allows you to customize objects. Personalize objects with new colors and textures. The Create a Style tool is fully explained later in this chapter.

Eyedropper Tool E: The Eyedropper tool copies the color or texture of an object so you can easily place it on another object. You can also use this tool to copy decorations, such as wallpaper. Click on the tool and then click on the object/surface you want to replicate. Then, click on the object/surface you want to copy the texture or color set to.

Sledgehammer Tool K: Want to destroy an object, wall, or floor? Click on the Sledgehammer tool. Once the cursor turns into a hammer, click on an object to immediately destroy it. Simoleons are instantly returned to your bank, minus any depreciation.

NOTE

The Sledgehammer tool has also been upgraded from previous *The Sims* games: it now can delete many things at once. To delete multiple objects, click down on an object you want to delete, then hold and drag over an area, and it will delete any objects within the highlighted area. If you want to delete lots of flooring, click and hold on a floor tile, then drag out over an area of floor tiles you'd like to delete. Similarly, if you'd like to delete many walls, click on a wall segment, then drag along an entire wall or drag out over multiple rooms to delete all the walls in the highlighted area.

Day/Night Toggle L: Want to see how a room or outdoor setting will look at night? This toggle instantly snuffs out the sun or toggles it right back on. Use this tool when placing lights around your property to see if you are casting the right amount of illumination on your stuff.

Indoor Grid Placement G: The Indoor Grid is useful for placing objects inside a room or planning your wall layout. Clicking on this button drops a white grid over your property. To remove it, just click the button again.

Undo C + Z / **Redo** C + Y: To undo or redo your previous design decisions, use these buttons. There is no penalty for undoing an object placement. However, once you exit either Build Mode or Buy Mode, you can no longer undo your previous choices.

Build Mode

1 **Foundation**	6 **Windows**	11 **Fences**	15 **Trees/Flowers/Shrubs/Rocks**
2 **Floor Covering**	7 **Roof**	12 **Gates**	16 **Terrain Tools**
3 **Walls**	8 **Stairs**	13 **Pool**	17 **Water Tool**
4 **Wall Covering**	9 **Arches**	14 **Fireplaces**	18 **Terrain Paints**
5 **Doors**	10 **Columns**		

TIP

Remember what we said about being able to build a castle with a moat? You can use the Terrain tool to sink a moat around your house. As the ground sinks, it automatically fills with water.

Build Mode is how you physically construct a house or make changes to your property. Use Build Mode to lay down a foundation, build walls, and place a roof on your house. Want to add a window or wallpaper? Head to Build Mode. You can also buy doors and windows in Build Mode. Landscaping tools are available from the Build Mode tab, such as the ability to physically manipulate terrain.

Buy Mode

1 **Show Room**	5 **Kitchen**	8 **Living Room**	11 **Kids Room**
2 **Sort by Room**	6 **Bathroom**	9 **Dining Room**	12 **Outdoor**
3 **Household Inventory**	7 **Bedroom**	10 **Study**	13 **Objects**
4 **Object Buy Field**			

Outfit your new digs with the latest furniture and gadgetry in Buy Mode. You can view this object catalog either by room or by object function. To view by rooms, click on the small room icon in the upper-left corner. To sort by function, click the chair icon. (To view your current household inventory, click on the box.) Once you choose how to view the catalog of objects, just click on individual items to see a close-up view of the object, a short description, price, and any functions or pertinent properties.

Buying a Lot

After creating your Sim or choosing a pre-made one from the Sim Bin, you and your §20,000 can look over Sunset Valley's available properties. You see a mix of empty lots and pre-fabricated houses. The pre-fab houses are more expensive than empty lots, and the prices go up even more if you choose to purchase a pre-fab house that is completely furnished.

When shopping for a lot, scroll around the overhead map of Sunset Valley and check out all of your available options. Lots with a purple diamond are empty. Purple house icons indicate a pre-fab house for sale. Lot prices are affected by the distance from the city center and size. Choice real estate

in exclusive neighborhoods such as the trio of empty lots on Redwood Parkway also goes for a premium. Buying one of these lots will set you back immediately, but location is everything. If you live in the tony part of town, you are likely to attract some pretty swank friends.

> **Tip**
>
> Moving onto a beachfront lot has the extra benefit of giving your Sims the Beautiful Vista moodlet, which is a major happiness bonus. See the Simology chapter for a full list of moodlets.

When you click on a lot, you see the address and lot size. The larger the lot, the more expensive i is. It's not necessarily a bad thing to splurge on your lot, because while you may build a humble abode at first with your paltry earnings, you will likely need the room to expand in the future.

> ### BROWNIE BITES
>
> Consider your Sim's interests when buying property. If you have a Sim with social traits, move into a bustling neighborhood with other families. Or if your Sim likes to fish, why not move into the lot on Waterfall Way? Into gardening? Buy a lot with extra space for horticultural studies. Skimping on land at the beginning of your game is rarely a good idea. You can always make more money and build out a house or buy cool doodads to fill it with later on. Land, on the other hand, is a premium commodity in Sunset Valley.

Lot Prices

Marker	Price	Street Name	Size
A	§14,700	15 Summer Hill Court	60 x 60
B	§6,800	477 Sunnyside Blvd.	29 x 29
C	§2,700	9 Sun Song Ave.	19 x 30
D	§5,400	180 Redwood Pkwy.	40 x 30
E	§5,400	130 Redwood Pkwy.	40 x 30
F	§3,000	100 Redwood Pkwy.	24 x 29
G	§1,800	365 Oak Grove Rd.	30 x 30
H	§2,400	74 Landgraab Ave.	30 x 40
I	§1,800	99 Landgraab Ave.	29 x 29
J	§3,200	415 Skyborough Blvd.	40 x 40
K	§2,400	17 Maywood Lane	29 x 39

Marker	Price	Street Name	Size
L	§1,200	18 Maywood Lane	19 x 29
M	§3,200	299 Skyborough Blvd.	40 x 40
N	§3,384	53 Waterfall Way	35 x 47
O	§1,800	2200 Pinochle Point	30 x 30
P	§1,800	2250 Pinochle Point	30 x 30
Q	§1,800	2300 Pinochle Point	30 x 30
R	§1,800	2350 Pinochle Point	30 x 30
S	§1,200	2450 Pinochle Point	29 x 30
T	§2,400	2400 Pinochle Point	40 x 30
U	§3,200	2500 Pinochle Point	40 x 40

Creating a House

Build Mode

So, you've decided to build your own place in Sunset Valley. Construction day is here and you are ready to break ground. Erecting a house in Sunset Valley is much easier than real life because the only contractor you need is your mouse. Let us take you through the process of building a basic, single-story house. While building a house, you should be acquainted with these two buttons, located near the camera controls right on the main section of the toolbar:

 Change Wall Mode [Home] **and** [End]: Toggle through three different views of your house—walls down, cutaway walls, and walls up.

 Change Floors [Pg Up] **and** [Pg Dn]: Scroll up and down the different floors of your house with these two buttons.

Walls down view

Cutaway walls view

Walls up view

> ### TIP
> To build a second story in a house, use the Change Floors buttons to go up a story and lay down a floor.

Laying Down a Foundation

Once you purchase a lot, it's time to plan out your house. If this is your very first house and you are working with the Simoleons afforded at the beginning of the game, you need to think small. Frugality is a beneficial state of mind when planning your first house—if you blow all of your Simoleons on a monstrous foundation right away, you won't have an adequate amount of money left over to fill the house with essential objects. So, throttle back those mansion-sized dreams (for now) and lay down the foundation for a modest house. Foundation is just §4 per square.

To lay the foundation, click on the actual foundation pictured under the house in the Build Mode menu. This turns the cursor into an arrow tool for creating the foundation. To stretch the foundation across your lot, hold down the left mouse button. When you have the foundation set up, release the mouse button to instantly pour the cement. You can extend the foundation is different directions by laying down extra pieces. You absolutely do not have to make the foundation a rectangle.

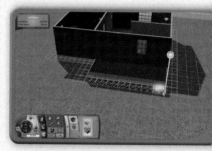

There are two types of foundations, too. The second is the deck foundation. Use this foundation to create simple or elaborate outdoor decks for your Sim's house. You can use the diagonal tool to create walkways through a garden or around a uniquely shaped pool.

Both the regular and deck foundations can be used to create a flat surface over uneven terrain. Use the Change Floor button to raise or lower the working level when laying foundation. If you have a drop-off on your property, foundations are perfect for building houses overlooking a bluff. Multi-layered decks are quite attractive, too. Just make sure you connect the multiple stories with a set of stairs.

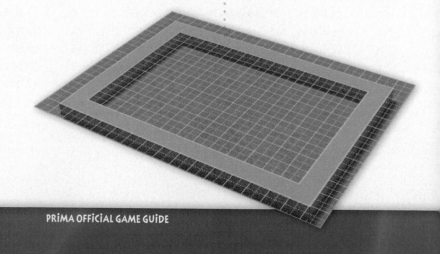

BROWNIE BITES

You can use the foundation to create a basement under your house. I found this is particularly useful if you have a large household of Sims living under one roof. To create a basement, you need to either work on already lowered terrain or sink the terrain yourself with the Terrain tools in Build Mode. To create a basement with the foundation, follow these simple steps:

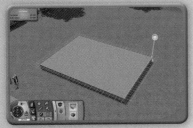

1. Lay a foundation slab with the Foundation tool.

2. Next, hold down [Control] to "hollow out" the foundation, leaving a ring of foundation to serve as the walls of your basement.

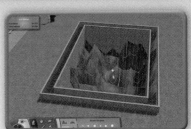

3. Switch to the Terrain tools in Build Mode (more on those in a moment) and sink the terrain as deep as you want the basement.

4. Use Change Floor to drop down to the level you want to designate as the floor of the basement and then switch over to the Level Terrain tool from the Terrain tools kit. Level the entire floor of the basement by dragging the tool over the sunken terrain.

5. When the terrain is flat, you now have the outline of your basement. Drop a layer of foundation into the basement along the bottom level. Now you can dress up the basement with flooring and paint or paper the walls. Or you can leave it all dank and creepy-like. Your choice.

6. Don't forget to install some stairs leading down to your basement. Once you have built the ground floor on top of your basement, connect the two stories with stairs.

Walls

After laying the concrete, it's time to put up some walls. Return to the main Build Mode tab by clicking on the arrow to the left of the foundation options. Now, click on the wall of the house in the Build Mode menu. The cursor changes to an arrow with a small wall icon on top. You now have three ways to erect walls:

 Create Wall: Create walls manually by dragging the cursor along the edges of a foundation or directly across it.

 Create Room: Erect four walls to instantly create a room. Drag the cursor across the foundation to expand the pre-made room.

 Create Diagonal Room: This option creates a whole room, but does so along the diagonal of the square grid. Use this option to create unique rooms.

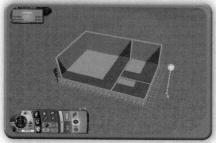

For this basic house, let's just create three separate rooms. Later, we'll make a wall to divide the kitchen from the living room.

There is no limit to the number of walls you can create—only your pocketbook controls that. Walls are §70 per panel. However, you need to create rooms large enough for a Sim to actually function inside. Shuffling your Sims into a broom closet will make them unhappy in record time. You need to make rooms large enough to fulfill needs, such as a bathroom that can fit a tub, sink, and toilet, or a bedroom that can at least host a bed.

TIP
Hold [Shift] to switch between Create Wall and Create Room. When you release [Shift], you automatically return to Create Wall.

Walls are required to build additional stories on to your house. To build a story or room on top of an existing story, you must have enough load-bearing walls to support the upper story. You cannot build a story on top of a room that's too big to support the weight of the upper floor. If you meet resistance while building an upper story, add an extra wall or column to the lower floor to increase support.

NOTE
You must install stairs to allow your Sims to reach the upper story.

NOTE
One of the coolest new features in Build Mode is the ability to drag walls to resize rooms. To do this, select the Hand tool and move your cursor over a wall (it also works with fences, decks, and foundations). If a green arrow appears, then you can click and hold, and then drag back and forth to resize the room. This is especially handy once you've built out an entire room and realize you need more space because it not only moves the walls, but it also fills in all the correct floor and wall patterns you've chosen. And it will move objects for you as well!

Wall Coverings and Floors

No Sim wants to live in a house with exposed cement slabs and naked drywall, so decorate these surfaces with wall coverings and flooring. (In fact, there is a negative moodlet called Unfinished Room that docks your overall mood.) Dozens of wall covering options range in price from §4 to §12 a panel. There are both interior and exterior wall coverings, but nobody is going to tell you that you cannot put siding in your living room. The wall coverings are divided into the following categories:

◆ Paint	◆ Masonry
◆ Wallpaper	◆ Rock & Stone
◆ Tile	◆ Siding
◆ Paneling	◆ Misc.

Click on a swatch of wall covering to see a larg[e] sample of the texture.

NOTE
You can choose to paint one panel at a time or paint all contiguous panels. The same choice is available for flooring.

Floor coverings are priced between §4 and §21 per square. There are multiple flooring categories that span carpeting to stone. The categories for floors are:

◆ Carpet	◆ Masonry
◆ Tile	◆ Linoleum
◆ Wood	◆ Metal
◆ Stone	◆ Misc.

TIP
Mix and match different floorings to create cool effects—especially in the same room. Try running wood along the walls and then fill in the center of a room with carpeting. Or mix carpet textures. Or make a checkerboard out of different types of stone.

Doors

Once you create the outer walls of a house or a room, you need to give your Sims access. You can either install a door or place an arch. Always place a door leading from the exterior to the interior of the house to discourage burglars or overly curious Sims from just wandering into your humble abode.

To install a door or arch, click on the door or arch picture in the Build Mode tool. Select the desired door or arch from the list of available options and then place it on the wall you desire.

CAUTION

Just leaving an open panel in a wall does not make a door or arch. These objects are required to differentiate one room from another.

Glass doors serve two purposes. Not only do glass doors allow access to a room or house, but they also allow in outside light, which many Sims find pleasing.

Windows

Windows are more than just decoration; they allow daylight into a house, which cuts down on the need for electrical lights. Sims can read by daylight if a couch is placed close enough to a window, for example. There are many window options in Build Mode, including massive windows the size of entire wall panels. These windows let in a lot of light, so if you have a Sim attuned for the outdoors, consider placing sizeable windows like this in your house so they can at least appreciate the greenery just beyond the four walls.

Stairs and Railings

The primary function of stairs is to connect two separate levels inside a house or connect an upper story (deck, etc.) to the ground outside a house. Stairs cost between §10 and §120 per segment. To create stairs, click on the stairs in Build Mode and then click on the place you want to start the staircase. Inside a house, the stairs will automatically "clamp" to the next level up. There must be sufficient room for the stairs in order to successfully purchase and install them. If the marker around the base of the stairs is red, there is not enough room for the stairs or they are not correctly connected to a landing on an upper story.

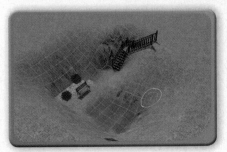

You do not have to build stairs in one single set when building on terrain. You can create connected stairs that make turns at landings by dragging in one direction on the terrain, then dragging in another direction without letting go. Outside, stairs automatically alter terrain to fit. If you have a lot on uneven ground, installing stairs on a slope is an attractive way to give your Sims easy access to all levels of the sloping surface. You can also use the "Stair Width" slider to determine how many tiles wide you'd like the stairs to be when you place them.

NOTE

You can have railings automatically added to stairs, choose your own railings, or opt for no railings at all.

Columns

Columns are both attractive and functional. An artfully placed column can really class up a room. However, columns are incredibly practical for load-bearing purposes. If you want to create an outdoor balcony on your house, use columns to support it. Columns can also be used inside a house to support an upper story above a large room. (Maybe you want a small ballroom on the third floor of your house?) Different columns support different areas of upper floors. The cheapest column, Column Contempo, can also support a four by four grid of flooring above it. The Column de Mish can support five by five.

NOTE

The prices of columns vary from §70 to §450.

Roof

No house is complete without a roof. When you first select roofs from the Buy Mode menu, you are dropped into Autoroof, which will place your desired roof on your house with a single click of the mouse. However, you can turn Autoroof off and manually place the roof on top of your dwelling as well as adjust the height with the slider bar.

There are 10 roof types (from flat to dome) and a host of roof textures. You can also choose diagonal roofs, such as a gabled roof. Roofs are free to put on your house, so experiment without worry of losing any Simoleons with roofing decisions you later regret.

TIP

At first, just use Autoroof to complete you house. When you expand your house or build a new, larger one, you can try out different kinds of roofs, or even mix-and-match for some pretty cool effects.

Fireplaces

Like columns, fireplaces are both decorative and functional. Some fireplaces must be installed next to a wall, but there are freestanding fireplaces like the Combustion Junction. Installing a fireplace in your house automatically runs a chimney up through the roof. You can share a chimney by installing fireplaces directly above and below each other on different floors of a house. Fireplaces can also be installed outside, too. They are attractive centerpieces of decks or outdoor sitting areas.

Fireplaces add Fun to a household and provide new interaction options (expensive fireplaces even have the ability to customize the color of the flames!) that affect your Sim's mood. To start a fire, click on it and choose the Light Fire option. When the fire is going, you can poke the fire to keep it going, which amuses your Sim. You can also warm your Sim by the fire for a comforting mood lift.

Before your Sim leaves home, make sure you put the fire out. If you leave a fire going while you are out, you risk setting the house on fire.

You can try to extinguish the flames yourself, but if you have installed a smoke alarm, the fire department will show up to help put ou the fire.

TIP

Handy Sims can fix up fireplaces with a special Fireproof upgrade so your house is never in jeopardy. For more information about the Handiness skill and possible upgrades, please see the Simology chapter.

Starting a fire induces the Cozy Fire moodlet, which adds 10 to your current mood. Warming your Sim by a fire induces the Warmed moodlet, which adds 25 to your current mood. You don't even need to stay next to the fire to enjoy the moodlet.

Gates and Fences

Fences make good neighbors. To add a fence to your property and create a yard or designated gardening space, choose the Fence tool from the Build Mode menu. There are several types of fences to choose from, priced from §5 to §165 per panel. Fences ar as simple as small rails on the ground (which a Sim can easily step over) to elaborate brick walls with a touch of dignified ivy. Fences can be laid out just like walls, including the ability to select the Create Yard option to automatically create a four-walled area by stretching the cursor across the ground.

NOTE

You can place fences on uneven terrain. However, you cannot build a fence on steep inclines or declines.

Decorate fences with outdoor lighting from Buy Mode. Lights can only be placed on fence posts, though.

You can also add gates to give Sims a way in and out of yards and gardens with tall fences. Gates cannot be placed on uneven terrain. There is also no rule about a fence needing to match a fence, although Sims definitely have an appreciation for complementary decor.

Swimming Pools

A swimming pool = instant party. Or, if your Sims love the outdoors, a good swim will increase their good mood. To build a swimming pool, choose the pool from Build Mode and stretch it across the ground just like you were laying a foundation. The swimming pool costs §80 per square, making it an expensive addition to a house, but the pool is a great way to meet people or give friends something to do in the sunshine.

Once you build a pool, you can install a ladder, which is selectable from the Pool Objects menu just below the Create Pool option. The Aquatic Ascent Ladder costs

§315, so make sure you have sufficient funds in your budget or else your pool will remain an attractive body of chlorinated water until you have §315 to spare.

NOTE

In addition to the ladder, you can add a pool rules, sign, a pool light, and a mosaic to the bottom of the pool.

Also, you do not need a ladder to get in and out of the pool. Sims can now exit the pool anywhere.

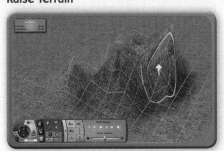

The Sea Underwater Pool Lights let you safely swim after dark. Which can be very romantic, by the way...

Terrain Tools

Terrain tools let you perform effortless landscaping that would normally require use of a bulldozer and earthmover over on our side of the screen. These tools let you sink ground, build mounds, and create ponds with just a click or two of the mouse. To use Terrain tools, select them from the Build Mode menu.

Raise Terrain

The Raise Terrain tool lets you lift the ground and create mounds, berms, or other inclines on your property. After selecting the Raise Terrain tool, choose the brush shape (circle or square, then size) as well as the brush softness, which affects the level of jaggedness on your newly created peaks. After selecting the shape and softness of your Raise Terrain

tool, run the new cursor over the ground and click the left button to lift the ground. Hold the button to keep pulling the terrain upward.

Lower Terrain

The Lower Terrain tool works exactly like the Raise Terrain tool, except this option sinks the ground to create holes or declines on your property. Like the Raise Terrain tool, you select the shape and size of your cursor and then adjust the softness of the terraforming.

Soften Terrain

Shifting terrain up and down can result in some pretty harsh-looking landscapes. To smooth over the rough edges and create a more inviting yard, run the Soften Terrain tool over your raised or sunken ground.

Level Terrain

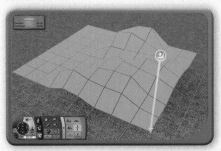

Want to flatten the surface of raised or lowered terrain? Use the Level Terrain tool. After selecting this tool, use the Change Floor button to raise or lower the "level" you are working on. Then, drag the Level Terrain tool over the landscaping you want to flatten out. Terrain that appears green will be leveled once you release the left mouse button.

25

Creating a House

Water Tool

The Water tool works similarly to the Lower Terrain tool, except that the hole created in the ground automatically fills with water. This is the easiest way to build a pond on your property. Hold the mouse button down to keep sinking a pond or move the cursor around your property while holding the left mouse button to increase the size of the pond.

> **NOTE**
> Sims will not swim in ponds, so don't think you can get away with building a cheap swimming pool via the Water tool.

Flatten Lot

Need to undo any of your terrain-altering landscaping? Hit the Flatten Lot tool to completely zero out any inclines and declines, turning the lot into a perfectly flat surface.

Terrain Paints

The default terrain on the ground is grass. However, you can easily change that with the Terrain Paints tool on the Build Mode menu. This tool lets you replace grass with basic flowers, gravel, sand, and other ground textures. After selecting Terrain Paints, choose the size and shape of your brush and the

softness of the edges around the brush. Then, select the desired texture. Once these are chosen, sweep the brush cursor over your property and press the left mouse button to lay down the new terrain.

Create a nice path to your front door with the Slate Stones texture.

The Raked Sand texture turns your backyard into a zen paradise.

Foliage

The exterior of your house can be further beautified by foliage such as trees, shrubs, and flowers. You can also buy rocks to place around your property to create a serene scene—or maybe a mystical stone circle? Trees cost between §65 and §400. Shrubs run between §5 and §95, making them much more affordable than trees. (They also take up much less room.) Flowers retail between §1 and §45. Any of these features can be arranged into artful landscapes or randomly placed on a lot to replicate the wild.

> **NOTE**
> You do not need to worry about upkeep on basic plants like shrubs and flowers in The Sims 3.

Buy Mode

There's just no way around it: everybody loves *stuff*—and in The Sims 3, there is a lot of it you can buy and place inside and outside your house to make your Sims happ Buy Mode is where you go to instantly shop for your Sim's furniture, appliance, and decorating needs.

> **TIP**
> Buying news objects in Buy Mode can positively affect your Sims' mood. When a Sim enters a room with two or more new objects, it gets the New Stuff! moodlet.

When you enter Buy Mode, the action is temporarily paused so you can browse without penalty. Your Sims are more than happy to wait while you shop for them. Wh you buy an object, the Simoleons are not automatically deducted from your account. It's not until you place the object on your lot that the Simoleons disappear from your account. Now, while you are in Buy Mode, you can return an object without losing any Simoleons by using the Sledgehammer tool However, the moment you step out of Buy Mode and back into life, you must factor depreciation into the sell-back value of your objects.

When you're placing an object in the house, the space needed to properly interact with th object appears around it. If the markers arour the object are green, the object can be placed If the markers are red, you cannot place the object there.

What's New

Creating a Sim

Creating a House

A Day in the Life

Simology

Relationships and Aging

Tour of Sunset Valley

Design Corner

Object Catalog

Community

TiP

Want to place an object anywhere, at any angle? Hold [Alt] while holding down the left mouse button and moving the mouse. Now you can rotate an object in very small increments.

DEPRECIATION AND APPRECIATION

As soon as you buy an object and then exit Buy Mode, the object loses value. The immediate value hit is significant, but not devastating: 15 percent. With each additional day, the object loses more value: 10 percent per day. The value of an object finally bottoms out at 40 percent of its original value. So, if you bought the SimmerChar Dual-State Stove for §400, the object would lose §60 on the first day. The next day, it would lose another §40. If you sold the object back after two weeks of use, you would get §160 back.

However, not everything in this world goes down in value upon purchase. Some art actually increases in value. And if your Sim is an artist, the paintings created on the easel will also grow in value over time. The masterworks of a true artist will skyrocket in value, so it can definitely pay to work on those painting skills.

BILLS

Every Monday and Thursday, the postal worker drops off a stack of bills in your mailbox. You have to pay approximately §6 for every §1,000 of stuff you own. For example, if you spent §14,500 on building and objects, your bills will come out to around §85. So keep this in mind when shopping. To pay your bills, click on the mailbox and choose the Pay Bills interaction or choose the Auto Bill Pay option.

You cannot ignore bills and hope they go away. You can pick up bills from your mailbox and attend to them in a timely manner. Bills change color as you ignore them, indicating the growing need to attend to them. Here's the color chart:

1 day old: Yellow

2 days old: Orange

3 days old: Red

If you do not pay your bills within three days—the normal bill cycle—you can count on a visit from the Repo Man on day four. The Repo Man will enter your house without warning and take objects without mercy until he has reached the number of Simoleons you currently owe. Once you enter day four of bills, you cannot quickly pay them and shoo away the Repo Man. It's too late by that time.

Rooms

You can have as many rooms in your house as your Simoleons allow, but some rooms are essential for your Sims to have a happy life: bathroom, bedroom, and kitchen. There are, of course, other rooms that would be absolutely appreciated by your Sims, such as a living room, dining room, or study, but these three are required for your Sim to live a functional life.

NOTE

The Objects Catalog chapter contains examples of each type of room and a full list of all objects associated with different rooms, such as kitchen, bedroom, and study.

Bathroom

The bathroom is positively critical for your Sims' well-being. Without a place to attend to hygiene and bladder needs, your Sims will not be able to function properly in polite society. You must install a toilet so your Sims can relieve themselves in a timely manner. A bathtub or shower is also essential for keeping clean. If your Sims do not wash on a regular basis, not only with their overall mood suffer, but relationships with friends and work will also take a hit. Install a sink and mirror in the bathroom, too, so your Sim can brush teeth as well as primp and pose. Looking good is often akin to feeling good, you know.

Creating a House

Kitchen

Other Rooms

When you create a bathroom, make sure you leave enough room along the side of the bathtub for a Sim to bend over and turn on the faucet. If you put something too close, like a counter, just use the Hand tool to move it over and create the needed space.

Bedroom

Sims need their beauty rest. After a long day of work or play (or, hopefully, a nice combination of both), Sims get sleepy. While a Sim can take a catnap on a couch, to get the kind of rejuvenating rest needed to greet a whole new day and effectively perform at work, Sims need a bed. A modest bed will do the trick at first. You can place other useful objects in the bedroom, such as a dresser, but the bed is your top priority.

Sims do fancy checking themselves out. If you have a little money to spare, put a mirror in the bedroom. A dresser is useful, too, because it lets Sims change their outfits.

Sims need to keep hunger at bay to function, and that means they need to eat food. If Sims get too hungry, not only does their mood greatly suffer, but they can eventually pass out and lose valuable time recovering. Build a small kitchen for starters, with a refrigerator, stove, and sink. A dishwasher is useful to be sure, but dishes can be easily cleaned in the sink at first. A fridge by itself is not exactly helpful after a few days, so make sure you hit up the grocery store for food, especially if you plan on being a cook. You can also dine out, but it is much cheaper to eat at home.

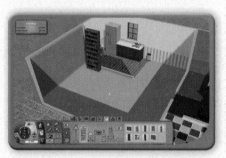

The kitchen does not need to be its own room with a door. It can just be a small nook off the living room to save money and space. However, noise from the kitchen will wake Sims within earshot, especially Sims who are light sleepers.

TIP

If your Sim is going to pursue a career in cooking, a kitchen is absolutely essential. Splurge on this room at the expense of other parts of the house.

As mentioned, there are several other rooms to create in a house, as indicated by the different categories of objects for sale in Buy Mode. If your Sim is going to be a writer, a separate study with a bookcase and computer is particularly useful. If your Sim household has children, build rooms for the wee ones so they have a place to call their own. A dining room is not a necessity, but in larger households, it is a great place for the household to come together and socialize.

You can also mix furniture from different rooms in Buy Mode—there is no hard and fast rule about a bookcase from the study collection having to be placed inside an actual study. Preserve money and space in the beginning by fusing rooms. A single Sim can afford to have a bookcase and computer in the living room.

NOTE

Many objects have properties that affect the mood of your Sim or are directly related to skill development. Object properties are fully detailed in the Object Catalog chapter.

Design Alternatives

When you click on an object category and start browsing through available objects, don't get too fixated on the immediate appearance or color choice of the objects. Most objects have several different design options, which appear in a small box when you left-click on a specific object. To choose one of the design alternatives, just left-click on that particular color scheme and it will be applied to the object when you place it on your lot.

Scroll through all the different object designs before settling on a purchase. And if none of these designs please you, then use the Create a Style tool to customize it to your liking.

HOUSEHOLD INVENTORY

You do not need to store all of your belongings in your house all of the time. You have a household inventory you can use to temporarily store unused objects. To store objects, left-click on the Household Inventory button. This expands a large inventory bar across the bottom of the screen. Now, use the Hand tool to drag objects into the Household Inventory bar. You can take objects out of the inventory by dragging items back into your lot. The Household Inventory is particularly useful when moving to a new house. When you choose to move and take your belongings with you, all of the objects are placed in Household Inventory.

Create a Style

So, you just bought a bed for your house, but you want to change the color of the duvet cover? It's easy to accomplish this design feat with the Create a Style tool. The Create a Style tool for changing the appearance of an object works quite similar to making adjustments to a Sim's clothes in Create a Sim. To change the colors or textures, left-click on the Create a Style button (the palette). Now, right-click on the object you want to alter.

When the Create a Style toolkit appears on the screen's right side, you see the current colors and textures used in the currently selected object. In the case of this bed, the pattern for the duvet cover, the wooden frame textures, and the metal knobs on the bed all appear on the pane to the right. To make changes to any of the textures, left-click on the desired texture. Now, you can either adjust the color with the color wheel or color palette or select a different texture from the texture box in the top-right corner.

The textures are divided into several categories, such as wood, metal, abstract, and geometric.

NOTE

To save a customized object, just click the folder icon in the upper-left corner, right below all of the pre-set versions of the object. Now you can grab a replica of it at any time.

If you want to make objects in a room match, you can easily apply the same textures and patterns from one object to another by

grabbing the texture pane and dragging it on to the object you want to match. You can either pull the entire set of textures on to the new object or grab a single texture (such as the wood from the bed frame) and then drag it on top of the piece of furniture you want to match. In this case, pulling the wood texture from the bed onto the dresser changes the pattern so the set now matches.

When you drag a pattern onto another object with multiple textures, you must designate which pattern you want to replace.

BROWNIE BITES

Take your time and have fun with the Create a Style tool. This is one of the easiest ways to customize the game to reflect your tastes and sensibilities. My favorite color is purple, so I really dug in and created a house that reflected my love for all things purple. I didn't go nuts and splash lavender, violet, and eggplant all over everything, but the Create a Style tool made it simple to place purple highlights in little nooks and crannies. It truly personalized the place and made it representative of me.

Furnished Lots and Pre-Set Lives

Sometimes, starting from scratch can be overwhelming, so why not ease a little stress by moving into a furnished house—or even a furnished life? Sunset Valley is a mature town with lots of developments and interesting households for you to investigate and even take control of in certain situations. If you are just starting *The Sims 3*, checking into a pre-built house is a good way to get ideas for your own dream house. Some of these furnished lots are pretty elaborate and may introduce design ideas you might have never considered before stepping over the threshold of these properties.

You can also skip Create a Sim entirely and jump into a life-in-progress with existing households in Sunset Valley. Each household has its own situation and scenario that gives the story some structure. As you try to fulfill the wishes and wants of the pre-built households, you will learn a lot about skill development, career management, and the general social structure of life in Sunset Valley. And if you choose, you can ignore the presented scenario and take these households in an entirely different trajectory. Their world is your oyster.

Finished Lots

Finished houses can be purchased either empty or completely furnished. Furnished homes are more expense than unfurnished homes, which puts a lot of them out of range of first-time buyers.

Marker	Property Name	# of Bedrooms, Bathrooms	Unfurnished Price	Furnished Price	Street Name	Size
A	Myrtle Bungalow	1br, 1ba	§17,408	§20,620	3 Sun Song Ave.	30 x 20
B	Mosquito Cove	1br, 1ba	§16,061	§22,273	36 Sim Lane	30 x 40
C	Pre-Fabulous	1br, 1ba	§9,970	§12,082	55 Water Lily Lane	20 x 30
D	Shotgun Style	2br, 1ba	§12,133	§15,020	58 Water Lily Lane	30 x 40
E	The Monotone	1br, 1ba	§12,290	§14,945	72 Water Lily Lane	20 x 30
F	"El" Urban Sprawl	2br, 1ba	§17,124	§23,279	60 Maywood Lane	40 x 30

Myrtle Bungalow

Mosquito Cove

Pre-Fabulous

Shotgun Style

The Monotone

"El" Urban Sprawl

Sunset Valley Households

Sunset Valley has a number of households that have already moved in and are waist-deep in their own complicated lives. Every household or life situation you can take control of is listed in this section, complete with all of the necessary information you need before slipping into the skins of these busy Sims. As mentioned, each household has its own scenario that you can attempt to unravel and complete, or you can just take over the household and live their lives however you please. You never know what trouble you might get into when you deviate from the set desires of your newly acquired household. (Trouble isn't always a bad thing, by the way. Some of the best fun in life comes from getting into—and out of—trouble.)

NOTE

There are many pre-made households you can select and play with, too. These households are not exclusive to Sunset Valley. They can be used in all towns associated with *The Sims 3*.

NOTE

Each household has a different difficulty rating (one through six). Six is the toughest difficulty. The reasons for the household's difficulty rating are partially explained by the scenario description.

NOTE

Certain parcels of land have amazing views that give Sims on them the Beautiful Vista moodlet. The following houses/lots give this mood boost: Alto, Crumplebottom, Frio, Koffi, Landgraab, Ursine, Wan-Goddard, and Wolff.

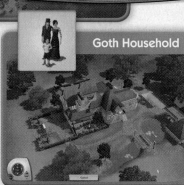

Goth Household

Goth Manor

Difficulty: 3
Budget: §50,000

Scenario: The Goths have lived in tow since time immemorial. The aura of glo from the nearby cemetery suits them, can a young boy named Mortimer gro up to be well-adjusted in such a place

House Name: Goth Manor
Address: 13 Skyborough Blvd.
Lot Size: 60 x 60
Rooms: 3br, 3ba

Unfurnished Cost: §129,943
Furnished Cost: §195,134

Marker	Household Name	Marker	Household Name	Marker	Household Name
A	Goth	I	Single Moms	Q	Roomies
B	Landgraab	J	Crumplebottom	R	Kennedy
C	Alto	K	Wolff	S	Alvi
D	Langerak	L	Wan-Goddard	T	Bachelor
E	Bunch	M	Ursine	U	Clavell
F	Wainwright	N	Frio	V	Andrews
G	Jolina	O	Koffi	W	Hart
H	Keaton	P	Working Friends	X	Steel
				Y	Sekemoto

Landgraab Household

Landgraab Estate

Difficulty: 3
Budget: §75,000

Scenario: The Landgraabs are old money (Nancy's family more or less founded the town), so it was no surprise that when she married Geoffrey, it was Geoffrey who changed his last name, not Nancy. Will young Malcolm be a mild-mannered doctor like his father or a voracious business tycoon like his mother?

House Name: Landgraab Estate
Address: 10 Summer Hill Court
Lot Size: 60 x 60
Rooms: 3br, 4ba

Unfurnished Cost: §203,724
Furnished Cost: §310,740

Alto Household

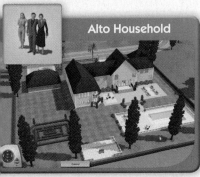

Villa Alto

Difficulty: 3
Budget: §75,000

Scenario: The Altos are new money. Their unscrupulous business practices have gotten them far in this town. Unofficially, they own most of the local shops. But how did their daughter become such a Goody Two-Shoes?

House Name: Villa Alto
Address: 20 Summer Hill Court
Lot Size: 60 x 60
Rooms: 2br, 2.5ba

Unfurnished Cost: §138,426
Furnished Cost: §272,848

Langerak Household

Tileicious

Difficulty: 4
Budget: §3,400

Scenario: Kaylynn Langerak cleans up after her brother and stay-at-home dad while her mother works all day. Now Kaylynn's Aunt Zelda has arrived with half-dead plants in tow and things are messier than ever.

House Name: Tileicious
Address: 14 Sierra Tango Street
Lot Size: 30 x 40
Rooms: 4br, 3ba

Unfurnished Cost: §92,472
Furnished Cost: §133,095

Wolff Household

Lone Wolff Manor

Difficulty: 2
Budget: §25,000

Scenario: Both the arts and having children are very important to Morgana Wolff, but she has just learned that her new husband, Thorton, actively dislikes both. Oops. Can these newlyweds save their young marriage? Should they even try?

House Name: Lone Wolff Manor
Address: 505 Sunnyside Blvd.
Lot Size: 40 x 40
Rooms: 1br, 4ba

Unfurnished Cost: §126,663
Furnished Cost: §217,093

Bunch Household

Peep's Peak

Difficulty: 5
Budget: §3,300

Scenario: Here's the story: two working parents juggle family, household chores, and their careers while their four children run wild. What is the right balance for this household of six to stay sane?

House Name: Peep's Peak
Address: 16 Maywood Lane
Lot Size: 40 x 30
Rooms: 4br, 4ba

Unfurnished Cost: §35,628
Furnished Cost: §51,694

Wainwright Household

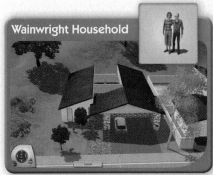

Minihaus

Difficulty: 2
Budget: §2,900

Scenario: Susan and Boyd are techno-geniuses who spend all of their available time with electronics. When their daughter, Blair, was a child, they bought every toy she asked for in the hopes that she would amuse herself and give them more free time for their hobbies. Now that Blair has moved out on her own, the Wainwrights are thinking of converting her old room for the next project.

House Name: Minihaus
Address: 53 Maywood Lane
Lot Size: 30 x 20
Rooms: 2br, 1ba

Unfurnished Cost: §35,869
Furnished Cost: §74,065

Jolina Household

House Plan B

Difficulty: 1
Budget: §1,000

Scenario: Jamie Jolina is as intelligent as she is beautiful. Can she prove to the world that two traits can coexist?

House Name: House Plan B
Address: 91 Landgraab Ave.
Lot Size: 30 x 20
Rooms: 2br, 1ba

Unfurnished Cost: §24,264
Furnished Cost: §30,496

Single Moms Household

Asilomar

Difficulty: 4
Budget: §3,700

Scenario: Fiona Marsh is used to living alone with her teenage daughter, River. But when Fiona's best friend needed a place to live with her own young daughter, Fiona readily invited the two to live in her home. Will Molly be the perfect housemate or Fiona's biggest regret?

House Name: Asilomar
Address: 330 Oak Grove Road
Lot Size: 30 x 30
Rooms: 3br, 2ba

Unfurnished Cost: §38,795
Furnished Cost: §63,850

Wan-Goddard Household

Raggio del Sole

Difficulty: 2
Budget: §2,100

Scenario: Pauline and Hank are certain that they will be 2-gether 4-ever becau they have so much in common: parties, the beach, and music. The only questic is whether or not they can maintain the lifestyle.

House Name: Raggio del Sole
Address: 1 Sun Song Ave.
Lot Size: 20 x 30
Rooms: 2br, 1.5ba

Unfurnished Cost: §36,629
Furnished Cost: §49,773

Keaton Household

Low Fat Ranch

Difficulty: 2
Budget: §4,500

Scenario: Avid outdoorsy Sims, Marty and Justine Keaton both have active careers and active hobbies. What effect will the impending arrival of their first child have on their lifestyle?

House Name: Low Fat Ranch
Address: 86 Landgraab Ave.
Lot Size: 40 x 40
Rooms: 2br, 1ba

Unfurnished Cost: §31,700
Furnished Cost: §45,660

Crumplebottom Household

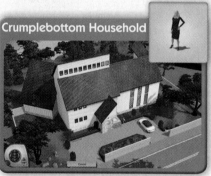

August Moon

Difficulty: 1
Budget: §20,000

Scenario: Agnes Crumplebottom hadn't even changed her last name to her husband's when an unfortunate accident on her honeymoon ended the marriage. Between her growing bitterness and her husband's ghost scaring away gentleman callers, only the bravest Sim would ever try to win her heart and fortune now.

House Name: August Moon
Address: 230 Redwood Pkwy.
Lot Size: 30 x 40
Rooms: 2br, 2ba

Unfurnished Cost: §73,560
Furnished Cost: §135,686

Ursine Household

Pescadero

Difficulty: 1
Budget: §1,500

Scenario: Claire Ursine is a reclusive angler living by the ocean. Since she lives alone, she is hopeful that no one will notice her unexpectedly changing waistline.

House Name: Pescadero
Address: 5 Sun Song Ave.
Lot Size: 30 x 20
Rooms: 2br, 1.5ba

Unfurnished Cost: §30,397
Furnished Cost: §40,311

What's New

Creating a Sim

Creating a House

A Day in the Life

Simology

Relationships and Aging

Tour of Sunset Valley

Design Corner

Object Catalog

Community

Frio Household

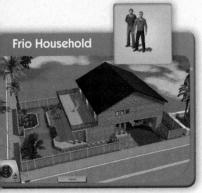

Ocean Vista Cottage

Difficulty: 2
Budget: §1,200

Scenario: The Frio brothers are cool—but in very different ways. Connor is shy and seems aloof; Jared is downright cold to people after he befriends them. Can anything be done to change them into the next level of cool: awesome?

House Name: Ocean Vista Cottage
Address: 7 Sun Song Ave.
Lot Size: 30 x 20
Rooms: 2br, 2ba

Unfurnished Cost: §43,375
Furnished Cost: §70,932

Working Friends Household

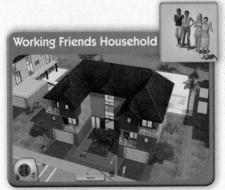

Metropolitan Lofts

Difficulty: 3
Budget: §2,850

Scenario: Four women trying to make their way in the world have come together to share this house. Madison and Monica are best friends forever, Tori is a best-friend wannabe, and Ayesha is the tomboy who couldn't care less.

House Name: Metropolitan Lofts
Address: 270 Sunnyvale Blvd.
Lot Size: 30 x 20
Rooms: 3br, 2ba

Unfurnished Cost: §55,388
Furnished Cost: §101,760

Kennedy Household

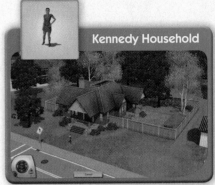

Cottage Cheese

Difficulty: 1
Budget: §1,300

Scenario: Erin Kennedy is a long-term military career woman who has recently transferred to town. Making friends has always been difficult for her, and she worries that things might be the same in this town. Will her fears come true?

House Name: Cottage Cheese
Address: 67 Water Lily Lane
Lot Size: 30 x 30
Rooms: 1br, 1ba

Unfurnished Cost: §29,063
Furnished Cost: §37,313

Koffi Household

Sur la Plage

Difficulty: 1
Budget: §3,500

Scenario: Gobias Koffi is a well-meaning single Sim who just hasn't met the right woman. Is this because he actually prefers the company of his male friends?

House Name: Sur la Plage
Address: 433 Sunnyvale Blvd.
Lot Size: 30 x 30
Rooms: 1br, 1.5ba

Unfurnished Cost: §82,416
Furnished Cost: §135,519

Roomies Household

Cosmopolitan Lofts

Difficulty: 4
Budget: §3,050

Scenario: Can five young adults from five different backgrounds really stand living together in a single house? Just about every personality is represented in this wacky household...but who is the exceedingly plain guy who doesn't socialize with the others? And how did he manage to get his own room?

House Name: Cosmopolitan Lofts
Address: 260 Sunnyvale Blvd.
Lot Size: 30 x 40
Rooms: 5br, 3ba

Unfurnished Cost: §79,787
Furnished Cost: §107,992

Alvi Household

Flava-ful

Difficulty: 3
Budget: §600

Scenario: Young Miraj Alvi wishes that his teenage brother would stop giving their dad such a hard time. Is there some way he can help the two make amends?

House Name: Flava-ful
Address: 43 Water Lily Lane
Lot Size: 20 x 30
Rooms: 2br, 1ba

Unfurnished Cost: §22,412
Furnished Cost: §32,087

Bachelor Household

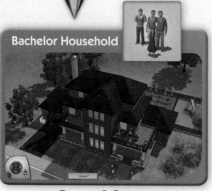

Greener & Greener

Difficulty: 3
Budget: §3,100

Scenario: The Bachelors are a tightly knit household and Simis sees to it that everything—and everyone—is in its place. Now if only the other neighborhood kids were as well behaved as Michael and Bella.

House Name: Greener & Greener
Address: 12 Sim Lane
Lot Size: 40 x 30
Rooms: 3br, 3ba

Unfurnished Cost: §68,020
Furnished Cost: §104,507

Clavell Household

Victor's Abode

Difficulty: 2
Budget: §2,800

Scenario: Xander Clavell is a party animal still living in his parents' house. Buster is tired of Xander's mooching and wants him out. Will Bessie have to choose between her son and her husband?

House Name: Victor's Abode
Address: 306 Skyborough Blvd.
Lot Size: 30 x 20
Rooms: 2br, 2.5ba

Unfurnished Cost: §62,485
Furnished Cost: §95,070

Hart Household

Primrose

Difficulty: 3
Budget: §2,400

Scenario: Bebe Hart has a hard time as the only responsible person in the entire Hart lineage. It's no secret in the neighborhood that both of her parent are slightly insane, so Bebe feels that th neighbors' eyes have been scrutinizing her for ages, just waiting to see if she'll crack too.

House Name: Primrose
Address: 303 Skyborough Blvd.
Lot Size: 30 x 40
Rooms: 2br, 2ba

Unfurnished Cost: §35,624
Furnished Cost: §65,291

Sekemoto Household

Plus Plus

Difficulty: 3
Budget: §2,550

Scenario: Yumi Sekemoto has recently moved in with her son, Leighton, to help him raise his toddler, Sam.

House Name: Plus Plus
Address: 24 Sim Lane
Lot Size: 30 x 30
Rooms: 3br, 3ba

Unfurnished Cost: §30,509
Furnished Cost: §44,349

Andrews Household

Stalwart Mission

Difficulty: 2
Budget: §1,400

Scenario: Beau Andrews is an inventive slob who spends most of his time watching television. Victoria is an artistic bookworm who spends most of her time reading. How is it that these two seem to be living happily ever after?

House Name: Stalwart Mission
Address: 378 Skyborough Blvd.
Lot Size: 20 x 30
Rooms: 1br, 1.5ba

Unfurnished Cost: §42,301
Furnished Cost: §57,471

Steel Household

Garden Cottage

Difficulty: 1
Budget: §1,000

Scenario: Christopher Steel is lucky by nature. Things have always come easily for him, which is starting to get boring. Now that he's in a brand new town w no friends, how will he fare?

House Name: Garden Cottage
Address: 373 Skyborough Blvd.
Lot Size: 30 x 40
Rooms: 2br, 1ba

Unfurnished Cost: §24,784
Furnished Cost: §32,111

ch member of the Sunset Valley households you can play as has their very own unique personality that helps shape their wishes and behaviors.
e this table to check out each household member before diving in and living out their lives:

HOUSEHOLDS

m Name	Age	Trait 1	Trait 2	Trait 3	Trait 4	Trait 5
ck Alto	Adult	Mean-Spirited	Family Oriented	Hydrophobic	Workaholic	Ambitious
ta Alto	Adult	Evil	Charismatic	Snob	Schmoozer	Ambitious
lly Alto	Teen	Good	Artistic	Vegetarian	Easily Impressed	
bal Alvi	Adult	Couch Potato	Neurotic	No Sense of Humor	Angler	Absent-Minded
J Alvi	Teen	Evil	Childish	Inappropriate	Snob	
iraj Alvi	Child	Family Oriented	Neat	Good		
eau Andrews	Adult	Couch Potato	Can't Stand Art	Slob	Inappropriate	Good Sense of Humor
ctoria Andrews	Adult	Good	Hopeless Romantic	Artistic	Ambitious	Bookworm
mis Bachelor	Adult	Family Oriented	Handy	Inappropriate	Neurotic	Frugal
ocasta Bachelor	Adult	Coward	Loner	Over-Emotional	Green Thumb	Angler
ichael Bachelor	Teen	Athletic	Loves the Outdoors	Schmoozer	Friendly	
ella Bachelor	Child	Lucky	Brave	Good		
rlo Bunch	Child	Excitable	Athletic	Loves the Outdoors		
han Bunch	Teen	Bookworm	Genius	Charismatic	Good	
ack Bunch	Adult	Schmoozer	Perfectionist	Loves the Outdoors	Green Thumb	Good Sense of Humor
udy Bunch	Adult	Neat	Light Sleeper	Perfectionist	Over-Emotional	Family Oriented
sa Bunch	Teen	Kleptomaniac	Inappropriate	Snob		
arlene Bunch	Child	Brave	Daredevil	Unlucky		
essie Clavell	Elder	Family Oriented	Artistic	Neat	No Sense of Humor	Good
uster Clavell	Elder	Grumpy	Family Oriented	Heavy Sleeper	Loner	Frugal
ander Clavell	Young Adult	Party Animal	Inappropriate	Commitment Issues	Mooch	Hot-Headed
gnes Crumplebottom	Young Adult	Grumpy	Loner	Hopeless Romantic	Bookworm	Frugal
onnor Frio	Young Adult	Absent-Minded	Bookworm	Unflirty	Loner	Good
ared Frio	Young Adult	Natural Cook	Heavy Sleeper	Mean-Spirited	Inappropriate	Party Animal
orneila Goth	Adult	Charismatic	Grumpy	Neat	Perfectionist	Unflirty
unther Goth	Adult	Frugal	Grumpy	Charismatic	Workaholic	Brave
Mortimer Goth	Child	Artistic	Grumpy	Ambitious		
ebe Hart	Teen	Bookworm	Frugal	Good	Technophobe	
us Hart	Adult	Easily Impressed	Family Oriented	Charismatic	Childish	Insane
orie Hart	Adult	Loser	Absent-Minded	Childish	Insane	Over-Emotional
amie Jolina	Young Adult	Flirty	Virtuoso	Party Animal	Genius	Bookworm
ustine Keaton	Young Adult	Loner	Perfectionist	Good	Neat	Hot-Headed
Marty Keaton	Young Adult	Athletic	Loves the Outdoors	Friendly	Neurotic	Great Kisser
rin Kennedy	Adult	Brave	Can't Stand Art	Technophobe	Unflirty	Athletic

HOUSEHOLDS, CONTINUED

Sim Name	Age	Trait 1	Trait 2	Trait 3	Trait 4	Trait 5
Gobias Koffi	Adult	Never Nude	Childish	Over-Emotional	Loser	Flirty
Geoffrey Landgraab	Adult	Good Sense of Humor	Family Oriented	Hopeless Romantic	Loves the Outdoors	Charismatic
Malcolm Landgraab	Child	Bookworm	Ambitious	Good		
Nancy Landgraab	Adult	Workaholic	Charismatic	Snob	Perfectionist	Ambitious
Dustin Langerak	Adult	Slob	Family Oriented	Friendly	Handy	Clumsy
Kaylynn Langerak	Child	Neat	Perfectionist			
Iliana Langerak	Adult	Neat	Workaholic	Schmoozer	Perfectionist	Daredevil
Parker Langerak	Teen	Flirty	Great Kisser	Schmoozer	Slob	
Zelda Mae Langerak	Young Adult	Childish	Flirty	Green Thumb	Party Animal	Easily Impressed
Leighton Sekemoto	Young Adult	Family Oriented	Good	Frugal	Ambitious	Brave
Sam Sekemoto	Toddler	Excitable	Artistic			
Yumi Sekemoto	Elder	Neurotic	Family Oriented	Inappropriate	Perfectionist	Neat
Christopher Steel	Young Adult	Great Kisser	Angler	Natural Cook	Daredevil	Friendly
Claire Ursine	Young Adult	Angler	Loves the Outdoors	Kleptomaniac	Loner	Hot-Headed
Boyd Wainwright	Adult	Computer Whiz	Genius	Couch Potato	Slob	Neurotic
Susan Wainwright	Adult	Computer Whiz	Genius	Couch Potato	Snob	Workaholic
Pauline Wan	Young Adult	Flirty	Ambitious	Party Animal	Commitment Issues	Loves the Outdoors
Hank Goddard	Young Adult	Commitment Issues	Schmoozer	Charismatic	Loves the Outdoors	Great Kisser
Morgana Wolff	Young Adult	Workaholic	Family Oriented	Artistic	Charismatic	Good
Thorton Wolff	Young Adult	Commitment Issues	Frugal	Perfectionist	Dislikes Children	Ambitious
Sandi French	Toddler	Slob	Excitable			
Molly French	Adult	Flirty	Daredevil	Hopeless Romantic	Party Animal	Slob
River McIrish	Teen	Good	Neat	Perfectionist	Artistic	
Fiona McIrish	Adult	Genius	Handy	Vegetarian	Charismatic	Bookworm
Stiles McGraw	Young Adult	Loner	Light Sleeper	Frugal	Neat	Loves the Outdoors
Blair Wainwright	Young Adult	Loner	Childish	Hopeless Romantic	Genius	Good
CyclOn3 Sw0rd	Young Adult	Absent-Minded	Inappropriate	Genius	Couch Potato	Computer Whiz
Emma Hatch	Young Adult	Charismatic	Natural Cook	Unflirty	Artistic	Good Sense of Humor
Tamara Donner	Young Adult	Flirty	Daredevil	Mooch	Hot-Headed	Charismatic
Ayesha Ansari	Young Adult	Athletic	Genius	Artistic	Frugal	Brave
Madison VanWatson	Young Adult	Ambitious	Clumsy	Snob	Excitable	Childish
Monika Morris	Young Adult	Snob	Schmoozer	Great Kisser	Angler	Absent-Minded
Tori Kimura	Young Adult	Charismatic	Workaholic	No Sense of Humor	Snob	Natural Cook

What's New | Creating a Sim | Creating a House | A Day in the Life | Simology | Relationships and Aging | Tour of Sunset Valley | Design Corner | Object Catalog | Community

Cheat Sheet

There are some incredible shortcuts in *The Sims 3* that give you extra controls over the fates of your Sims as well as the town around them. You can boost their household funds, change their traits, give them promotions, and more. To input a cheat, press Control + Shift + C at the same time. A blue bar appears at the top of the screen. Type the cheat and press Enter to make it take effect.

Some cheats can be toggled on and off. Some cheats cannot be undone, too, such as adding money to your household funds, so be sure you want these shortcuts before you start using them.

GENERAL

Command	Effect
help	Lists all commands available at the moment.
enableLlamas [on/off]	Gives a message that says, "Llamas enabled."
jokePlease	Posts a random (and silly) joke on-screen.
fullscreen [on/off]	Toggles between full-screen and windowed modes.
resetSim <firstname> <lastname>	Resets the named Sim with neutral motives, no moodlets, and teleports Sim back home.
fps [on/off]	Toggles framerate indicator in the upper-right corner of the screen
quit	Exits the game.
testingCheatsEnabled	Enables cheat functionality

MONEY & LIFETIME POINTS

Command	Effect
kaching	Adds §1,000 to active household's funds
motherlode	Adds §50,000 to active household's funds
freeRealEstate	Ignores the cost when buying a lot for the current game.
hazaam	Gives 2,500 Lifetime Happiness Points to active Sim.

BUILD & BUY

Command	Effect
moveObjects [on/off]	Removes footprint limitation for all object placement in Buy Mode and Build Mode. Removes limitations placed on hand tool for when objects are in use, or are normally non-movable objects.
constrainFloorElevation [true/false]	Allows all terrain adjustments regardless of objects, Sims, and other structures on them. Walls, floors, and objects will move with the terrain, allowing you to create sloped walls and floored hills. However, placing new walls/floors will still flatten terrain, and placing objects will still require the terrain to be flat initially if the objects normally require it.
disableSnappingToSlotsOnAlt [on/off]	When on, objects will not snap to slots while holding Alt.
hazaam	Gives 2,500 Lifetime Happiness Points to active Sim.

VISUALS

Command	Effect
hideHeadlineEffects [on/off]	Hides all meters and effects in the game, such as the plumbbob and skill meter.
fadeObjects [on/off]	Toggles whether objects fade when the camera gets close to them.
slowMotionViz <level>	Puts the game in slow motion. Optional parameter, value 0 = normal speed and 8 = slowest.
snapObjectsToGrid [true/false]	Toggles how objects snap to the grid. If true is given, behavior is normal. If false is given, then by default, objects do not snap to the grid (and holding Alt will snap them to the grid).
snapObjectsToAngle [true/false]	Toggles how objects rotate. If true is given, behavior is normal. If false is given, then by default, objects do not snap to 45 degree angles when rotating them (and holding Alt will snap them to the 45 degree angles).

SIMS

Command	Effect
Modify Traits	Interaction to bring up a trait-modification window. Can set/clear traits.
Add to Household	Add the active Sim to the current household.
Set Age	Set the age of the Sim.
Edit in CAS	Takes the Sim back into Create A Sim and allows you to make physical and personality changes.

CAREER BUILDINGS

Command	Effect
Force Opportunity	Click on career building you work at to force an opportunity.
Force Event	Click on a career building to give you a random career event.
Force All Events	Click on career building to display all events for the career consecutively.

MAILBOX

Command	Effect
Force Service Sim…	Force a specific Service Sim to show up.
Force Visitor	Force a neighbor to show up.
Make Me Know Everyone	Make the selected Sim know every other Sim that exists in the town. Sets them to acquaintances.
Make Friends For Me	Make a few random friends for the selected Sim.
Set Career…	Give the selected Sim any career at any level.
Make Happy	Set the mood/moodlets of everyone in the house to perfect. Remove all negative moodlets.
Make Motives Static/Dynamic	Make motives static/dynamic for the entire household.

A Day in the Life

• • •

With Create a Sim and Build Mode you've conjured the elements of your new life—now it's time to live it! There is a general flow of life in Sunset Valley, a place where dreams are never too far out of reach as long as you keep your Sims happy. Before barreling into this alternative life, you need to know how events unfold so that when surprises happen, they do not actually catch you by surprise. To ready you for Sunset Valley, let us introduce all of the essential terms and concepts that affect your Sims' lives and show you a sample sliver of the lives of two different Sims under the roof: Catherine and Chris Browne.

REQUIRED READING

Before starting your new story, you need to know these terms, as you will see them a lot in this chapter as well as those that follow. This chapter is a general overview of how the game unfolds. Deeper explanations of these concepts follow in the next three chapters.

◆ **Wishes:** Every Sims has desires, both immediate and long-term. When you created a Sim, you gave it a Lifetime Wish. However, Sims also come up with smaller wishes each day that they would love for you to help them fulfill. Fulfilled wishes boost your Sim's mood and award Lifetime Happiness points.

◆ **Lifetime Happiness Points:** These are the ultimate barometer of your Sim's fulfillment. When you complete a wish, your Sim earns Lifetime Happiness points. You also earn these points when you boost your Sim's mood over a certain threshold. Lifetime Happiness points can be traded in for Lifetime Rewards, which affect your Sim's personality and aptitude.

◆ **Skills:** Sims can learn a variety of talents, such as writing, fishing, painting, and athletics. These skills are often tied into careers or hobbies. Certain activities increase your skill ranking. You can track your Sims' skills in their Skill Journals.

◆ **Careers:** In order to maintain their households, Sims must have a constant source of income. Careers provide that. There are a multitude of career tracks in Sunset Valley, from athlete to journalist. Sims can also seek out part-time jobs or turn their skills in moneymaking opportunities, such as penning books from home. Each career has several levels of promotion.

◆ **Opportunities:** From time to time, Sims encounter opportunities that result in rewards when completed. Opportunities are typically related to careers and skills, but special opportunities pop up just by exploring Sunset Valley and talking to people. Rewards include job promotions, physical objects, Simoleons, or relationship boosts.

◆ **Moodlets:** *The Sims 3* introduces a new measurement of your Sim's happiness—moodlets. Moodlets are factors that affect your overall mood. They are good, bad, and neutral. Most moodlets have a timer that denotes how long they affect overall mood. Some negative moodlets can be eliminated by correcting behavior or environment. To make your Sims' life better and earn more Lifetime Happiness points, adjust your Sims' life so they experience more positive moodlets.

◆ **Needs:** As in *The Sims™ 2*, Sims have individual needs like Bladder, Hunger, Hygiene, Social, Fun, and Energy. These needs are affected by environment, activities, and relationships. While mood and moodlet take center stage in making sure your Sim is happy, don't neglect basic needs. When buying objects for your lot, be sure to keep an eye on how certain objects affect specific needs. For example, a nicer bathtub or shower will increase your Sim's Hygiene rating.

◆ **Socials:** Socials are the interactions that take place between Sims. There are literally hundreds of socials. Not all socials are available right away. Some are unlocked by developing skills. Other socials are activated by the traits you give your Sims. Use socials to direct a conversation and engage other Sims, paying attention to their likes and dislikes so you can build better relationships. Who knows what could happen? Playfully teasing the right Sim could lead to a lifelong love, while joking with a sourpuss could result in a new nemesis.

The Essentials

While *The Sims 2* revolved a lot around time management, *The Sims 3* is primarily a happiness factory. There are many roads to happiness (and a few highways to misery, too) and you'll get the most out of the game by finding the best ways to get your Sims to feel good about themselves. To do this, you need to understand the best and easiest ways to deliver your Sims' dreams, such as helping them build careers, develop skills, or seek out exciting opportunities. Use this chapter to get a firm grip on all the basic tools for creating happiness so that when you move into Sunset Valley, you minimize the frowns that are bound to happen when exploring a whole new life.

A Day in the Life

BROWNIE BITES

Because there is no linear Point A to Point B structure in *The Sims 3*, you have an unprecedented degree of freedom with your Sims. You can focus on a career with one Sim and focus on a family with another. You can put an entire clan under one roof with a zillion different interests pulling the household in multiple directions or design a power couple with a singular purpose.

I played the game with several different families and was consistently amazed at how the smallest decision-making tweaks would result in a whole new life trajectory for my Sims. For example, I had one Sim who seemed happy as a clam when painting, but after meeting somebody in downtown Sunset Valley who loved fishing, the Sim told me she wanted to take a fishing class. By developing the Fishing skill, I banked a ton of Lifetime Happiness points because I had a whole new avenue to make my Sim happy. Whether out at the pond or in front of easel, this Sim was just high on life.

Wishes

The Wish panel

As soon as your Sims arrive at their new lot, they start expressing wishes to you via the Wish panel at the bottom of the screen. In addition to their Lifetime Wish, Sims can have up to four active wishes awaiting fulfillment. When a Sim has a new wish, it appears in the arched bubble on top of the Wish panel. To promise a wish and add it to your Sims active wishes, left-click on the wish. To deny a wish, right-click on it. There is no punishment for denying a wish. Your Sim will just forget

about it. That doesn't necessarily mean a new wish will take its place right away. You may have to wait a while before your Sim conceives of a new wish.

CAUTION

You cannot undo a wish denial, so think before you right-click on that little dream.

 Incoming wishes can stack up without penalty. Use arrows to cycle through your Sim's wishes before committing to them or denying them.

TIP

Exploring Sunset Valley and talking to other Sims often results in your Sim coming up with new wishes.

To learn more about a wish, just move the cursor on top of it. The full details of the wish appear in a box. The box explains what the wish is, what needs to happen to fulfill the wish (you can sometimes get hints here), and how many Lifetime Happiness points the wish is worth once fulfilled. Wishes with loftier or more time consuming goals are worth more Lifetime Happiness points. For example, with the Chat With Sim wish is worth 150 points, the slightly more time-consuming Read 3 Books wish is worth 900 points. The monumental Have First Child wish banks 6,000 Lifetime Happiness points, but that wish sends your life on an entirely new course.

Wishes include activities such as:

- Chatting with a specific Sim
- Kissing a Sim your Sim is interested in
- Taking a class
- Raising a skill level
- Buying a specific object
- Starting a new career
- Getting a promotion at a current career
- Banking a specific amount of Simoleons
- Throwing a party

- Going to a community location
- Going to an event at a location

Once you have added a wish to the Wish panel, it stays there until you either fulfill it or throw it away. You throw a wish away with quick right-click, and there is zero penalty.

 Some wishes are directly related to your Lifetime Wish. These wishes appear with a starburst behind them, indicating that you should definitely consider prioritizing them once promised. Fulfilling these wishes will get you closer to your Sim's overall goal in life.

Wishes are not universal across age groups. Sims of differing ages will want different things. A child will never have a desire to join a specific career track, but instead want to be talked to, played with, or receive a new object like a toy. Teen Sims start to mingle wishes with young adult and adult Sims, although you will see slight variations on wishes—many are socially-oriented, too. Because Sims can undergo personality changes as they age, some wishes do not survive the move between age groups. The desire to have a baby will disappear when your adult Sim moves into the elderly age bracket.

Skills

Sims are not mentally static creatures. Their minds are hungry for knowledge and new skills. Skills not only help unlock new wishes for you to promise your Sims, but skills also help Sims advance careers and money-making enterprises, result in new social interactions, and keep a positive mood so those Lifetime Happiness points keep rolling in. Skills are also a good way to cultivate a unique personality in each of your Sims. Why fill a house with a bunch of Sims who are great at the guitar when you can have a parade of talents, like logic, cooking, and painting, too? There are 10 different skills to develop in *The Sims 3*.

What's New | Creating a Sim | Creating a House | A Day in the Life | Simology | Relationships and Aging | Tour of Sunset Valley | Design Corner | Object Catalog | Community

...ese skills can be initiated by several ...ethods, such as taking classes at specific ...cations in Sunset Valley, by picking up a ...ook that specializes in a skill, or by engaging ...the activity related to the skill itself. Here are ...e 10 skills and where you need to go to ...arn them:

- **Athletic:** Llama Memorial Stadium
- **Charisma:** City Hall
- **Cooking:** Hogan's Deep-Fried Diner or Little Corsican Bistro
- **Fishing:** EverFresh Delights Supermarket
- **Gardening:** Landgraab Industries Science Facility
- **Guitar:** Wilsonoff Community Theater
- **Handiness:** Fort Gnome Military Base
- **Logic:** Landgraab Industries Science Facility
- **Painting:** Community School for the Gifted
- **Writing:** Doo Peas Corporate Towers

...king a skill class is typically one of the first ...ishes your Sims dream up when they ...ove to Sunset Valley, so don't deny them. ...se their eagerness to jump-start their ...evelopment. Classes cost §400 to attend, ...ut you acquire the first level of a skill faster at ...class than if you pick up a beginner's level ...ill book at the local bookstore. Beginner-...vel books are cheaper, though. However, ...you gain skill levels, you can buy more ...xpensive books designed specifically for ...rtain skill tiers that help advance your Sim to ...e next skill level.

...eading a book about a specific skill takes longer than a class, but it is a good way to advance a skill set during off-hours.

TIP

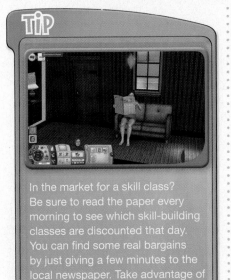

In the market for a skill class? Be sure to read the paper every morning to see which skill-building classes are discounted that day. You can find some real bargains by just giving a few minutes to the local newspaper. Take advantage of the savings!

Some skills are directly related to a Sim's traits. An athletic Sim will naturally be predisposed to the Athletic skill. The Sim will excel at the skill that matches up with their respective trait. Here are the traits that match up with skills, so you can see what your Sim potentially has a leg up on when they first move into Sunset Valley:

- **Athletic:** Athletic
- **Charisma:** Charismatic
- **Cooking:** Natural Cook
- **Fishing:** Loves the Outdoors, Angler
- **Gardening:** Loves the Outdoors, Green Thumb
- **Guitar:** Artistic, Virtuoso
- **Handiness:** Handy
- **Logic:** Genius
- **Painting:** Artistic
- **Writing:** Bookworm, Artistic

CAUTION

Don't try to take on too many skills. Developing skills takes time and if you try to master too many, you'll likely end up mastering none. Pick a couple and get really good at those. If you want to explore another skill, why not add a new Sim to the household by making a special friend?

Each skill is split into 10 different levels of mastery. As a Sim masters a skill, they learn new things, like talents and socials. New opportunities can also result from advancing a skill. Each skill level takes longer to learn than the last. You will likely tear through the first two levels of a skill. However, as you climb the rungs of the skill, the time needed to develop the skill increases. (You can speed up the process by maintaining a high mood, too. Happy Sims learn things faster.) By the time you reach levels 8, 9, and 10, plan on devoting dozens of game hours (not real world hours) to the pursuit of skill mastery.

TIP

To speed the skill development process, spend your Lifetime Happiness points on the Fast Learner Lifetime Reward. This kicks up the rate at which new skills are acquired for the remainder of the Sim's life.

43

A Day in the Life

Performing actions related to a skill is a good way to not only cultivate a skill, but also work on a money-making plan related to the skill. Let's use the Writing skill as an example. Once you have the first level of the Writing skill, you can start on a novel. While your Sim works on the novel, she is also practicing writing. When the Sim pushes back from the computer, it results not only in a ream of pages, but a nice bump toward the next skill level. The same goes for cooking. While cooking a dish, particularly a new recipe learned by advancing to the next skill level in cooking or by buying a new recipe from the bookstore, you add to your Cooking skill.

NOTE

A full list of activities that improve skills is located in the Simology chapter.

TODDLER SKILLS

Toddlers have their own skills to develop, too. Toddlers need to learn the following skills to be well-rounded Sims: walk, talk, and potty training. These skills are taught to toddlers through social interactions. When controlling a grown-up Sim, left-click on the toddler and choose Teach to Walk, Teach to Talk or Potty Train. The adult will sit with the toddler and patiently help them master the skill. The toddler is not the only Sim that benefits here, either. Unless a Sim has the Dislikes Children trait, they will get a positive moodlet for helping the child. If you successfully teach all three skills to the toddler, you can choose the toddler's extra trait when it becomes a child.

Track Skill Development

It's easy to monitor your Sim's skill development. When your Sim is engaging in an activity that improves a skill, the Skill meter appears above its head. This is a blue meter. (The meter that tracks progress on a specific activity, such as exercise or fishing, is green.) The meter fills from the bottom up. When the meter fills to the top, your Sim's skill improves to the next level. Any new actions, talent, or socials unlocked by raising the skill level appear on-screen to the right.

If for any reason you must interrupt the Sim who's developing a skill, you do not lose any progress. The Skill meter remains in the exact same place the next time you work on the skill level.

The Skill panel is an easy place to track your Sims' skill levels. Any skill the Sim has learned appears in the Skill panel. A meter next to the skill shows which level the Sim is. Move the cursor over the meter to see how close the Sim is to the next level. Click on the page to the right of each skill measurement to read the Skill Journal. The Skill Journal offers a detailed look at that specific skill, such as how long the Sim has been working at the skill, and how many of a certain object/item related to that skill the Sim has made.

The Skill Journal also displays skill-specific challenges associated with that skill. Challenges are requirements that, when met, result in improved results or financial rewards for activities related to that skill. For example, one of the challenges for the Writing skill is Specialist Writer. A Sim who writes five novels in a specific genre earns the reward of penning more hits and best-sellers in that particular genre, which results in more royalties. Each skill challenge is associated with a title, such as Body Builder or Comedian.

Use the Skill Journal to track progress on a skill and look at any skill-specific challenges.

Skills as Careers

Not every Sim needs to run out and get a full-time job. Sims can develop skills to the point that they start bringing income into the household. Skills that result in money-making opportunities are also a good way to augment the income of a Sim who has a full-time gig but doesn't make a lot of Simoleons because they have not earned many promotions just yet.) The Writing skill, for example, can be developed into an authoring career. As Sims develop the Writing skill, they learn how to create genre novels. Some genres are worth more on the market than others, so advancing the writing skill to get at those more lucrative genres is a good plan.

NOTE

For a complete list of all of the skills, the benefits of achieving each skill level, and the best way to master each skill, please see the Simology chapter.

Careers

While some Sims will find great fulfillment out of pursuing skills, others need a more conventional source of income: a career. Careers are not just places to report to five or so days a week and earn Simoleons. Careers help define Sims by affecting moods, inspiring wishes, and offering opportunities that affect the previously two mentioned facets of a Sim's personality.

There are many career tracks in Sunset Valley for your Sim to pursue, and like skills, some of them are natural picks for your Sim depending on the traits selected in Create a Sim. Because some Sims are inclined toward specific careers—an athletic Sim will likely want to be a professional athlete—watch the incoming wishes when you first move to Sunset Valley to see what your Sims want to be. Some Sims will immediately tell you what career they want to join. Other may need it coaxed out of them over time by interacting with other Sims or by developing skills associated with certain careers. Many careers are also directly tied into a Sim's Lifetime Wish, such as reaching level 10, the highest level, of a specific career.

Here are all of the available careers in Sunset Valley, and where you need to go in order to apply for a job:

- **Business:** Doo Peas Corporate Towers
- **Criminal:** Outstanding Citizen Warehouse Corp.
- **Culinary:** Hogan's Deep-Fried Diner or Little Corsican Bistro
- **Journalism:** Doo Peas Corporate Towers
- **Law Enforcement:** Police Station
- **Medical:** Sacred Spleen Memorial Hospital
- **Military:** Fort Gnome Military Base
- **Music:** Wilsonoff Community Theater
- **Political:** City Hall
- **Professional Sports:** Llama Memorial Stadium
- **Science:** Landgraab Industries Science Facility

To apply for a job, just show up!

TIP

Mercifully, there is no interview process when you seek a new career. You just need to go to the associated building and select Join.

NOTE

Unlike *The Sims 2*, elder Sims do not have to partake in part-time work. They can pursue a full career.

You can also check the newspaper for jobs. At least three will be offered, complete with full listings that detail schedules and wages. You can also look for work on the computer.

When you get a job, expect to slide into the bottom spot on the totem pole. There are 10 levels of advancement inside a career. Depending on your job performance, though, you can earn promotions that result in more money and better shifts. In fact, it seems the more promotions you get, the less hours you work. But because you are earning more Simoleons, working fewer hours does not hammer your pocketbook.

The Sims 3 — A Day in the Life

The Career Panel is the best place to check out your Sim's current career status. Here, you can see your current position at the career, the current wage, and current work schedule. From the Career panel, you can also see little hints for how to get ahead at work. To the right of the work schedule is a set of performance ratings. Use these hints to focus your Sim's energies on the right skills and needs. If you go to work in a bad mood, you are likely to be passed over. But if you keep your spirits high at home and report to work with a wide smile, you may enter the fast-track to the corner office.

From time to time, you also get opportunities directly related to your career that will help with advancement. Sometimes your coworkers or your boss will offer a task that will make you look good. Maybe your boss will give a book to take home and read. Or your coworkers will ask you to please come to work smelling so fresh and so clean. If you meet the requirements for these opportunities, the next time you head to your place of employment, the achievement will be duly noted. More often than not, a promotion is not too far behind.

> **TIP**
>
> Another good way to get ahead at work? Befriend the boss! Check out the Relationships chapter for tips and tricks for starting and maintaining great friendships.

You decide how your Sim will behave at work. Select an attitude from the drop-down

menu to direct your Sim's workplace ethic. How your Sim chooses to spend his or her time at work can have a serious effect on the chance of a promotion. You can work on skill development related to your job while at work, too, by choosing a workplace behavior that matches one of your skills. For example, if you work at the stadium and choose to hit the gym while there, your Athletic skill goes up.

> **NOTE**
>
> Career promotions often unlock new workplace behaviors, which in turn give you more options for how to spend your work day.

A carpool picks you up from your house approximately 30 minutes before your shift starts. Be home to catch the lift. If you miss the carpool, you better hail a cab so you aren't late.

Demotions and Terminations

> **CAUTION**
>
> If your performance at work is suffering for reasons such as mood and hygiene, you can be demoted. (Look at the performance descriptors on the Career panel for signs of what needs improvement.) Your boss will give you a two-day warning that the demotion is coming unless you turn things around. If one of the performance ratings hits zero, you are instantly demoted. If you are at the bottom level of the ladder, you will be fired. Typically, this happens over the phone, but if you opt not to even answer that, your career just ends with a brief on-screen note. If you have received a few promotions, you will be demoted before finally being fired.

INVEST

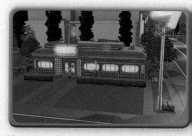

You can also earn money by investing in a business, such as Hogan's Deep-Fried Diner. The initial investment is §6,000, but if the joint does well, you will see a handsome return on your money. Every week, you earn a share of the profits. It's an interesting alternative to a regular career—not bad for an artist who wants to spend more time in front of the canvas than the fry machine. Of course, that initial outlay might put a Sim in rough economic shape for a little while. Fortunately, there is no time limit for when you can invest in a place. You can wait until you have a substantial nest egg before splurging on the business opportunity.

After a while, you can increase your investment so you own the entire business. You now get all of the profits. With ownership, you can now rename the business to whatever you want and fire employees. Firing employees gives your relationship a serious hit, though, so keep that in mind before handing out pink slips.

Paid Time Off

Under certain circumstances, Sims get paid time off from work. Should a Sim become pregnant, she does not have to report to work and there is no threat of losing her job because of the absence. Male Sims off for paternity leave get a similar deal. While taking time off because of the new family, Sims receive notices saying how much they earned for that day when they would have normally worked.

46

What's New

Creating a Sim

Creating a House

A Day in the Life

Simology

Relationships and Aging

Tour of Sunset Valley

Design Corner

Object Catalog

Community

art-Time Jobs

ens can work, but they cannot get a career ecause they are still in school. To make a le extra money on the side, teens can seek t part-time work at jobs like the bookstore supermarket. Part-time work does not quire the same degree of management as full career. Part-time jobs are tricky because ey can interfere with homework time, but metimes a household needs all of the help can get.

dult and elder Sims can also partake in part-ne jobs, but children younger than teens bsolutely cannot get a part-time job of any rt.

chool

ds don't get full-time careers like their arents. Instead, they must go to school uring the week just like kids (should) do on his side of the computer screen. Excelling at chool is not all that different from excelling at career. Students should show up for school lean and in a good mood. While at school, ou set the tone for students just like you vould at a career, choosing from options like Work Hard, Slack Off, and Talk to Friends.

ds are sent back to their lots with homework hat must be completed by the next day order to get good grades. Doing well in chool can result in you being able to select e trait that opens up when they turn into eens. Students that do poorly in school or re caught napping can earn detention, which eeps them after school and negatively affects heir mood.

> **NOTE**
>
> For more information on school, please see the Simology chapter, which also details all of the different career tracks.

Opportunities

Just as in real life, opportunities can come out of nowhere and serve to shape your destiny. In *The Sims 3*, opportunities are a major driving force in Sunset Valley. They give Sims chances to reach goals and increase their happiness. The opportunities you typically encounter are related to your Sims' current careers, skills, or social circles. Each completed opportunity results in a reward of some form, such as extra money, skill advancement, or promotions at work.

> **NOTE**
>
> You get many opportunities from interacting with other Sims, so it pays to be social.

When an opportunity arises, the story temporarily stops and you are given a chance to review the opportunity and either accept or reject it.

Some opportunities are time-sensitive. If you are offered an opportunity with a time limit, such as participating in a certain event, you are told the deadline for completing the opportunity. To earn the associated reward, you must finish the opportunity by the deadline. You cannot just start the opportunity with five minutes to go. The required action must be finished when the timer reaches zero. You are absolutely not required to participate in an opportunity. You can ignore an incoming opportunity with no consequence save for the dismissal of the potential reward.

> **NOTE**
>
> To discard an opportunity you have already accepted, just right-click on it in the Opportunities panel.
>
> Each career and skill has a set of smaller opportunities associated with it. For a full list of opportunities and their corresponding rewards, please see the Simology chapter.

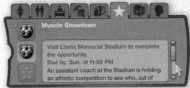

To track your active opportunities, use the Opportunities panel. There are three opportunity categories in *The Sims 3*: Career, Skill, and Special. Career opportunities are directly related to your full- or part-time work. Completing these opportunities advances your career and often results in a hasty promotion. Skill opportunities are tied to one of the skills you are currently developing. Usually, another Sim in the community will have a request that calls on your skill expertise. The third type of opportunity, the Special opportunity, is outside your career or skill. These opportunities are received from other citizens or spotted in the newspaper.

> **TIP**
>
> Don't stress out over opportunities. You can only have one active opportunity of each type at a time.

Opportunities are actually quite useful for getting outside a set routine that Sims often fall into. Some opportunities require to you to do an activity or visit another part of the city. The reward, however, is usually related to your current career or skill set.

A Day in the Life

Mood Maintenance

The immediate measurement of a Sim is mood. A Sim's happiness, neutrality, or misery is quickly identified by their current mood, which is displayed in the Mood meter that occupies the center of the screen, right next to the portrait of the active Sim. The Mood meter is shaped like an upside-down exclamation point. Good mood is represented by green. As the Sim dips toward neutral or tense feelings, the color of the meter turns yellow. When the meter displays red, your Sim is seriously troubled. You need to pay immediate attention to the Sim and rectify whatever situation or interaction is upsetting the Sim.

The portrait also chips in with mood management by mirroring the Sim's current mood. A happy Sim is represented with a smiling portrait. A sad or disturbed Sim wears the kind of frown that you simply must try to turn upside-down.

CAUTION

If the Mood meter is red, your Sim is more likely to fail at tasks such as cooking or painting. Your Sim may even become unresponsive to your suggestions and commands.

Your constant goal is to push your Sim's mood into the "bubble" at the top of the Mood meter. If you can keep your Sim happy long enough to push the mood rating into that bubble, the Sim begins earning Lifetime Happiness points. The stream of Lifetime Happiness points continues until the Sim's mood drops back out of the bubble. While you earn a lot of Lifetime Happiness points

by fulfilling wishes in nice-sized chunks, if you can keep a trickle coming in via the Mood meter, you'll be surprised how soon you can start buying Lifetime Rewards.

Moodlets

Managing mood in *The Sims 3* is considerably easier than in *The Sims 2* thanks to the introduction of moodlets. Moodlets show you exactly what is affecting your Sim's overall mood at any given time. Moodlets are not necessarily passive indicators—your actions and commands greatly influence your Sim's moodlets.

The Moodlet panel is directly next to the Mood meter. All current moodlets are shown here. To learn more about each moodlet, mouse over it to see a fuller description.

Because moodlets contribute to your Sim's overall mood, you need to pay close and constant attention to the Moodlet panel. Some moodlets require direct attention, particularly the negative ones, which appear with a red outline. There are two types of moodlets: positive and negative. To keep your Sim happy, you need to do things that bring about more positive moodlets. Moodlets have varying degrees of effect on overall mood, so it's always best to seek out activities that bring about the biggest positive effect on overall mood. Fulfilling a wish is a good way to cause a positive moodlet. But minor things can also promote a positive moodlet, such as having your Sim brush his teeth, thus receiving the Minty Breath positive moodlet.

Because no mood-influencing factor is eternal, moodlets have timers on them. While a moodlet is active, its full

effect is seen in the overall mood. There is no decay over time. Pay attention to the time on a moodlet and try to make sure your Sim will experience another positive event before a good moodlet runs out. Some moodlets are actually warning that a negative impact on the overall mood is about to take place unless the factor that inspired the upcoming negative

moodlet is removed. For example, a moodlet showing that a Sim is hungry and has to use the bathroom appears with a timer. If the need is addressed before the timer counts down, the chance of suffering the negative moodlet associated with these activities is avoided. If the need is not addressed in time and the negative moodlet occurs, it's too late to rectify the situation.

Let's say your Sim hasn't eaten in a while and the Hungry moodlet appears. You have two hours to feed the Sim. If you fail to feed the Sim, the Hungry moodlet is replaced by Very Hungry, which knocks down the overall mood. Even if you fed the Sim right after the Very Hungry moodlet, you still must suffer the hit to overall mood.

Negative moodlets bring down the overall mood. Sometimes, you just have to ride a negative moodlet out and try to offset it with a positive moodlet. However, some negative moodlets can be nullified by performing an action. The Sore moodlet brings down the overall mood as long as it is active, for example. If another Sim was to give the sore Sim a brief massage (which is a social), the Sore moodlet vanishes.

TIP

For a full list of all moodlets and their individual values, please see the Simology chapter.

Needs

Needs are not as central to *The Sims 3* as they were in previous games. While the needs of a Sim are still important to overall mood, the introduction of moodlets offers a more interactive way to deal with a Sim's specific needs. Still, you should check in on needs to make sure your Sim is taken care of. If you wait until your Sim's Bladder rating drops low enough that she has to use the bathroom within a set amount of time, the Has to Pee moodlet appears. Now the timer is on to get to a bathroom before the Has to Pee moodlet devolves into passing out entirely from bladder failure.

What's New | Creating a Sim | Creating a House | A Day in the Life | Simology | Relationships and Aging | Tour of Sunset Valley | Design Corner | Object Catalog | Community

ere are six needs to monitor:

◆ Bladder ◆ Hunger

◆ Energy ◆ Hygiene

◆ Fun ◆ Social

ese needs are addressed not only with tivities such as eating or taking a bath, ut also through the purchase of certain bjects. Many objects affect needs, such as new toilet, mirror, or bathtub. When you e shopping in Buy Mode, mouse above an bject to see what needs it addresses and ow. The higher the need rating, the more the bject does to address the specific need. r example, not all tubs and showers are eated equal. The more expensive the tub or ower, the more it improves a Sim's Hygiene ing when the Sim interacts with it.

ch need in the Needs panel is ccompanied by a meter. This meter easures the current level of satisfaction for at need. The Hunger meter, for instance, ows you if the Sim needs to eat. The nount of hunger satisfaction is seen in green. the meter is mostly green, the Sim is not ngry. However, if the meter drops to the 50 ercent level, the background of the meter rns yellow. This means the need should be ddressed before it slips into the negative, hich is red. Once a need drops into the d, a negative moodlet occurs and the verall mood takes a dip.

elationships and ocializing

ishes, opportunities, and moods are all ffected by one very important facet of e Sims 3: socializing. Hermits have their ace in Sunset Valley, but for Sims to get the ost out of life, they must venture outside e front door and start interacting with other tizens. Making friends in Sunset Valley is an asy way to make Sims happy—unless they e total misanthropes. By interacting with

other Sims, you may see new opportunities pop up or have your Sims discover new wishes on the basis of seeing other Sims having fun with a specific object or activity.

As Sims meet people, they are added to the Relationships panel. Here, you can monitor the progress of a relationship by looking at the two meters directly below the portraits. The green meter on the right fills as a relationship with a Sim improves. If the relationship sours, the meter on the left turns red. Directly below the meter are small indicators that show the current status of the relationship and any factors that help describe the relationship, such as spouse (little rings) or family (a small collection of people).

When you first encounter a new Sim, the Sim is characterized as an Acquaintance. As a relationship improves or decays, the descriptor of the relationship changes. Here are three categories of relationships and the different descriptors:

Positive: Acquaintance, Friend, Good Friend, Best Friend, Distant Friend, Old Friend, Romantic Interest, Fiance, Spouse

Negative: Rival, Enemy, Old Enemy, Ex-Friend

Neutral: Stranger

Relationships are affected by socializing with Sims via conversations. When you initiate a conversation, you can choose from a litany of available actions and conversation pieces. These are called "socials." Socials can be positive, neutral, and negative. Every Sim will have a different set of available socials.

When a conversation is struck, your interaction with the other Sim appears in the screen's upper left. The Relationship meter under the portrait of the Sim in the Relationship panel now appears on the main screen. Below the meter, you see how the other Sim views your Sim. These ratings help put your relationship in context and guide how you should steer the conversation to reach a desired effect. If another Sim thinks you are funny, then keep up the jokes. If the Sim thinks you are interesting, perhaps you can steer this thing toward romance. And if the other Sim thinks you are dull or drab, you need to correct course. Try finding out what the other Sim is interested in and talk about it, or throttle back whatever thing you are doing that is upsetting the other Sim. For example, if you flirted with a Sim and they regarded you as creepy, then you need to not flirt anymore. Try normal conversation for a while so the other Sim accepts you as just being social or polite.

AGING

Another factor that affects wishes, relationships, skills, careers, and opportunities is aging. As your Sims grow older, they get new traits that shape personality and affect wishes and opportunities. A new trait when a teen turns into a young adult can help shape a career.

For a full explanation of aging and how it affects your story, please see the Simology chapter.

BROWNIE BITES

Okay, so that's the basic rundown of all the essentials you need to know before moving into Sunset Valley. Is that all you need to know? Hardly. And that's why there are a lot of pages in this guide following the one you are on now. But I wanted to explain the basics right up front so that when we go deeper in the following chapters, you understand how all of the life-defining factors work in tandem with each other. Just know this: nothing in *The Sims 3* is an island—everything is connected.

Now that you get the concepts of wishes, opportunities, and mood, let's follow a household on the first part of their journey and see how all of these factors fit together. And not just any household, either. Meet the Brownes: Catherine and Chris. He's an athlete and a social butterfly. She's a Bookworm with a passion for writing and cooking. Will they find a natural pace that works for them? Or will they find themselves at each other's throats, with Catherine occasionally furious that somebody doesn't make much of an effort to learn how to cook, doesn't pick up the dishes, and gets up super-early even though the other person was up late working on a book...

Ahem.

Meet the Brownes

Here's the magic couple: Catherine and Chris Browne. They are just about to move into their new house in Sunset Valley. It's a humble house with just a few rooms. Many of the objects in the house are the base-level offerings, like the tub and fridge. After all, that §20,000 needs to last, because neither is starting with a high-paying career.

However, the goal is to change all of that. But Catherine and Chris will go about it in very different ways. While Chris is going to seek out a career with a regular payday and schedule, Catherine is going to work from home by honing one of her skills. Each Sim's traits affect the chosen Lifetime Wish, which in turn affects how skill development and careers are handled. Here's the trait breakdown of each Sim so you can see how these selections affect the course of a life in Sunset Valley, from work to wishes.

Catherine Browne
- **Trait 1:** Bookworm
- **Trait 2:** Hopeless Romantic
- **Trait 3:** Artistic
- **Trait 4:** Ambitious
- **Trait 5:** Lucky
- **Lifetime Wish:** Illustrious Author

Chris Browne
- **Trait 1:** Loves the Outdoors
- **Trait 2:** Athletic
- **Trait 3:** Charisma
- **Trait 4:** Schmoozer
- **Trait 5:** Ambitiou
- **Lifetime Wish:** Become a Superstar Athlete

Now, without further ado, let's get these two moved into their new house and see how they go about life...

Getting Settled

Creating a house for the Brownes via Build Mode and Buy Mode doesn't take too much time. Because funds are limited, nobody goes crazy with construction. The house is modest with just three designated rooms—the kitchen is just sectioned off from the living room with an incomplete wall. Because I have a plan for each Sim's career and skills, I make sure to place an object for each of them that addresses their different tracks. Their living room sports a treadmill for Chris and a computer for Catherine. Both of them could interact either object, of course, but the objects will definitely have primary users. Once the house is finished, it's time to start assigning careers and building skills.

Chris immediately takes a job at the stadium because his Lifetime Wish is to be a Superstar Athlete, which is level 10 of the Professional Sports career track. Because Chris has the Athletic trait, he can develop the Athletic skill faster than other Sims. This means he will have an easier time getting ahead at work. Right away, he's put to work training on the treadmill. Catherine, on the other hand, is offered a Business career. Because she wants to be an author and painter, I reject the career and instead start training her on the computer. Both Chris and Catherine immediately wish to learn skills. He wants to learn the Athletic skill. She wants to learn the Writing skill. I tell Chris to work out on the treadmill and task Catherine with refining her writing on the computer. Because each has a trait strength, both develop the first level of the skill within minutes.

NOTE

Now, I could send Catherine to a writing class down at Doo Peas Corporate Towers, and if she wanted to spend the §400, she would have the Writing skill. But money is tight so I stick with the computer.

TIP

Raising Chris's Athletic skill to level 1 increases the number of available workout options. Now I choose to Pace Yourself on the treadmill so he can work out longer.

After working out, Chris develops the Grungy moodlet. If I don't give him a bath, this moodlet will continue to drag down his overall mood. Plus, if he really gets stinky, Catherine will develop the Disgusted moodlet.

Each Sim had a wish to learn their respective skills. So now that I've fulfilled those wishes, each Sim earns the Fulfilled moodlet, which gives them a +15 mood boost. This pushes Catherine up into the bubble on the Mood meter, so she starts earning Lifetime Happiness points. As a result of starting her Writing skill track, Catherine hits me with another wish: Reach Level 5 of Writing Skill. That will give her +1,500 Lifetime Happiness points, so I promise it to her.

After Chris gets out of the tub, I sent him to the stadium to join the Professional Sports career, which also fulfills a wish. He starts at the very bottom of the ladder: Rabid Fan. This only pays him §13 per hour. Oh well—nobody becomes the star quarterback on day one, right? When Chris returns home, I'll promptly put him back on the treadmill to keep building the Athletic skill.

Chris enters the stadium. When Sims visit certain community places, they sort of "vanish" for a while. You cannot follow them inside.

Because Chris is a social Sim, he immediately strikes up a conversation with Jared outside the stadium. I keep the conversation friendly but when I see that Jared thinks Chris is boring, I direct Chris to ask about Jared's career. Finding out that Jared is on the culinary track improves their relationship.

51

Meanwhile, Catherine is sent to and finishes her writing class to satisfy a wish and get her the Fulfilled moodlet again. As soon as she finishes the class, she hits me with a handful of wishes. She wants to Write a Novel and Write a Science Fiction Novel. I accept both wishes because doing one will fulfill the other.

Back at the house, the Brownes settle in for the night. Catherine is sent back to the computer to refine her Writing skill. When she reaches level 2, she can then start writing drama novels. (Many of the Writing skill increases unlock new genres.) Chris is hungry after his workout, so I have him grab a quick meal of cereal from the fridge.

> ## TiP
>
> Sims prefer prepared meals because it gives them the Good Meal moodlet and the cooker improves their Cooking skill while whipping up the meal. However, when money and/or time is tight, use the quick meals for a cheap solution to the hunger issue.

When your Sims tell you they are tired via the Tired moodlet, send them to bed. If you let them sleep until they are ready to get up, you enjoy the Fully Rested moodlet, which offers a long-lasting mood boost. You can get Sims up earlier, but you will miss out on the moodlet.

In the morning, I send Catherine into the kitchen to prepare breakfast for the pair. She does not have the Cooking skill yet because I have not ordered her to read a cookbook or take a class down at the bistro. So she burns the waffles I task her with making. Even though the waffles are burnt and neither of the couple particularly likes eating them, not only is hunger sated, but Catherine automatically starts developing her Cooking skill just by performing the activity. If I keep her and Chris in the kitchen to make meals, each one will naturally get better at cooking and soon start not only making better meals that offer Good or Great Meal moodlets, but they will unlock the ability to make new recipes or buy advanced cookbooks that teach new recipes.

Chris and Catherine are spouses, so they better act like it. Plus, Chris professed a wish to Chat with Catherine. Easy enough. Before Chris has to get ready for his first day

at the stadium, I make the pair talk to each other—and flirt, too. Because Catherine is a Hopeless Romantic, she has some extra socials like Kiss on Cheek, Whisper in Ear, and Leap into Arms. These socials quickly improv their relationship, which was already good to begin with. Feeling loved gives Sims positive moodlets, like Flattered.

While at work, Chris gets his first career opportunity: The Right Way to Riot. His boss gives him a book he should read. The reward is the favor of his boss and improved job performance—this usually leads to a promotion To complete this opportunity, I need to make Chris read the book at home during his down time. The next time he returns to work after finishing the book, the opportunity is complete and the benefits are awarded.

While Chris is at work, Catherine refines her writing at the computer. I want to raise her Writin skill level so she can write better and faster befor I tell her to start work on her first novel.

Chris is grungy when he comes home from wor He needs a bath to nullify that negative moodlet which is sure to gross out Catherine and bring h mood down. However, before Chris goes inside, tell him to check the mailbox and pay bills. I dor want a visit from the Repo Man.

BROWNIE BITES

Well, that wraps up the couple's first two days in Sunset Valley. Within just about 20 minutes of play, I have assigned a career to one Sim and started an at-home career for the other by improving a skill that can be turned into a money-maker. We've also demonstrated certain key activities that you need to complete every day:

- **Eating:** This is easy to forget, but your Sims will throw out lots of signs so you do not. Use quick meals if time is short, but to improve mood and the Cooking skill, have Sims prepare meals from recipes.

- **Bathing:** Sims who work outside the home, such as Chris, can get dirty fast. Try to get a bath in every day. Don't wait until you see the Grungy moodlet. Look at the Needs panel and when you spy Hygiene rating headed toward 50 percent, hit the bath. If you are extremely busy, invest in a nice shower as soon as possible to speed up hygiene.

- **Social:** Sims are naturally into other people. Because there is an extrovert in the house, I made sure to have Chris chat up people in town close to his job. Making friends is fun, but just as in real life, do not take loved ones or family for granted. They need social attention, too. Fortunately, Sims have wishes related to relationships. Attend to those wishes to earn Lifetime Happiness points, get social-related moodlet boosts, and discover new opportunities.

- **Bills:** Do not forget to pay your bills. Make it a habit to roll the mouse over the mailbox. If you see that you can interact with the mailbox, that means bills have arrived. Pay them as soon as possible.

Making the Most

The next morning, Chris comes up with a new wish: Visit the Park. This wish makes perfect sense in the context of his Loves the Outdoors trait. Not only will sending him to the park fulfill the wish, but he will also get the benefit of the Beautiful Park and One With Nature moodlets. Plus, while he's at the park, Chris can meet new Sims and be sociable. Since he is a Schmoozer, he can use the socials associated with that trait to start some nice friendly relationships.

Meanwhile, Catherine is back at the computer. I promised her the Reach Level 5 of Writing Skill wish and I want the 1,500 Lifetime Happiness points that go along with it. As a bonus, completing this wish opens up a promised wish slot I can put a new wish into, such as Write a Romance Novel. (By level 5 of the Writing skill, Sims can pen romance novels, which are the most lucrative genre. They also take the longest to write, though.)

Chris had a good day at work. He got a promotion! Now he's a Snack Hawker. The promotion came with a one-time bonus of §158 and a raise to §25 an hour. At home, I put him on the treadmill to keep on his Athletic skill before he grabs a quick bite, takes a bath, and goes to sleep.

When Catherine gets up in the morning and goes to the bathroom, she gets the Dirty Surroundings moodlet. The tub and toilet are filthy. To remove the problem and prevent Chris from suffering the same negative moodlet when he gets up, I task Catherine with cleaning the bathroom.

And the hits just keep on coming. After putting dishes in the dishwasher, the object pushes water all over the floor. Left-click on the puddle to mop it up.

The wishes are getting a little more varied now. Catherine wants to Buy a Cookbook, which is attached to her Bookworm trait and her recently acquired Cooking skill. (She got it while making waffles in the morning.) I sent Catherine to Divisadero Budget Books to buy a cookbook. Since her Cooking skill is only level 1, I have to buy a recipe she is capable of making. I settle on Ratatouille. As soon as she checks out, the wish is fulfilled. While Catherine is out, I also send her down to the supermarket to buy some groceries. Along the way, she meets some people on the street. Now she has some acquaintances. I don't engage her in too much conversation, though, because I want her to get home.

Alright, Catherine is ready to start her first book. There is a choice to be made here: What genre? I opted for romance because I know she has the time to work on it. And while writing such a lengthy novel, she will also develop her Writing skill at the same time. When it's all done, she'll have a good money-maker plus an advanced skill set.

While writing, I noticed sparks coming out of the dishwasher following cleaning up after the morning meal. Catherine takes a short break to call the Repair Technician, which costs §50. If she had any degree of the Handiness skill, I'd consider just having her tinker with it herself. But as a total novice, she risks injury.

The Repair Technician is just one of the many Service Sims (Non-Player Characters) you can call to take care of tasks or jobs, such as delivering a pizza or baby-sitting. For a full list of all of the Service Sims and their roles, please see the Community chapter.

When Chris comes home from work, I plop him down in the living room and open his personal inventory via the Inventory panel. By left-clicking on the book his boss gave him as part of the opportunity, I automatically command Chris to start reading. The meter over his head shows me how far into the task he is. Chris is not a Bookworm like Catherine, so it takes him longer to read a book than it takes her. When Chris finishes the book, he is not done with the opportunity. He still needs to report back to work. That's when his boss recognizes that he has completed the opportunity and issues the corresponding reward.

The next morning, I make another investment in Chris. One of his wishes is to Do a Strength

Workout, so I buy the Exercise Queen, which will not only help him with his Athletic skill, b also keep his stress down while he uses it. I move the treadmill to another wall and instal the weight resistance machine right in the living room. As soon as Chris starts working out on the Exercise Queen, the promised wish is fulfilled and he banks 450 Lifetime Happiness points.

While Chris works out, his cell phone rings. When he answers it, he gets another opportunity: Muscle Showdown. This is a skill opportunity—and it's a timed one. He needs to report to the stadium during his personal time before 11:58 on Sunday to participate in a competition.

Aren't they cute, reading on the couch together

Soon, Catherine gets a phone call. Word of her being a budding author has spread because she submits a few completed chapters of her book every few days for a small stipend. The call leads to the opportunity It's a Living. Here Catherine must write enough books so that she gets §500 a week in royalty checks. If she does, Connor Frio will hook her up with a publisher to increase the size of those checks. Here's where the decision to write the romance novel pays off. This novel will be worth §500 a week in royalties because it's the most lucrative genre. As soon as that book is finished, the opportunity will be fulfilled, too

Not too long after accepting the opportunit Catherine hit me up with the Learn Painting S wish. I accepted the wish and immediately set about fulfilling it because that helps on e other half of the Illustrious Author Lifetime ish. Both the Writing and Painting skills must e mastered up to level 10. Catherine is at vel 6 on Writing skill now. There's no better he than the present to start learning the inting skill. The next day, I'll send Catherine the Community School for the Gifted to ke the class. But I'll do something first that ight help with the tuition...

s a result of finishing the book related to the reer opportunity, Chris got a promotion work. It's a good day for our family. While ris comes home, Catherine makes dinner both will have a Good Meal and she can ost her Cooking skill a little bit.

ter dinner, I make sure Chris and Catherine ve some time alone. I use Catherine's peless Romantic socials to love up on ris and in turn, use Chris's Schmoozer cials to flatter Catherine. Everybody is ppy. Catherine turns in and I send Chris take a bath so he doesn't stink up the ace overnight.

While Chris is bathing, he comes up with a new wish: Buy Something Worth At Least §100. That's an easy wish to fulfill, so I left-click on it to promise it to Chris. Then, while Chris soaks with the duckie and works on his Duck Time moodlet, I bring up Buy Mode and look for something sensible to buy that meets the wish requirement. I chose the Tigervine Plant to give the home a nice little environment boost of +2. Adding this bit of decor actually helps with closing in on another easy-to-get moodlet that helps with overall mood: Decorated. A nicely furnished home with enough objects that raise the Environment rating past a certain point results in the Decorated moodlet, which is worth +10 mood.

NOTE

See the Simology chapter for a full description of how to achieve the Decorated moodlet, plus the two advanced versions of the moodlet: Nicely Decorated and Beautifully Decorated.

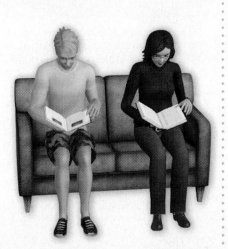

BROWNIE BITES

This has been a couple of full days for Catherine and Chris. What have we learned from observing this pair of lovebirds? For one thing, pay attention to wishes. Your Sims get new wishes every single day and many of them are small wishes that you won't have a problem fulfilling, such as wanting to raise a skill to a particular level, buy an object, or talk to somebody. You have only four promised wishes at a time, so you need to learn how to juggle wishes effectively to maximize the number of Lifetime Happiness points you bring in this way. Try to leave a slot open for these easy wishes. If you just leave them up in the bubble you will lose them when you go to sleep that night. The next day, your Sim will have forgotten about the wish. So try to balance longer term wishes that require a bit of time with those that are a breeze to fulfill.

Did you notice that Chris has received two opportunities while Catherine has only one? That's because Chris is out and moving around Sunset Valley on a regular basis and has a career where he constantly interacts with other people. Catherine will get opportunities, but it takes her much longer because she sticks closer to home to work on her novels. So, if you want more opportunities, make sure your Sims get out there and chat up the good people of Sunset Valley, in community locations like the park or at a career location.

A Day in the Life

Keep On Keepin' On

Good morning! Yesterday was a good day, but today will be even better. Catherine's Lucky trait gives her the Feeling Lucky moodlet, which boosts her mood for the entire day and wards off misfortune. (Today is a good day to try repairing something or make a difficult recipe. There is a good chance nothing will go wrong during either activity.) However, luck does not serve Catherine when she grabs the newspaper and scans it for discount classes. The only discount class for the day is Athletic. The Painting class will still be §400.

> ### TiP
>
> It doesn't take very long to read the paper and look for discount classes, so make sure to do it from time to time. If you spot a deal and have some free time, why not see if a new skill is a good fit for one of your Sims?

Chris has the day off, too. This is the perfect time to fulfill the requirements of the opportunity at the stadium. I sent Chris to the stadium and check him into the event, which is an option from the interactions menu. While Chris competes in the event, Catherine works on her romance novel. Chris naturally does

well at the event and scores an extra §500 for the household. Surely the boss will love this when word gets back to him on the next full day of work.

Back at home, Catherine takes some time away from the computer because she's feeling stressed out. Her Fun need has dropped precipitously low, so I tell her to read a book, which is something a Bookworm would enjoy. The trick, though, is I give her a cooking manual so her improves her Cooking skill while blowing off a little steam. While she reads, Chris works out. He improves his Athletic skill to level 5, which gives him the option while working out to "Push Self." This work out option increases the effectiveness of the activity and increases the skill even faster. But there is a catch. (There's always a catch...) The next day, Chris will have the Sore negative moodlet. I'll push Chris anyway because I have a secret weapon to combat this moodlet in the morning.

The next morning, Catherine loves up on Chris and offers a massage. The social negates the Sore moodlet and improves Chris's mood right away.

And just to make sure Chris knows he is loved, pick the Leap Into Arms social from Catherine' Hopeless Romantic socials. This improves their relationship.

Catherine's Feeling Lucky moodlet is definitely over because that night, the computer breaks Neither Sim has the Handiness skill, so a Repa Technician is summoned. There's §50 out the window...

At this point, Chris and Catherine have been together in this house for a week. They are very much in love and because they interact romatically regularly, they have a strong relationship. Because of this, each of them gets a new wish—and it's a big one: Have First Child. This wish will take a little time and will send their lives in a whole new direction But there is a significant pay-off for having th baby: 6,000 Lifetime Happiness points. That for each of them, too, if I promise the wish t both of them, which I do.

It's back to the book for Catherine, and Chri hits the weights because his Athletic skill is close to level 6. When Chris crosses that threshold and hits 6, a new social opens up: Train. Now, Chris can train other Sims on exercise equipment on the same lot as he is

is not a paid position, but it will help Sims
th a little extra weight lose it. See, this is
other reason you should always be working
skill development. Almost every new skill
vel brings with it new social, interactions,
d benefits.

This is actually kind of a weird scene—mainly
ecause it is eerily similar to my real world life.

NOTE

Catherine took the painting class,
so she better start developing
that skill. To develop the Painting
skill, jump into Buy Mode and
pick out the Artsy Easel for §300.
Install it in the house and now you
can left-click on it to choose the
Practice Painting interaction and
develop that skill.

The toilet got clogged again. Chris calls the
epair Technician. Before the technician leaves,
ough, Chris chats him up outside and makes a
new friend.

Catherine has been working hard on her
novel, pouring hours into each new chapter.
She's getting close, but stress kicks in again.
To improve her mood, I send her to the art
museum to look around and unwind. Seeing
a movie at the theater is another good way
to unwind. Plus, seeing a movie can result in
the Saw Great Movie moodlet, which boosts
Catherine's mood by +10 for 16 hours. Not a
bad deal for a §40 movie ticket.

Keeping working it, honey...

One of Catherine's recent wishes is to
improve her Cooking skill. That's an easy one,
so I promise it and then buy a new recipe
from the bookstore: Cookies. Those will be
fun to cook, right?

Wrong.

Fires will happen, especially with a stove.
Fortunately, Chris and Catherine were home
when it happened, so one of them was
able to put out the fire right away via the
interactions menu. Here, Chris sprayed foam
all over the fire and put it out. However, this
incident underlines the use of a fire alarm,
which I had installed in the kitchen anyway.
Had neither Chris nor Catherine been home,
this alarm would have summoned the fire
department to the house to put out the
flames before significant damage was done to
other objects in the house besides the stove.

The fire completely ruined the stove.
Insurance offered §165 to cover part of the
damages. However, I just had to click on the
Replace interaction to destroy the broken
stove and buy a brand-new one.

Well, it's taken about a week, but Catherine
is about to put the finishing touches on her
romance novel: Tender Was Her Flesh. As
soon as she does, she fulfills two promised
wishes: Write a Novel and Write a Romance
Novel. Each wish is worth 1,000 Lifetime
Happiness points. Not only does finishing the
romance novel fulfill those twin wishes, but it
also completes the opportunity: It's a Living.
The romance novel is a big hit. Catherine will
receive six royalty payments over the next
six weeks. Each payment is §4,494. That's
a massive payday for the household. Now
Catherine can devote more time to painting
and start really developing that skill.

With Chris's career going well and Catherine's torrid romance novel flying off the shelves, it's now time for, well, *business time*. To have a baby, Catherine and Chris need to love on each other a little bit and make sure their relationship is really heated. Once they have snuggled, kisses, and nuzzled, I chose the Try for Baby social from the Romantic social menu. This social inspires the pair to make WooHoo.

What is WooHoo? Well, when a man and a woman love each other very much, the man... oh, go ask your parents.

BROWNIE BITES

Well, will Chris and Catherine have a baby? Not every WooHoo results in a baby. You will know if WooHoo was successful if you hear a brief musical chime following the, uh, interaction. Within eight hours, the female Sim gets a little nauseous. If this happens, she's preggers and the couple will have a baby three days later. In this instance, WooHoo was just WooHoo and no baby came of it. The pair will have to keep trying to fulfill that wish of a first baby.

But in the meantime, life goes on with Chris and Catherine. The pair seems to be spending a lot on repairs, so it was time to enroll them in the Handiness skill class as Fort Gnome. And then to help build up that skill, Chris and Catherine read books on handiness from the bookstore. This is a bit safer than developing the skill by trying to actually fix things—especially electric objects.

Hopefully, this tour of the first two weeks in Sunset Valley with Chris and Catherine gives you an idea of the general flow of life in *The Sims 3*. Your Sims will keep you busy with a constant demand for wishes and a insatiable desire to develop skills. But life cannot be all about work. How *jejune*. You need to make sure your Sims relax with pastimes like books and fishing. They need to socialize. The need to visit community locations and meet people so they are exposed to new ideas and opportunities. That way, when Death finally does come a-callin', they can disappear into that Great Digital Beyond with a lifetime of happiness as their final thought.

Unless they come back as a ghost, of course...

Simology

• • •

"The human soul, as a part of the movement of life, is endowed with the ability to participate in the uplift, elevation, perfection, and completion."

—Alfred Adler, founder of Individual Psychology

ur Sims are not puppets or clockwork toys. tead they are shards of your own soul, ernate avatars that let you explore new uations and stimulae without the constraints this world's consequences. When you w life in Sunset Valley through that prism, liberating—and very exciting. It's an venture that could spin out into a million ferent possibilities.

at you put into these digital beings is at you get out of them. If you just check in e in a while and haphazardly pick traits or reers, you'll see an interesting story. But you nt an engaging one, don't you? After all, 's why you're holding this guide.

s chapter explains all of the different ors that go into the development a Sim's personality. That personality olves. Sometimes the changes are subtle. metimes they are drastic. Use Simology help guide your Sims through their lives. , life is random and Sunset Valley is full of prises. Just like your life.

aits

ts are the building blocks of a Sim's rsonality. When you fashion a Sim, the last g you do is imbue them with a set of traits. ts determine Lifetime Wishes, career tracks, development talents, social graces, and re. Almost every facet of the Sim's life is cted by the choices you make assigning ts, so choose wisely.

ait List

e this list of traits to determine the best difers for your Sims. This list explains the

strengths and weaknesses of each trait as well as the unique features that having the trait brings into a Sim's life.

Absent-Minded

Description: Absent-Minded Sims get lost in their thoughts and occasionally forget what they are doing or where the are going.

Benefits: None

Shortcomings: Sim will often stop in mid-action, disrupting progress and losing valuable time.

Unique Features: Absent-Minded Sims sometimes turn off the television when they finish watching—even if other Sims are still watching.

Ambitious

Description: Ambitious Sims dream big and are more rewarded when their wishes are satisfied in life. They are driven to move up the corporate ladder more quickly, but fall prey to low mood if they don't quickly receive the promotion they desire.

Benefits: Ambitious Sims enjoy improved performance at work. Fulfilled wishes are worth more Lifetime Happiness Points.

Shortcomings: Sim gets the Anxious to Advance negative moodlet if promotions or skill level advancements dont come at a regular pace.

Unique Features: To keep Ambitious Sims happy, make time to advance skills. Stay on top of goals at work, too.

Angler

Description: Anglers catch fish better than any other Sims. They also enjoy fishing more than anyone else.

Benefits: Anglers catch more fish and gain Fishing skill faster than normal Sims.

Shortcomings: None

Unique Features: Anglers start their lives with a Fishing skill book in their personal inventories. Fishing lowers their stress and decreases the need for Fun.

Artistic

Description: Artistic Sims are naturally gifted artists with a paint brush. They make pretty good writers or musicians.

Benefits: Artistic Sims gain the Painting skill faster than normals Sims. They also gain the Writing and Guitar skills faster, too, but not as fast as the Painting skill.

Shortcomings: None

Unique Features: Artistic Sims automatically interact with guitars and easels more often. Trait introduces Talk About Art social.

Athletic

Description: Athletic Sims are the best athletes in town. They can push themselves harder and longer than others, and will do so to feel the burn.

Benefits: Athletic Sims earn the Athletic skill faster than normal Sims. Athletic Sims also take longer to get the Fatigued moodlet.

Shortcomings: Do not like to listen to other Sims complain about exercise or athletic activities.

Unique Features: Athletic Sims cannot possess the Couch Potato trait. Athletic Sims get the Talk About Exercise social.

Bookworm

Description: Bookworms have a passion for reading that surpasses their other desires. They also tend to become good writers.

Benefits: Bookworm Sims read faster. Bookworm Sims also write faster whether working on the Writing skill, writing novels, or doing homework. They get increased Fun from reading, which helps dispel the Stressed Out moodlet.

Shortcomings: None

Unique Features: Bookworm Sims get an increased environmental bonus from a room with a bookcase. They receive a Talk About Books social.

Brave

Description: Brave Sims are fearless individuals who will fight fires, wrangle Burglars, and work to protect those around them.

Benefits: Brave Sims will fight and defeat Burglars. If a fire breaks out on the lot with the Brave Sim, the Brave Sim will not panic. He/she will immediately grab a fire extinguisher and put out the flames. Brave Sims do better in the Military and Law Enforcement careers.

Shortcomings: None

Unique Features: Brave Sims can sometimes demand a raise from their boss with success. Brave Sims are not scared by ghosts. Brave Sims cannot pick the Loser or Coward traits.

Can't Stand Art

Description: Sims who Can't Stand Art will never appreciate the latest masterpiece or expensive home decor. They are the anti-connoisseur.

Benefits: None

Shortcomings: Sims with this trait have a negative reaction to all art. They do not like to talk about art either.

Unique Features: Sims get the negative Can't Stand Art moodlet whenever they are around art.

Charismatic

Description: Charismatic Sims love to socialize and often know the perfect thing to say. They also like to throw parties.

Benefits: Charismatic Sims start with a Charisma skill building book and gain the Charisma skill faster than other Sims. Charismatic Sims fare well in almost all conversations. It's a useful trait for the Political career because it boosts the chances of contributions. Social-oriented tones in career have greater effect on performance.

Shortcomings: None

Unique Features: Charismatic Sims are great in conversations, which makes it easier to make friends. They're good at everything from Debate Politics to Boast About Fishing. Cannot have the Loser trait at the same time.

Childish

Description: Childish Sims find it difficult to "act their age." They love playing with children's toys, see things through the eyes of a child, and need to be constantly entertained.

Benefits: Childish Sims get benefits from having children's toys around, such as environmental boosts. They can also play with toys.

Shortcomings: Childish Sims are easily bored in conversations. They are particularly sensitive to repeated socials.

Unique Features: Childish Sims are not afriad of ghosts. Childish Sims can fish in swimming pools.

Clumsy

Description: Clumsy Sims muck up life with shoddy footwork and poor planning.

Benefits: None

Shortcomings: Clumsy Sims drop food, trip, and lose fish while reeling them in from the water.

Unique Features: Clumsy Sims drop engagement rings when proposing. It's actually cute...

Commitment Issues

Description: Sims with Commitment issues don't really want to settle down into a long-term relationship or lifelong career. Marriage is out of the question.

Benefits: None

Shortcomings: This Sim reacts poorly to many relationship-oriented socials, like proposing marriage.

Unique Features: Commitment Issues Sims must have a high romantic relationship with another Sim to accept marriage proposal. This Sim will desire to change careers just when things are getting good at work.

Computer Whiz

Description: Computer Whizzes love spending time on the computer. They are great at tinkering with computers, and can even make money as hackers if they choose.

Benefits: If the Sim has the Handiness skill, they almost instantly repair computers without fail. Unlocks the Hack interaction, which offers a new revenue stream. Sim gets greater pleasure out of Play Computer Games interaction.

Shortcomings: None

Unique Features: Unlocks Talk About Computers social.

Couch Potato

Description: Couch Potatoes are perfectly happy sitting on the couch to watch TV and eat junk food. They'll ne additional prodding to lead active live:

Benefits: Comfy moodlet is 50 percer stronger. Watching TV improves Fun ne quicker than other Sims.

Shortcomings: Couch Potatos need to sleep longer.

Unique Features: Couch Potato Sims cannot have Athletic trait. Will not workout unless in a very good mood.

Coward

Description: Cowards are terrified of everything that can and will go bump in the night. They are scared of the dar and frequently faint in "dire" situations.

Benefits: None

Shortcomings: Gets the Scared moodlet when seeing any of the following—Burglar, ghost, fire, Grim Reaper. Runs from these things most times, but will occasionally faint.

Unique Features: The trait unlocks the Run Away interaction. Cowardly Sims cannot have the Brave or Daredevil trai

Daredevil

Description: Daredevils seek the extreme side of life, even if it means making an everyday chore extreme. Th also love fire.

Benefits: Quickly puts out fire when c the same lot. Daredevils never burn to death if on fire.

Shortcomings:

Unique Features: Many interactions no have the word "extreme" in them. Add the Watch This social, which asks other to watch as the Sim does something crazy. After being crazy, Sim enjoys the Adrenaline Rush moodlet. Cannot have Daredevil and Coward trait at same tim

Dislikes Children

Description: Sims who Dislike Children do not want to have anything to do with children. No talking, no playing, an certainly no reproduction.

Benefits: None

Shortcomings: Sims reacts poorly to Sims with children or on a lot with children.

Unique Features: Dislikes Children Sims are in a bad mood any time they are around young Sims.

Easily Impressed

Description: Easily Impressed Sims are easily astounded by everyday stories and are always pleased with the smallest of accomplishments.

Benefits: Easily Impressed Sims are always receptive to boasting socials.

Shortcomings: None

Unique Features: Discovering an Easily Impressed Sim is a goldmine for adulation. These Sims hang on every boastful word, whether it's about fishing or dancing.

Evil

Description: Evil Sims love the dark, take great delight in the misfortune of others, and prefer to lead a life as far away from goodness as possible.

Benefits: Evil Sims are not discouraged by a lack of light. These Sims also get positive moodlets from other Sims' misery, like Very Hungry or Smelly. Natural advanced performance in the Criminal career track.

Shortcomings: Other Sims are naturally wary of the Evil Sim once this trait is discovered, especially Good Sims or Sims in the Law Enforcement career.

Unique Features: Evil Sims cannot have the Good trait.

Excitable

Description: Excitable Sims get excited about everything. They enjoy an extra dose of self-satisfaction when good things happen.

Benefits: Excitable Sims get positive moodlets from many activities, such as going on dates, eating a favorite food, getting a promotion, or catching a fish.

Shortcomings: None

Unique Features: Excitable Sims cannot have Grumpy trait.

Family Oriented

Description: Family Oriented Sims make great parents. They love big families and being surrounded by their children.

Benefits: Family Oriented Sims can help children with walking and talking better than other Sims. These Sims also start out with even better familial relationships than other Sims.

Shortcomings: None

Unique Features: Family Oriented Sims have the Talk About Family social.

Flirty

Description: Flirty Sims are constantly looking for romance and are most often quite successful in this endeavor.

Benefits: Flirty Sims do exceptionally well with romantic socials and have more available right away. Massages from Flirty Sims have extra positive effects.

Shortcomings: None

Unique Features: Flirty Sims naturally drift toward flirting unless it would negatively affect a current relationship.

Friendly

Description: Friendly Sims smile frequently at other and are quick to make friends.

Benefits: Friendly Sims default to friendly socials and develop friendships faster. Friendly Sims have an easier time becoming friends with other Sims.

Shortcomings: None

Unique Features: Friendly Sims cannot have the Mean trait.

Frugal

Description: Frugal Sims love to clip coupons to save money, relish a good deal, and hate being wasteful.

Benefits: Frugal Sims get coupon-related interactions with newspapers and computers and enjoy the Got a Good Deal moodlet whenever a discounted object/service is purchased.

Shortcomings: Frugal Sims react poorly to purchasing expensive objects, even if they are beneficial to household or Sim.

Unique Features: Frugal Sims give less in campaign donations.

Genius

Description: Geniuses are brilliant logical thinkers, masters of chess, and excellent hackers. They savor pursuits of the mind.

Benefits: Genius Sims generally have accelerated learning with brain-related skills and activities, such as the Logic skill

or using a telescope. Genius Sims do well in the Science, Law Enforcement, and Medical careers and are naturals at chess.

Shortcomings: None

Unique Features: Genius Sims often automatically use the Contemplate interaction.

Good

Description: Good Sims go out of their way to help friends and family in need, are charitable with their money, and frequently comfort those around them.

Benefits: Good Sims don't react negatively to socials or interactions as often and try to see everything in a positive light. When Good Sims "help" another Sim in a negative mood, that Sims gets the Comforted moodlet.

Shortcomings: None

Unique Features: Good Sims cannot have the Evil trait. Good Sims get the Donate to Charity interaction with the mailbox. Donating results in the Charitable moodlet. Good Sims can only donate once per day.

Good Sense of Humor

Description: Sims with a Good Sense of Humor tell the best jokes.

Benefits: Sims with this trait have an easier time starting relationships with other Sims, even those with No Sense of Humor. Jokes have a greater impact on relationships with other Sims.

Shortcomings: None

Unique Features: Sims with a Good Sense of Humor also respond well to jokes.

Great Kisser

Description: Great Kissers kiss better than any other Sim. They give kisses that are not easily forgotten.

Benefits: Kisses from Great Kissers are more readily accepted by other Sims and have larger positive effects on the relationship.

Shortcomings: None

Unique Features: None

Green Thumb

Description: Green Thumbs are the best gardeners. They find solace and comfort in their gardens and can revive plants in the worst conditions.

Benefits: Green Thumb Sims learn the Gardening skill faster than other Sims and start off with a Gardening skill book in their personal inventories. They create higher quality harvestables and can revive dead plants.

Shortcomings: None

Unique Features: Green Thumb Sims have the Talk to Plants interaction with their gardens. This interaction can remove the Lonely moodlet.

Grumpy

Description: Grumpy Sims are rarely in a good mood. They simply don't want to be happy.

Benefits: None

Shortcomings: Grumpy Sims naturally have decreased moods. It takes more work to make them happy.

Unique Features: Grumpy Sims cannot have the Excitable, Hot-Headed, Good Sense of Humor, or Neurotic traits.

Handy

Description: Handy Sims are the best tinkerers. They will never fail when repairing or upgrading a household item, which makes electrical objects far less dangerous.

Benefits: Handy Sims learn the Handiness skill faster and start out with a Handiness skill book in their personal inventory. Handy Sims never fail when repairing or upgrading objects.

Shortcomings: None

Unique Features: Objects repaired by Handy Sims have a lower chance of breaking again.

Hates the Outdoors

Description: Sims who Hate the Outdoors despise being outside and will remain indoors whenever possible.

Benefits: None

Shortcomings: These Sims get the Plagued by Outdoors negative moodlet when they are outside for longer than just a few minutes. (Travel to work is excluded.) These Sims make poor anglers because they don't like being outside.

Unique Features: They cannot have the Loves the Outdoors trait.

Heavy Sleeper

Description: Heavy Sleepers will sleep through any situation, no matter how loud or alarming. They also tend to snore.

Benefits: Heavy Sleepers are not awakened by loud appliances or music, letting them get a full night's sleep.

Shortcomings: Heavy Sleepers sleep through bad events, too, like burglaries and fires. Not even the alarms for these rouse the Sim.

Unique Features: Heavy Sleepers cannot have the Light Sleeper trait. They also get the Sleep at Work tone for careers.

Hopeless Romantic

Description: Hopeless Romantics passionately seek their soul mate. They want romance and true love, and surround themselves with cheesy romantic television and novels.

Benefits: Hopeless Romantics are more receptive to romantic socials and get an environment bonus if they are in the same room as a romantic interest in their lives.

Shortcomings: The Stood Up and Heart Broken negative moodlets are more potent with Hopeless Romantic Sims.

Unique Features: Hopeless Romantics have more fun reading romance novels and if they are writers, they create higher quality romance novels.

Hot-Headed

Description: Hot-Headed Sims are quick to anger. Broken household objects, conversations gone awry, or even the slightest negative moodlet will send them into a boiling rage.

Benefits: None

Shortcomings: Negative moodlets related to anger are more potent. Hot-Headed Sims have increased negative reactions to getting fired and broken objects.

Unique Features: Hot-Headed Sims react poorly to negative socials, such as Mock or Break Up.

Hydrophobic

Description: Hydrophobic Sims are terrified of swimming. They loathe every second they have to spend in the pool.

Benefits: None

Shortcomings: This Sim hates the water and will experience negative moodlets whenever around it.

Unique Features: Hydrophobic Sims never automatically get in the pool. They will not play with the rubber duckie in the bath, excluding them from Duck Time moodlet.

Inappropriate

Description: Inappropriate Sims talk about the wrong thing at the wrong time, never think to dress properly, and never think to apologize when they've wronged someone. They enjoy mocking others with harsh words.

Benefits: Inappropriate Sims can rummage through other Sims' trash can to find cool things (and trash).

Shortcomings: Inappropriate Sims cannot Apologize—they simply do not have this social option. They have the Make Fun Of social that is just cruel to other Sims.

Unique Features: Inappropriate Sims cannot have the Friendly trait.

Insane

Description: Insane Sims respond to events in life unpredictably. They say what they want, do what they want, and even wear what they want, even if it doesn't make sense to anyone else.

Benefits: Insane Sims are not frightened by ghosts.

Shortcomings: Insane Sims have a random response to a marriage proposal, no matter the level of the relationship.

Unique Features: Insane Sims will sometimes put on inappropriate outfits for occasions, like formal wear for going to bed. Insane Sims can fish in swimming pools. Insane Sims have the Talk to Self social, which removes the Lonely moodlet.

Kleptomaniac

Description: Kleptomaniacs "accidentally" end up with things owned by others. They often permanently borrow items from work, school, or even their neighbors' homes.

Benefits: None

Shortcomings: Kleptomaniac Sims often come home with stolen objects, which can severely damage relationships.

Unique Features: Stolen objects are tagged with the object's origin.

Kleptomaniacs get the Return to Owner interaction with stolen objects that results in Returned Stolen Object moodlet.

Light Sleeper

Description: Light Sleepers toss and turn throughout the night and are awakened by the slightest sound or bump.

Benefits: Light Sleepers always wake up when a Burglar arrives.

Shortcomings: Light Sleepers have trouble getting Fully Rested and are easily woken by music, children, and noisy objects.

Unique Features: Can use the Research Sleep techniques interaction on computer, but this has no specific benefit. Light Sleepers cannot have the Heavy Sleeper trait.

Loner

Description: Loners enjoy time spent alone more than time spent with others, Quite shy, they never approach anyone who isn't a close friend. They prize their solitude and get nervous around large groups.

Benefits: Loner Sims do not mind being by themselves. In fact, they get the Enjoying Solitude moodlet.

Shortcomings: Loners get the Too Many People negative moodlet in social situations.

Unique Features: Loner Sims cannot have the Party Animal trait.

Loser

Description: Losers encounter woe and misfortune throughouts their lives, beginning with school and continuing into their career. They will fail, and fail often. They won't get mad even when life falls apart. They'll just cry.

Benefits: Loser Sims will get a nice mood bump from the Winner moodlet in the rare event they actually win a game.

Shortcomings: Losers rarely win at games, such as chess or videogames. Losers complain more often in conversations.

Unique Features: Loser Sims cannot have the Charismatic or Brave traits.

Loves the Outdoors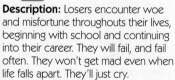

Description: These Sims love spending time outdoors and find special joy amid nature.

Benefits: Sims get great moodlets for being outside and love careers like

Athletic, Science, and Military, and enjoy talking about the outdoors.

Shortcomings: Loves the Outdoors Sims need to be outside more often, which can be disruptive at times.

Unique Features: Sims cannot have the Hates the Outdoors trait at the same time.

Lucky

Description: Lucky Sims are closely followed through life with comforting sense of luck. They win often and they win big.

Benefits: If a Lucky Sim gets at least four hours of straight sleep, they have a chance at the Feeling Lucky moodlet. This staves off misfortune, like fires, broken objects, and burglaries. Lucky Sims also have a greater chance of getting raises at work.

Shortcomings: None

Unique Features: Lucky Sims have increased chances at winning chess games or videogames.

Mean-Spirited

Description: Mean-Spirited Sims love to fight, mostly because they never lose in a brawl. They take satisfaction with every new enemy made and dream of new ways to be nasty to others.

Benefits: Mean Sims always win fights. Of course, that means they had to get into a fight in the first place. Every enemy a mean Sim has contributes to the Sim's overall mood. In other words, the more enemies they have, the better mood they'll be in.

Shortcomings: Mean-Spirited Sims regularly make enemies and often veer toward negative socials.

Unique Features: Mean-Spirited Sims cannot have the Friendly trait.

Mooch

Description: Mooches can mooch food and money from their neighbors, who for the most part, just go along with it.

Benefits: Mooch Sims can actually get free food and Simoleons from other Sims.

Shortcomings: While many Sims just roll with it, not everybody likes a Mooch.

Unique Features: Mooch Sims have the Have Snack interaction on other Sim's lots and the Mooch interactions in conversations.

Natural Cook

Description: Natural Cooks can improve any dish, making their food the most delicious.

Benefits: Natural Cooks learn the Cooking skill faster than other Sims and start off with a Cooking skill book in their personal inventory. They never start kitchen fires and never burn food.

Shortcomings: None

Unique Features: Natural Cooks can learn recipes just by trying foods on other lots.

Neat

Description: Neat Sims always find the time to clean, regardless of their mood. They are easily devastated by filthy surroundings, but will never leave a mess behind.

Benefits: Neat Sims will automatically clean up their surroundings and clean objects more thoroughly.

Shortcomings: Neat Sims get negative moodlets around dirty surroundings or unclean Sims.

Unique Features: Neat Sims have the Clean House interaction, which sets them to clean every filthy/dirty surface or object in a house.

Neurotic

Description: Neurotic Sims will freak out at the most minor of provocations. They become stressed easily and can be difficult to mellow. Luckily, they take solace in sharing their worries with others.

Benefits: Neurotic Sims have a self-interaction to freak out, which gives them a mood boost for a while (at the mood expense of nearby Sims).

Shortcomings: Neurotic Sims take longer to shake stress. Sims can automatically Freak Out after an unfortunate event, such as burning food or breaking an object.

Unique Features: Neurotic Sims can use a new Freak Out interaction that is disruptive to nearby Sims. At the end of the Freak Out, they get the Tranquil moodlet.

Never Nude

Description: Never Nudes despise nudity and will never completely remove their clothing.

Benefits: None

Shortcomings: None

Unique Features: Never Nude Sims wear swimwear into the bath or shower.

No Sense of Humor

Description: Sims with No Sense of Humor tell terrible jokes, so they tend not to tell them. They don't enjoy the jokes of others, either. Humor is simply wasted on them.

Benefits: None

Shortcomings: No Sense of Humor Sims have weak reactions to jokes or humorous socials.

Unique Features: No Sense of Humor Sims cannot have the Good Sense of Humor or Schmoozer traits.

Over-Emotional

Description: Over-Emotional Sims experience great mood swings when both good and bad things happen. They are constantly shedding tears of joy, whether it's at a wedding or just on the couch watching romantic television.

Benefits: Over-Emotional Sims get an extra bump out of positive moodlets.

Shortcomings: Over-Emotional Sims also get an extra dip out of negative moodlets.

Unique Features: Over-Emotional Sims have extreme reactions to events such as getting a raise/promotion, having a child, or getting married.

Party Animal

Description: Party Animals love to party, and others love to party with them. When a Party Animal hosts a party, everyone comes and has a great time. Wooo!

Benefits: Any Sim invited to a party from a Party Animal will attend regardless of relationship. These Sims have a greater chance bringing gifts to a Party Animal's party.

Shortcomings: None

Unique Features: Party Animals have the Wooo! social. If the other Sim reacts positively, the Party Animal gets the Awesome Party and Life of the Party moodlets.

Perfectionist

Description: Perfectionists spend more time cooking, writing, or even painting, but what they eventually finish is noticeably better than average. Perfectionists accept nothing shy of perfection.

Benefits: Perfectionist Sims have the chance to make higher quality painting, novels, recipes, and homework.

Shortcomings: If a Perfectionist Sim is making a high-quality piece of art or food, the action takes longer.

Unique Features: The Perfectionist Sim always makes the bed after waking up from sleep.

Schmoozer

Description: Schmoozers are really good at befriending neighbors and co-workers, and sucking up to their bosses. They love to flatter and are very good at it.

Benefits: Schmoozer Sims more effectively socialize/suck-up with co-workers and bosses.

Shortcomings: None

Unique Features: Compliments from Schmoozers are always accepted and always improve a relationship. The Chat social is replaced with Schmooze.

Slob

Description: Slobs constantly leave messes in their wake. To make matters worse, they won't offer to pick up or clean. Luckily, common filth won't offend their senses.

Benefits: Slob Sims are not negatively affected my messes or bad smells. Slob Sims can eat spoiled or burnt food without negative effects.

Shortcomings: Objects used by Slobs get dirtier faster than when used by other Sims.

Unique Features: Slobs can use the Lick Dish Clean interaction.

Snob

Description: Snobs are very hard to impress, though they love hearing about themselves and will never turn down a compliment. They dream of owning only the finest things and being associated with the highest echelon of neighborhood Sims.

Benefits: Snob Sims love mirrors and expensive objects. They also always accept compliments regardless of relationship.

Shortcomings: Snobs are very hard to impress in conversations.

Unique Features: Snobs often wish to make money, date wealthy Sims, take well-paying jobs, and buy new objects -- particularly mirrors!

Technophobe

Description: Technophobe Sims hate television. They rarely watch television and always look for alternate entertainment.

Benefits: None

Shortcomings: Technophobes have negative reactions to computers and televisions.

Unique Features: Because Technophobes do not like computers or televisions, they have a difficult time repairing them and have a harder time learning the Writing skill.

Unflirty

Description: Unflirty Sims do not appreciate romantic advances and are difficult to woo. It's not that they don' want to love, it's just difficult for them.

Benefits: None

Shortcomings: Unflirty Sims have negative reactions to romantic socials, such as kisses or flirtatious jokes.

Unique Features: Unflirty Sims cannot have the Flirty trait. They also have few romantic socials.

Unlucky

Description: Things rarely go right for Unlucky Sims. They lose at everything they touch.

Benefits: The Grim Reaper sometimes takes pity on Unlucky Sims who die of accidents and revives them.

Shortcomings: Unlucky Sims occasionally get the Feeling Unlucky moodlet after four hours of sleep, wh affects their chances of burning food, setting fires, and losing games.

Unique Features: Unlucky Sims canno have the Lucky trait.

Vegetarian

Description: Vegetarian Sims never choose to eat meat and doing so mak them ill.

Benefits: Vegetarians live longer than other Sims.

Shortcomings: Vegetarian Sims who eat meat earn the Nauseous moodlet.

Unique Features: Vegetarian Sims cannot prepare recipes with meat in them. Vegetarians can also cook vegetarian versions of some recipes, such as veggie burgers and tofu dogs.

Virtuoso

Description: Virtuosos have a natural gift with musical instruments and make the best musicians. **Benefits:** Virtuosos learn the Guitar skill faster than other Sims and start with a Guitar skill book in their personal inventory. They earn more Simoleons from tips.

Shortcomings: None

Unique Features: Virtuoso Sims tend to sing in the shower.

Workaholic

Description: Workaholics love to work and rarely become stressed from working. Their mood suffers when they miss work, but they can make it up by working from home. Workaholics make the best employees.

Benefits: Workaholics finish homework faster and have fun doing it. Workaholics have a better chance at getting raises at careers. They get the Likes Work moodlet when working.

Shortcomings: Workaholics suffer from the Missing Work moodlet if they accidentally miss a shift.

Unique Features: Workaholics can check in at work via the cellphone. These Sims can also work from home on the computer, which helps with career advancement.

HIDDEN TRAIT

There is a hidden trait that can only be earned through genetics: Pyromaniac. The Pyromaniac trait is sometimes given to children of Firefighters. Pyromaniacs can set objects on fire and get a positive moodlet from doing so. Of course, this ruins the object. Pyromaniacs can also take a fruit and turn it into a Flame Fruit, which Pyromaniacs have fun eating.

Mood

A Sim's mood of is the ultimate real-time determination of your success. A happy Sim means you are doing a good job on the big things, like fulfilling wishes and advancing careers, and also on the small stuff, like potty breaks.

Keeping your Sim's mood up is critical for banking Lifetime Happiness Points. Use the information in this chapter—the list of moodlets below as well as tip and tricks for advancing skills, fulfilling wishes, and advancing careers—to keep your Sims' moods high. By doing so, you can grab some awesome Lifetime Rewards that make life in Sunset Valley sweeter than honey.

BROWNIE BITES

If you're like me, you reacted to negative moodlets with horror at first. What am I doing wrong?!? Relax. You are not causing permanent damage to your Sims. In fact, negative moodlets are excellent teaching tools. Whenever I spotted a negative moodlet, I made a mental note to avoid the activity in the future that caused the downer.

Besides, pain is part of life. Without it, you're missing discovery opportunities. If you've ever had your heart broken, you know that once you get past the awful first week, you are already a better person because you learned about love's fragility. You can apply that lesson to the next relationship—and if you're smart, the next partner will benefit from your previous hurt.

Use that in *The Sims 3*. Let your darlings stumble. (But don't push them.) And when they do fall down, pick them up, dust them off, and send them back out into Sunset Valley all the wiser.

Moodlets

The mood system in *The Sims 3* uses an easy-to-read system of moodlets that instantly show all of the contributing factors to your Sim's overall mood. Use these moodlets to direct your household and make adjustments to behaviors, activities, or objects. If a Sim is Disgusted, look around for something unpleasant like dirty dishes or rotten leftovers. However, if you note that your Sims are happy about getting a compliment from a smooth Sim (the Flattered moodlet), then make sure they talk to that Sim more often for a good ego-stroke.

Here are three lists of all of the moodlets your Sims might experience during their lives. Each moodlet entry lists the effect on the overall mood and the duration of the effect. Most moodlets are self-explanatory. As you explore the careers, skills, socials, relationships, and objects sections of this guide, you'll find examples of how to generate these moodlets—and how to potentially avoid the bad ones.

Positive Moodlets

Aim for these moodlets in your daily activities. They all have a positive effect on your mood. Don't ignore the small ones in pursuit of the big scores. A simple moodlet like Minty Breath could be the 100 Lifetime Happiness Points you need for a coveted Lifetime Wish.

POSITIVE – MOODLETS

Moodlet	Effect	Duration in Hours	Description
Minty Breath	5	4	Sims love to be around those with Minty Breath. It sure beats the alternative.
Feeling Lucky	5	23	Today is Sim's lucky day. Who knows what good will happen?
Heard Theater Music	10	Variable	The music pulsing from the inside of the theater sounds awesome. Perhaps tickets are still available!
Educated	10	Variable	Exploring the local halls of culture and learning may teach even the most studious individual a thing or two.
Impressed	10	0	Touring public place sometimes reveals unexpected and impressive sights.
Let Off Steam	10	Variable	Having a friendly ear to complain to helps when you need to vent.
Decorated	10	Lasts as long as Sim is in room	Sims enjoy well furnished homes. By the looks of things, this place isn't so bad!
Brightened Day	10	3	Good Sims know exactly what to say to make someone's day better.
Had a Nice Nap	10	5	Having a great, refreshing nap may be just enough to hold back the onset of sleep.
I Am Beautiful	10	4	Recognizing beauty, even one's own, is just a benefit of vanity.
New Car Smell	10	2	Ah, that new car smell is so factory fresh!
Fascinated	10	2	Some Sims take joy in things ordinary Sims might otherwise overlook.
Got a Good Deal	10	8	Saving a few Simoleons is pure satisfaction!
Saw Great Movie	10	16	Sims have a special place in their hearts for movies on the silver screen, and a special place in their stomachs for the buttery popcorn.
Flattered	10	Variable	Compliments are quite flattering!
Intrigued	10	Variable	Juicy gossip satisfies eager ears!
Attractive	10	Variable	When a Sim looks this good, it's difficult for others not to notice. Wowza!
Hilarious Conversation	10	Variable	Some Sims should be stand-up comedians with the humor they're dishing out.
Tranquil	10	8	Nothing can stress or anger Sims who have reached their happy place.
Squeaky Clean	10	0	Experience the clean sensation of practicing personal hygiene!
Cheered Up	15	3	Gobs of sobs are stopped by the kind words of others.
Duck Time	15	5	Rubber duckies make hygienic cleansing fun!
Calmed Down	15	3	Sometimes all an Angry Sim needs is an understanding voice to help them get through a bad mood.
Enjoying Solitude	15	0	Introverted Sims like it best at times when others completely and utterly stay away.
Buzzed	30	3	Caffeine can really wake a Sim. Use this time wisely, because after the high comes the low...
The Life of the Party	15	3	Not only do party animals love to party, but other Sims love to party with them. Wooo!
Excited	15	3	Excitable Sims tend to get, well, excited.
Great Kiss	15	3	Great kissers give amazing smooches.
Inspired	15	4	A genuine and original work of art can inspire and render viewers speechless upon experiencing.
Oddly Powerful	15	5	The feeling of power is...intense! Science has bestowed Super Sim capabilities!
Fiendishly Delighted	15	6	Sims of the Evil persuasion take pleasure in the misfortune of others.
Fulfilled	15	6	The satisfaction of having a wish come to fruition feels great!
Returned Stolen Property	15	8	Kleptos enjoy returning things even more than...ending up with them. After all, it's more difficult to do the right thing, even when it follows the wrong thing.
Fresh Start	15	24	Moving into a new location provides a clean slate many dream of!
Likes Work	10	0	Work isn't quite the daily grind for everyone. Bring on the overtime!
Out After Curfew!	15	Variable	Being out after curfew is totally radical.
Pristine Picture	15	Variable	The pixels are dancing daintily on the television, perfectly in harmony within the highest resolutions money can buy.
Cozy Fire	15	5	Sims enjoy the warm cheery glow of their fireplaces...poke them for extra warmth!

POSITIVE – MOODLETS, CONTINUED

Moodlet	Effect	Duration in Hours	Description
Pumped	15	4	If Sims work out long enough, they get Pumped. Workouts are even more effective while Sims are pumped.
Sweet Venue/Party	15	Variable	The choice in venue for this party is excellent. It sure beats the standard house party.
Adrenaline Rush	15	3	An Adrenaline Rush will keep this Sim pumped and running around everywhere for some time to come!
Feeling Calm	15	Variable	It turns out it was just anxiety getting the best of your Sim. The object wasn't left turned on and impending disaster wasn't looming. But, double checking helps to calm the anxiety.
Comforted	15	3	A quick cry on the shoulder helps the sadness go away.
Sugar Rush	15	Variable	Filling up on sugary goodness makes everything more fun!
New Stuff!	20	2	Sims love getting new things for their homes!
My Love!	20	Variable	Sims in love swoon and flutter about like fools oblivious to the world around them.
Pregnant	20	Lasts until birth	The wonder of creating new life makes pregnancy an exciting time for most Sims.
One With Nature	20	Variable	Outdoorswomen find themselves quite happy when not tucked away indoors.
New Home	20	24	It's a new place to call home!
Read a Masterpiece	20	24	Turning the last page of a masterpiece is like falling in love...it's a beautiful thing.
Saw Great Game	20	16	The fans are rowdy, the food is messy, but when combined with a sports game, it's an experience Sims love!
Cuddle Time	20	5	Teddy bears make excellent sleeping companions.
Exhilarating Shower	20	4	It makes sense that if a Sim uses quality plumbing, they get quality showers.
Awesome Party	20	3	Party plus Party Animal usually equals Awesome Party. It's simple math!
Great Adventure	20	3	Sim had such an amazing time! How could this adventure possibly be topped?!
New Friend	20	8	Meeting someone new and hitting it off well enough to call them a friend is spiffy!
Nicely Decorated	25	Lasts as long as Sim in room	Well designed décor stands out in a good way and tends to make everyone happier.
Entertained	25	Variable	Sim is entertained.
Winner!	25	8	Sims never tire of the thrill of victory.
I'm the Greatest!	25	8	It doesn't really matter how you got there. Being at the top means being at the top; you are the best!
Virtually Victorious!	25	8	Success! Sims love the (virtual) taste and smell of (virtual) victory.
Saw Great Concert	25	16	Sims unanimously agree that experiencing a concert is well worth the potential inner-ear damage.
Saw Great Play	25	16	Sims love to watch people on stage doing funny and unexpected things right before their eyes. Sometimes they get the strangest feeling of déjà vu.
Honor Student	25	24	Hard work and a nose to the books pays off with the satisfactory acceptance into the Honor Roll.
Warmed	25	3	There is nothing like the feeling of a warm flame to make a Sim happy.
Saw Great Symphony	30	16	A feast for the ears, Sims devour the mellifluous melodies of symphonies with jubilee.
Threw a Great Party	30	24	Sims love a great party and the host who throws them.
Celebrity	30	Variable	Sims love being recognized by their fans. Celebrity status is so cool!
Superior Equipment	30	Lasts as long as Sim near object	Food made with top-of-the-line equipment just has that superior flavor!
Beautifully Decorated	40	Lasts as long as Sim in room	Rooms adorned with the most expensive sculptures and paintings improve life dramatically.
Having a Blast	40	Variable	Sim is having so much fun it's almost criminal.
First Kiss	40	24	A Sim's first kiss can leave them glowing for a long time.
First Romance	40	48	Love has bloomed for the first time. Could this be the real thing?
Wedding Day	40	24	Sims love to celebrate this incredibly important day with a party...just make sure everything goes to plan!
Celebrated Birthday	40	24	Birthday parties are the best!

67

POSITIVE – MOODLETS, CONTINUED

Moodlet	Effect	Duration in Hours	Description
Father of the Bride	40	24	Seeing a daughter married makes a father so proud.
Father of the Groom	40	24	Seeing a son married makes a father so proud.
Mother of the Bride	40	24	Seeing a daughter married makes a mother so proud.
Mother of the Groom	40	24	Seeing a son married makes a mother so proud.
Charitable	50	24	It feels great to help out other Sims, especially when they are in need.
Newly Engaged	50	24	With a ring on the finger, vows and true love forever aren't far behind.
Just Married	50	48	Sims always enjoy the joyful period following the marriage. Let's hope the love lasts...
Divine Meal	75	168	Sim has experienced a meal so exquisite, so divine, that it defies description. (i.e., Ate Ambrosia)
It's a Boy	80	24	Bouncing baby boys are delightful additions to any family!
It's a Girl	80	24	Gurgling baby girls are delightful additions to any family!
It's Triplets	80	24	Three babies! Hope your Sims wanted a big family.
It's Twins	80	24	Wow, your Sims were lucky enough to have twins. Double trouble!
Good/Great/AmazingMeal	Variable on cooking skill	Variable	Yummy! Sim enjoyed that meal more than the standard fare.
Comfy	Variable on quality of the chair	Variable	Nothing beats a good seat for comfort except perhaps a better seat.
Well Rested	Variable on quality of the bed	Variable	It's easy to wake up on the right side of the bed when you get plenty of time in the bed.
Beautiful View	Variable on trait	Variable	Would you look at that view!
Beautiful Vista	Variable on trait	Variable	This...house...is...incredible! Somebody really knows how to live.
Enjoying Music	Variable on music preference	Variable	It's hard not to enjoy a beat this solid.
Fit Atmosphere	Lasts as long as Sim is in gym	Variable	Exercising at the gym really improves the quality of the workout.

Neutral Moodlets

Neutral moodlets did not affect your Sim's mood, but they indicate activities that could have a bearing on mood soon, such as being a little hungry or having to go to the bathroom.

NEUTRAL – MOODLETS

Moodlet	Duration/Effect	Description
Learning Quickly	Indicates sped-up learning	Sim is picking up on this skill really quickly–how satisfying!
Cozy Fire	Lasts as long as Sim is in front of fire	Sims enjoy the warm cheery glow of their fireplaces...poke them for extra warmth!
Has to Pee	Alerts that Sim must use bathroom	Your Sim needs to go. Like, "go."
Hungry	Alerts that Sim must eat	Your Sim's a wee bit peckish. The stomach growling isn't far behind.
Sleepy	Alerts that Sim must go to bed	Get Sim to bed soon, to avoid the wrath of the truly tired.
Stuffed	Sim is completely full	Forcing Sims to eat when they are not hungry may lead to loss of appetite and weight gain.
Garlic Breath	Whoa! It might be time to scrub away that garlic with a toothbrush	Whoa! It might be time to scrub away that garlic with a toothbrush.
Fatigued	Variable	Activity of the athletic variety naturally leads to a little muscle fatigue.
Baby is Coming	Indicates birth is soon	Uh oh! The water has broken, contractions have started, and the baby is on its way! Get the mother to a hospital soon or sit tight until the baby arrives!
Power Study	Indicates sped-up homework/learning	That quiet library atmosphere makes reading, studying, and working so much more efficient!

What's New | Creating a Sim | Creating a House | A Day in the Life | Simology | Relationships and Aging | Tour of Sunset Valley | Design Corner | Object Catalog | Community

Negative Moodlets

Negative moodlets pull overall mood down, so side-step the ones that can be avoided. Those that cannot be avoided can sometimes be alleviated, though, through socials or activities. Cure the Sore moodlet, for example, with a nice massage.

NEGATIVE – MOODLETS

Moodlet	Effect	Duration in Hours	Description
On Fire	-200	1	Contrary to popular belief, being on fire is not healthy and can lead to symptoms including panic, burns, and death. Best find some water quickly!
Starving	-80	0	Allowing Sims to starve is quite cruel! Get Sim some food immediately to avoid an unnecessary death.
Heart Wrenching Scene	-60	Lasts until leaving	Witnessing a break up is truly heartwrenching. Hopefully the two Sims can reconcile and find new love elsewhere…
Betrayed	-50	24	Being cheated on is tough to move past. Talking it out with the other Sim would speed the healing process.
Mourning	-50	48	The death of a loved one affects those closest to them. Sims can mourn at a tombstone or move it to a graveyard to feel more at peace.
Heart Broken	-50	48	A broken heart is an affliction only time and tears can heal.
Vile Surroundings	-40	Lasts until leaving or cleaning	This room is so fetid and foul. Sims were not meant to endure such a lax household cleaning philosophy!
Exhausted	-50	0	At this level of sleep deprivation, even the floor looks like a good bed to this Sim.
Failing	-40	18	Having to stare at a failing grade on a report card just stings. Homework completion and a good mood will improve low marks.
Desolate	-50	0	When Sims get really, really lonely, they need to talk to somebody. Anybody.
Singed	-40	0	Fire burns quickly, but it will burn a Singed Sim even faster, so avoid hot situations.
Singed Electricity	-40	0	Sims find it unenjoyable to be electrocuted, especially because it may stop their heart. Until this wears off, Sims should steer clear of further potentially electrifying activities.
Horrified	-35	8	Terrible things have been seen underneath the mausoleum. Explorers beware.
Stressed Out	-40	Variable	Sim is in desperate need of some entertainment. The daily grind has ground the enjoyment of life to a halt!
Really Has To Pee	-30	0	The bladder situation has only gone from bad to worse; find a bathroom soon!
Missed the Wedding	-30	24	It's a bad, bad, bad idea to miss the wedding. It takes two to tango and your Sim missed the dance.
Rejected Proposal	-30	6	It hurts to propose and be rejected. The good news is that Sims can try again as many times as they like. Of course, each rejection will hurt just as much.
Fired	-30	Variable	Ouch! Getting thrown out of the workplace never feels good. Time to find a new job…
Missing Work	-30	0	Workaholics don't get stressed from working, but from not working.
Lost a Friend	-25	Variable	The loss of a friend hurts, but can be easily rectified by giving them a call and rekindling the friendship.
Scared	-25	3	Scaredy-cats are scared of pretty much everything, but they really show it when their life flashes before their eyes.
Virtually Terrified!	-25	3	Yikes! That snaggle toothed monster looked far more realistic than expected. Who knew monster breath would be so…fragrant…in virtual reality.
Too Many People	-15	0	Certain Sims may not feel too comfortable around large groups.
Nauseous	-25	2	Sim isn't feeling so hot. You may want to keep her around a bathroom.
Filthy Surroundings	-30	Lasts until leaving or cleaning	The grime and muck is really starting to pile high. It won't be long before it starts paying rent.
Plagued by Nature	-20	0	It's often best for Sims who Hate the Outdoors to spend as little time out there as possible.
Stir Crazy	-15	Lasts until leaving house	Sims should leave the house frequently for sanity's sake. Shake well with a community marinade for best results.
Tired	-40	0	When Sims get too tired, their mood begins to go south.
Very Hungry	-40	0	Gnawing hunger is not a good feeling for Sims. Feed regularly to avoid.
Hydrophobic	-20	Lasts until away from water	There's just too much water for Sim to enjoy this moment.
Drowning	-40	Lasts until taken out of water	Sims breathe air. Anything else gets a little…suffocating.

NEGATIVE – MOODLETS, CONTINUED

Moodlet	Effect	Duration in Hours	Description
Stuff Taken	-15	24	Sims really like their stuff, and when someone grabs it, they take it quite personally.
Rejected By Ex	-20	6	Sims don't like getting rejected, especially by someone who used to like them. Sims will have less luck socializing while they stew over a rejection.
Witnessed Betrayal	-20	6	Witnessing the romantic betrayal of a loved one is quite devastating.
Detention	-20	4	Aww shucks! Nobody likes spending time in detention!
Embarrassed	-20	3	Situations like this should be avoided at all costs...they're hard to live down.
Aching Back	-20	4	An aching back is quite the nagging problem. A massage would surely help.
Buzz Crashed	-10	3	Caffeine buzzes wear off eventually, leaving a sad Sim. Walk it off or have another cup!
Disgusted	-5	Lasts until leaving or cleaning	Revolting sights and smells will have this effect on Sims, so it's best to move them away.
Afraid of the Dark	-15	0	Heading inside or finding a bit of sunlight will take care of this cowardly affliction.
Disappointed	-15	24	Some Sims just hate it when they blow a chance to impress others.
Caught After Curfew	-15	3	It's so unfair! Why don't parents understand?
Offended	-15	3	Offense, when given, will require a healthy dose of time to forgive and forget. Or the dreaded apology.
Humiliated	-15	3	Humiliation tends to rear its ugly head just behind the heap of insulting comments.
Threw a Lame Party	-15	8	Some Sims throw awesome parties. Others throw parties that compare roughly with a stomach virus.
Crying Baby	-15	Lasts until leaving or baby stops crying	If the baby can't be quieted, it's best to get as far away as possible.
Feeling Anxious	-15	Variable	Neurosis overtakes some Sims with a feeling of anxiety that can only be solved by confronting the problem head on.
Anxious to Advance	-15	0	It's been a long time since a promotion has been earned or a skill has been improved... too long!
Overworked	-15	12	All work and no play makes it so that Sim needs to lay off putting in all that extra effort.
Upset	-15	3	It's hard to endure the rough patches with those you care about.
Itchy	-15	4	There's just no way to scratch the cursed itch!
Bad Night's Sleep	-15	6	Sleeping on a cheap bed would make any Sim grumpy.
Dirty Surroundings	-15	Lasts until leaving or cleaning	Garbage, filth, and grime do not improve one's surroundings.
Enemy!	-10	Lasts until Sim leaves	The presence of garbage would be preferred to that of a hated enemy!
Unfinished Room	-10	Lasts until room finished	This room needs proper flooring and wall covering of some sort to be considered complete.
It's Dark	-10	Lasts until room brightens	A little light would certainly improve things. Perhaps some windows to let natural light in, as well?
Strained	-15	Variable	Sim could stand a few hours of fun to iron out the stress.
Sore	-10	6	Sims may occasionally feel a little pain, but the results are usually worth it. Sometimes a massage can help...
Technophobia	-10	3	Some Sims really can't stand watching TV no matter what the channel.
Can't Stand Art	-10	3	One Sim's art is another Sim's garbage. Some Sims just don't appreciate the finer things in life.
Rude Awakening	-10	1	Loud noises and ruckuses will disturb sleeping Sims. Keep those stereos off and the conversation somewhere else, and don't light the bedroom on fire.
Dislikes Children	-10	Last until Sim or child leaves	Some Sims just don't find children to be adorable bundles of joy.
Rude Guest	-10	4	Sims don't like it when other Sims are rude, especially houseguests!
Rejected First Kiss	-10	6	It's sad when a Sim gets rejected for a first kiss. Very sad. A rejected sim needs time to cool off before their social skills will be back on track.
Bad Reception	-10	Variable	Cheap television sets don't always provide the most pristine picture.
Tired From Moving	-10	6	It's been a long day, but it's good to be home and settled in.
Creeped Out	-10	Variable	Ewww! Someone sure is acting creepy!
Cold Shower	-10	3	Freezing jets of water will dull any mood. Perhaps it's time to upgrade the shower...

NEGATIVE – MOODLETS, CONTINUED

Moodlet	Effect	Duration in Hours	Description
Tastes Like Fridge	-10	Variable	Every bite shouldn't contain flavors from everything else in the fridge. Quality fridges never have this problem!
Uneven Cooking	-10	Variable	At least the left-most portion was cooked correctly…right? Maybe a nicer stove would burn better.
Lonely	-15	Lasts until Sim finds company	Communication is a must for Sims. A quick chat will fix things right away.
Smelly	-10	Lasts until shower	Sims don't like to stink. More importantly, Sims don't like other Sims that stink.
Grungy	-5	Lasts until shower	Yuck! That layer of grime growing might mean it's time for a bath or shower.
Wasted Food	-5	Variable	Don't throw away good food! There are starving children in Strangetown!
Creepy Graveyard	-5	Variable	Graveyards are terrifying places filled with dead bodies, the ghosts of the bodies, and fear.
Boring Conversation	-5	3	Yawn! Will they ever stop talking?
Feeling Unlucky	-5	23	Today is NOT Sim's lucky day. Nothing good can come of this.

BROWNIE BITES

The best way to earn Lifetime Happiness Points and get those essential Lifetime Rewards—as well as keep your Sim happy—is to maximize moodlets. Do things that will make your Sims repeatedly content and your will bank plenty of Lifetime Happiness Points. Here are some little tips and tricks:

- Take a stereo with you to the park. Pull it out and play your Sim's favorite music. You get the Enjoying Music and Beautiful Park moodlets.

- Learn the Cooking skill and make high quality meals. Place extra servings of a perfect meal in the fridge (a good fridge) so you can eat these perfect leftovers for days and keep getting the Amazing Meal moodlet.

- Give your Sim the Over-Emotional trait for a 20 percent increase on every moodlet. If you make sure they get positive moodlets, their overall mood will soar.

- Buy the Moodlet Manager Lifetime Reward to remove negative moodlets.

- Achieve level 10 in the Culinary career to get a mysterious new fridge. Sims who walk past this fridge get the Superior Equipment moodlet.

- Have somebody in the household learn the guitar so everyone nearby gains the Enjoying Music moodlet.

- Grow a Flame Fruit and carry it with you at all times. You get the Warmed moodlet.

- Install a fireplace in your house and direct Sims past it to pick up the Cozy Fire moodlet.

- Go see movies at the theater. It is a cheap way to get a long, positive moodlet: Saw a Great Movie.

- Wonderful paintings created by Sims who master the Painting skill add huge environmental boosts to rooms. Add in some rare fish and precious gems and you have rooms that inspire the Beautifully Decorated moodlet on a regular basis.

- Buy the rubber duckie from the supermarket so you can enjoy the Duck Time moodlet every time you take a bath.

- Brush your teeth regularly for the Minty Breath moodlet.

- If you have multiple Sims in your household, have them stop and compliment each other for a moment to get the Flattered moodlet.

NOTE

Have a Loves the Outdoors Sim? Send them outside to fish and explore daily for the One with Nature moodlet.

Wishes

Sims want to feel fulfilled. Their dreams and goals define their lives. These aspirations are communicated to you through wishes. The essentials of wishes were covered in the previous chapter. Once a wish is fulfilled, it adds Lifetime Happiness Points to your Sim' total.

There are two types of wishes: Lifetime Wishes and regular wishes. The Lifetime Wish is an overarching dream that gets assigned in the Create a Sim tool. Regular wishes are the day-to-day goals that are met by doing smaller things, like achieving certain skill levels, getting promotions, buying objects, or socializing with specified Sim.

Lifetime Wishes

When you first conjure up a Sim in Create a Sim you select a Lifetime Wish. Each Sim has five possibilities, determined by the traits you give them. Satisfying a Lifetime Wish takes a lot of work, but is worth *a lot* of Lifetime Happiness Points. Not every Lifetime Wish is worth the same number of points, though. Here are all of the Lifetime Wishes:

Become a Creature-Robot Cross Breeder

◆ Reach Level 9 in the Science Career

The complexity of circuitry and oddity of organics perennially perplex the scientific community. Your Sim must have excellent Handiness expertise and enough experience with gardening and fishing to know what organic beings need to thrive when fused with machines.

The Emperor of Evil

◆ Reach Level 10 of the Criminal Career (Evil branch)

Your Sim can become the leader of the world's most diabolical organization. Strong evil office relationships are a must, as is possessing enough Athletic ability.

Leader of the Free World

◆ Reach Level 10 in the Political Career

The Leader of the Free World must be a passionate and charismatic politician who can raise immense campaign funding. It is an unenviable position where a Sim must constantly adjust to unexpected problems. The world needs great leaders—like your Sim.

The Perfect Garden

◆ Plant and Grow X Different Species of Perfect Plant

The most delicious fruits and vegetables are harvested from a perfect plant. Perfect plants grow from only the best seeds, which drop from the branches of generation-spanning plants that have been well tended and loved. Only fanatically patient outdoorsmen can plant such a garden.

Swimming in Cash

◆ Have X Simoleons in Household Funds

Simoleons fuel the world and for some fiscally minded Sims, personal happiness as well. Scrimping and saving to live in an efficient home, working hard at work, and succeeding at lucrative personal side projects will allow your Sim to swim in the metaphorical pool of money.

Illustrious Author

◆ Master the Painting Skill

◆ Master the Writing Skill

The arts delight most Sims. However, for each successful artist there are dozens of has-beens and failures. Your Sim can write and paint toward a lifetime of artistic success, but it won't be easy.

Celebrated Five-Star Chef

◆ Reach Level 10 of the Culinary Career

Bustling kitchens filled with fiery stoves and flamin' hot dishes are in store for Sims desiring the Five-Star Chef epithet. Your Sim will need to build relationships with kitchen staff and develop Cooking skills.

Presenting the Perfect Private Aquarium

◆ Have at Least X Different Species of Perfect Fish in Fishbowls

The ultimate fishermen can reel in incredibly majestic fish; so large they're practically bursting out of their scales. Truly dedicated fishermen spend hours casting and re-casting until the fruits of the deep blue are caught. Your Sim can create an amazing private aquarium by catching the most magnificent fish for a private collection.

Super Popular

◆ Be Friends with X Sims

Popularity is a sign that the community enjoys the friendship of your Sim. Unselfish socialization is a worthwhile pursuit.

International Super Spy

◆ Reach Level 10 in the Law Enforcement Career (Special Agent branch)

The forces of justice and order need champions to foil the nefarious plans of those who would do the citizenry harm. Only Sims in peak physical condition who use logic to solve troubled situations and look smashing in evening wear need apply at the Police Department.

Golden Tongue, Golden Fingers

◆ Master the Guitar Skill

◆ Master the Charisma Skill

Kindly spoken words and softly strummed strings are the fastest way to a Sim's heart and an excellent way to make friends. Charisma is a highly social endeavor, whereas guitar is for those who love learning and performing music. A master of both is an irresistible charmer.

The Culinary Librarian

◆ Learn Every Recipe

By mastering the Cooking skill and perusing t bookstore for recipes, your Sim can becom a walking library of culinary expertise.

Become a Grand Master in Chess

◆ Chess Legend

◆ Master the Logic Skill

Logic is cold and calculated, and chess is the battleground for those who adhere to it. A Sim who can master the path of logic and reach the coveted rank of Chess Grand Master will forever be enshrined in memory.

Renaissance Sim

◆ Reach Level 10 with 3 Different Skills

True scholars are not satisfied with mastering a single subject. Reach the top level of sever skills to become a Renaissance Sim.

Surrounded by Family

◆ Raise X Children from Babies to Teens

For family focused Sims, the pitter patter of little feet makes parenthood worthwhile. A house full of children can mean a tight budget, little personal time, and few luxuries but there's always somebody to play with o something new to teach.

Jack of All Trades

◆ Reach Level 5 of 4 Different Careers

Being tied to a single job isn't for everyone. Your Sim will be a jack of all trades, or at leas four, by climbing halfway up the corporate ladder of four careers.

Living in the Lap of Luxury

◆ Have Household Net Worth of X Simoleons

A life of extreme wealth is one of comfort and privilege, but also one of fulfillment. If your Sim owns a fabulously furnished home and has enough money to live in luxury, satisfaction will be had.

Star News Anchor

◆ Reach Level 10 in the Journalism Career

Great Charisma and an epic level of literary eloquence are required to succeed in the fast-paced field of journalism.

old Digger

◆ See Ghost of Wealthy Spouse

...me paths to acquiring wealth are more ...vious and selfish than others. Gold Diggers ...ek to marry the incredibly wealthy and ...arn to see the premature demise of their ...ouse. It's the only way to really enjoy the ...oney—alone and rich.

...rfect Mind, Perfect Body

◆ Master the Athletic Skill

◆ Master the Logic Skill

...eking personal perfection through rigorous ...ental and physical training is a noble goal ...at guarantees a lifetime of challenge. Your ...n may one day stand on the peak of ...ysical Sim achievement, but not without ...ch sweat and mental strain.

...aster of the Arts

◆ Master the Guitar Skill

◆ Master the Painting Skill

...e artisan can paint images that incite the ...morless to laugh and the inarticulate to ...oquence. The addition of Guitar skills can ...ke your Sim the envy of the community.

...come an Astronaut

◆ Become an Astronaut in the Military Career

◆ Reach Level 10 in the Military Career

...tronauts are incredible pilots who have ...dured years of rigorous athletic training. An ...ronaut's thirst for adventure is quenched ...ly by daring space missions.

...rensic Specialist: Dynamic DNA ...ofiler

◆ Reach Level 10 in the Law Enforcement Career (Forensic branch)

...ecial Agents in the field require the best ...ta to apprehend criminals and only the ...est analytical minds will suffice. After all, ...minals leave only so many useful clues, ...aking the work challenging. Students of ...gic with a knack for Painting make the best ...rensic analysts.

...come a Master Thief

◆ Reach Level 10 in the Criminal Career (Thief branch)

...htning quick reflexes (honed at the gym of ...ourse) and impeccable teamwork will take ...ur Sim far, but only the most cat-like thieves

reach the rank of Master Thief. The path begins with the local crime organization and leads to pilfering the world's jewels!

The Tinkerer

◆ Master the Logic Skill

◆ Master the Handiness Skill

Logic and Handiness are natural bedfellows, partners of invention and discovery. Logic leads to great finds like eerie nebulas, whereas Handiness unlocks interesting household improvements.

Rock Star

◆ Reach Level 10 in the Music Career (Rock branch)

The path of rock appeals to many a young Sim, but the perilous journey is completed by few. Your Sim must join the music career, survive the early years of rock servitude, and master the guitar to become the greatest rock star the world has ever known.

Heartbreaker

◆ Be the Girlfriend/Boyfriend of X Different Sims

Why settle for a long-term romantic relationship or monogamy when there are so many attractive Sims out there? Your Sim can find a lifetime's enjoyment by seeing many different Sims. Just keep your Sim's many former lovers at a reasonably safe distance.

Hit Movie Composer

◆ Reach Level 10 in the Music Career (Symphonic branch)

The composer must be well-liked by the musicians of the symphony, a master of music, and one who truly understands logic to grasp the science of sound.

CEO of a Mega-Corporation

◆ Become a CEO in the Business Career

Your Sim can become a purveyor of profits and margins that make board members smile. Your Sim must successfully schmooze co-workers and the ever-present boss to ascend the corporate hierarchy.

Become a Superstar Athlete

◆ Reach Level 9 of the Athletic Career

Earning a championship jersey means developing the utmost athletic perfection and a tight bond with teammates, thus fostering victory even when the game seems lost.

World Renowned Surgeon

◆ Reach Level 10 in the Medical Career

Only the greatest surgeons defeat disease. Your Sim must be able to make logically brilliant, split-second decisions at the operating table. The medical profession is only for incredibly dedicated Sims who are mentally above the rest.

Wishes

Not every wish is worth the same number of points to all Sims. Some wishes are worth more than others. However, here is a complete list of wishes you may encounter during your Sims' lifetimes and how you can satisfy the wish:

Simology

WISHES

Wish	Requirement
Watch TV	It doesn't matter if there's nothing on TV. Sims just need to tune in to tune out sometimes.
Improve Grades	Your Sim wants to buckle down and improve the grades being earned from school. Grades can be improved by showing up to school in the right mood and finishing all homework.
Have X Grandchildren	The pitter-patter of little feet warms the heart of an older Sim. Your Sim wants granchildren!
Become Friends with Someone	Friends almost always stand together through thick and thin. Your Sim wants to have a Friend, so meet someone new and build a friendship.
Determine Gender of Baby	Doctors have certain abilities that should be shared. Your Sim wants to determine the gender of someone's baby so the new parents will know how to decorate the baby's room.
Have X Rich Friends	The world becomes a much more dazzling and wondrous place when you are friends with the wealthy. Your Sim dreams of having lots of friends that are loaded! Look for the nicest houses and befriend the owners!
Throw a Campaign Fundraiser	Campaign Fundraisers are great social gatherings that bring constituents together for the sake of donations. Your Sim wants to throw a campaign fundraiser party. Start calling potential donors!
Make §X from Hacking	Encryption and firewalls are nothing to the skilled nocturnal hacker. Set your Sim in front of a computer at night to make some easy money.
Tutor a Sim for School	Teaching impressionable young minds is a valuable service to the community. Your Sim wants to help another Sim with schoolwork.
Visit the Art Gallery	Art is good for the soul, and your Sim's soul is in need of help. Take in some culture at the art gallery!
Win X Fights	The rough and tumble lifestyle earns few friends and a few bruises. Even so, your Sim boldy hopes to win some fights. Dukes up!
First Kiss	There's nothing quite like the dizzying delight and nervous anticipation of a first kiss with someone new.
Return Stolen Object	Kleptomaniacs cannot control their urges. Stealing things is a sickness! Your Sim wants to make amends by returning the stolen object to its rightful owner.
Repair Something	It's no use having broken objects in the home! They don't work and they just ruin a tidy house. Your Sim wants to repair a broken household object.
Talk to Tummy	A new life is growing inside someone close to your Sim. Your Sim wants to talk to the tummy to say something to the baby!
Play Game with Sibling	Games are a great way to pass the time and playfully prove one's dominance over family members. Your Sim wants to play a game with a sibling.
Pick up a Baby or Toddler	Sims want to pick up and hold their little ones close.
Do a Cardio Workout	Bend, flex, and keep the heart rate up! Your Sim wants to burn a few calories using the treadmill, taking a jog, or using the Fitness Channel on TV.
Donate Money to Charity	You can't take it with you, so you might as well try to do some good with it! Your Sim wants to mail a check to a charity.
Play Catch	Tossing the ball around is a great pastime many Sims enjoy. Your Sim wants to play catch outdoors with someone.
Sit on Couch	Your Sim wants to sit on the couch for a bit. Click the couch and select Sit to direct your Sim to do this.
Have Private Wedding	The pizazz of a wedding party is sometimes outdone by a more intimate private ceremony. Your Sim dreams of having a private wedding. Pick a special place and have your Sim ask the spouse-to-be to have a private wedding.
Make Something Fireproof	A home that cannot burn is a safe home! Your Sim dreams of a fire-free existence and wants to upgrade a flame producing household item to be fireproof. Start with the stove!
Break Up	Things aren't going so well with the current relationship and your Sim thinks it might be time to call things off. Perhaps the two lovers can still be friends after the break up?
Boast About Fishing Feats	Your Sim really knows how to handle a rod and reel and wants everyone to know. Go on, boast a little bit!
Cook X Different Recipes Perfectly	Preparing one Perfect meal is a bit of a task. Your Sim has lofty aspirations of preparing many. Best of luck!
Flirt with Someone Else	Old flames can sometimes burn low. Your Sim wants to light things up with someone new.
Donate §X to Undermine Charity	Nothing is as wickedly satisfying as confounding do-gooders. Your Sim wants to mail a check to help undermine a charity.

What's New | Creating a Sim | Creating a House | A Day in the Life | **Simology** | Relationships and Aging | Tour of Sunset Valley | Design Corner | Object Catalog | Community

WISHES, CONTINUED

Wish	Requirement
Make at Least §X per Week in Royalties	There's nothing like regular income! Your Sim wants to have money coming in from book royalties.
Earn a Promotion	Hard work pays off in the career climb. Your Sim dreams of reaching the relative safety of the next career ledge by receiving a promotion, earned by pushing just a little harder at work!
Get Ingredients for a Recipe	Knowing how to prepare a recipe doesn't matter if your Sim doesn't have the right ingredients. Your Sim wants to prepare a recipe. Travel to the supermarket and purchase everything called out in the recipe!
Work Out Until Fatigued	Your Sim wants to work out until the body can take no more and fatigue sets in. Purchase some exercise equipment, go for a jog, or work out in front of the TV.
Work Out for X Hours Straight	Your Sim wants to push the envelope and feel the burn! You can do it!
Do a Strength Workout	The muscle groups are begging for a workout and your Sim is eager and ready to comply. Muscle up with the TV's fitness channel or using the workout bench.
Calm Someone Down	When Sims are filled with rage, the best cure is to calm them down. Your Sim hopes to calm an angry acquaintance down with some soothing words.
Work at Home	Your Sim can't get enough of work, and wants to put in some overtime on the computer.
Get Demoted	Too much success can be scary for some Sims. Your Sim would like to relieve the pressure by getting demoted.
Propose Truce	Personal rivalries between Sims often reach a point when a truce is in order. Your Sim wants to let bygones be bygones and propose a truce with a nemesis.
Eat at the Bistro	The restaurant's menu offers some of the most elegant dishes in town...at reasonable prices! Your Sim wants to eat at the restaurant.
Catch X Fish	Your Sim hopes to spend some time at the beach or lake with a fishing rod in hand to catch several fish.
Work Out X Times	Good personal fitness leads to a healthy lifestyle. Your Sim values a strong ticker and wants to get in quite a few good workouts. Check out the Fitness Channel, or purchase gym equipment!
Calibrate for Higher Cooking Quality	An upgraded stove can greatly increase the quality and flavor of food prepared on it. Your Sim wants to Calibrate the Stove for Higher Quality to make every meal fantastic!
Start Working Out	Your Sim wants to spend a little time working out. It's never a bad time for personal fitness! Purchase some exercise equipment, go for a jog, or workout in front of the TV.
Eat recipe	Your Sim has a craving to eat something—cooked just right, of course!
Make a Smooth Recovery	One inappropriate remark doesn't need to end the conversation! Your Sim wants to use a Smooth Recovery to fix things. Go on, be smooth.
Invite Sim to Park	The park makes a great (and cheap) hangout. Your Sim thinks it would be great to take another Sim to the park.
Play Guitar an Hour a Day for X Days	Your Sim wants to develop a guitar habit! There's no better way to improve a skill than daily practice, so find an hour each day!
Boast About Gardening Glory	The gardening skills of your Sim should not go unnoticed. Your Sim wants others to know! Go on, boast a little bit!
Avoid People for X Hours	Loners prefer to be alone for a little while, as it helps them relax. Your Sim wants to avoid others for several hours to get back to equilibrium.
Stay Inside for X Hours	The outside world can be so busy, harsh, and bright. Your Sim wants to lay low for a bit.
Meet Someone New	There's a town full of interesting Sims for your Sim to meet. Your Sim wants to meet someone new!
Play Chess	Chess is a match of wits and cunning that often concludes without bloodshed. Your Sim wants to practice or play chess with someone.
Have First WooHoo	Your Sim wants to have a first WooHoo with someone close! Sounds like fun for a romantic evening.
Scrap Current Painting	Artistic Sims needs fresh inspiration and that old canvas is definitely not doing it. Your Sim wants to Scrap Current Painting on the easel.
Have Triplets!	Not one, not two, but three babies at once... oh my! Your Sim is a glutton for punishment (and love) and dreams of triplets. Surround your Sim with baby things, look into fertility treatment, and hope for a lot of luck!
Adopt a Child	Your Sim wants to start a family by adopting a child. Have your Sim call the Adoption Agency via the phone to adopt right away!

WISHES, CONTINUED

Wish	Requirement
Point Out Flaws	Some Sims like to be truly nasty toward their neighbors with a few insulting comments. Your Sim wants to point out someone's flaws.
Eat Stu Surprise	Stu Surprise is an icky dish that contains so many flavors that it becomes palatable. Your Sim wants to eat Stu Surprise made with grapes and garlic.
Teach Toddler to Walk	Crawling toddlers are even cuter when they can bobble about like basic bipeds! Your Sim wants to teach the toddler to walk...one wobbly step at a time!
Win a Fight	It's never fun to lose, especially when you're the one on the ground! Your Sim wants to win a fight. Sims that win tend to be good athletes, or just downright mean.
Win a Ranked Chess Match	Your Sim hopes to reign supreme on the highly dangerous Ranked Chess Circuit. Use the phone to invite over your next opponent.
Give Inspirational Speech	Politicians of great renown should use their oratory abilities to inspire the masses. Your Sim wants to give an inspirational speech...for liberty!
Buy an Exercise Machine	Pumping iron is the fastest way to turn a Sim's body into a muscular machine. Your Sim wants to bulk up! Buy an exercise machine from the Buy Catalog.
Eat Dim Sum and Canned Soup	Cravings cannot be explained, so there's no point looking for an explanation. Your Sim dreams of eating Dim Sum and canned soup.
Give Medical Advice	Expectant mothers frequently seek medical advice for their not-yet born children. Your Sim wants to give medical advice to a pregnant Sim.
Play the Guitar	Six strings of acoustic enjoyment are calling to your Sim's talented fingers. Your Sim wants to play guitar for a bit to relax.
Console Someone	Sims going through hard times need a friendly, consoling voice. Your Sim wants to console someone with a few kind words.
Learn Bait for a Fish	Some fish bite more often when the correct bait is attached to the lure. Your Sim wants to learn the bait for a certain fish. Read bait books purchased from the bookstore, or experiment with different types of bait to see what works!
Adopt a Boy	Your Sim dreams of adopting a baby boy to bring into the family. Baby boys are a wonderful addition to any family and will surely bring years of joy for your Sim!
Prepare a Meal Using Freshly Caught Fish	Properly prepared fish can taste simply wonderful, assuming the dish is without scales or that fishy taste! Your Sim aspires to prepare a recipe that contains freshly caught fish. Catch the ingredients and start cooking.
Make an Object Self-Cleaning	Handy Sims can tinker and upgrade some objects to be self-cleaning. The object will never be dirty again! Your Sim wants to upgrade an object to be self-cleaning.
Improve Relationship with Boss	Dreams can sometimes be made from just a little schmooze. Your Sim wants to meet up with the boss and improve their relationship, at least a little bit.
Tutor Someone in a Skill	Tutoring is a great way to teach others about a topic quickly. Your Sim wants to tutor someone in a skill such as cooking or fishing.
Catch a X Kilogram Fish	Only the biggest catches are worth mentioning. Your Sim wants to catch a certain sized fish of which to be proud.
Train Someone	Some Sims need a mentor to prod them along while exercising. Your Sim wants to personally train someone. Make sure your Sim owns exercise equipment, invite the trainee over, and start training!
Get a Job	Your Sim envisions a bright future with one of the fine employers throughout the town. Check the newspaper or computer for open positions. You can also go to Map View and filter by Jobs to find opportunities by location.
Wooo! Someone	Parties are ragin' awesome, but they are even better when the Wooo! gets thrown around. Your Sim wants to Wooo! other Sims to spread the fun.
Go Shopping	Your Sim has the shopping bug. There's only one cure! Send your Sim to the bookstore or supermarket in town to buy some items for the home.
Clean Entire House	The home is appallingly dirty! Your Sim thinks it's time to clean up the trash, puddles, and grime that have amassed since the home was last cleaned.
Earn a Raise	The sweet ka-ching of a raise is floating in your Sim's head. Dreaming big really pays off, assuming your Sim puts in the extra effort at work.
Compliment Someone's Personality	Someone around has a great personality, and your Sim wants to let that Sim know.
Take a Class in the X Skill	Your Sim wants to take a Writing skill class to learn the skill. Visit the Business Office to enroll in the class.
Take a Class in the X Skill	Your Sim wants to take a Painting skill class to learn the skill. Visit the School to enroll in the class.

WISHES, CONTINUED

Wish	Requirement
Take a Class in the X Skill	Your Sim wants to take a Logic skill class to learn the skill. Visit the Science Facility to enroll in the class.
Take a Class in the X Skill	Your Sim wants to take a Handiness skill class to learn the skill. Visit the Military Base to enroll in the class.
Take a Class in the X Skill	Your Sim wants to take a Guitar skill class to learn the skill. Visit the theater to enroll in the class.
Take a Class in the X Skill	Your Sim wants to take a Gardening skill class to learn the skill. Visit the Science Facility to enroll in the class.
Take a Class in the X Skill	Your Sim wants to take a Fishing skill class to learn the skill. Visit the Supermarket to enroll in the class.
Take a Class in the X Skill	Your Sim wants to take a Cooking skill class to learn the skill. Visit the Bistro to enroll in the class.
Take a Class in the X Skill	Your Sim wants to take a Charisma skill class to learn the skill. Visit City Hall to enroll in the class.
Take a Class in the X Skill	Your Sim wants to take an Athletic skill class to learn the skill. Visit the Stadium to enroll in the class."
Move In with Someone	Moving in with someone is a big deal that shouldn't be taken lightly. Can a relationship survive the move? Your Sim hopes to move in with someone.
Meet All Co-Workers	The office is full of friendly faces all waiting to be introduced to your Sim. Your Sim wants to meet everyone to improve the workplace and meet some new people.
Cheer Someone Up	Sadness will accompany Sims following rough patches like a broken heart or the death of a loved one. Your Sim wants to cheer someone up with a few kind words.
Write a Best-Seller	Sales aren't always an indication of quality, but they don't hurt! Your Sim wants to write a best-selling book.
Buy a X Worth at Least §X	Your Sim wants to improve the house with a new purchase. Start shopping!
Beat Up Someone	Your Sim isn't feeling so great. But beating up another Sim will make it all better!
Grow Ingredients for Meal	Home cooked meals prepared using fresh, home grown ingredients put the phrase "yum" in the dictionary. Your Sim wants to grow ingredients in the garden.
Stay on the Honor Roll for X Days	Your Sim wants to remain on the honor roll for a few days, but it won't be easy! Keep your Sim in a good mood and make sure all the homework is completed on time.
Water Plants	Your Sim's garden plants are thirsty! Your Sim wants to water the plants before they get sick and die.
Brighten Day	Good Sims have the innate ability to brighten one's day with a few kind words. Being the good sort, your Sim wants to brighten someone's day!
Prepare Meal with X	Fruits and vegetables can really bring the best flavors forward and delight the palate. Your Sim dreams of preparing a meal that contains fruit or vegetables. Buy them at the supermarket or grow them at home!
Attend a Protest	Your Sim wants to express a little political thought and attend a protest! Protests are typically held at City Hall on the weekends. Let your Sim join in to be heard.
Freak Out!	Sometimes you just have to freak out! Your Sim wants to let the neurosis take hold and freak out.
Grow Up!	Your Sim dreams of growing up! It'll take some scraped knees, exploration, and a healthy dose of good parenting. The special day isn't too far into the future!
Conduct an Interview	Your Sim needs a few questions answered in order to write a story. Track someone down and hold that interview for the answers you need.
Hold Hands	Your Sim longs for the familiar squeeze of a loved one's hand. Hand holding is always good for the soul, assuming there are no sweaty palms!
Eat Something at the Public Pool	Sims shouldn't eat and swim at the same time, but they can certainly swim after eating. Your Sim wants to prepare something tasty to eat at the public pool.
Finish Current Painting	Your Sim wants to put the final brush strokes to canvas to see if the current work is indeed a masterpiece. If it isn't, better to finish the current painting and move onto a new piece!
Wedding Congratulations	Dear friends or strangers, it doesn't really matter. Your Sim wants to offer Wedding Congratulations to a happy new couple!
See a Sim Age Up Well	A kid's job is to grow up well! Toddlers need to learn all their basic skills and be kept safe and happy. Teens and children need to be successful in school. Growing up well helps prepare kids for their next stage in life!
Teen Insult	Teens can be so cruel! Your Sim really wants to hit someone where it hurts.

77

Simology

WISHES, CONTINUED

Wish	Requirement
Eat Stu Surprise	Stu Surprise is an icky dish that contains so many flavors that it becomes palatable. Your Sim wants to eat Stu Surprise made with hot dogs and tomato.
Earn §X in Royalties Per Week	Prolific writers of great renown can typically live off their royalty checks. Your Sim wants to become a professional writer by earning money in royalty checks per week.
Practice Speech	Practice makes perfect, and your Sim will a need a mirror for this kind of practice.
Help a Sim with Homework	Your Sim has been there before, and wants to ease another Sim's burden by helping with homework.
Eat Stu Surprise	Stu Surprise is an icky dish that contains so many flavors that it becomes palatable. Your Sim wants to eat Stu Surprise made with cheese and limes.
Go Inside	Bugs and wide open spaces don't appeal to everyone. Your Sim wants to go inside the house.
Befriend All Co-workers	Your Sim hopes to improve the workday grind by befriending all co-workers. It's a good way to network, improve sanity, and find friends for after-work events.
Eat Stu Surprise	Stu Surprise is an icky dish that contains so many flavors that it becomes palatable. Your Sim wants to eat Stu Surprise made with peppers and apples.
Join Special Agent Career Branch	Foiling the nefarious plans of madmen is a staple of the Special Agent's life. Your Sim hopes to become one and should look forward to making the choice after being promoted past Lieutenant.
Mop Puddle	Puddles are blights on otherwise sightly floors. Your Sim wants to mop up the offending moisture before it spreads!
Listen to Tummy	A new life is growing inside someone close to your Sim. Your Sim wants to listen to the tummy to hear what the baby is up to!
Compliment Appearance	Physical appearance is often noteworthy. Your Sim wants to compliment another on their appearance.
Sleep Over at Someone's Home	Sleepovers are great fun, plus you don't need to make the bed! Your Sim thinks it'd be worthwhile to sleep over at someone's house. Become friends with someone and wait for the invitation.
Divorce	Enough is enough! Sometimes Sims wonder how their life might have been different if... Well, there's no time like the present.
Confess Attraction	Keeping secrets can get Sims all worked up. Your Sim can't hold it in any longer and wants to tell that certain someone.
Ask Someone to Stay Over	Inviting someone to a sleepover is a recipe for late night fun! Your Sim wants to ask someone to stay over, perhaps to see how long sleep can be avoided!
Spend §X at the Day Spa	Sims living a life of luxury need places to spend their Simoleons. Spend some money on day spa packages for a completely pampered experience.
Buy Something	Your Sim thinks it's time to spice up the house just a touch with something new.
Be Mean	Sometimes it's fun to hurt someone else's feelings. Your Sim wants to try out a mean social on someone.
Get Attention from Dad	It's okay to crave attention from time to time, because that nourishment helps little Sims grow up to be great! Your Sim desires a little attention from Dad. See if he wants to play or chat!
Ask for Campaign Donation	The political machine won't pay for itself. Money is needed to fuel city politics! Your Sim thinks it's time to talk to the neighbors and ask them for campaign donations.
See Game at Stadium	It's time to root, root, root for the home team! Your Sim hopes to see a game at the local stadium—quick, before the season ends!
Visit the Park	The park is full of outdoor pleasures for Sims of all ages. Your Sim dreams of visiting the park. BBQs, picnics, tag—there's so much fun to be had!
Write a Book Worth at Least §X a Week in Royalties	There's nothing like regular income! Your Sim wants to have money coming in from book royalties.
Hang Out in Room for X Hours	Some Sims get attached to a specific room. Your Sim would prefer not to leave for a while.
Fight!	Grrr! Your Sim wants to get in a fight! Provoke another Sim enough and that fight will happen soon enough!
Make a New Outfit for Myself	Fashions can fade in a matter of days. Your Sim wants to stay ahead of the trends by Planning an Outfit on the dresser.
Take It Easy at Work	There are some days when the boss isn't looking over your shoulder. Your Sim dreams of slacking off at work...if only for today! Pick the "Take It Easy" option once your Sim gets to work to take it easy.

WISHES, CONTINUED

Wish	Requirement
Join Thief Career Branch	Stealing the world's most dazzling jewels is what thieves do best. Your Sim has a keen eye for thievery and can make the choice to be a thief after being promoted past Con Artist.
Throw a Birthday Party	Birthdays are best celebrated among friends and family...with cake! Your Sim wants to throw a birthday party. Throw a Birthday Party using the phone.
Check Self Out in Mirror	Hey there, good-looking! Your Sim wants to Check Self Out in a mirror.
Steal Something	There's no better discount than the five-fingered kind! Your Sim wants to swipe something.
Start Writing a Book	Your Sim has a few ideas floating around and wants to start writing a book. Set aside some time to write and use the computer to transfer the idea to print!
Use an Object	Sims can be very object oriented, and right now, your Sim wants to use an object.
Master a Skill	Mastering a Skill takes great patience and dedication, but your Sim aspires to be the best. Have your Sim practice the skill and complete Opportunities, and great things will happen.
Mooch a Few Simoleons	Your Sim wants to "borrow" some money to use for...something. Ask a friend if it's okay to mooch a little money.
Become BFF	Your Sim wants to become best friends with a Sim. Discover what they have in common and they'll be BFF in no time!
Eat an Outstanding Quality Meal	Eating wonderful food is just one of the many joys of knowing how to cook. Your Sim yearns to eat an Outstanding meal. Obtain high quality ingredients and refine your Sim's Cooking skill.
See Child Become a Scientist	The life of a scientist is a rewarding one filled with gizmos, lab adventures, awards, and a decent pay. Your Sim dreams of seeing someone close reaching level 3 in the Science career. The science facility is always looking for new scientists...
Tutor Someone in a Skill	Tutoring is a great way to teach others about a topic quickly. Your Sim wants to tutor someone in a skill such as Cooking or Fishing.
Talk About Great Outdoors	Ah, the great outdoors! It's just so great, some Sims just have to talk about it!
Marry a Rich Sim	When love cannot sustain the relationship, perhaps heaps of money can! Your Sim dreams of marrying a rich Sim...hopefully for the right reasons? Your Sim should search the town for the nicest home and fall in love with its owner.
Make Out	Sometimes, it's just time to make your move. Your Sim thinks now is that time.
Find Own Place	Every Sim aspires to home ownership. Nobody likes being cooped up with friends or worse, parents! Your Sim wants to find a place to live. Look up potential homes on the computer!
Ask if Single	The romantic landscape of the town is vast and exciting, but some Sims are off limits. Your Sim wants to ask someone about their partner to see if they're available...or taken!
Prepare a Perfect Meal	It's important to prepare a meal that really gives the palate something worth remembering. Your Sim wants to prepare a Perfect meal. Purchase or grow high quality ingredients and refine your Sim's Cooking skill.
Catch Something without Bait	It takes a fisherman of great skill to catch a fish without the perfect bait to lure them to the hook that spells their doom! Your Sim wants to catch something without using bait.
Join Rock Career Branch	Sims enamored with guitar solos should take the path of Rock. Your Sim has quite the stage presence and may want to pick the Rock branch after being promoted past Music Talent Scout.
Go to the Bookstore	The bookstore is a great place to visit in town. Your Sim wants to visit the bookstore, perhaps to sign up for a class or purchase some new reading material!
Cook Someone's Favorite Meal	Friendly cooks learn to prepare their friends' favorite meals. Your Sim wants to please someone by preparing that Sim's favorite dish.
See Child Be a Genius	Sims that have a great upbringing and work hard in school get the best traits...like being a genius! Your Sim hopes to see a child become a genius.
Buy Something New	If you don't have something, that's why you need it! Your Sim wants to own something new.
Decorate House With at Least X Paintings	Your Sim wants to decorate the house with paintings. A range of great paintings is available in Buy Mode, but Artistic Sims might want an easel to create and display their own artwork.
Propose Going Steady	Your Sim is ready to settle down with an exclusive boyfriend or girlfriend. Perfect the timing and ask the question before your Sim's significant other gets away!
Find Out if a Sim is Rich or Not	Your Sim wants to know about the personal wealth of someone else. Converse with potentially rich neighbors or visit their homes to find out!

WISHES, CONTINUED

Wish	Requirement
Talk About New Job	The contract is glossy and the pay still good; your Sim just wants to talk about the new job with anyone who will listen.
Prepare a Meal Using Fish	Properly prepared fish can taste simply wonderful, assuming the dish is without scales or that fishy taste! Your Sim aspires to prepare a recipe that contains fish. Get the right ingredients and start cooking.
Become Best Friends with Someone	Best Friends always laugh at your jokes and, when needed, will offer a shoulder to cry on. Your Sim dreams of having a Best Friend, but it'll take time and dedication.
Go to the Library	Some Sims can't get enough of the quiet and that dusty book smell! Your Sim wants to visit the library.
Adopt a Girl	Your Sim dreams of adopting a baby girl to bring into the family. Baby girls are a wonderful addition to any family and will surely bring years of joy for your Sim!
Retire	Easy Street is calling with promises of lazy afternoons, sleeping in, and no bosses making demands. Your Sim dreams of retiring and collecting that lovely pension. Give the office a call to make retirement a reality.
Paint a Masterpiece	A painting masterpiece is such a rare, beautiful thing that cannot be taken for granted. Your Sim wants to paint a Masterpiece. A strong Painting skill and luck will bring this about.
See a Concert	The neighborhood enjoys quite a few good concerts from time to time. Your Sim really wants to see a concert at the theater. Check the theater on Fridays and Saturdays to see if there is a concert!
Reach the Top Level of a Career	For some, the only acceptable path is straight to the top. Your Sim aims to reach the top of a career. An admirable goal, to be sure! Work hard and do whatever management requests and your Sim will go far!
Go Out on the Town	Some Sims just don't like to stay in one place for too long. You Sim wants to get away from their home lot for a bit.
Mooch Food	If there's one thing better than food, it's free food! Your Sim wants someone else's food.
Become a Star Chef	Sometimes, merely cooking for friends and family isn't as great as being known as a star! Your Sim hopes to move up to become a Star Chef by working diligently on their culinary skills.
Ask for a Promotion	Your Sim seeks a promotion, because the current title and pay grade just won't cut it! Your Sim should butter up the boss and ask for a promotion.
Weed Plants	Your Sim's garden plants are overgrown with weeds! Your Sim wants to weed the plants before they get sick and die.
Eat a Perfect Quality Meal	Eating wonderful food is just one of the many joys of knowing how to cook. Your Sim yearns to eat a Perfect meal. Obtain high quality ingredients and refine your Sim's Cooking skill.
Hug Someone Amorously	Sometimes a friendly squeeze isn't enough. Your Sim dreams of hugging someone amorously to set the mood for romance!
Finish Current Book	Your Sim hates leaving a book unfinished and wants to type through to the last page of the current writing project. Your Sim needs to figure out how it will end!
Debate Politics	It can be like walking into a minefield, but your Sim wants to debate politics with another Sim.
Watch the Cooking Channel	Sims can learn about new recipes, cooking tips, and the right home appliances for cooking by watching the cooking channel. Your Sim wants to watch the cooking channel on TV.
Cuddle	Sims love feeling loved! Whether on a sofa or relaxing in bed, a cosy cuddle will do wonders for a relationship!
Play Guitar for X Hours	Let your Sim play a few uninterrupted hours of beautiful or not so beautiful guitar music!
Find Some Seeds	Your Sim wants more seeds to plant and has heard that some can be found in the town. Send your Sim exploring to find some seeds!
Set the Burglar Free	It's true the burglar tried to rob your Sim, but that shouldn't sour the relationship. Your Sim wants to set the burglar free! Hurry – go to the burglar before the police officer heads off to the station.
Visit Theater	The theater packs a punch of entertainment for Sims. Your Sim really wants to visit the theater to see what it offers. Send your Sim to the theater to check things out!
Reach Level X of a Skill	Learning is an exciting pursuit many Sims enjoy. Your Sim wants to improve a skill so they can do more things with the knowledge! Practice the skill and complete opportunities to improve the skill.
Visit the Neighborhood Pool	The town pool is just a splash away from refreshment and fun for your Sims! Your Sim wants to visit the pool. Have your Sim call some friends and meet up at the pool!
Repair Something	It's no use having broken objects in the home! They don't work and they just ruin a tidy house. Your Sim wants to repair a broken household object.

WISHES, CONTINUED

Wish	Requirement
Become More Muscular	Your Sim wants to build strong muscles—time to hit the weights! Of course, change won't come overnight.
Have Someone Else Do My Homework	Why should your Sim do the homework when someone else can do it? Your Sim dreams of letting someone else do the work for a change.
Throw a House Party	Your Sim wants to throw a party at home. Throw a house party using the phone.
See Child Earn an A	Seeing young Sims come home from school with an A on their report cards is a moment for parents to cherish. Your Sim dreams of seeing someone close earn an A. Make sure your Sim's child completes the homework and good grades will follow!
Have Twins!	Two babies...oh my! Your Sim wants to try raising two newborns at once. Surround your Sim with baby things, look into fertility treatment, and hope for a lot of luck!
Play Tag	Proving your speed, agility, and ability to outlast any pursuer is an important challenge of childhood. Your Sim wants to play tag with friends!
Go Swimming	Swimming is always a refreshing, healthy choice of entertainment, whether it's at home or at the public pool. Your Sim wants to go swimming!
Buy a Fishbowl	Hey, fishy fishy fish! Your Sim thinks it's time to get a pet to take care of and give a witty name. Buy a fishbowl out of the Buy Catalog.
Throw a Wedding Party	Your Sim dreams of throwing a wedding party filled with friends, family, music, and food! Throw a wedding party on the phone.
Fall in Love	Don't hold back on the romantic gestures, your Sim wants to fall in love!
See a Sim Get Strong	Strength for yourself is one thing. Strength for another Sim...now that's strong!
Play a Game with Someone	Games are a great way to pass the time and playfully prove one's dominance over friends and family. Your Sim wants to play a game with someone!
Learn a New Composition	There are so many great songs for guitarists to play. Your Sim wants to learn a new composition. Send your Sim to the bookstore to buy some new sheet music!
Serve a Great Meal	Preparing a solid meal for others brings joy and satisfaction to the best cooks. Your Sim dreams of serving a Great meal for others. Rustle up some high quality ingredients, invite some Sims over, and cook away!
Clean Something	A filthy home makes it difficult for Sims to remain happy. Your Sim would like to clean up the grime and lingering funk with some quick cleaning.
Scrap Current Novel	Every writer has a dud or two in their repertoire. Your Sim shouldn't be too ashamed to scrap a novel in progress and start over on the computer.
Grow a Great Plant	The sight of thriving greenery is so rewarding. Your Sim wants to grow a great plant.
Discover X Stars	Enterprising astronomers can eventually discover stars and other celestial bodies by Searching the Galaxy on a telescope. Your Sim wants to discover some stars!
Make an Object Unbreakable	Handy Sims can tinker and upgrade some objects to be unbreakable. The object will never break again! Your Sim wants to upgrade an object to be unbreakable.
Talk to Someone	Sims love to chat with each other to spread the news and share the latest joke. Your Sim wants to have a conversation with someone.
Talk About a Skill	Sims love discussing things that are important and interesting to them. Your Sim wants to talk about skills with other Sims. Strike up a conversation and learn what other Sims like to do!
Potty Train Toddler	Potty training is the best way to avoid any accidents...at least the stinky kind! Your Sim dreams of a day when the toddler is potty trained. Buy a potty chair and have your Sim teach the toddler good bathroom practices!
Prepare an Outstanding Meal	It's important to prepare a meal that's simply delicious. Your Sim wants to prepare an outstanding meal. Purchase or grow high quality ingredients and refine your Sim's cooking skill.
Make Fun of Sim	It may not be the nicest thing to do, but some Sims just have it coming.
Give Massage	The act of giving a massage is hard work, but your Sim wants to give one as a labor of love or to help cure a backache!
Become Good Friends with Someone	Good Friends happily reside a little above regular Friends, but a bit below Best Friends. Your Sim hopes to soon call a Friend a Good Friend.

Simology

WISHES, CONTINUED

Wish	Requirement
Use Charming Introduction	Sims with Charisma skill can do a Charming Introduction to really start a relationship on the right foot. Your Sim wants to use a Charming Introduction on a new Acquaintance!
Become a World-Class Chef	Your Sim dreams of cooking at the very top of the world, at least the culinary world! Earning the title of World-Class Chef in town would really be a dream come true for your Sim.
Learn a Skill	Your Sim seeks to learn something new to enrich and enlighten! Have your Sim take an interesting class in town to perhaps pick up a new skill!
Cook	Your Sim dreams of doing a little cooking. It's the only activity that results in delightful edibles!
Reach Level X of a Career	Your Sim seems ambitious, or at least hopes to earn more Simoleons! A bit of dedication and a steadfast adherence to the directic of management will take aspiring Sims far!
Announce Pregnancy	A new life is growing and friends and family should know about the little bundle of joy! Your Sim dreams of announcing the pregnanc to those most important!
Borrow Ingredients	Your Sim has a hankering to prepare a new dish, but doesn't have the ingredients specified in the recipe! Ask a neighbor to see if you can borrow the ingredients.
Visit the Graveyard	Oooo, spooky! Your Sim has aspirations of visiting the graveyard. It's a bit of daring few have the courage to actually do, but the rea question is—will your Sim go at night?
Paint X Paintings	Your Sim is convinced that time in front of an easel is time well spent. Your Sim wants to paint a number of paintings.
See a Fiery Ghost	Fire is a fascinating extension of nature, both in this life and the afterlife. Your Sim wants to see the ghost of someone who died by fire.
Prepare a Meal	Your Sim has a hankering to cook something and wants to start preparing it right away. Get the right ingredients from the supermarket and start cooking!
Compliment Someone's Cooking	Someone around is a great cook, and your Sim wants to talk about it!
Put a Fish in Fish Bowl	Sims like to catch fish and put them in a fish bowl to cherish forever... assuming the fish is fed. Your Sim wants to catch a fish and put it in a fish bowl.
Clean the Dishes	The dishes are piling up, which is a problem for Sims that hope to use them for upcoming meals. Your Sim wants to clean the dirty dishes.
Tell Flirtatious Joke	Sometimes humor is the best way to make your move. Your Sim thinks the flirtatious joke is the best way to go.
Flirt	Some eyelash batting, a slight brush of the hand...not all Sims are flirty but your Sim has the desire to Flirt with someone!
Question Someone	Your Sim needs answers, and someone has the info. After questioning someone, you can write a report about them.
Change Jobs	There are always greener pastures, right? Your Sim dreams of a fresh start with new employers. It's time to change jobs!
Fertilize Plant with Fresh Caught Fish	Good gardeners fertilize plants with the best nature has to offer. Your Sim wants to fertilize a plant with some freshly caught fish.
Ask Someone to Leave	Some guests tend to wear out their welcome. Your Sim would really like to ask unwanted guests exit the premises, immediately!
Visit Someone's Home	Your Sim wants to pay a visit to a friend at home. Ring the bell at the Sim's home to pay a visit!
Donate §X to Charity	You can't take it with you, so you might as well try to do some good with it! Your Sim wants to mail a check to help out a charity.
Have X Simultaneous Romances	Plate spinning is hard enough, and those are just plates! Your Sim wants to top that by dating multipe Sims at once. Oh, the peril!
Win a Game	Your Sim needs the boost that only being a winner can provide. Find someone for your Sim to play a game against and hope for the best...or a little luck.
Be Invited to a Party by Someone	It's time for a party...or so your Sim hopes. Your Sim wants to be invited to a party by a neighbor, so make friends with someone nearby and wait for their invitation!
Buy Something on Sale	Who can resist a good deal? Look out for sales at the bookstore or supermarket and have your Sim buy something even if they don' need it.

WISHES, CONTINUED

Wish	Requirement
Catch a Great Fish	The highest quality fish are caught by the best fishermen, and only if they continue casting until quality is caught. Your Sim wants to catch a Great fish.
See Child Become a Professional Athlete	Professional Athletes are the stars of the town, both on and off the field. They earn huge paychecks and always have a winning spirit, which is why your Sim dreams of seeing someone close become at least a level 5 Rookie in the Professional Sports career! The stadium is always looking for potential all-stars...
Mock a Sim	It's not the nicest thing to do, but sometimes it just makes you feel better about yourself.
See Someone Become a Criminal Mastermind	Living the life of evil and nefarious deeds promises riches and power to those who make it to the top. Your Sim dreams of seeing someone get to level 9 of the criminal career. The criminal warehouse is always looking for new recruits...
Skip Work	Long hours and poor pay will push anyone toward some off time. Your Sim dreams of a little rest and relaxation by skipping work. When the time comes to leave...just don't go!
Get Married	Marriage is a life-defining moment that only comes after courtship and a healthy romance. Your Sim dreams of tying the knot with a soul mate.
Hire a Maid	The house is messy and could use a little...attention. Your Sim really wants to hire a maid to help out around the home. Send your Sim to the phone and sign up for the maid's service!
Use an Object	What's the point of having things if they aren't used? Give it a spin!
Wash Hands X Times	Cleanliness improves hygiene, state of mind, and other Sims' opinion of your Sim. Your Sim wants to do some hand washing at a sink.
Earn X Simoleons Through Gigs	It's not easy living off your guitar. Get on the phone and call around for gigs at private parties or restaurants. Making cash will be easy when this Sim becomes a Rock Star.
Grow an Outstanding Plant	The sight of thriving greenery is so rewarding. Your Sim wants to grow an outstanding plant.
Leap Into Someone's Arms	How romantic! Your Sim wants to leap into another Sim's arms. Careful, there!
Throw a Great Party	Your Sim dreams of throwing a great party. Invite some close friends to the party, serve lots of refreshments, and keep the party jumpin'!
Serve Home Cooked Meal at a Party	Your Sim has the culinary chops to really wow the guests at a party. Your Sim wants to throw a party that's catered with home cooked food! Pick a fantastic recipe, buy the ingredients, then serve enough food for the guests.
Go to the Day Spa	Spend some time at the day spa for a completely pampered experience.
Go Fishing Before 6 AM	The early bird catches the worm, or in this case, the early Sim brings in the big fish. Your Sim wants to wake up extra early to fish out of the calm, pre-dawn waters.
Learn All Recipes	Culinary masters know of a recipe for every occasion and gastronomic desire. Your Sim dreams of learning all recipes. Master your Sim's Cooking Skill and purchase all recipes from the bookstore!
See Teen Graduate	Your Sim can't wait for someone to graduate from school. Life post-graduation is full of excitement and new adventures! Graduation comes to all Sims eventually, it just takes time and dedication.
Read a Skill Book	Learning new things opens the doorway for a variety of activities. Your Sim dreams of learning more about a skill. Send your Sim to the bookstore to buy a book on the topic!
Win X Games	Winning isn't everything, but it's hot on the mind of your Sim at the moment. Your Sim wants to win at some games like videogames or chess.
Propose to Someone to Spend the Night	Inviting someone to spend the night is a big step in taking the relationship to the next level! Your Sim wants to ask someone to spend the night, and get to know them a little better.
Grow Perfect Plant	Your Sim is eager to grow the very best produce. Plant some seeds, fertilize, weed, and water them and hope your Sim's skill is enough to grow perfection.
Be Worth More than §X	Financial security for some means a nice house and expensive furniture, as well as some funds in the bank. Your Sim's net worth is the household's cash plus the value of their lot.
Declare Someone a Nemesis	Relations have broken down and the only recourse is to declare the foe a nemesis. Your Sim thinks this is what it takes to come out on top!
Breakup with Someone	Things aren't going so well with the current relationship and your Sim thinks it might be time to call things off. Perhaps the two lovers can still be friends?

WISHES, CONTINUED

Wish	Requirement
Upgrade X Objects	Household items can be upgraded by handy Sims to have new functionality and "improvements." Your Sim wants to upgrade several objects around the house.
Paint Something Brilliant	Brilliant paintings, though not quite Masterpieces, are still awe-inspiring displays of creativity. Your Sim wants to paint something Brilliant.
Discover a Star	Enterprising astronomers can eventually discover stars and other celestial bodies by Searching the Galaxy on a telescope. Your Sim wants to discover a star!
Serve an Outstanding Meal	Preparing a solid meal for others brings joy and satisfaction to the best cooks. Your Sim dreams of serving an Outstanding meal for others. Obtain high quality ingredients and refine your Sim's cooking skill, then invite some Sims over and cook.
See a Ghost	The dead still exist...in a sense. Your Sim wants to see a ghost–how daring! Visit the graveyard at night or hang around the gravestones of deceased family members.
See Someone Have a Child	Becoming a parent is a life changing event for any Sim. Your Sim wants a close friend to have a child to raise and love.
Catch a Perfect Fish	The highest quality fish are caught by the best fishermen, and only if they continue casting until quality is caught. Your Sim wants to catch a Perfect fish.
Have X Enemies	Friends are overrated to some mean Sims. Your Sim is ready to argue, fight and insult to get some enemies!
See a Sim Get Married	You know a Sim is all grown up when they form their own family. Your Sim wants to see another Sim get married.
Learn X More Traits for a Sim	Meets and greets often reveal interesting tidbits about other Sims. Your Sim desires to learn more of someone's traits to better know them.
Start a Painting	Your Sim has a vision that just might make a fantastic painting. Set aside some time to break out the brush and canvas and begin a new painting.
Buy Something	Your Sim wants to buy something that'll really improve the house. Look in the Buy Catalog, but use the Family's Funds wisely!
Make the Bed	An unmade bed is the first step to a messy home. First it's an unmade bed, then it's a filthy bathroom! Your Sim wants to make the bed to tidy up.
Grow X Fruits or Vegetables	The time to grow fresh produce is now! Your Sim is eager to begin planting. Plant and care for several seeds until they reach maturity. Good luck with the harvest!
Befriend the Boss	Your Sim dreams of fast promotions and a corner office, so it's smart to build a relationship with the big cheese. Meet the boss after work for dinner, or just hang out together!
Go Steady with Someone	Your Sim is ready to settle down with an exclusive boyfriend or girlfriend. Perfect the timing and ask the question before your Sim's significant other gets away!
Talk About Self	Every Sim has a favorite subject, and your Sim wants to tell someone all about it!
Buy Something to Plant	Plantable foodstuffs can be purchased in the supermarket to plant at home. Your Sim hopes to buy something to plant in the garden.
Mooch a Lot of Simoleons	Your Sim wants to "borrow" some money to use for...something. Ask a friend if it's okay to mooch a lot of money.
Catch an Outstanding Fish	The highest quality fish are caught by the best fishermen, and only after many attempts. Your Sim wants to catch an Outstanding fish.
Skip School	There are days when school just doesn't appeal...at all. Your Sim wants to play hooky and skip school. When the bus comes around to pick up your Sim, don't get on!
Buy a Book	Reading is one of the most relaxing ways to entertain Sims. Your Sim wants to buy a book. Send your Sim to the bookstore to find a real page turner!
Give Friendly Introduction	Your Sim wants to give another Sim a warm welcome.
Buy a New Recipe	Your Sim knows enough about the culinary arts to prepare a new recipe. Send your Sim to the bookstore to see what delightful recipes can be purchased!
Insult Someone	Ooh, feel the burn! Your Sim really wants to hit someone where it hurts.
Have First Romance	Taking a relationship up the romantic ladder is rewarding, adventurous, and good for the soul. Your Sim dreams of a special first romance that will never be forgotten! Flirt, hold hands, and plant the smooch at the perfect moment!
Eat Stu Surprise	Stu Surprise is an icky dish that contains so many flavors that it becomes palatable. Your Sim wants to eat Stu Surprise made with watermelon and blowfish.

WISHES, CONTINUED

Wish	Requirement
Write an Autobiography	After writing a few biographies, your Sim wants to take a pass at writing an Autobiography. Your Sim should think back on personal history and write something truly spectacular.
Become an Uncle	The role of the uncle is to spoil you and teach you some crucial life skills that your parents would never want you to learn. Your Sim dreams of becoming an uncle one day, which will happen if the eventual parents have aspirations of parenthood!
Go to School	Your Sim wants to go to school to learn and meet new friends. Let your Sim jump onto the bus when it arrives, then off to school it is!
See a Play	Comedies, dramas, and musicals, all on stage. Your Sim wants to see a play. Check the theater on weekends to see if there is a play showing!
Paint X Masterpieces	Masterpieces are rare samples of pure creative genius. Your Sim dreams of painting multiple Masterpieces, but it'll take dedication, a mastery of the skill, and a lot of luck.
Earn X Simoleons in Tips	Guitarists can earn a little spare change from tips, assuming they are skilled with an acoustic guitar. Your Sim wants to earn some Simoleons in tips.
Throw X Great Parties	Your Sim likes to throw a great parties, but it's time to step it up. Your Sim wants to throw a number of great parties. Get on the phone to get the party started!
See Child Become a Doctor	Doctors are wonderful members of the community who give back with every cut of their scalpel. Your Sim dreams of seeing someone close put on the white coat of a level 5 Resident doctor one day. The hospital is always looking for talented medical professionals…
Win X Ranked Chess Matches in a Row	The professional chess circuit is not for the faint of heart. Your Sim hopes to win a string of bold victories on the circuit. Can your Sim survive the march of the pawns?
Bore Someone to Death	Your Sim wants to bore someone to death with nonsensical rambling. Find a victim for your Sim and bore them to death. Don't worry, they won't really die!
Become an Aunt	The role of the aunt is to spoil and tell embarassing stories the parents don't want their child to hear. Your Sim dreams of becoming an aunt one day, which will happen if the eventual parents have aspirations of parenthood!
Catch X Kilograms of Fish	The best commercial fishermen judge their catches by the weight of fish brought in. Your Sim wants to be measured against the best by catching a heavy load of fish.
Play Outside	The outdoors are beckoning your Sim to leave the indoors behind and enjoy the great outdoors. Your Sim wants to have fun in the sun!
Boast About Party	Great parties should be discussed at length the following day. Your Sim worked hard throwing a great bash and wants to brag a little!
Propose to Move In with Someone	Moving in with someone is a big deal that shouldn't be taken lightly. Can a relationship survive the move? Your Sim hopes to move in with someone.
Cook Something with Perfect Ingredients	A well made meal is tasty, but it's even better when prepared with perfect ingredients. Your Sim dreams of eating something made with perfect ingredients.
Sell Something	Simoleons can be earned in a variety of ways. Send your Sim to the store to sell some of the stuff your Sim is carrying, or delete household items in Buy Mode.
See a Symphony	The symphony is so romantic and wonderful, a buffet of sound for a Sim's ears. Your Sim dreams of seeing a symphony. Check the theater on weekends to see if there is a symphony!
Quit Job	When it's time to move on, it's time to move on. Your Sim hopes to give notice and quit the current job. Simply quit at the work place, or tell the boss face to face!
Have Sleepover	Your Sim hopes to have a super fun sleepover with friends soon. Late night movies and snacks plus mischief are good times for all! Use the phone to invite the Sim over.
Argue	Blood is boiling and it's time to vent. Your Sim desires an argument, so pick a victim and give them a tongue lashing!
Cook Something	Your Sim thinks a home cooked meal sounds absolutely delicious. Buy the ingredients and prepare something!
Scare Someone	Sims tend to get jumpy when it's dark outside or mischievous individuals are wandering about. Your Sim wants to sneak up on someone and Scare them.
Accuse Someone of Cheating	A lack of faithfulness can rupture any relationship. Your Sim desires the truth more than anything and thinks a face-to-face accusation is the only way to fix things.

85

WISHES, CONTINUED

Wish	Requirement
Play with Baby	Little gurgling babies are so cute! They're just begging to be played with! Your Sim wants to play with a baby.
Ask for Recipe	Exciting new recipes can be learned from a multitude of sources... you neighbors for one! Your Sim wants to ask a neighbor for a recipe to see what they have to offer.
Return Stolen Object	Kleptomaniacs cannot control their urges. Your Sim wants to make amends and return the stolen object to its rightful owner. Stolen objects can be returned in person or through the mail.
Go Fishing	Local bodies of water are beckoning to your Sim. The fish are biting, your Sim just knows it! Pick a nice fishing spot and cast away!
Kiss X Sims	The joys of a good smooch shouldn't be overlooked! Your Sim wants to kiss, or be kissed.
Have First Child	Becoming a parent is a life changing event for any Sim. Your Sim dreams of starting a family with someone. It's a noble endeavor that promises a lifetime of experiences!
Become Old Friends with Someone	Old Friends have sustained a friendship for a long, long time. Your Sim wants to have an Old Friend, so put in the time with a Friend and grow old together.
Be in a Steady Relationship	Your Sim is ready to settle down with an exclusive boyfriend or girlfriend. Pick the right time and place, but ask the question before your Sim's significant other gets away!
Uncover Conspiracy	Conspiracies are everywhere if you look hard enough or are just crazy enough to find them. Your Sim wants to uncover a conspiracy by looking in books, watching TV, or going straight to City Hall for clues!
Paint	There's something satisfyingly soothing about painting on the easel. Your Sim wants to do a little painting.
Sneak Out After Curfew	Your Sim wants to sneak out after curfew for a little excitement. Parents don't need to know! Sneak outside into town, but avoid parents and cops!
Hire a Baby-sitter	Parents need a break from the little ones every now and then. Get on the phone and call for the services of a Baby-sitter for a day or...every day!
Have a Child	Children make families, and your Sim wants a bigger family. Add a child to your family through adoption or pregnancy right away!
Throw a Formal Party	It's time for everyone to put on their suits and fancy duds! Your Sim wants to throw a formal party. Throw a formal party using the phone.
Buy Something	Your Sim thinks it's time to spice up the house with just a touch with something new. Your Sim really thinks it'll liven up the house!
Write a Novel	Your Sim's creativity needs an outlet! Writing a novel on the computer should help.
Read X Books Total	Your Sim seeks to read an entire library's worth of books! It will take time and several trips to the library or bookstore, but your Sim wants to read away!
Brag About Being a Doctor	Doctors are simply awesome. The power of life and death is in their hands, plus they wear scrubs! Your Sim wants to brag about the MD inscribed on the business card.
Eat at a Restaurant	There are times when Sims don't want to cook at home, especially when there are fine dining establishments in town. Your Sim wants to eat at a restaurant!
Lecture Teen	Teens tend to be rebellious. They stay out late, ignore their parents, and act unruly. Your Sim wants to lecture a teen to set them straight!
Grow Bait for Fish	Some fish begin biting when the right bait is dangling from the hook. Grow some bait to use while fishing to improve your Sim's chances of catching the big one!
Procure a Portrait of Self	Many desire to see themselves painted gloriously, framed, and hung on a wall! Have another Sim paint a portrait of your Sim!
Get a Part-Time Job	Sims who need more free time should obtain a part-time job. Your Sim wants to get a part-time job at a business like the supermarket or bookstore.
Catch Something with Live Bait	Your Sim wants to experiment with live bait to catch something. Pick the correct bait, make sure it's still wriggling, and cast away.
Join Evil Career Branch	Scum and villainy lie in the future for Sims bent on world domination. Your Sim thinks specializing in Evil is the right side of life. Your Sim can make the choice for evil after being promoted past Con Artist.
Buy a New Car	True freedom is experience behind the wheel of a new car. Your Sim wants to buy a new car to get around town faster and in style!
Harvest a Wild Plant	Gardeners with a sharp eye and eager hands can take advantage of public produce just waiting to be plucked. Your Sim wants to harvest wild fruits and vegetables found in the town.
Get Pumped	Good athletes are pumped after a long workout. Your Sim wants to work out long enough to get that adrenaline-fueled feeling.

WISHES, CONTINUED

Wish	Requirement
Beg for Job Back	The job was lost, but there's no use mulling over past mistakes. Your Sim really wants the job back! Get your Sim's old boss in a good mood and start begging!
Kiss Someone for the First Time	Romance is in the air! Your Sim wants to have that first special kiss with someone.
Have First Kiss	A first kiss is something so wondrous, so pure, but it can only be enjoyed once. Your Sim dreams of the perfect first kiss, but with whom?
Admire Someone	Sims like to recognize their friends and family with respect and admiration. Your Sim wants to pay some respect with a little verbal admiration.
Copy Homework	It's easy to finish the homework if it is just copied from another Sim! Your Sim wants to find another Sim's homework to copy. Be careful—your Sim might get caught!
Prepare a Great Meal	It's important to prepare a meal that really zings! Your Sim wants to prepare a Great meal. Purchase high quality ingredients and refine your Sim's cooking skill.
Have a Funeral	Sims gather together to say goodbye and mourn the passing of a Sim. Your Sim wants to call their friends on the phone and invite them to a funeral.
Catch an Excellent Fish	The highest quality fish are caught by the best fishermen, and only if they continue casting until quality is caught. Your Sim wants to catch an Excellent fish.
Find a Rock	Valuable meteorites, gems, and metals can be found throughout the town, but only if your Sim has sharp eyes! Your Sim wants to find a rock, so look in every nook and crevice.
Invite a Sim to a Party	It's party time, and your Sim wants to get social! Invite that special Sim to party!
Get Married at a Wedding Party	Marriage is a defining moment in a Sim's life. Your Sim dreams of tying the knot at a wedding party filled with friends, family, music, and food! Throw a wedding party on the phone.
Have X Garden Plants	Feeling blue? Feeling green is better! Your Sim wants to plant a few things in the garden.
Serve a Perfect Meal	Preparing a solid meal for others brings joy and satisfaction to the best cooks. Your Sim dreams of serving a Perfect meal for others. Obtain high quality ingredients, perfect your Sim's Cooking skill, then invite some Sims over and cook away!
Become a Grandparent	Little ones are double the fun when your only role is to spoil and love them! Your Sim dreams of becoming a grandparent. Hopefully, the parents have dreams of parenthood!
Catch X New Types of Fish	There are only so many fish species in the water, but your Sim hopes to catch a large number of them. Catch several new types of fish to satisfy your Sim.
Upgrade Something	Things can always work just a teeny bit better. Your Sim wants to upgrade something.
Ask Someone to Behave	A Sim's home is a sacred place that should be respected by visitors. Your Sim wants to put a stop to the nonsense by asking neighbors to behave while visiting!
Get a Specific Object	If you don't have something, that's why you need it! Your Sim wants to own something new.
Earn Some Money	Your Sim wants to earn a little money, maybe to save, maybe to spend! Have your Sim go to work, or even have them sell something at a store.
Join Symphonic Career Branch	The conductor's baton must be wielded with cunning and precision! Your Sim wants to join the symphonic branch and can do this after being promoted past Music Talent Scout.
Call Repair Technician	Broken things around the house have a way of staying broken...unless they get fixed. Your Sim really wants to call a repair technician to get things back to normal. Send your Sim to the phone to schedule the repair technician's service!
Catch Something	Your Sim wants to go fishing, and more importantly, catch something.
Make an Enemy	It's an all-out war! Don't hold anything back, your Sim wants to make an enemy!
Stay Out After Curfew	It doesn't matter that it's past curfew, your Sim wants to stay out! Parents don't need to know, but make sure your Sim avoids the cops!
Eat Sushi and Hot Dogs	Cravings cannot be explained, so there's no point looking for an explanation. Your Sim dreams of eating sushi...and hot dogs.
Talk About Celestial Object	Your Sim discovered an astronomical phenomena and wants to discuss it with others. Find a friendly ear and Talk About Celestial Objects!

WISHES, CONTINUED

Wish	Requirement
Have Sleepover	Your Sim hopes to have a super fun sleepover with friends soon. Late night movies and snacks plus mischief are good times for all! Use the phone to invite the Sim over.
Learn a New Recipe	The pursuit of knowledge often leads to a satisfied stomach when you're a cook. Your Sim wants to learn a new recipe to expand their menu.
Boast About Culinary Prowess	Your Sim is quite the chef and wants everyone to know. Go on, boast a little bit to friends!
Mourn a Sim	The loss of someone dear is never easy. Your Sim wants to Mourn at the tombstone or urn.
Fertilize Plants	Fertilized plants tend to produce higher quality fruits and vegetables for harvest. Your Sim thinks it's a good idea to fertilize the plants in the garden using fish, fruits or vegetables.
Have a Child with Someone	Becoming a parent is a life changing event for any Sim. Your Sim dreams of starting a family with someone. It's a noble endeavor that promises a lifetime of experiences!
Get a Massage	"Your Sim wants some pampering. Whether it's from another Sim or the spa in town, it's sure to put them in a good mood!
Stop Being Friends with Someone	The friendship just isn't working out and it may be best for all parties to just go separate ways. Your Sim wants to stop being friends with someone. Be mean...or just let the relationship die from neglect.
Order Pizza	Pizza is delicious and your Sim wants to enjoy the warm delights of a freshly delivered pizza. Send your Sim to the phone to order a pizza!
Teach Toddler to Talk	Cute gurgles and gibberish can soon be replaced by whole, grammatically correct sentences! Your Sim wants to teach a toddler to talk to move past the "goo goo" and "gaa gaa."
Get on the Honor Roll	Persistently earning good grades could land your Sim on the Honor Roll. Your Sim dreams of joining the ranks of the best students in school. Dedication is the key!
Chat with Someone	Sometimes it's nice just need to talk and listen. Your Sim wants to find someone for a nice chat.
Have a Girl	Becoming a parent is a life changing event for any Sim. Your Sim dreams of having a baby girl. It's a great adventure that promises a lifetime of experiences!
Have a Boy	Becoming a parent is a life changing event for any Sim. Your Sim dreams of having a baby boy. It's a great adventure that promises a lifetime of experiences!
Throw X Parties	Your Sim wants to get down and have a few parties with friends. Get on the phone to invite people to the party!
Eat Cobbler with Fruit	Fresh cobbler is delicious, like happiness baked in a crust of sugar and glee. Your Sim wants to eat cobbler paired with just the right fruit. Yummy!
Have X Total Children	For family focused Sims, the joys that pitter and patter about on two legs make all the struggle and hardship of parenthood worthwhile. A house full of children can mean a tight budget, little personal time, and few luxuries, but there's always somebody to play with or something new to teach.
Talk About Exercise	Even fit Sims can't exercise all the time...unless they exercise their mouths!
Ask Someone to Clean Home	Your Sim's home is an absolute mess! Your Sim wants to ask others to clean up to eliminate that smell!
Have X Friends	The world becomes a much more friendly and interesting place with Sims you can call friends. Your Sim dreams of having lots of friends.
Ask About Career	Learning about your neighbors is a great way to build community. Your Sim wants to ask someone what they do for a living.
Buy a Treadmill	The cruel taskmaster that is the treadmill is beckoning your Sim. The best cardio workout money can buy is available for purchase in the Buy Catalog.
Tutor Someone	Tutored Sims tend to earn higher grades in school and lead successful lives. Your Sim wants to tutor someone. Meet up with the Sim that needs tutoring and get to it!
Kiss Someone	Romance is in the air, and your Sim wants some. Pucker up!
Just Be Friends with a Sim	Friendships that blossom into something more are great...but sometimes it's best to keep things casual.
Throw a Birthday Party	Someone's birthday is coming up, and your Sim wants to help celebrate! Throw a Birthday Party using the phone.
Earn an A in School	Hard work and dedication in school will get Sims far. Your Sim desires an A grade to proudly display for all. Make sure your Sim always gets to school in a good mood and finishes all of the homework and that A will come!

WISHES, CONTINUED

Wish	Requirement
Brush Teeth X Times	Minty fresh breath is a blessing for those around your Sim. Your Sim wants to brush the chompers at the sink.
Read a Pregnancy Book	The bookstore sells several informative books for expecting parents. Your Sim wants to read one of the pregnancy books available, so that when the time comes, everyone is ready!
Tell Sim You Named a Star After Them	Some Sims appreciate gifts that aren't tangible. Your Sim wants to tell someone about the star named after them.
Have a Child	Becoming a parent is a life changing event for any Sim. Your Sim dreams of parenthood and starting a family with someone else. It's a noble adventure that promises a lifetime of experiences!
Snuggle Baby or Toddler	Babies and toddlers require so much attention in their formative years. Your Sim wants to snuggle a little one to give them lots of love.
Eat at a Restaurant	Home cooked meals are delicious, but it's enjoyable to dine out on the town from time to time. Your Sim wants to get dinner at a restaurant. Send your Sim into town for a fine meal that won't be forgotten!
Earn X Simoleons	Simoleons pave the way for nice things and a comfortable lifestyle. Your Sim dreams of earning some Simoleons—quite ambitious.
Grow Something	The best produce is in season and your Sim is eager to begin planting. Plant some seeds, watch them grow, and enjoy the harvest!
WooHoo with Someone	Your Sim hopes to take the relationship with someone to the next level with a WooHoo.
Have More than X Simoleons	Money money money! It doesn't make the world go around, but it can make life easier at times. Your Sim wants to have a pile of Simoleons. Time to get to work!
Eat Ice Cream and Spaghetti	Cravings cannot be explained, so there's no point looking for an explanation. Your Sim dreams of eating ice cream and spaghetti.
Chat with Toddler	Goo goo, ga ga! Toddlers aren't the best conversationalists, but talking to them can be rewarding in its own way.
Play Video/Computer Games	For some Sims, reading a book is fun and relaxing. For others, it's sinking a few hours into PallyQuest Online!
Be a Winner, for Once!	Losers rarely win at anything. Life's not fair! Your Sim wants to win at a game just this once. Perhaps your Sim can find another loser?
Work Out for X Hours	Your Sim wants to spend a few hours working out. Purchase some exercise equipment, go for a jog, or work out in front of the TV.
Invite Someone to Movies	You don't talk during a movie, but it's still a strangely social experience. Your Sim wants to invite another Sim to the movies.
Give Friendly Hug	Sometimes a hug is the best way to show that you care.
Eat Something at the Park	Park picnics are fun for the whole family, or even alone. Your Sim wants to prepare a meal to take to the park for consumption.
Buy a object worth at least §X	The home always looks best with nice things. Your Sim specifically wants to improve the house with something expensive. Start shopping!
Serenade Someone with Guitar	One of the best reasons to learn the guitar is the romantic advantages it provides. Your Sim wants to woo someone with a guitar serenade.
Spend X Simoleons	What's the fun in earning money if you can't spend it? Your Sim wants to spend some Simoleons. Doesn't sound too hard!
Resurrect a Sim	Parting permanently with loved ones is too much for some Sims to bear! Your Sim wants to resurrect someone. Preparing a dish of Ambrosia should do the trick...
Write a Romance Novel	Ah, love! To capture the greatest emotion on paper is no easy task. Your Sim wants to write a romance novel on the computer.
Buy Something New	Your Sim thinks it's time to spice up the house with just a touch with something new. It'll liven up the house!
Buy Something Worth at Least X Simoleons	The most valuable objects are the best, and your Sim wants something pricey!
Talk to Self	Insanity has its perks, like the ability to carry on a conversation entirely with yourself. Your Sim wants to have a self-chat.
Kiss Someone	Romance is in the air, and your Sim wants some. Pucker up!
Steal Candy from a Baby	Evil Sims love taking what's not theirs, especially when the victim can do nothing but cry. Your Sim wants to steal candy from a baby.
Go Out on the Town	Some Sims just don't like to stay in one place for too long. You Sim wants to visit some other place in town.

WISHES, CONTINUED

Wish	Requirement
Apologize	Harsh words were exchanged and maybe a few punches, but that shouldn't end a friendship forever. Your Sim wants to apologize and repair the relationship!
Ask a Sim About Their Day	Sharing is caring! Your Sim wants to ask another Sim about their day.
See Child Get on Honor Roll	The Honor Roll is a big deal for parents that want to see their children succeed in life. Your Sim hopes to see a child get on the Honor Roll. Children that focus on homework and work hard in school tend to end up on the coveted Honor Roll.
See a Sim Become Evil	If there's one thing more evil than evil itself, it's seeing another Sim turn to Evil. Bwah hah hah hah ha!
Have Father Read a Pregnancy Book	The bookstore sells several informative books for expecting parents. Your Sim wants the baby's father to read one of the pregnancy books available, so that when the time comes, everyone is ready!
Play Guitar at a Party	Want to be the life of the party? Put a guitar in your inventory, head to a party, and start jamming! You can host your own party too!
Buy Something Worth At Least §X	The home always looks best with nice things. Your Sim specifically wants to improve the house with something expensive. Start shopping!
Call Off Wedding	Perhaps getting married wasn't the best idea. It might be better for all parties, or at least your Sim, if the wedding is called off! Your Sim should have a heart-to-heart chat with the other Sim involved.
Improve a Skill	Learning is an exciting pursuit many Sims enjoy. Your Sim wants to improve a skill so they can do more things with the knowledge! Practice the skill until your Sim gains a level.
Get Pregnant	When two Sims dream of starting a family they make the ultimate plunge and Try for a Baby! Your Sim dreams of becoming pregnant! Hopefully her partner shares the sentiments.
Repair Something	Broken objects are of no practical use and can be dangerous! Your Sim wants to repair a broken household item to return it to normal.
Toddler Toss in Air	Airborne babies may not be the best idea in the world but they seem to enjoy it! Your Sim wants to toss a toddler in the air!
Eat a Great Quality Meal	Eating wonderful food is just one of the many joys of knowing how to cook. Your Sim yearns to eat a Great meal, something prepared just right with quality ingredients.
Mooch §X	Nothing's better than getting money that you didn't have to earn yourself. And, in a certain way, mooching IS work.
Learn a Recipe Containing Fish	Recipes that contain fish swim well with a Sim's stomach. Your Sim wants to learn to prepare a recipe that contains fish as an ingredient. Send your Sim to the bookstore to see what recipes are available!
Criticize Family	It may be rude, but some families have it coming!
Go to the Supermarket	The supermarket stocks everything Sims need to prepare a delicious meal, as well as a few fun household items. Your Sim wants to visit the store to see what there is to see.
Catch a New Type of Fish	The first fish caught is always the one best remembered. There's nothing like hooking a new species! Your Sim wants to catch the first of a certain type of fish.
Serve a Perfect Meal	Perfection is something rarely obtained, but often sought. Your Sim dreams of serving a perfect home cooked meal. Obtain really high quality ingredients, refine your Sim's Cooking skill, and give it a shot!
Take Out the Trash	The trash can has filled up and it's time to take the garbage out to the curb! Your Sim wants to empty the trashcan.
Hang Out with Someone	Your Sim wants to spend some quality time with a friend or loved one. Track that Sim down, or use the phone to arrange a meeting.
WooHoo with Someone	WooHoo is a lot of fun! Your Sim wants to WooHoo with someone special.
Join Forensic Analyst Career Branch	Forensic analysts love evidence gathering and lab coats. Your Sim thinks this may be the right path and should look forward to making the choice after being promoted past Lieutenant.
Play Guitar in the Park	Everyone loves a performance in the park. Just put a guitar in your inventory, find a good spot, and start strumming!
Garden	Toiling underneath blue skies with fingers deep into the dirt is satisfying for gardeners. Your Sim hopes to do a little gardening for agricultural excitement.
Mooch Food	Your Sim is hungry... or not, and wants to mooch a little food from a friend. Ask a friend to mooch some food.
Do Homework	Completing homework daily is the key to good grades. Your Sim hopes to make the honor roll and wants to finish the assigned homework.

WISHES, CONTINUED

Wish	Requirement
Watch a Movie	The best movies are always showing at the theater. Your Sim hopes to catch a flick soon. Check the theater to see if there is a movie showing. Don't forget weekend matinees!
Write X Best Sellers	Best selling books are the best way to earn huge royalty checks. Highly skilled writers that know the ins and outs of a genre tend to write the most best sellers.
Work on Book	Your Sim hates to leave the keyboard idle for long. Your Sim wants sit down at the keyboard to put a few more pages in ink.
Have X More Children	Big families are full of love, though there's always a stampede of hungry Sims at dinner. Your Sim dreams of having a number of children.
Paint a Portrait of a Sim	Sims make such excellent artistic subjects. Your Sim wants to paint a portrait of someone.
Retire	Easy Street is calling with promises of lazy afternoons, sleeping in, and no bosses making demands. Your Sim dreams of retiring and collecting that lovely pension. Give the office a call to make retirement a reality.
Invite Sim to Restaurant	Sharing a meal can be an intimate experience. Your Sim would like to invite another Sim to a restaurant.
Get Attention from Mom	It's okay to crave attention from time to time, because that nourishment helps little Sims grow up to be great! Your Sim desires a little attention from Mom. See if she wants to play or chat!
Learn a New Recipe	The pursuit of knowledge often leads to a satisfied stomach when you're a cook. Your Sim wants to learn a new recipe to expand their personal menu.
Work on Homework with Someone	Homework can be daunting and not fun at all. Your Sim hopes to work on the homework with someone else, because learning together is always more enjoyable. Make sure someone that can help is around and do the homework together.
Insult Home	Not everyone can keep up with the Goths! Your Sim is seeing green, feeling mean, and wants to insult some neighbor's home.
Grow Something	The best produce is in season and your Sim is eager to begin planting. Plant some seeds, watch them grow, and enjoy the harvest!
Tickle Toddler	What better way to make the little one shriek than a good tickle? Your Sim is feeling playful and wants to tickle a toddler!
Buy an Easel	Every blank canvas has the potential to become a masterpiece by your Sims. Your Sim wants to buy an easel to see what visions can be brought to life with paint.
Clean Something	It's satisfying to scrub something…anything to clean up the house a little bit! Your Sim wants to clean up!
Write a Science Fiction Novel	Aliens alone aren't enough to make a good science fiction novel. The lasers must singe the reader as a new galaxy is brought to life. Your Sim wants to write a science fiction novel.
Have a Deep Conversation	Sometimes a casual chat isn't enough. You need a deep conversation to really express your feelings.
Write X Novels	Your Sim wants to be known and respected as a prolific writer. Your Sim wants to write novels… better get busy behind the keyboard!
Sell Something	Simoleons can be earned in a variety of ways. Send your Sim to the store to sell some of the stuff your Sim is carrying, or delete household items in Buy Mode.
Catch an Insect	The town is full of all sorts of creepy crawlies to catch! Your Sim wants to find a butterfly or beetle to call their own. Look around to start a bug collection.
Catch a Record Size Fish	Your Sim wants to beat a personal best and catch a record size fish. Check the Skill Journal to see what your Sim is up against and start casting!
Tell Intriguing News Story	Only the best journalists can tell a tale that keeps the listener in rapt attention. Your Sim wants to tell someone an intriguing news story.
Have a Great Birthday Party	Great birthday parties include friends, great food, and several slices of cake! Your Sim hopes to have a great birthday party!
Buy Something with a Coupon	Frugal Sims love to save money wherever possible. Your Sim wants to use a coupon clipped from the newspaper to purchase something at a discount!
Hack	Computer whizzes have the urge to get away with geeky delinquent behavior under the cover of night. Get them to the nearest computer!
Talk About Gardening	Sims with green thumbs can't get enough chat about their favorite subject.
Play with Someone	It's fun to play with others—who knows what will happen! Your Sim hopes to play with someone soon… perhaps a game of Tag!
Ask Someone to Move In	Homes can always accommodate new inhabitants, assuming the Sims inside are emotionally prepared. Your Sim dreams of asking someone to move in!

WISHES, CONTINUED

Wish	Requirement
Throw a Party	Your Sim feels the need to par-tay! It doesn't matter what kind, people just need to show up in the mood for fun! Throw a party using the phone.
Talk About Cooking	Even food enthusiasts can't cook all the time. But when you're not cooking, you can always talk about cooking!
Be in a Fire	Daredevils like to feel the extreme side of life. Leave the fireplace on or cook on a cheap stove to experience the worst of household disasters!
Compliment Athleticism	Physical appearance is often noteworthy. Your Sim wants to compliment another Sim's athleticism.
Yell At Someone	It may not be the nicest thing to do, but sometimes you just have to let someone have it!
Take a Bubble Bath	Your Sim needs a little pampering time. The grocery store stocks the bubbles!
Catch X Fish	Your Sim dreams of catching the big fish, or perhaps enough of a certain kind of fish to equal a single big one. The weight of the fish will add up, it just takes dedication!
Invite a Sim Over	What's the point of having a home if you can't entertain guests? Your Sim wants to invite someone over to chat and have a good time.
Repair X Objects	It's no use having broken objects in the home! They don't work and they just ruin a tidy house. Your Sim wants to repair a broken household object.
Go to Work	Some Sims dream of long vacations, others wealth or nice furniture. Your Sim dreams of going to work, which is a noble and productive desire!
Feel Tummy	Your Sim wants to feel the tummy of a pregnant Sim. Maybe the baby will kick!
Cry on Shoulder	If you have to cry, it's best to have company. Your Sim wants to find a nice shoulder to cry on.
Paint Something Worth X Simoleons	A painter is truly established when pieces of art sell for a worthwhile amount.
Use a Telescope	The night sky is beautiful and mysterious. Your Sim wants to explore the logical patterns of the stars.
Play with Toy	Kids just want to have fun! Play with toys like toy blocks, stuffed animals, and toy ovens to fulfill this wish.
Get Out!	An overwhelming and uncontrollable desire to leave often compels some to just go elsewhere. Your Sim wants to leave the current location for someplace else…now!
Play Guitar for at Least X Sims	Nothing gets an aspiring Rock Star going like a cheering crowd! Perform in front of many Sims to fulfill this wish.
Imply Mother is a Llama	Ooh, feel the burn! Your Sim really wants to hit someone where it hurts.
Ask Someone to Go Inside	Your neighbors seem friendly and have impeccable taste! Your Sim wants to ask them if it's okay to take the conversation inside their home!
Play with Fire	Daredevils cannot get enough of fire! Your Sim wants to play with fire in the fireplace!
Eat Stu Surprise	Stu Surprise is an icky dish that contains so many flavors that it becomes palatable. Your Sim wants to eat Stu Surprise made with steak and eggs.
Go Home	The town is exciting but nothing beats home after a long day. Press the arrow on a Sim's thumbnail to send them home.
Bathe	That smell certainly isn't the hip new fragrance, nor will anyone confuse it as such. Your Sim thinks it's time to take a bath…for everyone's sake.
Buy a Skill Book	Your Sim wants to try something new in life. One of the easiest ways to do that is to purchase a skill book from the bookstore!
WooHoo with X Sims	Your Sim is in a romantic mood and wants to WooHoo. More than once.
See Sim Earn Passing Grades	Someone isn't doing so well in school and that's just not acceptable. Your Sim hopes to see the child earn passing grades sometime soon! Children who attend school in a good mood and finish the assigned homework earn high grades.
Propose Marriage	Marriage is a life-changing step, as it defines who wakes up next to you forever. Your Sim wants to tie the knot with a soul mate. Pick the Sim and pop the big question.
Get Fired	Too much success can be scary for some Sims. Your Sim would like to relieve the pressure by getting fired.

WISHES, CONTINUED

Wish	Requirement
Work Out	Your Sim wants to spend a little time working out. It's never a bad time for personal fitness! Purchase some exercise equipment, go for a jog, or work out in front of the TV.
Ask for a Raise	More money, fewer problems, or so your Sim hopes! Your Sim has worked hard and thinks it's time for a raise. Your Sim should butter up the boss and ask for a raise.
Eat Stu Surprise	Stu Surprise is an icky dish that contains so many flavors that it becomes palatable. Your Sim wants to eat Stu Surprise made with Flame Fruit and Vampire Fish.
Find Own Place	Every Sim aspires to home ownership. Nobody likes being cooped up with friends or worse, parents! Your Sim wants to find a place to live. Look up potential homes on the computer!
Own X Books	Knowledge is power, so the more books, the better!
Tell Dirty Joke	Some Sims appreciate a little blue humor, and your Sim is no exception.
Spend Time with a Baby	Every parent has the inescapable urge to spend time with their new baby. Your Sim wants to spend time with the baby. Cuddling and playing are quality time for parent and baby!
Write a Masterpiece	Every writer's dream is to write the perfect book that will be remembered forever.
Become Friends with Someone	Friends will stand by your Sim's side...mostly. Your Sim wants to have a Friend, so find someone to converse with and build a friendship.
Buy a Couch	Your Sim wants some place to sit and relax after a long day of moving. Buy your Sim a couch by going to Buy Mode and selecting something nice!
Catch Every Type of Fish	Your Sim dreams of catching every fish that swims in the local bodies of water. Seek out the best fishing spots, bring some bait, and get to it!
Go Jogging	Your Sim seeks the solace and pace of a neighborhood jog. Pick the route and strap on some sneakers.
Finish a Book	Reading is one of the most relaxing forms of entertainment for some Sims. Your Sim wants to read a book from cover to cover. Grab one from the bookshelf, visit the library, or purchase a new one from the bookstore!
Earn §X Per Week in Royalties	While some write as a purely creative outlet, the best and most persistent writers can make quite a healthy living as authors. Royalties don't grow on trees, so your Sim must be willing to push through years of lousy checks to earn enough to live comfortably.
Prepare a Meal with Fresh Ingredients	Nothing tastes better than a meal prepared with fresh fruits, vegetables, or fish! Your Sim dreams of just such a dish, so send your Sim into the world to do a little gardening or fishing, then prepare the meal!
Donate Money to Undermine Charity	Nothing is as wickedly satisfying as confounding do-gooders. Your Sim wants to donate money to undermine a charity.
Become Disliked by Someone	Though most Sims prefer to be liked, it takes a particularly mean spirited Sim to desire to be disliked. Your Sim wants to be insulting and mean to become disliked by others.

Lifetime Happiness Points

When you boost your mood into the bubble at the top of the Mood meter, you start accumulating Lifetime Happiness Points. Lifetime Happiness Points are also earned by fulfilling wishes. Lifetime Happiness Points are traded in for Lifetime Rewards, which are a series of special skill, traits, and objects with unique properties.

Gather as many Lifetime Happiness Points as possible—this is a great way to measure to the progress of your Sim and see how well they are doing life. And those Lifetime Rewards are fantastic to have, especially the objects like the Moodlet Manager and the Food Replicator. If you are playing out a multi-generational household, these special objects are passed down and greatly benefit future generations.

LIFETIME REWARDS

Lifetime Reward	Cost	Function
Steel Bladder	10,000	Never have to go pee
Change Lifetime Wish	10,000	Pick a new Lifetime Wish to replace current one
Dirt Defiant	15,000	Hygiene concerns be gone!
Hardly Hungry	25,000	Don't have to eat as often
Professional Slacker	5,000	Does not lose career performance for using the Slack Off tone at work
Speedy Cleaner	5,000	Sim can clean objects faster
Fast Metabolism	5,000	Change body shape faster
Multi-Tasker	10,000	Increased career performance / Do homework faster
Extra Creative	30,000	Paintings are always higher-than-average quality
Acclaimed Author	30,000	Increased royalty checks (from Writing)
Super-Green Thumb	20,000	Harvestables are of universally higher quality
Never Dull	15,000	Always interesting (never boring when socializing)
Discount Diner	5,000	Free restaurant meals
Complimentary Entertainment	5,000	Free theater shows
Bookshop Barginer	10,000	Cheaper books
Office Hero	5,000	Popular w/ peers (Increased Relationship Gain during "Hang with Co-Workers")
Vacationer	15,000	Reduce performance decay for missing work
Legendary Host	5,000	Everyone Invited shows up to your parties and they have a higher quality
Haggler	15,000	Permanent shopping discount (at stores)
Long Distance Friend	20,000	No relationship decay when apart from LTRs
Fast Learner	15,000	Develop skills faster
Attractive	10,000	Sims with appropriate preference start in a high relationship to you
Observant	5,000	Instantly learn traits when socializing (tunable number of traits learned)
Opportunistic	10,000	Increase opportunity rewards (earn 2x reward)
Fertility Treatment	10,000	Increases chance of conception and chance of twins or triplets.
Mid-life Crisis	20,000	Change traits
Collection Helper	40,000	This adds marks on Map View that help spot collectibles like metals and beetles.
Body Sculptor	30,000	Instantly change body shape with this wish
Mood Modifier	60,000	Remove negative moodlets...most of the time
Food Replicator	50,000	Freely duplicate meals without the shopping or cooking time
Teleportation Pad	75,000	Quick way of getting from home to specific destiniations

Mood Modifier

Food Replicator

Teleportation Pad

TIP

If your Sims are so good at Cooking that they regularly make perfect meals, zero in on the Food Replicator to keep making perfect meals ad infinitum. This is a great way to give all Sims on the lot the powerful Amazing Meal moodlet.

CAUTION

Buying the Hardly Hunger Lifetime Wish sounds like a good idea, but be careful. If you don't want to eat, then you miss out on the great Meal-related moodlets.

Skills

Sims love to learn—they are just waiting for a little nudge from you. Sims can pick and eventually master a variety of skills, from writing to gardening to learning how to play the guitar. Learning a skill is a good way to shape a Sim's personality, especially if aligned with a specific trait, such as the Gardening skill and the Green Thumb trait. Skills are also a great way for Sims who do not want traditional career to make money and contribute to the household. Some skills can also be treated as part-time jobs, like growing harvestables in the garden or working on a novel during off hours. Skills also contribute to a Sim's mood in many positive ways.

Development

Any Sim can learn any skill. All it takes is a time commitment and a drive to be the best. Sure, some traits help a Sim learn. The Bookworm trait lets Sims read faster, which helps speed the process of learning from books. But in general, any skill can be learned as long as the Sim works at it.

There are ways to speed skill development though, and some skills actually help out with the development of other skills. Skills such fishing and gardening are intertwined because the fish caught while practicing the Fishing skill can fertilize harvestables that boost your Gardening skill. Quality fish caught with higher Fishing skill also boost the quality of recipes cooked while practicing the Cooking skill.

Speed skill development so you can learn more skills and make your Sim well-rounded. Use these tips to maximize time spend developing skills:

- Some skills can be first learned by reading a book or taking a class, which gives you a full level boost. Learn the first few levels of a skill by doing. When the levels are getting harder to attain, attend a class or pick up a book. You will reduce the time required to reach that next level.
- Use public equipment whenever possible to save money. The Athletic skill, for example, is improved by using gym equipment. You can buy gym objects, but why not head to the 28 Hour Wellness Gym and use their stuff for free? While there, you can also meet other Sims and begin socializing.
- Sims learn a little faster when they are in a good mood, so do things that give Sims positive moodlets before and while trying to master a skill. For example, learning the Logic skill by playing chess at the park can give your Sim the Comfy and Beautiful Park moodlets.
- Buy the Fast Learner Lifetime Reward. Sims with this reward learn skills faster than other Sims.
- Cheap equipment can slow skill development. At first you may only be able to afford a cheap stove, for example. But when you can afford it, trade up. Your Sim will learn a little faster.

The local library stocks skill development books. Pop inside and check the shelves closest to the front doors.

Skill Journal

Sims don't start out with any skills. When a skill is first learned, it is added to the Skill panel, and an entry in the Sim's Skill Journal tracks the development of the skill. The journal charts more than current skill level, though. Skills that produce tangibles, such as Writing or Painting, have each created work logged in the journal. Other journal entries track time spent doing various activities. The Athletic page of the Skill Journal, for example, tracks the amount of time a Sim has spent on exercise.

The Skill Journal also details skill challenges, which are specific titles bestowed on a Sim if they manage to complete a set of requirements. Sims who complete a skill challenge are rewarded with a special benefit. A Sim who repairs a specific number of electrical objects earns the Electrician challenge title and is never electrocuted

again. The journal takes the guesswork out of each challenge because the requirements are expressly detailed.

EARLY START

Toddlers cannot develop skills quite like grown Sims, but playing with toys gives them a head start. When a toddler starts playing with the toy xylophone, the Skill meter appears. What's going on? The toddler is getting a hidden skill boost to the Guitar skill. Now, if that Sim picks up the guitar as a teen or beyond, they will be extra talented.

Athletic

Want to feel the burn? Develop the Athletic skill to positively affect your Sim's health in a variety of ways, from body shape to longevity. There are two types of exercise: strength and cardio. Using the weights improves muscle definition, while cardio drops pounds.

Acquire by: Take Athletic Class, Use Exercise Equipment, Swim, Read Athletic Book, Workout with TV, Workout with Stereo

Development tools: Shut-In Treadmill, Exercise Queen, Pool, TV, Stereo

Available Ages: Teen, Young Adult, Adult, Elder

Development Benefits

Developing the Athletic skill is essential for the Professional Sports career, but is also useful for the Law Enforcement career. If Sims want to excel at work, they must honing this skill on home equipment, at the gym or pool, or on the machines at the stadium. Sims can also exercise at home with the TV or a stereo, but the workout is not as effective as one with dedicated equipment. The higher the Sim's skill, the longer they can exercise without earning the Fatigued moodlet.

Here are the benefits of developing the Athletic skill:

Level 1: As soon as Sims hit the first level of this skill, they can choose to jog to locations as exercise.

Level 3: Sims can earn the Pumped moodlet from extended workouts once they reach level 3.

Level 5: Once Sims reach level 5 of the development ladder, they also run faster when directed around town on foot via the Go Here interaction.

Level 6: At level 6, athletic Sims learn the Train interaction, which lets them help other Sims improve their Athletic skill. It requires an exercise machine. When another Sim is getting trained by a level 6 athlete, the exercising Sim loses weight and gains Athletic skill faster than if they were exercising alone.

As the Athletic skill is developed, Sims earn new "tones" for workouts. These special tones modify a workout, which can lead to earning or avoiding certain moodlets. The Don't Break a Sweat tone is good for minimizing the amount of Hygiene decay so the Grungy moodlet doesn't kick in as soon. Use these tones to get the best possible workout for the current situation:

Don't Break a Sweat (Level 1): Bad Hygiene is a real problem with extended workouts. Use this tone to work out without a heavy Hygiene decay.

Good Pacing (Level 3): Good Pacing lets you increase the length of a workout before the Fatigued moodlet takes effect.

Push Self (Level 5): Use Push Self to increase the speed of building muscle, dropping pounds, and gaining skill. However, after Push Self is used, Sims wake up with the Sore moodlet.

Quick Burst (Level 7): Quick Burst allows your Sim to get a lot of body shape change and skill much faster than usual, but the Sim gets fatigued and sore much more quickly as well. Working out with other tones until fatigued will always yield more skill and body shape change than working out until fatigued using Quick Burst, but Quick Burst give you faster skill gains.

Work out with the TV at home to improve your Athletic skill.

Skill Challenges

- **Body Builder:** Body Builders have dedicated at least 60 hours to strength workouts. This dedication pays off, because they are never fatigued after strength workouts.

- **Marathon Runner:** Marathon Runners must run at least 500 kilometers before they earn this title. However, accomplishing this incredible feat guarantees them a longer, healthier life.

- **Fitness Nut:** Fitness Nuts have spent 75 hours focusing on cardio workouts. All that time experiencing the burn means they are no longer fatigued after cardio workouts.

Charisma

Everybody knows someone who can breeze into a room, seamlessly enter any conversation, and suddenly become the focus point of attention. The key to such feats is charisma. This skill is essential for Sims who want to effectively socialize. Tuning this skill unlocks new social interactions that simplify befriending other Sims and developing meaningful relationships.

Acquire by: Take Charisma Class, Read Charisma Manual, Practice Speech in a Mirror

Development tools: Books, Socials, Mirror, Parties

Available ages: Teen, Young Adult, Adult, Elder

Development Benefits

Enhancing the Charisma skill opens exciting new avenues of conversation as well as a special social that guarantees a smooth recovery from any conversational snafus. However, developing the skill requires more than just taking a class and then practicing your charismatic moves with a book or by talking into the mirror. It requires making friends and maintaining relationship during the course of the skill development. Each level of the skill requires a specific number of friends and relationships. Without these connections, you cannot advance up the skill tree, no matter how long your practice that wolfish grin in the mirror.

Here are the number of friends and relationships required to develop the Charisma skill:

CHARISMA – DEVELOPMENT

Level	Required Friends	Required Relationships
1	0	0
2	0	2
3	1	3
4	2	4
5	3	6
6	4	8
7	5	10
8	6	15
9	8	20
10	10	25

Practice your Charisma skill by working on your speech in the mirror.

Charismatic Sims get additional greetings that start a conversation right, such as Amusing Introduction and Friendly Introduction. These greets are more potent than regular greets. As the skill develops, more greet modifiers appear that increase the social weight of the greeting and can steer the conversation. Here are the modified greetings with each advancing level:

CHARISMA – GREETINGS

Level	Greet Modifier	Type of Greet
1	Friendly	Friendly
2	Amusing	Funny
3	Interesting	Impressive
4	Flirty	Romantic
5	Affectionate	Romantic
6	Funny	Funny
7	Impressive	Impressive
8	Hilarious	Funny
9	Loving	Romantic
10	Hot	Romantic

TIP

If you ever want to truly manipulate a conversation, boost the Charisma skill. Greeting modifiers get you much closer to the desired outcome of any social interaction.

Three special socials unlock as you develop the Charisma skill. Once you reach a specific level, you learn these new socials:

Charming Introduction (Level 1): Sometimes, introductions are the toughest part of the conversation. Sims with high Charisma levels become more adept at introductions, as seen by the modified greets. Once charismatic Sims reach level 10, their Charming Introduction rockets them into Friend status right away.

Get to Know (Level 3): This social helps with discovering the traits and interests of other Sims. Once learned, this social becomes more powerful as the Sim approaches level 10 of the skill. Eventually, there is no possibility of rejection when inquiring about traits and interests.

Smooth Recovery (Level 5): Oops. You said the wrong thing. If you have the Smooth Recovery social, you can try to revive the conversation. It may not always work, but as the skill nears level 10, the chance of success increases.

TIP

The Charisma skill is helpful for Mooches and Sims in the Political career.

Skill Challenges

- **Celebrity:** Celebrities are Acquaintances with at least 25 local Sims. Celebrities build relationships faster due to a hefty starting relationship bonus.
- **Personable:** Personable Sims have learned at least 50 traits of their friends and neighbors. They learn traits more quickly when conversing with new people.
- **Super Friendly:** Super Friendly Sims can honestly say they have at least 20 friends.

It seems like an impossibly large number of relationships to juggle, but for Super Friendly Sims, friendships never decay.

- **Everybody's Best Friend:** To be Everybody's Best Friend, have at least 10 Best Friends. Your Friends skip Good Friend and jump immediately to Best Friends.
- **Comedian:** Comedians have successfully told 100 jokes, which amounts to quite a few laughs. Jokes told by Comedians rarely fall flat.

Cooking

Save for using the bathroom and sleeping, no activity is more crucial to a Sim than eating. Food is a central part of every Sim's life, so having a Sim around who can actually cook is a boon to everybody's mood. However, very few Sims are awesome in the kitchen right away—even those with the Natural Cook trait. Cooking must be practiced. It's hard work, but it has great rewards. Very few things offer a pick-me-up quite like a good meal.

Acquire by: Class, Prepare Meals, Read Cookbook

Development tools: Books, Meal Preparation Interactions, Foodstuffs, Recipes

Available Ages: Teen, Young Adult, Adult, Elder

NOTE

Children can only get snacks out of the fridge. They cannot cook.

Development Benefits

Sims must eat to survive. At first, Sims have access to just a handful of recipes, but can also just grab quick meals out of the fridge. Quick meals have zero prep time, are eaten quickly, and reduce hunger. However, quick meals and snacks do not help develop the Cooking skill, nor can they be served to groups of Sims like a full meal.

TIP

Ditch the cheap stove as soon as possible so you stop getting the Uneven Cooking moodlet.

The shortcomings of quick meals make developing the Cooking skill so important. Not every member of a household needs to excel at the skill, but a general acquaintance with it is very useful. Prepared meals build the Cooking skill while being made, can serve groups of Sims, and if made well, can improve mood.

CAUTION

Prepared meals are not without risk. An under-developed Cooking skill or a brand-new recipe can result in icky food that actually causes moods to temporarily drop.

TIP

The quality of your kitchen appliances also affects the development of the Cooking skill. Cooking on a cheap stove takes longer than on a good stove.

Quality of Food

As the Sim develops the skill, the food they make improves. The more recipes learned also improves the variety of dishes served, which has a positive effect on every Sim who eats them. When a Sim first tries to cook a recipe, there is a good chance they will fail and create a disgusting version of the dish. It is still edible, but it hits Sims with a negative moodlet. The more the dish is cooked and the level of the Cooking skill increase the recipe's quality. Eventually, a dish the Sims once botched will provide great happiness

r Sims, inspiring moodlets like Good Meal
d Amazing Meal.

BROWNIE BITES

Here's a little something that will make your Cooking career all the more beneficial to household happiness: recipe repetition. There is no downside to making the same meal over and over. There is no negative moodlet called "Hot Dogs Again?!?"

Now, the more you make a specific recipe, the better you get at it. This sub-skill is not tracked anywhere you can see, but it is indeed tracked. Some recipes are bound to cause culinary delight in Sims, like lobster. But if you make waffles repeatedly, one day you'll make waffles so perfect that Sims will get the same mood boost out of them as a gourmet food like lobster.

ecipes Learned

vo types of recipes are opened by eveloping the Cooking skill: learned recipes nd acquired recipes. Learned recipes are urchased in the bookstore, but cannot be pened until the skill at a specific level. The cquired recipes are those automatically

gifted when the Sim reaches a specific cooking level.

LEARNED RECIPES

Recipe Name	Level Required
Autumn Salad	0
Waffles	0
Mac and Cheese	0
Pancakes	1
Peanut Butter and Jelly	1
Hot Dogs	1
Goopy Carbonara	2
Grilled Cheese	2
Spgahetti	4
Sushi Roll	4
Stu Surprise	5
Hamburger	6
Key Lime Pie	7
Grilled Salmon	8
French Toast	9
Dim Sum	9
Lobster Thermador	10

ACQUIRED RECIPES

Recipe Name	Level Required
Ratatouille	1
Fish and Chips	3
Cookies	3
Fruit Parfait	4
Cheesesteak	5
Cobbler	6
Eggs Machiavellian	7
Tri-Tip Steak	8
Stuffed Turkey	9
Baked Angel Food Cake	10
Ambrosia	10

You cannot make any recipe at any time of day, Sims have particular tastes for meals at certain times of the day. They want pancakes for breakfast, salad for lunch, and meat or pasta for dinner. Here are the meal times:

3 AM-10 AM: Breakfast

9 AM-3 PM on Weekends: Brunch

12 PM-5 PM: Lunch

5 PM-3 AM: Dinner

Anytime: Dessert

The Costs of Cooking

Quick meals and snacks are free so that no Sim goes hungry. However, making prepared meals actually costs Simoleons. If Sims have the required ingredients in the fridge, no cost appears next to a recipe when selected from the interaction with the refrigerator. If a recipe requires ingredients not in the fridge, then the cost of the needed ingredients is displayed next to the dish in the menu. Selecting that dish automatically deducts the required funds from the household account. There is no need to drop everything and run

for EverFresh. You also won't need to start spending money right away, because fridges come with a few basic ingredients.

Skill Challenges

◆ **Star Chef:** Star Chefs have prepared at least 50 meals, so they clearly know their way around the kitchen. The dishes they prepare are higher quality and thus more pleasing.

◆ **World-Class Chef:** World-Class Chefs have prepared at least 75 dishes and are masters of the kitchen. World-Class Chefs prepare meals significantly faster.

◆ **Menu Maven:** Menu Mavens have learned to prepare all recipes. Recipes are earned by improving the Cooking skill and can be purchased at the bookstore. Menu Mavens prepare higher quality food.

Fishing

The waters around Sunset Valley ripple with life. Thousands of fish swim through the blue, hoping for a nice bit of food to drop. What's that pointy thing sticking out of the snack? Who cares, let's grab this grub...

The Fishing skill is good for three things: keeping food on the table, earning money, and relaxing. Sims with the Angler trait have a head start on other Sims who pick up a rod-and-reel, but any Sims can take a class to advance the Fishing skill or just plop a bobber in the water and start learning through experience.

Acquire by: Take Fishing Class, Read Fishing Book, Fishing

Development tools: No tools needed

Available ages: Child, Teen, Young Adult, Adult, Elder

Development Benefits

The Fishing skill begins one of three ways: reading a book, taking a class, or just going out to a body of water and using the Fish interaction. Once the Fishing skill is underway, the skill increases either by continued reading or continued fishing. Just having a hook under the surface is enough to develop the skill, but this is a slow way to learn. The skill actually gets a bump when you catch a fish. And the bigger the fish, the bigger the skill bump.

TIP

Certain traits in addition to Angler affect the Fishing skill. Loves the Outdoors Sims get great moodlets from just being outside and fishing. Hates Outdoors, Easily Bored, or Clumsy dampen the ability to catch fish. If a Sim has any of these traits, perhaps they should pick up the guitar instead of the rod.

When a fish is hoisted out of the water, the Sim holds it up and the weight of the fish is automatically logged in the Skill Journal. If it's a new type of fish, that is also noted.

Once the Sim reaches level 3 with the Fishing skill, they can choose the Bait interaction at the water's edge to use a specific type of bait while fishing. Bait is essential if a Sim hopes to catch more than just the basic fish in the water, such as the Goldfish. Gaining levels also unlocks the ability to catch certain fish. However, just unlocking a type of fish does not guarantee actually catching it.

Using any bait slightly increases the chance of catching all fish. It also drastically increases the chance of catching the fish that loves that specific bait type.

Higher quality bait (nice, perfect, etc.) will tend to catch bigger fish, but only for fish that specifically like that bait. So use perfect bait to catch the biggest fish.

You can also use bait to catch fish that are somewhat higher level than your Sim's Fishing skill. Sims can catch fish up to 3 levels higher than their skill by using the right bait, although it will be harder to catch those fish until the Sim is higher skill.

Each fish has one favorite type of bait, and you should use that bait to catch that fish. Learn what that bait is by experimenting with different types of bait or by reading bait books purchased from the bookstore.

Bait is not enough though. Certain fish exist only in certain locations, so you have to find where a fish lurks before you can catch it. Use the Inspect Water interaction to get an idea of the types of fish in the water. Inspect will show only those fish that your Sim is high enough level to catch.

FISHING

Fish	Skill Level Required	Commonality	Locations Found	Preferred Bait	Minimum weight	Maximum weight	Value at min weight	Value at max weight	Skill Points for Catching
Minnow	0	Common	Lakes, Ocean	Apple	0.1	0.5	5	11	120
Anchovy	0	Common	Ocean	Tomato	0.1	0.5	5	11	120
Goldfish	1	Common	Lakes	Lettuce	0.1	2	6	16	132
Alley Catfish	1	Uncommon	Lakes, Ocean	Cheese	0.1	5	6	20	132
Jellyfish	2	Common	Ocean	Grapes	0.1	10	8	19	140
Rainbow Trout	2	Common	Lakes	Egg	1	10	9	18	140
Red Herring	3	Common	Lakes, Ocean	Hot Dogs	1	10	5	5	160
Tuna	3	Common	Ocean	Onion	2	40	11	25	160
Piranha	4	Uncommon	Lakes	Watermelon	5	15	14	30	185
Tragic Clownfish	4	Uncommon	Laes, Ocean	Bell Pepper	5	40	13	32	185
Siamese Catfish	5	Common	Lakes, Ocean	Minnow	3	25	14	41	220
Blowfish	5	Uncommon	Ocean	Potato	5	40	13	47	220
Salmon	6	Common	Ocean	Lime	10	50	14	45	255
Black Goldfish	6	Common	Lakes	Goldfish	5	25	16	49	255
Shark	7	Uncommon	Lakes, Ocean	Red Herring	1	150	7	70	295
Swordfish	7	Common	Ocean	Anchovy	20	60	17	60	295
Angelfish	8	Uncommon	Lakes, Ocean	AlleyCatfish	2	60	21	85	340
Vampire Fish	8	Rare	Graveyard	Garlic	25	80	55	225	1,000
Robot Fish	9	Rare	Science Facility	Piranha	250	1,000	50	275	1,000
Lobster	9	Common	Lakes, Ocean	Tuna	5	50	25	120	400
Deathfish	10	Rare	Graveyard	Angelfish	20	80	200	1,000	1,500

DEATHFISH

Deathfish are the rarest and most valuable fish. They're found only in the graveyard, and only between 12 AM and 5 AM. They are very hard to catch, so your Sim should be level 10 Fishing skill and use their favorite food, Angelfish, as bait.

What to Do with Fish

Okay, so you caught some fish. Now what? here are five things you can do with fish: eat,

sell, use it as bait, use it as fertilizer for your garden, or keep it as a pet. Eating the fish is the most natural. Just place the fish in the refrigerator to keep it fresh. Fishing Sims can make quite a bit of cash selling "sea kittens" to the EverFresh market. Fish can be used as bait to catch other fish, too.

Place fish around your house for nice environmental boosts.

Fish also make good pets, especially if keeping fish is related to a Lifetime Wish. Buy the Shrinkomatic Bowl from Buy Mode

and place them around the house to store caught fish by left-clicking on the bowl and choosing Stock. Pay attention to them—fish in bowls must be fed regularly. A dead fish left unattended starts to stink, which results in the Disgusted moodlet.

Fish have environmental bonuses, too. The rarer and larger the fish, the more it contributes to the room's decor. Keep nice, rare fish in bowls to get the Nicely Decorated moodlet.

Skill Challenges

- **Amateur Ichthyologist:** Amateur Ichthyologists have caught at least one of every fish type. Their deep understanding of marine life helps them catch the bigger fish.

- **Commercial Fisherman:** Commercial Fisherman have caught at least 350 fish. They catch more fish in less time than normal Sims.

Gardening

Gardening is a great skill for Green Thumb Sims, Sims who want to cook, and Sims who like the outdoors. This skill tree lets you turn a backyard into a harvestable-growing paradise. But gardening is a lot of work and takes time to master.

TIP

The Gardening skill is a great way to make extra money on the side.

Acquire by: Take Gardening Class, Read Gardening Book

Development tools: Gardening Books, Seeds

Available ages: Teen, Young Adult, Adult, Elder

Development Benefits

Learn the Gardening skill by taking a class or reading a gardening book. You can also plant a seed and cultivate it to start developing the skill. Once the skill has been acquired, Sims can choose the Plant interaction from seeds and other harvestables in their personal inventories. Once a seed has been planted, Sims can water it. As they continue leveling, they unlock two more critical interactions: Weed and Fertilize.

NOTE

One clever thing you can do with a growing harvestable is talk to it. Talk to Plant is available if a Sim has the Green Thumb trait...or the Insane trait.

TIP

Sims can also View growing plants. If a Sim has the Loves the Outdoors trait, they will get a positive mood boost for standing outside and enjoying the fresh air while admiring the garden.

Here are the unlockable interactions or specials for the development of the Gardening skill:

Weed (Level 2): Once the Weed interaction is unlocked, Sims can pull up choking weeds before they damage a harvestable. The higher the skill level, the less time it takes to clear weeds around a plant.

Fertilize (Level 3): Fertilizing is key to growing the best harvestables. No one fertilizer is better for a particular plant. The quality of the fertilizer is what affects the potential growth of the harvestable.

Uncommon Seeds (Level 5): Once the Sim reaches this level, they can plant uncommon seeds.

Revive Plant (Level 6): If a Sim has the Green Thumb trait, this interaction is unlocked at level 6. A dying plant can be rescued with a pretty high success rate by using this interaction on it.

Rare Seeds (Level 7): Once the Sim reaches this level, they can plant rare seeds.

Special Plants (Levels 8, 9, and 10): At level 8, you get the first of three special gardening opportunities from the chef at the bistro. There is one opportunity per level: 8, 9, and 10. Once all three have been completed, the Sim receives Omni Plant seeds and the ability to plant them.

CAUTION

Do not use the Deathfish for fertilizer. It will kill your plant!

NOTE

What's an Omni Plant? Imagine a plant that grows into whatever fertilizer you give it. Give the Omni Plant a book and the Omni Plant will soon blossom great texts.

TIP

Grow garlic and watermelon for simple cash crops. Just keep planting the highest quality of these harvestables and churn that garden until it becomes a money machine.

The better care you give a plant and the higher your Gardening skill level, the better quality fruit a plant produces. Plants range from horrifying to perfect, just like prepared recipes from the Cooking skill. Better quality harvestables, are worth more when sold. Some gardening opportunities require plants of specific qualities, too. Nurturing excellent harvestables is the best way to advance this skill.

NOTE

To pick produce from a plant or tree, choose the Harvest interaction when left-clicking on the plant. It's that easy.

TIP

Dead plant clogging up your home garden? Use Dispose to dig it up and get rid of it, clearing room for a new start.

To raise the best harvestables, you must show no mercy with your plants. Keep growing as many as you can and Dispose of the lowest quality ones, so you keep breeding higher quality harvestables. Combine this tactic with raising your skill level to keep growing better harvestables. Using quality harvestables in your cooking improves the quality of recipes, which in turn gives out better meal-related moodlets.

TiP

Watering takes time. Install a sprinkler to water an entire area at once. If you can, get a Sims with the Handiness skill to upgrade the sprinkler so it auto-waters. Then you can completely put watering out of your mind.

..eeds

..ms need seeds to grow harvestables. Not all ..eeds are easy to grow into successful plants, ..hough. Sims must level up the Gardening ..kill to plant all types of seeds: common, ..ncommon, and rare.

..any seeds can just be bought from ..verFresh, such as grape or tomato. Just buy ..e fruit and then plant it. However, Sims ..an also find seeds by exploring Sunset ..alley. Every morning, there are new seeds ..n new locations, so look around daily to see ..hat's on the ground. The farther away from ..ouses and commerce buildings Sims look, ..e more likely they are to find uncommon ..nd rare seeds. Seeds are unknown when ..ound. To discover what the seed will grow, ..must be planted and nurtured. Once you ..row a harvestable from a found seed, you ..ecognize that seed in the wild.

TiP

There are a few amazing trees and plants out there, including the coveted Money Tree. The Money Tree gives off Simoleons if it is properly cared for, but it's a high-maintenance plant.

Money Tree

Life Fruit

CAUTION

If you do not take good care of the Money Tree, it will explode into bills that must be paid!

Death Blossom

Flame Fruit

TIP

Grow the Flame Fruit and then keep one in your pocket to enjoy the Warmed moodlet wherever you go.

Once you have unlocked it, you can order more Omni Plant seeds through the mailbox.

Fertilizer

There are many different types of fertilizer to use on your plants to help them grow into high-quality harvestables. Here's a full list of the best fertilizers:

FERTILIZERS

Ingredient	Effectiveness	Fish	Effectiveness
Cheese	1	Anchovy	1
Burger Patty	1	Goldfish	1
Egg	1	Alley Catfish	1
Lettuce	1	Rainbow Trout	2
Tomato	1	Minnow	3
Onion	1	Jellyfish	3
Potato	1	Tuna	3
Apple	1	Salmon	4
Lime	1	Black Goldfish	4
Grapes	1	Swordfish	4
Watermelon	2	Red Herring	5
Steak	3	Tragic Clownfish	5
Bell Pepper	3	Siamese Catfish	5
Garlic	3	Piranha	5
Flame Fruit	3	Blowfish	5
Life Fruit	4	Shark	6
		Lobster	6
		Angelfish	7
		Vampire Fish	7

TIP

You can also use fish that you reel in as cheap, free fertilizer to really get your garden growing.

Skill Challenges

- **Master Planter:** A Master Planter must plant every type of plant available. Once you have mastered the varieties, you can reduce weed growth significantly on future plants.

- **Botanical Boss:** Botanical Bosses must harvest at least 75 perfect fruits and vegetables. The plants of Botanical Bosses almost never die from neglect.

- **Master Farmer:** Master Farmers have harvested at least 650 fruits and vegetables. The plants of Master Farmers remain watered and fertilized longer, meaning their gardens are more efficient.

Guitar

Who doesn't love the gift of music? A smooth jam lilting on a summer's breeze brings joy to all who hear it. So why not become the source of such aural pleasures by picking up the guitar and developing this skill. The Guitar skill can be enjoyed by any Sim, not just those who have embarked on the music career.

Acquire by: Take Guitar Class

Development tools: Guitar

Available ages: Teen, Young Adult, Adult, Elder

Development Benefits

To get started on the guitar skill, visit the Wilsonoff Community Theater and enroll in the guitar class. §400 later, your Sim now has the ability to strum a few bars on a six string. To advance this skill, though, you really need to pick up a guitar for the Sim's household. The guitar can slide into the Sim's personal inventory, though, so they can take it the park or the beach. The guitar is a great ice-breaker.

When you play in a communal location, Sims around you stop and listen. Even if you mess up and play a song poorly, you still start off on the right foot with Sims who were listening. Use socials on them quickly before the boost fades.

Once Sims know how to play, they only have a few available compositions. Only by leveling up the skill does the Sim learn more music and eventually reach a point where they can buy sheet music from the bookstore and really play some impressive tunes. As the skill improves, the Sim gets better at playing music and makes fewer mistakes. Here's the level progression of the Guitar skill:

Level 1–4: Sim learns at least two basic practice-level songs per level.

Level 5: Sim earns three new songs—real songs that other Sims enjoy listening to.

Level 6–10: Sim learns at least one new song per level and performs it without fail.

Level 5 is particularly important to this skill. At this level, the Sim stops just noodling around with the Play interaction and moves up to the Perform interaction. Other Sims get the Enjoying Music moodlet if around a performing Sim. Level 5 Sims can also Serenade other Sims, which is a romantic social that can aid a romantic conversation following the song's conclusion.

Guitar-playing Sims can also Play for Tips in public locations. This is not the most lucrative activity, but it does add some extra change to the household bank account. The higher your skill, the more you make in tips. To really make money with this skill, practice hard and be sure to socialize around Sunset Valley. Soon, you will receive opportunities to play at parties or venues. That's where the real money is.

Sheet Music

You can buy sheet music from the bookstore or earn it from opportunities and give it to your Sim to practice. To learn from sheet music, left-click on the music from the Sim's personal inventory and select the Learn interaction. The Sim starts playing the song and when the meter is full, the Sim knows the song by heart and can perform it.

SHEET MUSIC

Sheet Music	Level Required
Yes Ma'am, I Do	5
Flamenco Fever	6
A Perfect Moment	7
Improvise Here and Now	8
Dream Escape	9

Skill Challenges

Master Guitarist: Master Guitarists learn to play every song awarded to them and available for purchase at the bookstore. After learning so many songs, they receive a special master track!

Guitar Star: Guitar Stars must play at 10 parties and venues in the town to earn their title. Afterward, they earn more money for tips and performances.

Money Maker: Earn §5,000 playing the guitar to earn a new master track to perform. Money can be earned through tips or by completing opportunities.

Handiness

Stuff breaks. But when it does, it's usually inconvenient. Sims with the Handiness skill are suddenly valuable folks to have around. The Handiness skill is good for repairing broken objects, and can even ensure against future calamity.

Acquire by: Take Handiness Class, Read Handiness Book, Try to Repair an Object

Development tools: Handiness Skill Books, Tinkering with Objects, Repairing an Object, Upgrading an Object

Available ages: Teen, Young Adult, Adult, Elder

Development Benefits

Once the Handiness skill has been acquired via a course or a book, Sims can further develop it at home by either Tinkering with objects or attempting to Repair a broken object, such as a stove, stereo, dishwasher, or toilet. Any mechanical or electric object has the potential to break after every use. When an electrical object breaks, it typically smokes or sparks. A broken toilet is clogged and refuses to flush. When this happens, the Repair interaction becomes available.

This is the risk of trying to fix an electrical object when you have not developed this skill.

When the Repair option is selected, a handy Sim will start working on the object. Depending on the level of the Handiness skill, the Sim risks getting electrocuted by the object. This causes the Singed moodlet, which drops the overall mood. (Remove this moodlet with a bath or shower.) The higher the Handiness skill, the less chance the Sim will be shocked while repairing the object. Fortunately, one of the skill challenges (Electrician) can make a Sim invulnerable to electrocution.

A repaired object is not back to 100 percent. Once an object breaks, it has started its steady downhill slide. The chance of a repaired object breaking again goes up. The more it breaks and is repaired, the higher the chance of repeat breaks until the object finally goes absolutely kaput and must be replaced.

Upgrading

Once the Handiness skill reaches level 3, the Sim learns the Upgrade interaction. Upgrading lets a Sim add a new effect or function to an existing object. This is not a universal interaction once learned. Subsequent levels after earning the Upgrade interaction unlock extra upgrades the handy Sim can install.

Simology

Upgrades can provide many benefits, from making an object unbreakable or self cleaning or fireproof to strictly improving it, for instanc the stereo's speakers can be improved to produce a bigger Enjoying Music moodlet.

Here is the list of objects that can be upgraded, the function of the upgrade, and the level required to perform the upgrade:

UPGRADING

Level	Object	Upgrade	Failure Effect
3	Inexpensive Shower	Prevents ever getting Cold Shower moodlet	Causes puddle that must be mopped
3	Dishwasher	Silences noisy dishwashers that disturb other Sims	Dishwasher just makes louder noises while running
3	Doorbell	Change doorbell to a pleasing sound	Doorbell makes awful noise
3	Stereo	Increase area of effect	Electrocution
3	Window	Improves insulation which lowers bills	None
4	Stove	Make stove fireproof so it never catches fire	Stove catches fire and burns up
4	Coffeemaker	Add timer function so coffee is ready in morning	Electrocution
6	Trash Compactor	Improve capacity	Electrocution
6	Shower	Improve water pressure to cause the Exhilarated moodlet	Causes puddle that must be mopped
7	Gas Fireplace	Fireplace starts when Sim enters room	Fire breaks out in fireplace
7	Stove	Improves food quality	None
8	Stereo	Increase mood gain of Enjoying Music	Electrocution
8	Stereo	Wire House with Speakers so music plays in all rooms	Electrocution
8	Computer	Improves graphics to make games more fun for Sims	Electrocution
9	Grandfather Clock	Increase value of clock	Decrease resale value of clock
6 through 10	Television	Unlock extra channels. Higher the skill, the more channels unlocked.	Electrocution

At level 3, a Sim can add a self-cleaning upgrade (Self Cleaning) to objects that get dirty, such as the stove or refrigerator. At level 6 of the skill, Sims can upgrade any mechanical/electrical object so that it is unbreakable with the Prevent Breakage interaction. This upgrade takes time, but doing so helps develop the skill. Success with these upgrades is not guaranteed. If the upgrade fails (there's a small chance of this happening) then the object is either broken beyond repair or gets dirty and must be cleaned.

Finally, at level 10, the Sim gets a membership card to a guild. Build Mode objects are then 25 percent off.

Skill Challenges

- **Electrician:** Electricians have repaired at least 10 electrical objects. The experience gained means they will never be electrocuted by an electrical object again.

- **Plumber:** Plumbers have repaired at least 10 plumbing objects. They are so good at repairs that plumbing objects repaired by them never break again.

- **Tinkerer:** Tinkerers have finished at least 10 unique upgrades on household items. Installing the "Unbreakable" upgrade on multiple objects only counts as one unique upgrade, so it helps to experiment with different upgrade options! Tinkerers never fail when upgrading objects.

Logic

Intelligence is always a treasured asset, so pursue the Logic skill to improve your Sim's brainpower. The Logic skill involves the use of the telescope and chess set objects, but also gives Sims additional computer interactions.

> **Acquire by:** Take Logic Class, Read Logic Book, Play Chess, Use Telescope

> **Development tools:** Chess Set, Telescope, Logic Books, Computer

Development Benefits

The development of the Logic skill starts with attending the logic class at the Landgraab ndustries Science Facility, playing chess at a hess board (at home or in a public location), r reading a logic-related book. This skill as many benefits beyond the ability to win hess matches. For example, this skill unlocks he Solve the Unsolvable interaction with the omputer, which gives the logic-minded Sim chance to earn some Simoleons at home. This interaction is not a guaranteed success.)

As this skill is developed, it shortens the me it takes to develop other skills, with the exception of Athletic and Charisma. Teen and hild Sims also get a homework speed boost s this skill is developed. The higher the level, he faster homework is completed. (This is tremendous benefit with grades.) This kill also increases the chance of winning all arieties of games. Winning games gives Sims mood boost.

good measuring stick for the chance a logic im will beat another Sim is to compare Logic kill ranks. A Sim with level 5 will likely beat ne at level 4—but upsets can occur.

At level 3 of the Logic skill, Sims have a new nteraction with the telescope. They can now do more than just Stargaze, they can Search Galaxy. This is another money-making opportunity for Sims, as every new celestial oody found earns them a little extra cash from he science facility. New finds are logged in he Skill Journal, too. When a Sim finds a new object in the heavens, they can name it.

Playing chess against other Sims not only increases the Logic skill, but it also gives LTR a little boost.

Want to really impress somebody? Name a star after them.

At level 5, Sims unlock the ability to Tutor other young Sims: children and teens. Tutoring not only develops the Logic skill, but it helps he student and can provide a mood bump.

Tutored Sims always do better in school, so if a child suffers from lagging grades, interacting with a logic Sim is a great remedy. If the mentored student has the Logic skill, too, they develop the skill while being tutored, but at a slower pace.

TIP

There is a "hidden" Chess skill. Like other skills, the more you play chess, the better you get at it. You will soon start winning more and more games.

At level 5 Logic skill, Sims can start talking about the things they find while using the telescope. Talking about a celestial object is a friendly social that improves the building relationship between two Sims. However, for a real social bump, tell a Sim that you named a celestial object after them. This instant relationship builder helps with making over new friends or developing a romantic relationship.

At level 10 Logic skill, the Sim can tutor any other Sim from teen to elder in any of the skills with the exception of Athletic and Charisma. The catch is that the logic Sim must also have the skill they are teaching and they cannot teach past their current level. For example, if Catherine has level 5 Writing skill, she cannot tutor Chris past level 5. This development process is much faster than reading a skill-related book but not as fast as actually practicing the skill.

Skill Challenges

◆ **Grand Master:** Chess Grand Masters have reached the coveted fifth level of the competitive chess circuit. Those who engage Grand Masters in chess improve their abilities in Logic and Chess twice as quickly.

◆ **Celestial Explorer:** Celestial Explorers have discovered 20 celestial bodies through their telescope. Their extensive knowledge of the heavens allows them to discuss the stars with their friends and neighbors.

◆ **Teacher Extraordinaire:** Teachers Extraordinaire have spent at least 20 hours tutoring other Sims. Because of this, they are twice as effective when tutoring others.

◆ **Skill Professor:** Skill Professors have spent at least 30 hours tutoring other Sims in skills. Because of this, they are twice as effective when teaching skills to others.

Painting

One of the hardest skills to develop, painting is also one of the most rewarding. Watch in wonder as Sims create works of art before your very eyes, working from inspiration they gathered from themselves or your own input. Like writing, this is a personalized skill that requires a lot of direction from you. But once this skill is mastered, it's not only satisfying, but very lucrative. Great painting can sell for a pretty penny.

> **Acquire by:** Take Painting Class, Practice at Easel
>
> **Development tools:** Easel
>
> **Available Ages:** Children, Teen, Young Adult, Adult, Elder

Development Benefits

The painting skill is actually fairly easy to acquire, but it is not exactly cheap. You must either pay for a painting class at the community school or spring for an easel. With an easel, use the Dabble interaction on the easel to pick up a brush and just mess around. After a considerable amount of time, the skill is acquired. Once level 1 of the painting skill has been acquired, though, the development path is pretty clear: practice, practice, practice.

The Dabble interaction is replaced by Practice and you can choose the size of the canvas you want the Sim to practice on. The smaller the canvas, the faster the painting is completed. The size of the canvas also factors into the price a painting fetches, but more on that in a moment. The Practice interaction disappears when there is a canvas on the easel—then you can only continue practicing unless you chose to Scrap the Painting and start all over with a new one.

Once a Painting is completed, a Sim can either Sell it and earn a few Simoleons or Take it, and then pull it out of personal inventory to hang on a wall.

The Sims 3

At level 5 of the skill, Paint replaces Practice as the interaction with the easel. Now the Sim can start earning money with this skill. As soon as the Sim unlocks skill level 6, they can paint a Brilliant painting, which is worth a decent number of Simoleons and can add environmental bonuses to rooms and inspire the Decorated moodlet. At level 9, the Sim has the chance to create a Masterpiece painting, which is even more valuable than a Brilliant painting.

Value

The value of a painting is determined by several factors. The canvas size partially determines the value, as does the number of paintings a Sim has produced. Brilliant or Masterpiece paintings get massive value boosts, too. There is a degree of randomness in a painting's value. One somewhat morbid factor greatly enhances a painting's value: death. If the painter is deceased, the painting's appreciation accelerates.

> ### TIP
> At skill level 5, a Sim's paintings increase in value over time. Keep checking the painting to see its current appreciation.

BROWNIE BITES

This is a little sinister, but it's a great trick. If you have an elder Sim in the house, make them a painter. Concentrate on that skill. Make them painting factories. Get them to produce as many quality works as possible before they die. Then, once they do pass, all of their paintings are worth more!

Painting from Inspirations

In addition to the chances of painting Brilliant paintings or Masterpieces during the development of the skill, painters also unlock a handful of interactions that deal directly with the inspiration of a painting. Here are the interactions and their corresponding skill levels:

Paint Still Life (Level 5): When this interaction is chosen, you can direct what you want the Sim to paint from the immediate area around the Sim. Use a small frame to select the subject of the painting and then left-click to direct the Sim to start painting away.

Paint Portrait (Level 7): This interaction directs the painter to create the portrait of a Sim on the lot. The painting frame zeroes in on the Sim subject and you can manipulate it to decide the angle. Portraits take longer to finish than Still Life paintings.

Paint Memorized Scene (Level 8): Use the cellphone to take a photo of a scene somewhere in Sunset Valley. This then becomes the Memorized Scene. The Sims will start painting the scene.

Here are some examples of different paintings and different painting styles:

Skill Challenges

- **Brushmaster:** Brushmasters have painted at least 35 paintings, and as a result paint much faster than normal painters.

- **Proficient Painter:** Proficient Painters have proven their worth by painting at least six Brilliant paintings. They then paint far more Brilliant paintings and Masterpieces than less proficient painters.

- **Master Painter:** Master Painters have painted at least five masterpieces. Every painting they sell is worth much more than normal paintings.

Writing

Writing is another personalized skill that is deeply involving but also rewarding. Sims who learn the Writing skill unlock a world of possibilities when they sit down to the computer. Naturally, the Bookworm Sim has a jump on this skill thanks to the relevant trait. But any Sim with time and dedication can become a bestselling author.

Acquire by: Attend Writing Class, Read Writing Book, Practice Writing at Computer

Development tools: Computer, Books

Available Ages: Teen, Young Adult, Adult, Elder

Development Benefits

Once the Writing skill has been acquired, Sims have several new interactions at the computer. The Refine Writing Skill is a good way to continue developing the skill. No novels come out of this activity—just skill development. Once a writer reaches level 2 of the skill, they can start writing novels. Write Novel is one of three interactions available once this level is reached. While writing a novel, a Sim continues to develop the Writing skill. When the Sim pushes back from the computer, the development is added to the Skill meter. Continue Writing Novel and Scrap Current Novel are two more interactions that affect a novel-in-progress. A scrapped novel

What's New | Creating a Sim | Creating a House | A Day in the Life | **Simology** | Relationships and Aging | Tour of Sunset Valley | Design Corner | Object Catalog | Community

...osses out an incomplete work but the skill
...evelopment remains.

> ## NOTE
>
> When you first start a novel, you get to name it. If you complete the novel, you may see it on the shelves of the library!

...arious novel genres are unlocked as the skill
... further developed. The higher the genre
...n the skill tree, the more it is worth when
...ublished. Here are the genres, the levels
...equired to unlock them, and the reactions
...hey can cause it their readers:

NOVEL GENRES UNLOCKED BY WRITING

Genre	# of Books Required
Genre	# of Books Required
Fantasy	Write 3 Sci-Fi novels
Satire	Write 3 humor novels
Autobiography	Write 3 biographies
Vaudeville	Write 3 of each: drama, sci-fi, humor, mysery, romance

NOVEL GENRES UNLOCKED BY SKILL LEVEL

Genre	Level
Fiction	0
Non-Fiction	0
Science Fiction	1
Trashy Novel	2
Drama	3
Childrens Book	3
Humor	5
Historical	6
Mystery	8
Romance	10
Masterpiece	10

> ## TIP
>
> Good Sense of Humor Sims can write humor books at level 2. Hopeless Romantics can write romances at level 5. And to write a children's book, Sims must have level 6 of the painting skill.

> ## CAUTION
>
> You can only work on one novel at a time. If you want to start a new novel in a newly unlocked genre, you must scrap the current novel.

Royalties

While a Sim writes a novel, they regularly submit chapters to an agent and get a small stipend. It's enough to live on, but nothing extravagant. Once a novel has been completed, though, the royalties start rolling in. When the novel is finished, the Sim is immediately told if the book is good or not and if it is a success. The amount of royalties is listed, as well as how the amount will be paid out. (Typically, royalties are paid over the course of several weeks with lump sums dropped into the household account at a specific time on a specific day.)

The royalty amount is decided by: level of Writing skill, desirability of the genre (check the Skill Journal, which also tracks the number of books written and the amount pulled in so far), and a certain degree of randomness. The author's traits can also affect the amount of royalties paid. Here are the traits that boost the profitability of specific genres:

TRAITS – GENRES

Genre	Trait
Trashy Novel	Flirty
Drama	Commitment Issues
Sci-Fi	Computer Whiz, Genius
Humor	Good Sense of Humor, Inappropriate, Mean-Spirited
Satire	Grumpy, Hot-Headed, Over-Emotional
Mystery	Genius
Romance	Hopeless Romantic
Historical	Perfectionist
Children's Book	Artistic, Childish, Family Oriented
Vaudeville	Bookworm
Autobiography	Charismatic, Unlucky, Daredevil, Insane, Kleptomaniac

Every novel has a chance of becoming a Hit, Best-seller, or total Flop. Flop books are worth only half of a normal book. Hit books are worth double the value of a normal book. Best-sellers are worth triple a normal book's value.

> ## NOTE
>
> Hit books and Best-sellers provide more Fun to readers than normal or Flop books, no matter the relationship between the reader and the author.

Skill Challenges

- ◆ **Speed Writer:** Speed Writers are so prolific that they've earned §15,000 in royalties. Speed Writers write much faster than normal writers.

- ◆ **Prolific Writer:** Prolific Writers have written at least 20 books in their career. They are so well known that they tend to write far more Hits and Best-sellers than their counterparts.

- ◆ **Specialist Writer:** Writers must pen at least five novels in a specific genre to be known as a specialist. Such specialists write far more Hits and Best-sellers in their particular genre than most.

Simology

Careers

While everybody would prefer a life of leisure, you must find a source of income if you want to succeed. There are multiple ways to rake in the Simoleons, including the advancement of certain skills as detailed earlier in this chapter. However, there are more traditional ways of finding an income: careers.

When you first move into town, it's likely that your Sims will wish for a specific career. You do not have to honor such requests, but those wishes are usually born out of the specific traits you assigned that Sim, and often directly connected to the Lifetime Wish.

To sign up for a career, you simply report to the building that headquarters the job, such as the military base or police station. Applying is as easy as left-clicking on the location and then choosing the offered career. When your Sim reports to the job location, the career is immediately offered and the starting position/salary flashed on-screen. If you accept, you are given a schedule and expected to show up at the designated times.

There are multiple ways to advance a career. Promotions are the most common benchmark of success and always comes with a one-time Simoleon bonus, but there are social aspects to each career that involve getting to know co-workers, which has the potential to widen your circle of friends. While at work, you can set the "tone" for your performance, which affects how you interact with co-workers or approach the job itself. As you advance, your schedule changes and your salary rises. Typically, there are perks or benefits for hitting certain promotions.

NOTE

Many careers have specific outfits related to the job. Athletes will dress in team garb, for example, while business Sims will don a power suit.

Going to work in a good mood boosts your chances of promotion. Go see a movie the night before work to get the powerful Enjoyed a Great Movie moodlet that lasts almost the entire next day.

Use this chapter to check out all of the careers and see exactly what is expected and involved with each job. Each entry details the list of career ranks and promotion titles.

TIP

Go to work in a good mood to get promotions easier. Mood is always a metric used to when bosses hand out promotions.

TIP

Once you reach level 10 of a career, you can keep getting raises. Keep attending to your job and every time the performance meter fills, your Sim gets another raise

Retiring

Later in life, Sims can retire from a career and make a pension. This pension is smaller than the wages normally made at that promotion level, but it is a great way to pull in daily income for necessary food and objects whil pursuing skills.

Business

The business career unfolds exactly as you might expect. Sims dutifully report to work in the morning to attend meetings and climb the corporate ladder. As you approach the top of the career ranking, the requirements to reach each new promotion become harder to juggle. But that should be expected for a career with such incredible financial rewards. You cannot coast. You must work hard, appealing to both the boss and co-workers so that one day that corner office is yours.

Work Location: Doo Peas Corporate Towers

How Hired: Report to business tower, answer computer ad, answer newspaper ad

Work Week: The career is a Monday through Friday job with normal business hours. At first, the hours are a little longer. However, over time, those hours are spread out across meetings that are required as part of the job at different times.

Salary Progression: This career pays very little at first. However, when you move up the ranks, the Simoleon rewards grow exponentially. As you close in on the top levels of the career, the salary is huge.

BUSINESS CAREER

Level	Position	Work Days	Start Time	Length of Day	Average Daily Pay	Weekly Average Pay	Pension Pay	Metrics for Promotion
1	Coffee Courier	M, T, W, TH, F	8 AM	6	160	800	40	Mood, Relationship w/ Boss
2	Filing Clerk	M, T, W, TH, F	8 AM	6	208	1,040	50	Mood, Relationship w/ Boss
3	Report Processor	M, T, W, TH, F	8 AM	6	271	1,355	70	Mood, Relationship w/ Boss, Relationship w/ Co-Workers
4	Corporate Drone	M, T, W, TH, F	8 AM	6	353	1,765	90	Mood, Relationship w/ Boss, Relationship w/ Co-Workers
5	Department Head	M, T, W, TH, F	8 AM	7	530	2,650	130	Mood, Relationship w/ Boss, Relationship w/ Co-Workers
6	Division Manager	M, T, W, TH, F	8 AM	7	689	3,445	170	Mood, Relationship w/ Boss, Relationship w/ Co-Workers, Meetings Held
7	Vice President	M, T, W, TH, F	8 AM	7	896	4,480	220	Mood, Relationship w/ Boss, Relationship w/ Co-Workers, Meetings Held
8	CEO	M, T, TH, F	8 AM	6	1,434	5,736	280	Mood, Relationship w/ Boss, Relationship w/ Co-Workers, Meetings Held
9	Venture Capitalist	M, T, TH, F	8 AM	6	1,721	6,884	330	Mood, Relationship w/ Co-Workers, Meetings Held
10	Power Broker	M, T, TH	8 AM	3	947	2,841	400	Mood, Relationship w/ Co-Workers, Meetings Held

BUSINESS TONES

Tones	Description
Hold Meetings	Available to schedule meetings, slows performance growth
Meet Co-Workers	Build relationship with co-workers
Chat at Water Cooler	Build relationship with co-workers
Suck Up to Boss	Build relationship with boss
Power Work	Work hard to increase performance, but adds stress

Benefits and Rewards

To work your way up this career, you must have a good relationship with the boss. This can be achieved by the Suck Up to Boss tone, but this risks alienating co-workers. This turns into a problem later in the career when the relationship with co-workers becomes a metric for which your promotion is judged. Being charismatic can help with this career because after meeting co-workers on the job, you can then improve those relationships outside working hours.

TIP

The Business career is the easiest to master because it requires the fewest skills.

Once you reach the Division Manager promotion, you can start holding meetings and meeting opportunities come regularly. Making these meetings becomes a critical metric for making additional promotions. Here, the career starts to consume a lot of time and attention.

TIP

Don't worry about missing scheduled work hours to attend meetings. Meetings supersede scheduled work at the Doo Peas Towers.

NOTE

When you earn the CEO promotion, you ride to work in a limo.

One of the key benefits of this career comes at the top promotion to Power Broker. Now, you have complete control over working hours by choosing to hold meetings at your whim. You are paid for these meetings, too, so you have control over how much money is made during that specific day. A day full of meetings is very lucrative. This flexibility allows the Power Broker to pursue different skills or attend to a household without worrying about a heavy work schedule.

Criminal

Who hasn't harbored thoughts of engaging in criminal activity? The Criminal career in Sunset Valley allows you to try out being a bad guy. The Criminal career actually branches into two different tracks: Thief and Evil. Each of these branches has a different reward for reaching the top.

Work Location: Outstanding Citizen Warehouse Corp.

How Hired: Report to warehouse, answer computer ad, answer newspaper ad

Work Week: The Criminal career unfolds at night with a typical five-day work schedule.

Salary Progression: The Criminal career pays a poor salary until the highest level is achieved. However, there are special bonuses from time to time that result in big paydays.

CRIMINAL CAREER

Level	Position	Work Days	Start Time	Length of Day	Average Daily Pay	Weekly Average Pay	Pension Pay	Metrics for Promotion
1	Decoy	SU, M, T, F, S	10 AM	6	100	500	30	Mood, Athletic Skill
2	Cutpurse	SU, M, T, F, S	10 AM	6	140	700	40	Mood, Athletic Skill
3	Thug	SU, M, T, F, S	9 PM	6	190	950	50	Mood, Athletic Skill
4	Getaway Driver	SU, M, T, F, S	9 PM	6	240	1,200	60	Mood, Athletic Skill, Relationship w/ Accomplices
5	Bagman	SU, M, T, F, S	9 PM	6	310	1,550	80	Mood, Athletic Skill, Relationship w/ Accomplices
6	ConArtist	SU, M, T, F, S	9 PM	6	375	1,875	90	Mood, Athletic Skill, Relationship w/ Accomplices

CRIMINAL CAREER – THIEF

Level	Position	Work Days	Start Time	Length of Day	Average Daily Pay	Weekly Average Pay	Pension Pay	Metrics for Promotion
7	Safe Cracker	SU, M, T, F, S	9 PM	5	480	2,400	120	Mood, Athletic Skill, Relationship w/ Accomplices
8	Bank Robber	SU, T, F, S	9 PM	5	610	2,440	120	Mood, Athletic Skill, Relationship w/ Accomplices
9	Cat Burglar	SU, T, F, S	9 PM	4	900	3,600	180	Mood, Athletic Skill, Relationship w/ Accomplices
10	Master Thief	SU, T, F, S	9 PM	4	2,100	8,400	400	Mood, Athletic Skill, Relationship w/ Accomplices

CRIMINAL CAREER – EVIL

Level	Position	Work Days	Start Time	Length of Day	Average Daily Pay	Weekly Average Pay	Pension Pay	Metrics for Promotion
7	Henchman	M, T, W, TH, F	9 PM	6	650	3,250	160	Mood, Athletic Skill, Relationship w/ Leader
8	Evil Sidekick	M, T, TH, F	9 PM	6	850	3,400	170	Mood, Athletic Skill, Logic Skill, Relationship w/ Leader
9	Super Villain	M, T, TH, F	9 PM	5	1,200	4,800	230	Mood, Athletic Skill, Logic Skill, Relationship w/ Leader
10	Emperor of Evil	M, T, F	9 PM	5	2,100	6,300	300	Mood, Athletic Skill, Logic Skill

CRIMINAL TONES

Tones	Description
Work Hard	Work hard to increase performance, but adds stress
Take It Easy	Relax at work. Slower performance, but less stress.
Practice Illicit Activities	Increases athletic skill at work
Meet Accomplices	Build relationship with co-workers
Conspire with Accomplices	Build relationship with co-workers
Do a Side Job	Perform this tone to earn side cash
Grovel to Leader	Build relationship with boss

can also use the Do a Side Job tone to earn extra cash while at work, but this takes time away from getting to better know accomplices (the equivalent of co-workers in the criminal career), which is an important metric for earning promotions.

 TiP

If you also have the Athletic skill, you can improve it by selecting the Practice Illicit Activities tone.

Benefits and Rewards

The Criminal career sounds shady, but it has definite benefits. For example, no one will rob the home of a Sim who's on the Criminal career track. Criminal career Sims also occasionally come home with an object in their personal inventory, snatched while out on a job. The criminal Sim

s mentioned, the Criminal career splits into wo branches at the sixth level. Here, the Sim ust choose between the Thief branch or the vil branch.

hief Branch

he Thief branch of the Criminal career starts ou toward becoming the Master Thief. Right way, you earn the Sneak interaction for going a location. When you Sneak onto a lot, her Sims do not detect you. Sleeping Sims ill not wake up either, so you can actually b while performing this interaction.

TIP

To improve your chances of a promotion on the Thief track, be sure to work on your relationships with accomplices.

s soon as you reach the Bank Robber romotion, you receive a valuable piece art as a bonus. At the top of the career ack, the Master Thief, the Sim receives an xtremely valuable statue called The Fox. This atue can be placed on the Sim's lot, which ffers a huge environmental bonus. Whenever e Sim chooses to View the statue, they get e I Am the Best moodlet, which is a positive post to overall mood.

TIP

If you are arrested and must spend time in jail, you can work out and improve your Athletic skill. This gives you the Pumped moodlet.

Evil Branch

The Evil branch of the Criminal career has different rewards and a different means of reaching the top job: World Dominator. You must use the Grovel to Boss tone a lot to advance along the Evil track because the relationship with the boss is a metric used to doling out promotions.

At level 9—Super Villain—the Sim gets a black limo. But when you finally get that top promotion, you earn the Aura of Evil. This has a powerful effect on other Sims. Criminal Sims or Sims with the Evil trait get a relationship boost from the Aura of Evil. However, the Aura of Evil has a negative effect on Sims with the following traits: Cowardly, Loser, and Neurotic. These Sims are afraid of the Aura of Evil and will flee. Sims with the Good trait or in the Law Enforcement career will actually boo at the Aura of Evil Sim. Building a good relationship with these Sims is extremely difficult.

Culinary

Sims who want to pursue a career in the culinary arts should head to either the bistro

or the diner. This is not one of the higher paying careers, but it does come with a lot of perks, such as the consistent development of the Cooking skill while at work and discounts at the restaurant of employment.

CAUTION

Part-time work at the bistro or diner does not result in any of the benefits of entering the full Culinary career.

Work Locations: Little Corsican Bistro or Hogan's Deep-Fried Diner

How Hired: Report to bistro or diner, answer computer ad, answer newspaper ad

Work Week: Normal work week but with hours that start later in the day. Sims are typically reporting to work in late morning or early afternoon and do not come home until late.

Salary Progression: Starting pay is very low and increases only a little with each promotion. Even at high level, this is not a high-paying career.

CULINARY CAREER

Level	Position	Work Days	Start Time	Length of Day	Average Daily Pay	Weekly Average Pay	Pension Pay	Metrics for Promotion
1	Kitchen Scullion	SU, M, T, F, S	3 PM	6	148	740	40	Mood, Cooking Skill
2	Spice Runner	SU, M, T, F, S	3 PM	6	190	950	50	Mood, Cooking Skill
3	Vegetable Slicer	SU, M, T, F, S	3 PM	6	230	1,150	60	Mood, Cooking Skill, Relationship w/ Boss
4	Ingredient Taster	SU, M, T, F, S	3 PM	6	280	1,400	70	Mood, Cooking Skill, Relationship w/ Boss, Relationship w/ Co-Workers
5	Line Cook	SU, M, T, F, S	3 PM	5.5	460	2,300	110	Mood, Cooking Skill, Relationship w/ Boss, Relationship w/ Co-Workers
6	Pastry Chef	SU, M, T, F, S	3 PM	5.5	590	2,950	150	Mood, Cooking Skill, Relationship w/ Boss, Relationship w/ Co-Workers
7	Sous Chef	SU, T, F, S	3 PM	5.5	680	2,720	130	Mood, Cooking Skill, Relationship w/ Boss, Relationship w/ Co-Workers
8	Executive Chef	SU, T, F, S	3 PM	5	750	3,000	150	Mood, Cooking Skill, Relationship w/ Boss, Relationship w/ Co-Workers
9	Chef de Cuisine	SU, F, S	3 PM	5	1,005	3,015	150	Mood, Cooking Skill, Relationship w/ Boss, Relationship w/ Co-Workers
10	Five-Star Chef	SU, F, S	3 PM	4	1,400	4,200	200	Mood, Cooking Skill, Relationship w/ Boss, Relationship w/ Co-Workers

CULINARY TONES

Tones	Description
Work Hard	Work hard to increase performance, but adds stress
Take It Easy	Relax at work. Slower performance, but less stress.
Practice Cooking	Increases cooking skill at work
Meet Co-Workers	Build relationship with co-workers
Hang with Co-Workers	Build relationship with co-workers
Suck Up to Boss	Build relationship with boss

Benefits and Rewards

Because cooking is such an important part of every Sim's life, the Culinary career has benefits that extend far beyond a daily paycheck. The Culinary career offers the Practice Cooking tone, which lets you advance the Cooking skill while earning a paycheck. Using this tone may come at the expense of not hastening an improved relationship with the boss or with co-workers (essential to promotion), but being a good cook is a mood booster for your Sim and potentially all other Sims in a household.

CAUTION

While cooking at work improves the Cooking skill, remember that cooking a recipe at home also improves the quality of the recipe each time you cook it.

TIP

Improving your Cooking skill is an important part of the promotion game in the Culinary career. Make sure you practice at home and don't rely on too many quick meals or snacks.

Good food is a mood booster for all Sims, so the benefit of occasionally getting free meals from work to take back to the lot is a real happiness generator. This benefit does not happen until the Sim reaches Ingredient Taster. But once it happens, expect to see free meals on a regular basis. And if you have multiple Sims in a household, that free meal will have enough servings to satisfy all.

Dining out is another mood booster that benefits from the Culinary career. At the Sous-Chef level, Sims get a discount at the restaurant where they work. This saves money, especially on dates, which can get pretty

expensive after a while. Once the Sim reach Executive Chef, the discount extends to bot restaurants.

Sims in the Culinary career get two very cool equipment bonuses. At the Pastry Chef position, the Sim earns the food processor, which speeds up the cooking process at home. The real prize, though, comes at the final promotion: Five-Star Chef. The Sim is awarded the Master Chef Fridge. This fridge gives the Superior Equipment moodlet to ar Sim who walks near it. Also any recipe that uses food out of the fridge will come out hig quality.

Journalism

As a journalist in Sunset Valley, Sims must chase down the facts not only during work hours, but on their own time, too. Such dedication is as reward in it itself, for the pursuit of truth is the noblest professional of all.

> **Work Location:** Doo Peas Corporate Towers
>
> **How Hired:** Report to business tower, answer computer ad, answer newspaper ad
>
> **Work Week:** Regular work week, but the week is often augmented by regula opportunities
>
> **Salary Progression:** Low-paying caree at the beginning and not exactly an account-stuffer over time either. Cash bonuses at promotion times are strong, though.

JOURNALISM CAREER

Level	Position	Work Days	Start Time	Length of Day	Average Daily Pay	Weekly Average Pay	Pension Pay	Metrics for Promotion
1	Paper Boy	M, T, W, TH, F	8 AM	6	225	1,125	60	Mood, Writing Skill
2	Automated Spell-Checker Checker	M, T, W, TH, F	8 AM	6	259	1,295	70	Mood, Writing Skill
3	Freelance Writer	M, T, W, TH, F	8 AM	6	298	1,490	80	Mood, Writing Skill, Stories Written
4	Professional Blogger	M, T, W, TH, F	8 AM	4	301	1,505	80	Mood, Writing Skill, Stories Written
5	Anonymous Source Handler	M, T, W, TH, F	8 AM	5	482	2,410	120	Mood, Writing Skill, Charisma Skill, Stories Writter
6	Investigative Reporter	M, W, TH, F	8 AM	5	627	2,508	120	Mood, Writing Skill, Charisma Skill, Stories Writter
7	Weather Man	M, W, TH, F	8 AM	5	753	3,012	150	Mood, Writing Skill, Charisma Skill
8	Lead Reporter	M, W, TH, F	8 AM	5	942	3,768	180	Mood, Writing Skill, Charisma Skill, Stories Writter
9	Editor-In-Chief	M, W, TH, F	8 AM	5	1,178	4,712	230	Mood, Writing Skill, Charisma Skill, Stories Writter
10	Star News Anchor	M, W, TH, F	8 AM	4	1,532	6,128	300	Mood, Writing Skill, Charisma Skill, Stories Writter

JOURNALISM TONES

Tones	Description
Work Hard	Work hard to increase performance, but adds stress
Take It Easy	Relax at work. Slower performance, but less stress.
Practice Writing	Increases Writing skill at work
Discuss Latest News	Build relationship with co-workers
Hang with Co-Workers	Build relationship with co-workers
Suck Up to Boss	Build relationship with boss

Benefits and Rewards

Like other careers where a certain skill is in play, pursuing the Journalism career lets a Sim advance their Writing skill while at the office. Sure, this is to the exclusion of seeking better relationships with the boss or co-workers, but it also opens up more genre possibilities for writing lucrative novels at home in the Sim's spare time.

Joining the Journalism career also allows the Sim to develop a new genre for writing at home: stories and reviews. Stories and reviews are selected from the computer interaction list, just like choosing to write a novel. It does not take nearly as long to write a story or review as a novel, and no royalties are awarded for completing a story or review. However...

Writing stories and reviews are essential for promotions. If you want to reach the very top of the career track, you must spend considerable time outside the workday creating articles at home. These stories and reviews go into the Sim's personal inventory and are recognized at work. To get the material for writing stories and reviews, you must interview Sims around town. You should also visit the stadium to see sporting events and stop into the restaurants. These three things give you plenty to write about – but they take time to attend, and that's on top of the time it takes your Sim to write the story or review. At least visiting the stadium and going out to eat is a good mood boost, so there is a nice side benefit for taking the time to do your research.

Not every promotion takes stories and reviews into consideration, though. You really need to work on Charisma skill to keep getting ahead. The Charisma skill ranking is an important metric for promotion. This just adds to the career workload, as you must now juggle improving the Writing skill, improving the Charisma skill, and writing articles outside of work hours. Fortunately, the work hours in this career are slightly lower than others, giving you extra free time for these career-related pursuits.

When you finally reach the top of the career track—Star News Anchor—you unlock a new social: Tell Intriguing News Story. This social is perfect for situations where you want to boost a relationship with another Sim.

> **TIP**
>
> The Tell Intriguing News Story social can be used several times with another Sim before it loses its effectiveness.

Law Enforcement

Not everybody in Sunset Valley is on the up-and-up. With a criminal element afoot, the city needs its fair share of Law Enforcement officers. This career branches, and the two tracks lead to different rewards. The Law Enforcement career also uses a number of skills as metrics for promotion, so having a well-rounded Sim is a plus.

Work Location: Police Station

How Hired: Report to Police Station, answer computer ad, answer newspaper ad

Work Week: Sim maintains normal workweek hours (9 to 5), but the Special Agent branch cuts those hours by three per day and adds an on-call alert that sometimes requires work at odd hours.

Salary Progression: Decent wages until the career branches. The Special Agent branch gets higher bonus for promotions while Forensic Analysts get a higher daily wage.

LAW ENFORCEMENT CAREER

Level	Position	Work Days	Start Time	Length of Day	Average Daily Pay	Weekly Average Pay	Pension Pay	Metrics for Promotion
1	Snitch	M, T, W, TH, F	9 AM	6	235	1,175	60	Mood, Logic Skill
2	Desk Jockey	M, T, W, TH, F	9 AM	6	278	1,390	70	Mood, Logic Skill
3	Traffic Cop	M, T, W, TH, F	9 AM	6	329	1,645	80	Mood, Logic Skill, Relationship w/ Partner
4	Patrol Officer	M, T, W, TH, F	9 AM	6	389	1,945	100	Mood, Logic Skill, Relationship w/ Partner, Reports Written
5	Lieutenant	M, T, W, TH, F	9 AM	6	460	2,300	110	Mood, Logic Skill, Relationship w/ Partner, Reports Written

FORENSIC CAREER

Level	Position	Work Days	Start Time	Length of Day	Average Daily Pay	Weekly Average Pay	Pension Pay	Metrics for Promotion
6	Wiretap Reader	M, T, W, TH, F	9 AM	6	805	4,025	200	Mood, Logic Skill, Relationship w/ Partner, Reports Written
7	Crime Scene Technician	M, T, W, TH, F	9 AM	6	950	4,750	230	Mood, Logic Skill, Relationship w/ Partner, Reports Written
8	Sketch Artist	M, T, TH, F	9 AM	5	1,121	4,484	220	Mood, Logic Skill, Painting Skill, Reports Written
9	3D Crime Scene Modeler	M, T, TH, F	9 AM	5	1,323	5,292	260	Mood, Logic Skill, Painting Skill, Reports Written
10	DNA Suspect Reconstruction Simulator	M, T, TH, F	9 AM	5	1,985	7,940	380	Mood, Logic Skill, Painting Skill, Reports Written

SPECIAL AGENT CAREER

Level	Position	Work Days	Start Time	Length of Day	Average Daily Pay	Weekly Average Pay	Pension Pay	Metrics for Promotion
6	Vice Squad	M, T, TH, F	9 AM	5	690	2,760	140	Mood, Relationship w/ Partner, Athletic Skill, Reports Written
7	Undercover Specialist	M, T, TH, F	9 AM	5	815	3,260	160	Mood, Relationship w/ Partner, Athletic Skill, Reports Written
8	Special Agent	M, T, TH, F	9 AM	5	962	3,848	190	Mood, Relationship w/ Partner, Athletic Skill, Reports Written
9	Triple Agent	M, T, TH, F	9 AM	4	1,136	4,544	220	Mood, Logic Skill, Athletic Skill, Reports Written
10	International Super Spy	M, T, TH, F	9 AM	4	1,704	6,816	330	Mood, Logic Skill, Athletic Skill, Reports Written

LAW TONES

Tones	Description
Work Hard	Work hard to increase performance, but adds stress
Take It Easy	Relax at work. Slower performance, but less stress.
Chat with Partner	Build relationship with co-workers
Build Independent Case	Side work that can result in extra cash
Use Workout Facility	Build Athletic skill at work to expense of performance
Suck Up to Boss	Build relationship with boss

WRITING REPORTS

One of the metrics for doling out promotions is the number of reports written. Sims in the Law Enforcement track create reports on other Sims by conducting interviews with the Question social. (This social is not negative.) During the questioning, the interviewer discovers the other Sim's traits, which is actually quite useful for social situations outside the workday.

Benefits and Rewards

The Law Enforcement career takes a few interesting turns but comes with some exciting rewards and side benefits. One of the tones for work is to Build Independent Case, which detracts from dealing with co-workers or the daily workload, but is quite useful if successful. If after a lot of time building this case against a criminal, the case ends up being a success and the Sim has a chance at an immediate promotion. However, if the case fails, the Sim risks losing the respect of co-workers.

TIP

The current Logic skill level is what determines the chance of success, so build up that skill before trying out this tone.

At level 3, the Sim can apprehend Burglars, which goes a long way toward getting a promotion. At level 5, the Sim gets a police car, which improves travel time. At level 5, the Sim chooses a branch of the career to pursue. Each branch has an different end reward.

NOTE

To keep this fair, Sims can only use the Question social on each Sim once per promotion level. Otherwise, you could amass quite a file on the citizenry of Sunset Valley.

...ports can also come from rifling through ...rbage cans. Use this interaction to look ...ough another Sim's trash until you receive ...notice that you have enough information ...the person whose trash you were ...pecting to write a report.

...during these interactions, the discovers that ...subject is part of the Criminal career track, ...chance of promotion greatly increases.

CAUTION

Rummaging through the trash leads to the Disgusted moodlet. Be ready to shower after extensive garbage-sifting sessions.

...anching Career Rewards

...lvance the Logic skill to succeeded in all ...anches of the Law Enforcement career. Get ...rted with a logic book or chess set (home ...park) to get a jump on the first promotions. ...hen the career branches after the fifth

promotion, two more skills come into play. The Painting skill must be developed for the Forensics branch, and the Athletic skill must be advanced for the Special Agent branch. After the split, the Logic skill is still critical to getting promotions.

The Forensics branch has a reward as soon as you earn its first promotion: laptop. The laptop computer is placed in the personal inventory and can be used at home. The top reward for the career in a new computer interaction: Run Analysis. This is a lengthy interaction, but it results in a payday. This is a good way to make additional money when not at work.

The Special Agent branch of the career has two special rewards that are given out at level 10: Tell Impressive Story and Raid Warehouse. Tell Impressive Story is a special social. It immediately impresses the Sim it is directed at. The Raid Warehouse interaction directs the Sim to enter the warehouse at night and disappears for a few hours. If the raid is a success (based on mood, Athletic skill, and Logic skill), the Sim has the potential to earn two different rewards. A mild success at the warehouse results in a small monetary bonus. A big success results in a huge payday. Special Agents also unlock the Raid Warehouse interaction, which lets you raid the criminal headquarters at the warehouse. Depending on your mood and athletic skill, you can have a great, good, or bad raid. A great and good raid results in extra cash. A bad raid just brings your mood down.

CAUTION

Should the Raid Warehouse fail, the Sim is booted out of the warehouse and given the Sore moodlet. Get a massage to wash away those negative feelings.

Medical

The Medical career is not for a Sim who likes to keep a strict schedule. As this career develops, the schedule turns chaotic and occasionally disruptive thanks to the unpredictable needs of patients at the local hospital. If you don't mind the idea of being pulled into work in the middle of the night, then the Medical career's rewards may be worth the potential inconvenience. Especially the final reward for becoming a World Renowned Surgeon...

Work Location: Hospital

How Hired: Report to hospital, answer computer ad, answer newspaper ad

Work Week: In the beginning of this career, the hours are fairly normal. However, this soon changes when the Sim is given a pager and told to be "on call."

Salary Progression: This career doesn't pay well at first, but around level 5, the bonuses and salary start creeping up.

MEDICAL CAREER

Level	Position	Work Days	Start Time	Length of Day	Average Daily Pay	Weekly Average Pay	Pension Pay	Metrics for Promotion
1	Organ Donor	M, T, W, TH, F	9 AM	6	128	640	40	Mood, Logic Skill
2	Bed Pan Cleaner	M, T, W, TH, F	9 AM	6	150	750	40	Mood, Logic Skill
3	Paramedic	M, T, W, TH, F	9 AM	7	190	950	50	Mood, Logic Skill
4	Medical Intern	M, T, W, TH, F	9 AM	10	330	1,650	80	Mood, Logic Skill, Medical Journals Read
5	Resident	M, T, W, TH, F	9 AM	9	700	3,500	170	Mood, Logic Skill, Medical Journals Read
6	Trauma Surgeon	M, T, W, TH, F	7 PM	8	810	4,050	200	Mood, Logic Skill, Medical Journals Read
7	Gene Therapist	M, T, TH, F	9 AM	5	960	3,840	190	Mood, Logic Skill, Medical Journals Read
8	Infectious Disease Researcher	M, T, TH, F	9 AM	5	1,050	4,200	200	Mood, Logic Skill, Medical Journals Read
9	Neurosurgeon	M, T, TH, F	9 AM	8	1,800	7,200	350	Mood, Logic Skill, Medical Journals Read
10	Deadly Disease Specialist	M, T, TH, F	9 AM	5	2,400	9,600	460	Mood, Logic Skill, Medical Journals Read

MEDICAL TONES

Tones	Description
Work Hard	Work hard to increase performance, but adds stress
Watch TV in Ready Room	Relax at work. Slower performance, but less stress.
Chat with Medical Personnel	Build relationship with co-workers
Do Boss's Paperwork	Build relationship with boss
Sleep in Ready Room	Napping at work helps with energy
Suck Up to Boss	Build relationship with boss

Benefits and Rewards

The Medical career is one of the most stressful careers, so to advance, you need activities in the Sim's life that will counteract the Stressed Out moodlet. Mood is a major factor in promotions, so be sure to get sleep when possible (the Sleep in Ready Room tone helps out with this) and have an activity that lowers tension, such as reading, exercise, or socializing.

NOTE

The Medical career is a logic-based job, so install a telescope or chess set in the house to build the Logic skill when not at work. The telescope is great because you can make extra money by using the Search Galaxy interaction.

As soon as you reach the Medical Intern promotion, get ready for a hectic schedule. The Sim gets a beeper and has to come into work at odd hours. Shifts start growing,

too, so be ready to spend lots of time at the hospital as you work farther up the promotion ladder. Medical Interns earn the Give Medical Advice social, which helps out pregnant Sims. Pregnant Sims who regularly seek medical advice (or receive it) assist the development of the pregnancy, which can lead to the baby getting highly desirable traits.

TIP

If the medical Sim is the one who is pregnant, the Give Medical Advice benefits are automatic.

When you reach the Medical Intern position, you start receiving medical journals, too. These are critical for future advancement because the number of journals read is a metric for deciding promotions alongside mood and Logic skill. In your off time, be sure to read these medical journals because the game keeps track of this statistic.

TIP

The Medical career does not factor relationship with co-workers or the boss into promotions. The quality of work is what really counts.

At the Resident level, Sims get two new socials: Give Good Medical Advice and Brag About Being a Doctor. The Give Good Medical Advice has a greater benefit to

expectant mothers—in fact, the medical Sim can even deduce the sex of the baby. The Brag social impresses other Sims in conversation. If the other Sim is already romantically interested in the medical Sim, th romance is further enhanced.

The Neurosurgeon promotion turns Give Good Medical Advice into Give Amazing Medical Advice, which is even more beneficial to expectant mothers.

Finally, the World Renowned Surgeon promotion comes with a special tone: Play Golf. Use this tone at work to eliminate stres without detriment to career performance. This is a great tone that keeps the medical Sim much happier while pulling in great paychecks.

TIP

The Medical career is pretty stressful, so look into scoring the Professional Slacker Lifetime Reward to so you slack off at work without recriminations.

Military

Fortunately, peace has broken out in Sunset Valley and Sims in the Military career need not worry about shipping out to war. They do have a goal that takes them outside of town, though. Way outside of town. As in, into space.

Work Location: Fort Gnome Military Ba

How Hired: Report to military base, answer computer ad, answer newspaper ad

Work Week: Work at the base starts early and lasts until the later afternoon, but at least there are fewer work days a week.

Salary Progression: Sims starts with a modest salary, but the promotion to Flight Officer comes with a nice bonus

MILITARY CAREER

Level	Position	Work Days	Start Time	Length of Day	Average Daily Pay	Weekly Average Pay	Pension Pay	Metrics for Promotion
1	Latrine Cleaner	M, T, W, F	7 AM	7	280	1,120	80	Mood, Athletic Skill
2	Grease Monkey	M, T, W, F	7 AM	8	350	1,400	100	Mood, Athletic Skill
3	Grunt	M, T, W, F	7 AM	8	385	1,540	110	Mood, Athletic Skill, Handiness Skill
4	Squad Leader	M, W, F	7 AM	7	655	1,965	150	Mood, Athletic Skill, Handiness Skill, Relationship w/ Superior
5	Flight Officer	M, W, F	7 AM	7	754	2,262	170	Mood, Athletic Skill, Handiness Skill, Relationship w/ Superior
6	Wing Man	M, W, F	7 AM	6	868	2,604	190	Mood, Athletic Skill, Handiness Skill, Relationship w/ Superior
7	Fighter Pilot	M, W, F	7 AM	6	999	2,997	220	Mood, Athletic Skill, Handiness Skill, Relationship w/ Superior
8	Squadron Leader	M, W, F	7 AM	6	1,149	3,447	250	Mood, Athletic Skill, Handiness Skill, Relationship w/ Superior
9	Top Gun	M, W, F	7 AM	5	1,322	3,966	290	Mood, Athletic Skill, Handiness Skill, Relationship w/ Superior
10	Astronaut	M	7 AM	18	6,000	6,000	430	Mood, Athletic Skill, Handiness Skill, Relationship w/ Superior

MILITARY TONES

Tones	Description
Work Hard	Work hard to increase performance, but adds stress
Goof Off	Relax at work. Slower performance, but less stress.
Hang Out with Fellow Soldiers	Build relationship with co-workers
Suck Up to Superior	Build relationship with boss

Benefits and Rewards

To advance in the military career and earn benefits, Sims must develop two different skills: Athletic and Handiness. (Fortunately, the Handiness skill can be learned right on base through a class.) Other metrics contribute to the chance of promotion, too, including the relationships with fellow soldiers and base superiors. Naturally, mood is also a factor. Working hard and keeping these skills in active advancement leads to some fun rewards.

For example, as soon as the career begins, you start saluting other soldiers of superior rank. But at level 4, Squad Leader, inferiors start saluting you. When you reach the Top Gun rank, random Sims in Sunset Valley are also inspired to salute you. Citizen salutes are positive and will start any social encounter with an impressed context.

Sims now get the interaction to Show Sim the Jet, which can impress potential partners. The Show Sim the Jet social is activated and Sims can take dates to the base. Showing a date the jet results in an improved romantic context for the relationship.

CAUTION

There is a small risk with Show Sim the Jet. If you are discovered and kicked off the base for bringing a civilian in a secure area, you lose work performance.

Finally, at level 10, Sims become an Astronaut. Becoming an Astronaut changes the Show Sim the Jet interaction to Show Sim the Spaceship. Showing a Sim the Spaceship is a huge romance booster.

Music

Let a little music fill your life with this exciting career track. This career is not about the money—it's about the music. Or, at least it's about the music at first with the extra benefit of truckloads of Simoleons later on when you're filling stadiums with fans that cannot wait to hear your next overblown anthem.

The music career has two branches, the Rock and the Symphonic tracks.

Work Location: Wilsonoff Community Theater

How Hired: Report to theater, answer computer ad, answer newspaper ad

Work Week: This is a slower work week with fewer hours than other careers—and never any work on Sunday. When the career splits, the Rock branch moves to an evening shift closer to the weekends. The Symphonic branch remains closer to the original level with occasional concerts.

Salary Progression: Musicians make low pay in the beginning. Toward the top of the career ladder, musicians are very well-paid.

Simology

MUSIC CAREER

Level	Position	Work Days	Start Time	Length of Day	Average Daily Pay	Weekly Average Pay	Pension Pay	Metrics for Promotion
1	Fan	M, T, TH, F, S	15	6	125	625	30	Mood, Guitar Skill
2	Roadie	M, T, TH, F, S	15	6	148	740	40	Mood, Guitar Skill
3	Stagehand	M, T, TH, F, S	16	6	175	875	50	Mood, Guitar Skill, Relationship w/ Band
4	Band Manager	M, T, TH, F, S	16	5.5	263	1,315	70	Mood, Guitar Skill, Relationship w/ Band
5	Music Talent Scout	M, T, F, S	17	5.5	311	1,244	60	Mood, Guitar Skill, Relationship w/ Band

ROCK CAREER

Level	Position	Work Days	Start Time	Length of Day	Average Daily Pay	Weekly Average Pay	Pension Pay	Metrics for Promotion
6	Lyricist	M, T, F, S	6 PM	5	483	1,932	100	Mood, Guitar Skill, Relationship w/ Band Members, Concerts Performed
7	Backup Vocalist	M, T, F, S	7 PM	5	628	2,512	120	Mood, Guitar Skill, Relationship w/ Band Members, Concerts Performed
8	Lead Guitarist	T, F, S	8 PM	4.5	817	2,451	160	Mood, Guitar Skill, Relationship w/ Band Members, Concerts Performed
9	Pop Icon	T, F, S	9 PM	4	1,144	3,432	200	Mood, Guitar Skill, Relationship w/ Band Members, Concerts Performed
10	Rock Star	N/A	N/A	N/A	N/A	N/A	350	Concerts Performed

SYMPHONIC CAREER

Level	Position	Work Days	Start Time	Length of Day	Average Daily Pay	Weekly Average Pay	Pension Pay	Metrics for Promotion
6	Quartet Member	M, T, F, S	3 PM	5.5	467	1,868	90	Mood, Guitar Skill, Relationship w/ Musicians
7	Orchestra Seat	M, T, F, S	3 PM	5.5	608	2,432	120	Mood, Guitar Skill, Relationship w/ Musicians
8	Orchestra Lead	M, T, F, S	3 PM	5.5	791	3,164	160	Mood, Guitar Skill, Logic Skill, Relationship w/ Musicians
9	Conductor	M, T, F, S	3 PM	5	1,029	4,116	200	Mood, Guitar Skill, Logic Skill, Relationship w/ Musicians
10	Hit Movie Composer	M, T, F, S	1 PM	5	1,801	7,204	350	Mood, Guitar Skill, Logic Skill, Relationship w/ Musicians

Benefits and Rewards

Naturally, the key to advancing in this career is the development of the Guitar skill. Starting out with a class at the theater is a good way to get a head start on the career. At first, you do not even need the Guitar skill because you are just a Fan and Roadie. But keeping on top of the skill before it becomes critical to advancement has nothing but advantages. The Guitar skill is a constant metric for promotions no matter which branch you choose when you reach the sixth promotion.

To continue moving up the career ladder, you must maintain a good mood and have a good relationship with co-workers, who are called

band or orchestra members depending on the career path taken. Use of the Study Music Theory tone because it helps build the Guitar skill—and the Logic skill, which is

a critical measure for the Symphonic branch. In the Rock branch, you need to practice for gigs because performing concerts is a key to advancement.

MUSIC TONES

Tones	Description
Work Hard	Work hard to increase performance, but adds stress
Slack Off	Take it easy at work to reduce stress
Chill with Band/Musicians	Build relationship with co-workers
Meet Band/Orchestra Members	Meet co-workers
Study Music Theory	Build Guitar and Logic skills
Practice Performance	Prepare before a concert so it goes better

ock Branch

e next promotion following the Music Talent rout in the Rock branch is Lyricist. When you ach this promotion, you can start holding ncerts. Use this interaction on the theater d stadium to stage two- or four-hour ncerts that are measured as part of the omotion process. (This interaction is only ailable between noon and midnight.) Once u choose to hold a concert and enter the nue, other Sims will follow.

nce inside the Rock branch, the relationship other band members is no longer portant. After all, rockers could care less out what others think of them—they are e center of the universe. When the Sim comes the Backup Vocalist, they unlock e Wave interaction to use at any place here music is playing. It's a fun action that osts mood.

ep performing concerts and keep up e Guitar skill to reach the pinnacle of the anch: Rock Star. At this level, your carpool replaced by a pastel limo that will take u anywhere. At this level, the Sim can also ect venues and choose to Hold Autograph ssion, just like the Athlete career. The goal o sign as many autographs as possible with e other Sims on the lot. The more signed, e more money is awarded for the session.

Once the Sim achieves Rock Star, they no longer have a work schedule. Money is earned exclusively by holding concerts. To maximize pay-outs, hold the concert at the stadium. The concert takes longer than one at the theater, but the salary is double.

> **NOTE**
>
> Between levels 8 and 10 of the Rock branch, Sims have two new socials: Worship and Be Worshipped. This social is acutely positive, as even Sims who are as low on the relationship ladder as Acquaintance will engage the Sim.

Symphonic Branch

The Symphonic branch of the Music career unfolds a bit differently than the Rock branch. In this track, relationships with other musicians are very important, so be sure to use that tone to get ahead. Keep advancing the Guitar skill whenever possible, too.

Once you close in on the Orchestra Lead promotion, develop the Logic skill. (Practice Music Theory is a good way to boost the Logic skill while at work.) Once you reach level 8 of this career—Orchestra Lead—you earn free admission to activities at the theater. This is great for boosting moods.

The highest level of the career—Hit Movie Composer—comes with an object reward: 85g Audio Explosion. This high-end stereo boosts the Fun of Sims in its listening radius and can be used to develop the Athletic ability.

> **NOTE**
>
> Between levels 9 and 10 of the Symphonic branch, Sims have access to the Worship/Be Worshipped social. The effects are the same as they are in the Rock branch.

Politics

Politics is no career for the timid Sim. This is a highly social career track that requires a great deal of socializing with the people of Sunset Valley. Because this is such a social career, the Charisma skill is required. Also required: no fear of asking other Sims for money. Campaigns don't pay for themselves, you know.

Work Location: City Hall

How Hired: Report to City Hall, answer computer ad, answer newspaper ad

Work Week: This career works a normal work week at first, but as Sims advance in the career, they work fewer hours because the career requires so much socializing.

Salary Progression: Until level 5 of the career, political Sims do not make that much money. Once they reach the City Council Member position, the bonuses and salaries grow. This career will not make your Sim rich, though.

POLITICAL CAREER

Level	Position	Work Days	Start Time	Length of Day	Average Daily Pay	Weekly Average Pay	Pension Pay	Metrics for Promotion
	Podium Polisher	M, T, W, TH, F	9 AM	6	140	700	40	Mood, Charisma
	Ballot Counter	M, T, W, TH, F	9 AM	6	185	925	50	Mood, Charisma
	Campaign Intern	M, T, W, TH, F	9 AM	7	230	1,150	60	Mood, Charisma
	Yes-Man	M, T, W, TH, F	9 AM	6	270	1,350	70	Mood, Charisma, Relationship w/ Boss
	City Council Member	M, T, W, TH, F	9 AM	5.5	375	1,875	90	Mood, Charisma, Relationship w/ Boss, Campaign Money Raised

Simology

POLITICAL CAREER, CONTINUED

Level	Position	Work Days	Start Time	Length of Day	Average Daily Pay	Weekly Average Pay	Pension Pay	Metrics for Promotion
6	Local Representative	M, W, TH, F	9 AM	5.5	500	2,000	100	Mood, Charisma, Relationship w/ Boss, Campaign Money Raised
7	Mayor	M, W, TH, F	9 AM	5	650	2,600	130	Mood, Charisma, Relationship w/ Boss, Campaign Money Raised
8	Governor	M, W, TH, F	9 AM	5	800	3,200	160	Mood, Charisma, Relationship w/ Boss, Campaign Money Raised
9	Vice President	M, W, F	9 AM	4.5	1,200	3,600	180	Mood, Charisma, Relationship w/ Boss, Campaign Money Raised
10	Leader of the Free World	M, W, F	9 AM	4.5	1,900	5,700	280	Mood, Charisma, Campaign Money Raised

POLITICAL TONES

Tones	Description
Work Hard	Work hard to increase performance, but adds stress
Chat with Co-Workers	Build relationship with co-workers
Meet Co-Workers	Meet co-workers
Run Errands for Superior	Build relationship with boss
Suggest New Course of Action	Research new ideas that can possibly increase performance or relationships

Benefits and Rewards

At first, mood is the only metric used to measure performance and award promotions. But to get ahead, be sure to start practicing Charisma early on through various means, like taking a class at City Hall or practicing in the mirror at home. Having a good Charisma level will make it much easier to advance early in this career.

The Yes-Man promotion is given out to a Sim who has a good relationship with the boss, so use the Run Errands for Supervisor tone early on, too. Getting in good with the boss is preferable to being popular with co-workers. To move up to the City Council position, though, you need to start raising campaign contributions, which is another metric for promotion. The social Ask for Campaign Donation will usually result in a small Simoleon transfer, although hitting up a wealthy Sim will elicit a larger donation. Fortunately, this social is positive.

CAUTION

You cannot use the Ask for Campaign Contribution social on household members.

NOTE

Here is a naughty bit of business with campaign contributions. Every so often, you will be asked if you want to transfer money out of the campaign kitty and into the household account. This is risky. If caught, the Sim is expelled from the career.

TIP

Political Sims can throw Campaign Fundraisers, which are just like parties. (See the Relationships chapter for details on how to throw a party.) If the party is successful, the host receives campaign contributions at its conclusion.

Once you reach the Local Representative position, you have a new social: Give Inspirational Speech. You can use this positive social you can use on a single Sim or in a group setting. It gives everybody a positive impression of you and sets up healthy relationships. Yes we can, indeed.

At higher levels you get two nice benefits. At the Governor level, a black limo drives you everywhere. As Leader of the Free World, your Sim gains the Aura of Leadership, and other Sims wave at them wherever they go. This boosts the relationship with other Sims and can also result in the Celebrity moodlet.

Professional Sports

The Professional Sports career charts a cours from zero to hero. The Sims slowly become deeply involved with the local sports team. At first, they are a fan with a dream. Then, the join the team and start working up the ranks. Soon, shifts are replaced by sporting events where winning and losing has a direct effect on mood.

Work Location: Llama Memorial Stadiu

How Hired: Report to stadium, answe computer ad, answer newspaper ad

Work Week: Five day work week with evening shifts. Soon, two shifts a week are replaced by games that only last a few hours. During this period, the work week increases to six days to offset the fewer hours.

Salary Progression: The Professional Sports career starts with a low salary. However, as the Sim progresses, that changes. At the upper ranks, this is one of the most lucrative careers.

PROFESSIONAL SPORTS CAREER

Level	Position	Work Days	Start Time	Length of Day	Average Daily Pay	Weekly Average Pay	Pension Pay	Metrics for Promotion
1	Rabid Fan	M, T, W, TH, S	3 PM	6	75	375	30	Mood
2	Snack Hawker	M, T, W, TH, S	3 PM	6	150	750	60	Mood
3	Toddler Sports Coach	M, T, W, TH, S	3 PM	6	195	975	70	Mood, Athletic Skill
4	Minor Leaguer	M, T, F, S	3 PM	6	254	1,016	80	Mood, Athletic Skill, Relationship w/ Team
5	Rookie	M, T, F, S	3 PM	5	381	1,524	110	Mood, Athletic Skill, Relationship w/ Team, Win-Loss Record
6	Starter	M, T, F, S	3 PM	5	667	2,668	200	Mood, Athletic Skill, Relationship w/ Team, Win-Loss Record
7	AllStar	M, T, F, S	3 PM	4	801	3,204	230	Mood, Athletic Skill, Relationship w/ Team, Win-Loss Record
8	MVP	M, T, F, S	3 PM	4	962	3,838	280	Mood, Athletic Skill, Relationship w/ Team, Win-Loss Record
9	Superstar	M, T, F, S	3 PM	3	1,155	4,620	330	Mood, Athletic Skill, Relationship w/ Team, Win-Loss Record
10	Sports Legend	M, T, F, S	3 PM	3	1,386	5,544	400	Mood, Athletic Skill, Relationship w/ Team, Win-Loss Record

PROFESSIONAL SPORTS TONES

Tones	Description
Prepare for Game	Get ready for next game. Increases chances of winning next game.
Meet Teammates	Build relationship with co-workers
Hang with Teammates	Build relationship with co-workers
Slack Off in Locker Room	Take it easy at work to reduce stress
Work Out in Gym	Develop Athletic skill

Benefits and Rewards

Naturally, this is a great career for a Sim with both the Athletic trait and developing the Athletic skill. Once you reach the Toddler Sports Coach position, you can start using the Work Out at Gym work tone, which lets you continue developing the Athletic skill at work, albeit at a slower pace than at home on personal time. (Up until this promotion, reporting to work does not increase the Athletic skill.)

Sports professionals do not get the Stressed Out moodlet from work like other careers.

Once the Minor Leaguer position is reached, the Sim can begin interacting with other team members, which casts a wider net of Sims to socialize with and make friends. The Rookie promotion starts the game part of the career. Now work is often replaced by practice and the career keeps a running tally on the team's win-loss record. The higher the Sim's Athletic skill, the greater the chance at winning the game, which in turn improves the Sim's mood with the Winner moodlet. The chance of winning a game is also improved by the Prepare for Game tone.

Members of a Sim's household can see a sporting event for free.

Once the Sim reaches the top promotion—Sports Legend—two things happen. One, the Sim can now perform the Sponsorship Deal interaction at businesses for Simoleons at least once a week. Two, the Sim can also Hold Autograph Sessions at venues where they are handsomely rewarded for signing autographs for as many Sims on the lot as possible.

Science

A mind is a terrible thing to taste—er, waste. This career celebrates that organ between the ears, the cortex that pulses with thoughts and desires. The Science career requires a keen sense of Handiness and a real green thumb, as well as a desire to both observe and collect.

Work Location: Landgraab Industries Science Facility

How Hired: Report to business tower, answer computer ad, answer newspaper ad

Work Week: Normal work week: five days with average hours in the 9 to 3 range because of the extra time needed to advance skills.

Salary Progression: The science career offers a modest salary with moderate bonuses and increases over time. This is not a rich Sim's career, but the skills developed during the career can lead to alternate incomes.

SCIENCE CAREER

Level	Position	Work Days	Start Time	Length of Day	Average Daily Pay	Weekly Average Pay	Pension Pay	Metrics for Promotion
1	Test Subject	M, T, W, TH, F	9 AM	5.5	240	1,200	60	Mood, Gardening Skill
2	Lab Tech	M, T, W, TH, F	9 AM	5.5	288	1,440	70	Mood, Gardening Skill
3	Useless Contraption Manipulator	M, T, W, TH, F	9 AM	5.5	346	1,730	90	Mood, Gardening Skill, Handiness Skill
4	Fertilizer Analyst	M, T, TH, F	9 AM	5	485	1,940	100	Mood, Gardening Skill, Handiness Skill
5	Carnivorous Plant Tender	M, T, TH, F	9 AM	5	582	2,328	120	Mood, Gardening Skill, Handiness Skill
6	Aquatic Ecosystem Tweaker	M, T, TH, F	9 AM	5	699	2,796	140	Mood, Gardening Skill, Handiness Skill, Fishing Ski
7	Genetic Resequencer	M, T, TH, F	9 AM	4.5	839	3,356	160	Mood, Gardening Skill, Handiness Skill, Fishing Ski
8	Top Secret Researcher	M, T, TH, F	9 AM	4.5	1,007	4,028	200	Mood, Gardening Skill, Handiness Skill, Fishing Ski
9	Creature-Robot Cross Breeder	M, T, F	9 AM	4.5	1,209	3,627	180	Mood, Gardening Skill, Handiness Skill, Fishing Ski
10	Mad Scientist	M, T, F	9 AM	4.5	1,814	5,442	260	Mood, Gardening Skill, Handiness Skill, Fishing Sk

SCIENCE TONES

Tones	Description
Work Hard	Work hard to increase performance, but adds stress
Relax in Specimen Closet	Relax at work. Slower performance, but less stress.
Meet Fellow Scientists	Meet co-workers
Hang Out with Fellow Soldiers	Build relationship with co-workers
Assist Boss with Research	Build relationship with boss
Do Independent Experiment	Doing this tone builds toward promotion or at least performance boost

Benefits and Rewards

The benefits of the Science career are plentiful, but you must be attentive to skills to receive the promotions that award them. The immediate skill required for the career is Gardening which can be learned at the military base or through a book. Get a jump on gardening as soon as you join the career. Later in the career, two additional skill comes into play: Handiness and Fishing. At no point are relationships a metric for advancement because, warranted or not, scientists aren't exactly known for their social graces.

TIP

Do not wait until you close in on a promotion that requires Fishing or Gardening to start learning those skills. Develop those skills early.

One of the most useful tones in this career is Do Independent Experiment. While performing this tone, you do side experiments that have a chance of resulting in great things. These experiments take time, though. You will not complete one in just a day. If the project is a success, though, you might get an immediate promotion.

From time to time, scientists will come home with extras in their personal inventories, such as a fish or seed. They will be either common or uncommon fish or seeds. Upon reaching the Top Secret Researcher and Creature-Robot Cross Breeder promotions, though, the Sim receives a seed for a special plant. These seeds are rare and will grow into one of the following: Flame Fruit, Life Fruit, Money Tree, or Omni Plant.

Do Science to It!

Upon reaching the height of the career, the Sim receives a new interaction to perform on household objects: Do Science to It. This interaction works on seats, beds, electronics, and appliances. It acts like an upgrade. Once the interaction is complete, the Sim stands back to have a look at what was accomplished. If the upgrade goes well, the following may happen:

- Object gets environmental boost.
- Object broadcasts music, giving all Sims the area the Enjoying Music moodlet.
- Object earns random upgrade from Handiness upgrade list.
- Object starts broadcasting random moodlets that affect Sims in the room: Attractive, Beautiful Vista, Cheered Up, Comforted, Feeling Lucky, New Car Sme New Stuff, Oddly Powerful, Tranquil, or Warmed.

Conversely, this interaction can have negativ effects, too. These things can go wrong:

- Object catches fire and is burned until useless.
- Object randomly electrocutes Sims wh try to use it later.
- Object disappears—forever.
- Object breaks and must be repaired.
- Object starts broadcasting random negative moodlets that affect Sims in the room: Upset, Tastes Like Fridge, Stir Crazy, Offended, Buzz Crash, Horrified, or Disgusted.

What's New | Creating a Sim | Creating a House | A Day in the Life | **Simology** | Relationships and Aging | Tour of Sunset Valley | Design Corner | Object Catalog | Community

PART-TIME WORK

In addition to these full-time careers, Sims can pick up part-time jobs at the supermarket, cemetery, bookstore, or day spa. These jobs are for just four hours day, four days a week. These jobs are designed not to interfere with life too much. For example, a teen might take a job at the supermarket that starts after school at 4 PM and lasts until 8 PM. Or an adult could grab a late-night 6 PM to 10 PM gig helping bury bodies at the cemetery.

Part-time jobs include tones, just like the full-time jobs. However, because relationships and skills don't determine job performance, the tones are limited to: Business As Usual (average amount of work), Work Hard (put in extra effort), and Take It Easy (minimal effort). Each part-time job has only three career levels with minimal raises between each promotion. To get ahead at a part-time job, just show up with a good mood and put in a decent day's labor.

Part-time jobs can be quit via the cellphone. You can go back to work at the same place, but if you wait too long between quitting and going back, you lose any promotions and must start over.

Level	Position	Work Days	Start Time	Length of Day	Average Daily Pay	Weekly Average Pay	Pension Pay	Metrics for Promotion
BOOKSTORE CLERK								
1	Magazine Recycler	M,T,W,TH,F	16	3	90	450	30	Mood
2	Stocker	M,T,W,TH,F	16	3	150	750	40	Mood
3	Book Seller	M,T,W,TH,F	16	3	240	1,200	60	Mood
GRAVEYARD CLERK								
1	Grave Digger	SU,M,TH,F,S	18	3	98	490	30	Mood
2	Gatekeeper	SU,M,T,F,S	18	3	165	825	40	Mood
3	Undertaker	SU,M,T,F,S	18	3	263	1,315	70	Mood
GROCERY CLERK								
1	Shopping Cart Gatherer	M,T,W,TH,F	16	3	90	450	30	Mood
2	Bagger	M,T,W,TH,F	16	3	150	750	40	Mood
3	Produce Washer	M,T,W,TH,F	16	3	240	1,200	60	Mood
SPA RECEPTIONIST								
1	Receptionist 1	SU,M,W,TH,S	15	3	98	490	30	Mood
2	Receptionist 2	SU,M,W,TH,S	15	3	165	825	40	Mood
3	Receptionist 3	SU,M,W,TH,S	15	3	263	1,315	70	Mood
SPA SPECIALIST								
1	Clothes Folder	SU,W,TH,F,S	15	3	98	490	30	Mood
2	Fitting Room Guard	SU,W,TH,F,S	15	3	165	825	40	Mood
3	Seller	SU,W,TH,F,S	15	3	263	1,315	70	Mood

School

Children and teens have a different set of obligations from adult Sims—they must regularly attend school. Just showing up isn't enough, though. Students must complete homework to improve grades. Good grades are more than just a point of pride, too. Good grades lead to improved mood and the chance to select a new trait when the student ages up.

> **School Schedule:** Always Monday through Friday, but hours vary slightly depending on age. Children are in elementary school from 9 AM to 3 PM. Teens are in high school from 9 AM to 2 PM.

Much like a career, school has specific requirements for getting ahead and metrics for judging performance. For school, grades are the rating. Tones you use at school guide behavior and have a deep effect on performance. Here are the tones for school:

◆ **Normal Effort:** This tone puts in an average amount of work at school and does not add too much stress.

◆ **Work Hard:** Working Hard is a good way to increase performance, but it adds a lot of stress, which often results in the Stressed Out moodlet. After school, you need to relax and reverse the negative moodlet.

◆ **Slack Off:** Stressed students can reverse the effect by choosing this tone. Very little work gets done, so performance does not increase by much.

◆ **Meet New Friends:** This is a great way to socialize in school and develop budding relationships with new students. If you successfully meet another student, there is a good chance that you will either bring that new friend home or be invited to the friend's home. (See Friends After School below.)

◆ **Talk to Friends:** Talking to Friends at school is a good way to potentially increase your Sim's friendship rating of with another of the same age. This increases the chance you will be invited to a friend's house or invite a friend back to yours.

◆ **Sleep in Class:** If a student reports to school sleepy, then this tone becomes available to combat the effects of being tired. If the student is Exhausted, this tone happens automatically at random times. There is a risk of being caught while sleeping, though. If caught, the student is given detention.

◆ **Work Late on Homework:** If the student comes to school with incomplete homework, they can use this tone to try and finish it while at school. Overall performance will not rise as much as a Normal Effort, though.

Homework

The first time students go to school, they receive a small homework booklet. This booklet is placed in the student's personal inventory and can be used via the new Do Homework interaction. Completing homework is essential for raising grades at school, so make sure to allot extra time in the afternoons and evenings for homework.

> ### CAUTION
> Doing homework lowers the Fun need and can sometimes cause the Stressed Out moodlet.

When you choose to Do Homework, the student finds a seat somewhere on the lot and starts scribbling in the booklet. A meter appears over the student's head, just like a Sim trying to complete any task.

> ### TIP
> The Logic skill helps the student complete homework faster. Using the Ask for Help with Homework interaction also increases the speed of doing homework as long as the Sim invited to help is in a good mood.

If the student finishes their homework before the next school day, their performance goes up, Coupled with being in a good mood, this can raise a grade. If the homework is only partially done, the performance boost is only modest. If the student does no homework and does not work on it at all in school the next day, their performance takes a significant hit and grades can potentially fall.

> ### CAUTION
> You can actually cheat on homework, but it's risky. Use the Copy Sim's Homework interaction on the homework of another student. This tags your homework as cheating, and if you are caught, you're given detention.

Detention

A student caught sleeping in class or copying homework is punished with detention. Detention keeps the student after school for a few hours, which can interfere with a part-time job. While staying late, the student cannot choose their tone and they will not see any improvement in grades or performance. When detention is over, the schoolbus takes the student home.

> ### NOTE
> Detention also results in a mood hit due to the Detention moodlet.

Grades

All students start school the first day with a C. Doing well in school raises that to a B and then an A. Doing poorly drops it down to an F. Grades are the culmination of mood and homework completion. If you keep reporting to school with a good mood and complete homework, you will get an A. Keep

that A up for three days in a row to get the Honor Roll moodlet. Every day after getting the Honor Roll moodlet that you maintain the A, you keep the moodlet. If you drop back down to a C, though, you must maintain an A for three straight days to get the Honor Ro award back.

If you do not do homework, get caught cheating repeatedly, or go to school in a poor mood, your grade will slip down to an F. The first time you get an F, you are warned that unless measures are taken, there will be consequences. The next F results in the Failin moodlet.

Grades are very important during age transitions, so pay attention to the age of the student and try to have an A when the student moves into the next phase of life. If you have an A when the child becomes a teen or the teen becomes a young adult, th you get to select the trait awarded during th age transition. If the student has a F, then the student is assigned a bad trait. If the student has a C at the time of transition, then the trait is random—could be positive, could be negative.

Friends After School

Making friends at school satisfies the student Social need. Students sometimes bring another student home from school with the or are invited to another student's house to play. You choose whether or not to go hom with another student for a couple hours. Doing so and then engaging in socials at the friend's house is a good way to improve a relationship.

One factor that determines the chance of this happening in the distance between the homes of the students. Students who go to each other's houses will live within a reasonable distance from each other. The closer the other student, the more likely an invitation is.

Opportunities

From time to time, your Sims encounter special chances to earn extra money, boost work performance, and earn all sorts of goodies. These special events are called opportunities. We covered the basics of opportunities in the previous chapter—you can deny them without consequence, some of them are timed, and you can only have one opportunity at a time in the career, skill, and special categories.

Completing opportunities is a great way to make your Sim happy. So, here are full lists of every opportunity in Sunset Valley, broken down by skill and career. Each list details the name of the opportunity, hints for accomplishing it, and the reward.

Skill Opportunities

Developing a skill leads to opportunities that will further the skill. You may not see all of the opportunities associated with a skill as you develop it. You may only see two or three. But when you do receive a skill opportunity, definitely pursue it to advance the skill.

ATHLETIC SKILL

Opportunity	Hint	Reward	Extra Reward
Adonis in the Making	Train until you can't possibly become more muscular, then head back to the Stadium to earn your cash bonus.	§2,400	
Flex and Bend	Train [Sim Name] on the exercise machine for [X amount of time] to earn some cash and improve your relationship.	§350	Relationship w/ Sim +30
Bounce the Crowd	Work as Bouncer at the Theatre before time runs out to earn some cash on the side.	§500	
The Complete Circuit	Work Out using the TV or stereo, and swim for 30 minutes to earn a cash bonus.	§300	
Jog Everywhere	Jog [X amount of time] then return the device for a cash prize.	§550	
Add It Up	Improve your Athletic skill by one level, then return to the Stadium for a cash reward.	§350	
Going Pro	Go to the Stadium and get a job in the Professional Sports career to earn starting cash and performance bonuses.	§250	Performance +25
Bend and Flex	Train [Sim Name] for [X amount of time] to earn some cash and improve your relationship.	§250	Relationship w/ Sim +30
Frequent Fatigue	Work out until Fatigued X times then return to the Stadium to earn a cash prize.	§400	
Bursting with Energy	Work Out until you become Pumped to improve your Athletic skill.	Athletic Skill +5	Oddly Powerful Moodlet
Sprint to the Finish!	Work Out using the Quick Burst tone for [X amount of time] to improve your Athletic skill.	Athletic Skill +5	
The Health Seminar	Lecture at Seminar at the hospital before time runs out to earn some cash.	§250	Relationship w/ Sim +30
Muscle Showdown	Attend Competition at the Stadium before time runs out to improve your Athletic skills and win a cash prize.	§750	Athletic Skill +10
Push It!	Work Out using the Push Self option for [X amount of time] to improve your Athletic skill.	Athletic Skill +8	
No Sweat!	Work Out using the Don't Break a Sweat option for [X amount of time] to improve your Athletic skill.	Athletic Skill +5	

CHARISMA

Opportunity	Hint	Reward	Extra Reward
Bestest Friends	Become Best Friends with [Sim Name] to improve your Charisma skill.	Charisma Skill +10	
Just Business	Give Presentation at the Business Office before time runs out to earn some money and improve your Charisma skill.	§500	
Allow Me to Introduce Myself	Use Charming Introduction on a stranger to improve your relationship.	Relationship w/ Sim +25	

Simology

CHARISMA, CONTINUED

Opportunity	Hint	Reward	Extra Reward
A Charming Experiment	Assist Experiment at the Science Facility before time runs out to earn a cash reward.	§1,000	
Getting to Know…You	Get to Know [Sim Name] to earn some cash and improve your relationship.	Relationship w/ Sim +25	
Lobster Crisis	Negotiate Lobster Crisis at the Supermarket before time runs out to earn a cash reward.	§2,000	
Looking for a Friend	Become Friends with [Sim Name] to improve your Charisma skill.	Relationship w/ Sim +10	
Charismatic Cash	Improve your Charisma skill by one level and return to City Hall to receive a cash reward.	§1,000	
Tough Negotiating	Teach Negotiation at the Police Station before time runs out to earn a cash bonus and improve your Charisma skill.	§1,000	Charisma Skill +10
A Public Speaking Event	Give Speech at City Hall before time runs out to improve your Charisma skill.	Charisma Skill +10	
Smooth, Like Verbal Butter	Use Smooth Recovery to earn some cash.	§1,000	
Star Study!	See a Play or Concert at the Theatre to earn some cash and improve your Charisma skill.	§1,000	Charisma Skill +10
Muscle Showdown	Attend Competition at the Stadium before time runs out to improve your Athletic skills and win a cash prize.	§750	Athletic Skill +10
Push It!	Work Out using the Push Self option for [X amount of time] to improve your Athletic skill.	Athletic Skill +8	
No Sweat!	Work Out using the Don't Break a Sweat option for [X amount of time] to improve your Athletic skill.	Athletic Skill +5	

COOKING SKILL

Opportunity	Hint	Reward	Extra Reward
Hot Dogs, Please	Prepare Hot Dogs on the grill and bring them in your inventory to [Sim Name] to earn some cash.	§250	
A Life Giving Recipe	Deliver Ambrosia to the Hospital before time runs out to earn a cash reward, and save a life!	$3,000	
From One Chef to Another	Share Cooking Tips with [Sim Name] to improve your Cooking skill and boost your relationship.	Relationship w/ Sim +15	Cooking Skill +15
Fresh Cookies for Sale!	Deliver Cookies at the School to earn some money.	Variable §	Variable §
Excellence You Can Taste!	Prepare an excellent group meal and bring it to [Sim Name] before time runs out to earn some cash.	Variable §	
A Favorite Meal	Prepare [set recipe] and bring it to [Sim Name] before time runs out to earn money, improve your Cooking skill, and boost your relationship with [Sim Name].	Variable §	
The Greatest Food Ever	Prepare a great group meal and bring it to [Sim Name] before time runs out to earn some cash.	Variable §	
Burgerlicious	Prepare a group serving of Burgers on the grill and bring them in your inventory to [Sim Name] to earn some cash.	§400	
Great Gooey Cheesesteaks	Prepare Cheesesteak Sandwiches on the grill and bring them in your inventory to [Sim Name] to earn some cash.	§700	
Swim Into the Grill	Prepare a group serving of Grilled Salmon on the grill and bring it in your inventory to [Sim Name] to earn some cash.	§1,000	
One, Two, Tri-Tip Steaks	Prepare a group serving of Tri-Tip Steaks on the grill and bring them in your inventory to [Sim Name] to earn some cash.	§1,000	
Nice!	Prepare a nice group meal and bring it to [Sim Name] before time runs out to earn some cash.	Variable §	

COOKING SKILL, CONTINUED

Opportunity	Hint	Reward	Extra Reward
That's Outstanding!	Prepare an outstanding group meal and bring it to [Sim Name] before time runs out to earn some cash.	Variable §	
Perfection from the Pan	Prepare a perfect group meal and bring it to [Sim Name] before time runs out to earn some cash.	Variable §	
Borrowing Ingredients	Bring a tomato to [Sim Name] and Share Ingredients to earn some money and improve your Cooking skill and relationship.	§500	Cooking Skill +10, Relationship w/ Sim +15
Burgers for Sims in Uniform	Deliver Burgers to the Police Station before time runs out to improve your Cooking skill.	Cooking Skill +15	Relationship w/ Sims @ Police Station
The Dish Showdown	Enter Dish at the restaurant before time runs out to earn a cash prize.	Variable §	
Very Nice!	Prepare a very nice group meal and bring it to [Sim Name] before time runs out to earn some cash.	Variable §	

FISHING SKILL

Opportunity	Hint	Reward	Extra Reward
Monster from the Deep	Catch Behemoth at the Science Facility before time runs out to earn some money.	§4,000	
Say Hello to My Little Fish	Catch a Black Goldfish and Sell Black Goldfish at the Police Station to earn some money.	Variable §	§650
Funny Looking Fish	Catch a Tragic Clownfish and Sell Clownfish at the Theatre to earn some money.	Variable §	§250
Aquarium Fishing	Attend Fishing Competition at the Supermarket before time runs out to catch an assortment of fish.	§1,000	5 Random Fish
Fishing for Suits	Teach Fishing Seminar at the Business Office before time runs out to earn some money.	§1,000	
Piscine Perfection	Catch a perfect fish and Sell Fish at the Supermarket to earn some money.	Variable §	
An Excellent Catch	Catch an excellent fish and Sell Fish at the Supermarket to earn some money.	Variable §	
Heaps of Fresh Fish	Catch 15 fish, then Sell Fish at the Supermarket to earn some money.	Variable §	
Lobsters in Demand!	Catch a Lobster and Sell Lobster to the Supermarket to earn some money.	Variable §	§100
That's a Nice Fish!	The fish you caught was exactly what the Supermarket's rather odd patron was looking for! You really saved the supermarket's fishy hide, so it only makes sense to pay you for your help.	Variable §	
Lots of Fresh Fish	Catch 6 fish, then Sell Fish at the Supermarket to earn some money.	Variable §	
Fresh Fish	Catch 3 fish, then Sell Fish at the Supermarket to earn some money.	Variable §	
Plumber and Fisherman	Unclog Pipes at City Hall before time runs out to earn some money.	§500	1 Random Fish
Fish of Life and Death	Catch a Deathfish and Deliver Deathfish at the Science Facility to earn some money.	Variable §	§350
Robot Fish v2.0	Catch a Robot Fish and Sell Robot Fish at the Science Facility to earn some money.	Variable §	§350

GARDENING SKILL

Opportunity	Hint	Reward	Extra Reward
An Apple a Day	Deliver X Very Nice (or better) apples to the restaurant to earn some money.	Variable §	§250
A Bag of Produce	Harvest X Very Nice (or better) fruits and vegetables and Deliver Harvest to the restaurant to earn some fresh produce.	3 Random Rare Harvestables	1 Random Special Harvestables
A Just-In-Time Harvest	Harvest X Very Nice (or better) fruits and vegetables and Deliver Harvest to the Supermarket before time runs out to earn some money.	Variable §	§300
Excellent Veggies	Deliver X Excellent fruits or vegetables to [Sim Name] to earn some money.	Variable §	§400
Garlic Goodness	Deliver X Very Nice (or better) bulbs of garlic to the restaurant to earn some money.	Variable §	§500
Grape-Aid	Deliver X Very Nice (or better) grapes to the restaurant to earn some money.	Variable §	§250
Absolutely Great Produce	Deliver X Great fruits or vegetables to [Sim Name] to earn some money.	Variable §	§300
Extreme Life Insurance	Give [Sim Name] a Death Flower before time runs out to earn some money.	Variable §	§500

GARDENING SKILL, CONTINUED

Opportunity	Hint	Reward	Extra Reward
Lettuce Help Out	Deliver X Very Nice (or better) heads of lettuce to the restaurant to earn some money.	Variable §	§250
The Fruit of Life	Give [Sim Name] a Life Fruit before time runs out to earn some money.	Variable §	§500
Limes Are Key	Deliver X Very Nice (or better) Limes to the restaurant to earn some money.	Variable §	§350
A Nice Harvest	Deliver X Nice fruits or vegetables to [Sim Name] to earn some money.	Variable §	
Don't Cry	Deliver X Very Nice (or better) onions to the restaurant to earn some money.	Variable §	§350
Outstanding Tasting Ingredients	Deliver X Outstanding fruits or vegetables to [Sim Name] to earn some money.	Variable §	§400
Fruit Flambe	Grow 6 Flame Fruit of Nice quality and Deliver Produce at the Business Office before time runs out to earn some money.	Variable §	
Peppers on Parade	Deliver X Very Nice (or better) peppers to the restaurant to earn some money.	Variable §	§350
Perfect Produce	Deliver X Perfect fruits or vegetables to [Sim Name] to earn some money.	Variable §	§1,000
Fresh Taters	Deliver X Very Nice (or better) potatoes to the restaurant to earn some money.	Variable §	§350
Uncommonly Good	Bring 20 harvested items of Excellent quality to the restaurant and Deliver Produce to learn how to plant some interesting things.	Move to Outstandingly Rare Opportunity	
Outstandingly Rare	Bring 10 Excellent quality cheeses to the restaurant and Deliver Produce to learn how to plant some interesting things.	Move to The Omnificent Plant Opportunity	
The Omnificent Plant	Bring 10 Outstanding steaks to the restaurant and Deliver Produce to learn how to plant the Omni Plant.	2 Omni Plants Seeds	
Fresh Tomato Sauce	Deliver X Very Nice (or better) tomatoes to the restaurant to earn some money.	Variable §	§250
Ingredients Ripe for the Eating	Deliver X Very Nice fruits or vegetables to [Sim Name] to earn some money.	Variable §	
Seed Spittin' Made Easy	Deliver X Very Nice (or better) watermelons to the restaurant to earn some money.	Variable §	§300

GUITAR SKILL

Opportunity	Hint	Reward	Extra Reward
Local Musician Showdown	Play in Contest at the Theatre before time runs out to earn the cash prize.	§2,500	
I Got Your Back...Up	Perform with Symphony before time runs out at the Theatre to earn some money.	§1,000	
The Social Event of the Season	Play the guitar at [Sim Name]'s home during the party on [specific date] to earn some money.	§1,400	Relationship w/ Sim +2
In the End	Perform for Party at the Business Office before time runs out to earn some money.	§500	
Raise the Fun(d)	Perform for Fundraiser at the restaurant before time runs out to earn some money.	§1,000	Composition
Guitar Up!	Improve your Guitar skill by one level to receive a new composition.	Composition	
Tons of Tips	Earn [X amount of §] in tips to improve your relationship with [Sim Name] and earn some money!	§1,000	Relationship w/ Sim +2
Jammin' on the Streets	Earn [X amount of §] in tips to improve your relationship with [Sim Name] and earn some money!	§300	Relationship w/ Sim +1
Sorting the Section	Help Organize Music at the Bookstore before time runs out to earn some money.	§450	Composition
Some Hogan Rock	Attend Seminar at the Bookstore before time runs out to receive a little inspiration.	Buff, Inspired	
Musical Assembly	Perform at Assembly at the School to earn some money.	§500	
Guitar in the House	Play the guitar at [Sim Name]'s home during the party on [specific date] to earn some money.	§500	Relationship w/ Sim +2

HANDINESS

Opportunity	Hint	Reward	Extra Reward
Settle an Argument	Speak to [Sim Name] and Convince Technology is Great to earn some money and improve your relationship.	§250	Relationship w/ Sim +25
Fix the Election...Machines	Fix Election Machines at City Hall before time runs out to earn some money.	§1,400	
Fix Before Jail Break	Fix Lock Mechanism at the Police Station before time runs out to earn some money.	§800	
Negetized Plumbing	Fix Plumbing at the restaurant to earn some money.	§350	
De-Worming	Stop Wormholes at the Science Facility before time runs out to earn some money.	§2,400	
Substitute Instructor	Provide Handiness Instruction at the Military Base before time runs out to earn some money.	§800	
Bad Reception	Repair the TV and return it to [Sim Name] earn some money.	§500	
No Jams, No Fun	Repair the stereo and return it to [Sim Name] to earn some money.	§600	
Broken Laptop	Repair the laptop and return it to [Sim Name] to earn some money.	§1,200	
Handiness How-To	Give Handiness Presentation at the School before time runs out to earn some money.	§400	
Bring Back the Jams	Upgrade the stereo and bring it back to [Sim Name] to earn some money.	§600	
Shower Upgrade	Upgrade the shower and return it to [Sim Name] to earn some money.	§1,250	

LOGIC SKILL

Opportunity	Hint	Reward	Extra Reward
Taking Down Sinclair	Challenge Argyle Sinclair at the Theatre before time runs out to earn some money.	§2,500	
Fixing the Books	Assist Accountants at the Business Office to earn some money.	§750	
Settle an Argument	Speak to [Sim Name] and Convince Logic is Great to improve your relationship.	Logic Skill +10	Relationship w/ Sim +20
A Stimulating Experiment	Participate in Study at the Science Facility before time runs out to earn some money.	§600	
Becoming More Logical	Improve your Logic skill by one point and report back to the Science Facility to earn some money.	§750	
Logic 101	Teach Logic Class at the School to earn some money.	§600	
Puzzle Panic	Assemble Puzzles at the Supermarket to earn some money.	§400	
Riddle Away	Compete in Contest at the Bookstore before time ends to earn some money and improve your Logic skill.	§1,500	Logic Skill +10
Fixing the Celestial Hump	Search Galaxy on your own telescope to earn some money and improve your Logic skill.	§500	Logic Skill +10
Logic Tutoring	Skill tutor [Sim] and then report back to [location] to earn some cash.	§2,000	
Tutor Me Please	Tutor [Sim Name] to improve your relationship and earn some money.	§250	Relationship w/ Sim +30
The Great Argyle Sinclair	Watch Argyle Sinclair at the Bookstore before time runs out to earn some money.	Logic Skill +5	§2,000

PAINTING SKILL

Opportunity	Hint	Reward	Extra Reward
Interior Decor	Deliver Paintings worth at least [X amount of §] to the restaurant to earn some money and improve your relationship with the restaurant employees.	Variable §	Relationship w/ Sims at Restaurant
The Business of Decor	Deliver 10 Paintings to the Business Office to earn some money and improve your relationship with the office employees.	Variable §	Relationship w/ Sims at Business Tower
Painting the City	Deliver Paintings to City Hall. The city needs 15 paintings, for which they will pay you a large sum of money.	Variable §	Relationship w/ Sims at City Hall
The Study of Art	Submit a Painting worth at least §1,000 at the Science Facility to earn some cash.	Variable §	
A Large Painting	Paint a large painting and give it to [Sim Name] to earn some money.	Variable §	

Simology

PAINTING SKILL, CONTINUED

Opportunity	Hint	Reward	Extra Reward
A Medium Painting	Paint a medium painting and give it to [Sim Name] to earn some money.	Variable §	
Art Class	Teach Art Class at the School before time runs out to improve your Painting skill.	Painting Skill +10	Relationship w/ Sims at School
Fresco Fest	Assist Painter at City Hall before time runs out to increase the value of all of your future paintings.	Painting Value Boost	
Local Artists Gallery	View Gallery at the Business Office before time runs out to improve your Painting skill and increase the value of your next painting.	Painting Value Boost	Painting Skill +10
A Small Painting	Paint a small painting and give it to [Sim Name] to earn some money.	Variable §	
A Retreat to Inspiration	Attend Retreat at the Bookstore before time runs out to obtain a little inspiration.	Pumped Moodlet	

WRITING SKILL

Opportunity	Hint	Reward	Extra Reward
Your Autobiography	Write an Autobiography to improve your relationship with [Sim Name] and earn some money.	§500	Relationship w/ Sim +2
A History of One	Write a biography about [Sim Name] on your computer and deliver a copy to improve your relationship and earn some money.	Relationship w/ Sim +10	Variable §
Book Donation	Bring three books you've written and Donate Books at City Hall to be viewed as Charitable.	Charitable Moodlet	
Add a Little Drama	Write a Drama novel to earn some money and improve your relationship with [Sim Name].	§500	Relationship w/ Sim +2
Hopefully You Like Orks	Write a Fantasy novel to improve your relationship with [Sim Name] and earn some money.	§500	Relationship w/ Sim +2
The Prolific Writer	Write enough books to earn a weekly royalty of [X amount of §] to permanently increase your royalty checks.	10% Royalty Increase	
Correcting Past Mistakes	Write a book that earns [X amount of §] in weekly royalty checks to improve your relationship with [Sim Name], as well as to improve the quality of your future books.	Book Quality Increase	Relationship w/ Sim +2
A History of the Times	Write a History book to improve your relationship with [Sim Name] and earn some money.	§500	Relationship w/ Sim +2
It's a Living	Write enough books to earn a weekly royalty of [X amount of §] to permanently increase your royalty checks.	10% Royalty Increase	
A Masterpiece	Write a Masterpiece to improve your relationship with [Sim Name] and earn some money.	§1,200	Relationship w/ Sim +2
The Great Novelist	Write enough books to earn a weekly royalty of [X amount of §] to permanently increase your royalty checks.	10% Royalty Increase	
A Few Pages of Satire	Write a Satire novel to improve your relationship with [Sim Name] and earn some money.	§500	Relationship w/ Sim +2
To Boldly Go	Write a Science Fiction novel to improve your relationship with [Sim Name] and earn some money.	§250	Relationship w/ Sim +2
The Glory of Vaudeville	Write a book of Vaudeville to improve your relationship with [Sim Name] and earn some money.	§600	Relationship w/ Sim +2

Career Opportunities

As you work your way up the career ladder, opportunities directly related to the career will be offered. You are not required to accept these opportunities. Rejected them will not result in a demotion or termination. However, completing them will almost always lead to improved performance at work and/or a promotion. The promotion may not occur the moment you complete the opportunity, but the extra effort will be recognized and noted.

BUSINESS OPPORTUNITIES

Opportunity	Hint	Reward	Extra Reward
The Wright Opinion	Read The Wright Papers before time runs out to earn some cash.	§500	
The Goth Way?	Read The Goth Account before time runs out to earn some cash.	§500	
Graab It Up	Read Landgraab Financial before time runs out to earn some cash.	§500	
Bathroom Gallery	Bring a painting of your own creation to work with you to improve your office popularity.	Co-Worker Relationship +15	
Marketing Material	Bring a painting of your own creation to work with you to improve your job performance.	Performance +25	§500
The Face of the Company	Bring a painting worth at least [X amount of §] of your own creation to work with you to earn a cash bonus.	Performance +30	§2,000
Boardroom Beautification	Bring a painting worth at least [X amount of §] of your own creation to work with you to earn a raise.	Raise	
Sealing the Deal	Sign Acquisition Deal at the Business Office to earn a cash bonus and raise.	Raise	§2,000
Making Coffee the Executive Way	Read Caffeine Culture to improve your job performance and increase your relationship with your boss.	Performance +15	Boss Relationship +25
A Farewell to Paper	Read Going Paperless to improve your job performance and increase your relationship with your boss.	Performance +15	Boss Relationship +25
Inflate Away	Read Bloviation on Hyperinflation to improve your job performance and increase your relationship with your boss.	Performance +15	Boss Relationship +25
Special Is, Special Does	Read You Are Special to improve your job performance and increase your relationship with your boss.	Performance +20	Boss Relationship +25
You're Liable for This	Read Limiting Liability to improve your job performance and increase your relationship with your boss.	Performance +20	Boss Relationship +20
No Whistles Here	Read Woes of Whistle Blowing to improve your job performance and increase your relationship with your boss.	Performance +20	Boss Relationship +20
No Shelter Here	Read Yay, Tax Shelters! to improve your job performance and increase your relationship with your boss.	Performance +20	Boss Relationship +20
Handling the Restructure	Read ABCs of Downsizing to improve your job performance and increase your relationship with your boss.	Performance +20	Boss Relationship +20
Making Nice with the Newsies	Make [Sim Name] your [set relationship level] to earn a job performance increase.	Performance +25	
Outflanking the Military	Make [Sim Name] your [set relationship level] to earn a job performance increase.	Performance +35	
Hospital Delivery	Deliver Dossier at the Hospital to earn a raise.	Raise	
Scientific Documents	Deliver Dossier at the Science Facility to earn a raise.	Raise	
Political Influence	Deliver Dossier at City Hall to earn a raise.	Raise	
Top, Top Secret	Deliver Dossier at the Military Base to earn a raise.	Raise	
Branding Bonanza Brainstorm	Hold Meeting at the Stadium to improve your work relationships.	Co-Worker Relationship +20	
Squabbling Scientist Settlement	Hold Meeting at the Science Facility to earn a cash bonus and increase your job performance.	§500	Performance +20
Hospitality: A Conscious Choice	Hold Meeting at the Hospital to earn a cash bonus and increase your job performance.	§1,000	Performance +20
The Status of Statutes	Hold Meeting at City Hall to earn a cash bonus and increase your job performance.	§1,200	Performance +20
Military Intelligence	Hold Meeting at the Military Base to earn a cash bonus and raise.	§2,000	Raise
Seeking More Favorable Taxes	Lobby for Tax Reforms at City Hall before time runs out to earn a raise.	Raise	

BUSINESS OPPORTUNITIES, CONTINUED

Opportunity	Hint	Reward	Extra Reward
It's All About Who You Know	Make [Sim Name] your [set relationship level] to earn a raise.	Raise	
Schmoozing the Political Machine	Make [Sim Name] your [set relationship level] to earn a raise.	Raise	
Merging Toward Overtime	Stay at work until closing time to improve your relationship with co-workers.	Co-Worker Relationship +20	
A Fun Gathering of Suits	Throw a party with [Sim Name] on the invite list to increase your office popularity.	Co-Worker Relationship +20	

CRIMINAL OPPORTUNITIES

Opportunity	Hint	Reward	Extra Reward
Grabbing the Llama	Steal Llama at City Hall to attempt to steal one of the precious Golden Llamas.		§4,000
Bouncer Duty	Bounce Competition at the [set location] to work as a bouncer at the Criminal Dance Competition.	§1,500	Co-Worker Relationship +25
Welcome to the Family	Read Dos and Don'ts of the Dons and return to work.	Performance +15	Boss Relationship +25
Wallets Up for Grabs	Read Adapting to the Wallet Environment and return to work.	Performance +15	Boss Relationship +25
Evolution?	Read From Goon to Made Man: Thuggery Evolved and return to work.	Performance +15	Boss Relationship +25
Payment Options	Read Make 'Em Pay and return to work.	Performance +20	Boss Relationship +25
Labeling Things	Read Losing the Huckster Label and return to work.	Performance +20	Boss Relationship +20
Presenting a Portfolio to Clients	Read Snake Oil and Other Sound Investments and return to work.	Performance +20	Boss Relationship +20
Oh, It's Advanced Alright	Read Advanced Combinatorials and return to work.	Performance +20	Boss Relationship +20
Irreplaceable	Read Making Yourself Indispensable and return to work.	Performance +20	Boss Relationship +20
Nimble Like a Cat	Read The Mythical Hot Tin Roof and return to work.	Performance +20	Boss Relationship +20
The Coup	Read Hostile Takeover: When to Make the Move to improve your job performance and relationship with your boss.	Performance +20	Boss Relationship +20
Simoleons Under the Table	Drop Off Bribe at City Hall to earn a job performance increase at work.	Performance +20	Boss Relationship +20
Case the Joint	Case Joint at the [set location] to earn a job performance increase.	§1,000	Performance +25
A Package for You	Deliver Package at the [set location] to earn a cash reward.	§250	
Thief Like There's No Tomorrow	Attend Competition at the [set location] to compete in the Thievery Competition.	§2,000	Co-Worker Relationship +25
Friends for Life	Make [Sim Name] your [set relationship level] to earn a job performance increase and relationship boost with the boss.	Boss Relationship +25	Performance +25
Extra Muscle	Assist Heist at the [set location] before time runs out to earn a cash bonus.	§350	
Criminals, Partners, Friends	Make [Sim Name] your [set relationship level] to earn a job performance increase and favor with the boss.	Performance +20	Boss Relationship +25
Shouting Contest	Make [Sim Name] your [set relationship level] to earn a cash reward and a job performance increase.	§1,500	Performance +25
Counting the Loot	Stay late to improve your relationship with your the gang.	Co-Worker Relationship +20	
Tools of the Trade	Pick Up Tools from the [set location], then return to work with them to earn a raise.	Raise	Boss Relationship +20
The Most Evilest Plan	Execute Evil Plan at the Military Base to attempt to take over the world with your nefarious scheme.	§4,000	

CULINARY OPPORTUNITIES

Opportunity	Hint	Reward	Extra Reward
Working Alongside Friends	Make [Sim Name] your [set relationship level] before time runs out to earn a performance boost. Good Job!	Performance +25	
Overtime Hours	Stay at work late to help out and earn a relationship boost with your co-workers.	Co-Worker Relationship +20	
Learn a Recipe	Read the [recipe] recipe and return to work to earn a cash reward.	Cooking Skill +10	§800
Best of the Best	Prepare a dish, then return to work with it before time runs out to be rewarded based on the quality of the dish.	Cooking Skill +10	
Serving the Masses	Prepare two group servings of [set recipe] and bring them to work with you to earn boosts to your performance and Cooking skill.	Performance +25	Cooking Skill +15
Bring the Buffet	Prepare two group servings of [set recipe] and bring them to work with you before time runs out to earn boosts to your performance and Cooking skill.	Performance +25	Cooking Skill +15
Burners Down!	Prepare two group servings of [set recipe] and bring them to work with you before time runs out to earn boosts to your performance and Cooking skill.	Performance +25	Cooking Skill +15
Some Reading Material	Read Secrets of the Master Chef before time runs out to earn a job performance boost.	Performance +25	
All-New Bi-Pedal Dishwashing Machine	Clean all of the dishes in your inventory before your next shift to earn a job performance increase.	Performance +25	
A Sweet Jam	Play Gig at the restaurant before time runs out to earn a cash bonus.	§600	
A Mouthful of Rock	Play Gig at the restaurant before time runs out to earn a cash bonus.	§600	
Appetizing Music	Play Gig at the restaurant before time runs out to earn a cash bonus.	§600	
A Divine Meal	Prepare Ambrosia and bring it to work with you before time runs out to earn a raise.	Raise	
A Lot of Bad Apples	Plant the provided Bad Apple, then bring 10 apples that are of bad (or worse) quality to work before time runs out for a job performance boost.	Performance +20	
The Feast of Ages	Prepare Feast at City Hall before time runs out to earn a large cash bonus.	§3,000	
Blown Away	Use Sushi as bait to catch a Blowfish, then return to work with it to earn a raise.	Raise	
Insider Dining	Eat with Others at the restaurant to improve your work performance.	Performance +20	
Corporate Dining	Eat with Others at the restaurant to improve your work performance.	Performance +20	
On-the-Clock Dinner Date	Eat with Others at the restaurant to improve your work performance.	Performance +20	
The Evolution of Sushi	Catch 5 [fish types] and bring them to work before time runs out to earn boosts to your performance and Cooking skill.	Performance +30	Cooking Skill +20
Caterer of Festivities	Prepare three group meals, then Cater Party at City Hall with the meals before time runs out to earn a cash bonus.	Cooking Skill +10	
Catfish for the Chef	Catch an Alley Catfish using the cheese as bait, then return to work with the fish for a cash reward.	§500	Performance +20
Harvesting the Best	Plant the Great [harvestable] to grow an Excellent [harvestable], then bring it with you to work before time runs out to earn a raise.	Raise	
A Catering Fracas	Cater Event at the Business Office before time runs out to increase your relationship with your boss and earn a cash bonus.	Boss Relationship +20	§500
Catering Time!	Get to the party to help cater before time runs out.	Boss Relationship +25	§500
Spying on the Cuisine	Dine at the other restaurant alone or with a guest, then return to work to earn a job performance increase.	Performance +25	
Rock and Sushi Roll	Catch two fish and turn in the fish at the restaurant to earn a performance boost and a cash bonus!	Performance +25	§500
Cooking with the Best	Prepare a group meal using the Excellent ingredients provided, then bring it back to work before time runs out for a skill increase and to earn a Perfect ingredient.	Random Perfect Special Harvestable	Random Very Nice Special Harvestable

Simology

JOURNALISM OPPORTUNITIES

Opportunity	Hint	Reward	Extra Reward
Reform Bill Amended by Fisticuffs	Get Exclusive Story at City Hall before time runs out to earn a raise and a job performance increase.	Raise	Performance +35
ER Explosion Sends Bedpans, Doctors Flying	Get Exclusive Story at the Hospital before time runs out to earn a raise and a job performance increase.	Raise	Performance +35
Robot Fish Revolt	Get Exclusive Story at the Science Facility before time runs out to earn a raise and a job performance increase.	Raise	Performance +35
Why Did the Journalist Cross the Road?	Read Street or Sidewalk: A Cautionary Tale and return to work.	Performance +15	Boss Relationship +25
Check This	Read Faster Checking Through the Power of Word Processing and return to work.	Performance +15	Boss Relationship +25
The Right Way to Borrow	Read Avoiding Plagiarism and return to work.	Performance +15	Boss Relationship +25
Digitizing Your Notes	Read From Notepad to Laptop and return to work.	Performance +20	Boss Relationship +25
A Tad Vague	Read 101 Ways to Be Vague and return to work.	Performance +20	Boss Relationship +20
It Was All Yellow	Read The Finer Points of Yellow Journalism and return to work.	Performance +20	Boss Relationship +20
Weathering the Storm	Read Fronts and Barometrics: Excellence Through Jargon and return to work.	Performance +20	Boss Relationship +20
Right and Wrong	Read Right and Wrong and Its Use in Important Stories and return to work.	Performance +20	Boss Relationship +20
Broken News	Read How to Fix It When News Breaks and return to work.	Performance +20	Boss Relationship +20
Quite the Charmer	Improve your Charisma skill in order to improve job performance.	Performance +20	Boss Relationship +25
Military Mishap	Check Lead at the Military Base before time runs out to earn a job performance boost and raise.	Performance +30	Raise
Bad News Bookstore	Check Lead at the Bookstore before time runs out to earn a job performance boost and raise.	Performance +30	Raise
Supermarket Status	Check Lead at the Supermarket before time runs out to earn a job performance boost and raise.	Performance +30	Raise
Business As Usual?	Check Lead at the Business Office before time runs out to earn a job performance boost and raise.	Performance +30	Raise
Theatre Terror	Check Lead at the Theatre before time runs out to earn a job performance boost and raise.	Performance +30	Raise
Stadium Spectacular	Check Lead at the Stadium before time runs out to earn a job performance boost and raise.	Performance +30	Raise
Restaurant Revelation	Check Lead at the restaurant before time runs out to earn a job performance boost and raise.	Performance +30	Raise
Restaurant in Review	Check Lead at the restaurant before time runs out to earn a job performance boost and raise.	Performance +30	Raise
City Hall Caper	Check Lead at City Hall before time runs out to earn a job performance boost and raise.	Performance +30	Raise
Science Lab Slander	Check Lead at the Science Facility before time runs out to earn a job performance boost and raise.	Performance +30	Raise
Hospital Hijinks	Check Lead at the Hospital before time runs out to earn a job performance boost and raise.	Performance +30	Raise
Proof of Concept	Write an Article and bring it to work to earn a performance increase.	Performance +20	Boss Relationship +20
A Co-Worker in Need	Write a Hit Article and bring it to work before time runs out to earn a cash bonus and relationship boost with [Sim Name].	Co-Worker Relationship +20	§500
Today's (And Tomorrow's) Current Events	Read the new newspaper each day for 5 days to earn a job performance increase at work.	Performance +25	Boss Relationship +20
Friendship for a Story	Become friends with [Sim Name] to earn a raise and a job performance increase.	Performance +25	Raise

JOURNALISM OPPORTUNITIES, CONTINUED

Opportunity	Hint	Reward	Extra Reward
Extra-Curricular Activity	Write an Article and bring it to work to receive a job performance boost and cash reward based on the quality of the article.	Performance +20	§250
Hit Needed	Write a Hit Article and bring it to work to earn a job performance boost and a raise.	Performance +30	$1,000
Writing for the Enemy	Write a Hit Article and bring it to the Bookstore to earn a cash bonus.	§X	§250
Reading for Proof	Read the article before time runs out to improve your job performance and relationship with your boss.	Performance +25	Boss Relationship +25
Getting to Know You	Make [Sim Name] your [set relationship level] to earn a raise and a job performance increase.	Performance +25	Raise
An Officer and a Scumbag	Interview Source at the Military Base before time runs out to earn a job performance boost.	Performance +25	
To Catch a Clerk	Interview Source at the Bookstore before time runs out to earn a job performance boost.	Performance +25	
Supermarket Super Stocker	Interview Source at the Supermarket before time runs out to earn a job performance boost.	Performance +25	
The Business of Giving	Interview Source at the Business Office before time runs out to earn a job performance boost.	Performance +25	
Tenacious Thespian Tackles Teller	Interview Source at the Theatre before time runs out to earn a job performance boost.	Performance +25	
Sports Story	Interview Source at the Stadium before time runs out to earn a job performance boost.	Performance +25	
Restaurant Regulation	Interview Source at [location] before time runs out to earn a job performance boost.	Performance +25	
The Deadly Dinner	Interview Source at the restaurant before time runs out to earn a job performance boost.	Performance +25	
City Councilman Councils to the Contrary	Interview Source at City Hall before time runs out to earn a job performance boost.	Performance +25	
The Scientist	Interview Source at the Science Lab before time runs out to earn a job performance boost.	Performance +25	
The Ordinary Orderly	Interview Source at the Hospital before time runs out to earn a job performance boost.	Performance +25	
The Perfect Article	Write a Best-Seller article and bring it to work before time runs out to earn a job performance boost and cash bonus.	Performance +30	§1,000
Sit, Listen, and Learn	Attend Seminar at [set location] before time runs out to earn a job performance increase and relationship boost with your co-workers.	Performance +30	Co-Worker Relationship +30
A Party for the Promoted	Throw a party and invite [Sim Name] to improve your relationship with your co-workers.	Co-Worker Relationship +20	
Late Night Crunch	Stay at work late to improve your relationship with co-workers.	Co-Worker Relationship +20	
Rushing to Deadline	Stay at work late to improve your relationship with co-workers.	Co-Worker Relationship +20	
Extra Edit, Extra Hours	Stay at work late to improve your relationship with co-workers.	Co-Worker Relationship +20	
Channel Surfing	Watch TV for [X amount of time] to earn a cash bonus.	§350	
Writing: A Journalist's Friend	Gain some Writing skill in order to improve job performance.	Performance +20	Boss Relationship +25

LAW ENFORCEMENT OPPORTUNITIES

Opportunity	Hint	Reward	Extra Reward
A Tad Better Shape	Improve your Athletic skill to the next level to earn a job performance increase and relationship boost with your boss.	Performance +20	Boss Relationship +20

LAW ENFORCEMENT OPPORTUNITIES, CONTINUED

Opportunity	Hint	Reward	Extra Reward
Your Friendly Neighborhood Police Officer	Visit three neighbors at their homes to earn a job performance increase and relationship boost with your boss.	Performance +25	Boss Relationship +20
Extensive Case Work	Finish Case at City Hall before time runs out to earn a large cash bonus.	§5,000	
The Wrong Pair of Shoes	Read How to Avoid Concrete Shoes to earn a job performance increase and relationship boost with your boss.	Performance +15	Boss Relationship +20
The Right Desk	Read More Out Than In: Maintaining a Proper Desk Environment to earn a job performance increase and relationship boost with your boss.	Performance +15	Boss Relationship +20
Whistle While You Police	Read Advanced Whistle Techniques to earn a job performance increase and relationship boost with your boss.	Performance +20	Boss Relationship +25
To Fashionably Protect and Serve	Read Protect, Serve, and Look Good Doing It to earn a job performance increase and relationship boost with your boss.	Performance +20	Boss Relationship +25
The Donuts of a Leader	Read Free Donuts and Other Great Leadership Tips to earn a job performance increase and relationship boost with your boss.	Performance +20	Boss Relationship +25
Not Seeing Is, uh, Believing?	Read How Not to Be Seen and return to work.	Performance +25	Boss Relationship +25
Guess What?	Read Keep 'Em Guessing and return to work.	Performance +25	Boss Relationship +25
Spray the Scene	Read Effective Luminol Spraying Techniques and return to work.	Performance +30	Boss Relationship +20
Don't Squint	Read Avoiding Squint Jargon for Better Communication before time runs out to earn a job performance increase and relationship boost with your boss.	Performance +30	Boss Relationship +20
Police Conference	Attend Conference at City Hall before time runs out to improve your job performance.	Performance +30	
For the Children!	Lecture Children at the School before time runs out to earn a raise.	Raise	
Black Market Gnomes	Gather Intel at the Business Office before time runs out to earn a job performance boost and increase to your relationship with your boss.	Performance +15	Boss Relationship +20
Developing Informants	Make [Sim Name] your [set relationship level].	Raise	
A Fresh Set of Forensic Eyes	Solve Crime at the [set location] to earn a raise.	Raise	
Spruce Up the Place	Create an original painting, then bring it to work before time runs out to earn a job performance increase.	Performance +25	Variable Painting Reward
Working the Late Shift	Stay at work until closing time to earn a relationship boost with your boss.	Boss Relationship +20	
Stop Doomsday!	Disable Device at the [set location] before time runs out to earn a cash reward.	§5,000	
Undercover on the House	Go Undercover at the [set location] before time runs out to earn a job performance increase and boost to your relationship with your boss.	Performance +25	Boss Relationship +25

MEDICAL OPPORTUNITIES

Opportunity	Hint	Reward	Extra Reward
Battlefield Medicine	Advise Military at the Military Base before time runs out to earn a cash bonus.	$2,000	
Wanted: Blood	Work Blood Drive at the School before time runs out to earn a raise.	Raise	
Waste Management	Read Better Out Than In and return to work.	Performance +15	Boss Relationship +20
Respect the Woo Woos	Read Respecting the Ambulance and return to work.	Performance +20	Boss Relationship +25
Blood Is Not Blue	Read Blood Is Not Blue and return to work.	Performance +20	Boss Relationship +25
Shifting Responsibilities	Read The 36 Hour Shift and return to work.	Performance +20	Boss Relationship +25
You're Golden!	Read The Golden Hour and return to work.	Performance +25	Boss Relationship +25
It's a Genetic Thing	Read The ATGCs of Genetics and return to work.	Performance +25	Boss Relationship +25
So Infectious It Hurts	Read The Simmania Pandemic and return to work.	Performance +30	Boss Relationship +20

MEDICAL OPPORTUNITIES, CONTINUED

Opportunity	Hint	Reward	Extra Reward
Shades of Grey	Read Grey Matters to earn a job performance increase and a relationship boost with your boss.	Performance +30	Boss Relationship +20
An Apple a Day	Grow X nice apples and bring them to work with you to increase your relationship with your co-workers.	Co-Worker Relationship +20	Garden Skill +8
The Surgeon, the Pastry Chef	Prepare a group serving of a dessert and bring it to work to earn a relationship increase with your co-workers.	Co-Worker Relationship +20	Cooking Skill +10
A Donation of Children's Literature	Write a children's book, then bring it to work with you to improve your relationship with your co-workers.	Co-Worker Relationship +20	Writing Skill +5
Medical Conference	Attend Medical Conference at the Business Office before time runs out to earn a raise.	Raise	
Brain Trust	Donate Brain Tissue at the Hospital before time runs out to earn a raise.	Raise	
It Takes Heart	Donate Heart at the Hospital before time runs out to earn a raise and cash bonus.	Raise	§2,000
From Two to One	Donate Kidney at the Hospital before time runs out to earn a raise.	Raise	
The Giving Sort	Donate Mucous at the Hospital before time runs out to earn a raise.	Raise	
You Don't Really Need It	Donate Pancreas at the Hospital before time runs out to earn a raise.	Raise	
Co-worker Problems	Become Friends with [Sim Name] with you to improve your relationship with your co-workers.	Performance +25	
Friends in High Places	Become friends with [Sim Name] before time runs out to earn a raise.	Raise	
Lice!	Check Students for Lice before time runs out to earn a job performance boost.	Performance +20	
Friends in Good Places	Become [set relationship level]s with [Sim Name] to get a raise.	Raise	
To the Rescue!	Save Politician at the [set location] before time runs out to earn a cash reward.	§2,000	
Caring for the Careless	Stay at work until closing time to earn a job performance increase.	Performance +25	
The Appropriately Named Deathfish	Stay at work until closing time to earn a job performance increase.	Performance +25	
Timely Vaccinations	Vaccinate Scientists at the Science Facility before time runs out to earn a raise.	Raise	

MILITARY OPPORTUNITIES

Opportunity	Hint	Reward	Extra Reward
Promoting the Military	Promote Military at [set location] before time runs out to earn a cash bonus.	§2,000	
Escaping the Pit	Read Getting Out of the Pit and return to work.	Performance +15	Boss Relationship +20
Zen and Airplane Maintenance	Read Advanced Elbow Lubricant Techniques and return to work.	Performance +15	Boss Relationship +20
New Stripes, New Lingo	Read Learning to Speak Officer and return to work.	Performance +20	Boss Relationship +25
Piloting Made Simple	Read Learn to Fly in 21 Days! and return to work.	Performance +20	Boss Relationship +25
No Whining!	Read Dealing with Whining from Engines and Pilots and return to work.	Performance +20	Boss Relationship +25
Lots of Ugly	Read How to Take the Ugly for the Team and return to work.	Performance +25	Boss Relationship +25
More than Awesome Shades	Read Beyond the Aviator Glasses and return to work.	Performance +25	Boss Relationship +25
Cat Wrangler	Read Herding Cats and return to work.	Performance +30	Boss Relationship +20
Honk if You Love Goose	Read Coping with Geese and Vipers and return to work.	Performance +30	Boss Relationship +20
Military Contracts	Deliver Package at City Hall to earn a job performance boost.	Performance +20	
General Staff Stationery	Deliver Package at City Hall to earn a job performance boost.	Performance +20	
A H.O.R.S.E. of Course	Attempt H.O.R.S.E. at the Military Base before time runs out to earn a raise and a job performance boost.	Performance +25	Raise

139

MILITARY OPPORTUNITIES, CONTINUED

Opportunity	Hint	Reward	Extra Reward
You Can Be My Wingman	Join Air Show at the Military Base before time runs out.	Performance +25	Boss Relationship +25, Co-Worker Relationship +30
Flightless Birds	Stay late at work to earn a job performance boost.	Performance +25	
Militaristic Athletics	Compete in RELAY at the Military Base to increase your relationship with your co-workers.	Co-Worker Relationship +35, Boss Relationship +20	Performance +25
Congratulations on the Promotion	Throw a party with [Sim Name] on the invite list before time runs out to improve your relationship with your co-workers.	Co-Worker Relationship +20	
Stellar Performance	Throw a party with [Sim Name] on the invite list before time runs out to improve your relationship with your co-workers.	Co-Worker Relationship +25	
Saved Sims	Throw a party at your house with [Sim Name] on the invite list before time runs out to improve your relationship with your co-workers.	Co-Worker Relationship +25	
Finding New Recruits	Attend Recruitment Event at the School before time runs out to earn a job performance boost.	Performance +25	
The R.H.A.T. Race	Attempt R.H.A.T. at the Military Base before time runs out to earn a raise and a job performance boost.	Performance +25	Raise
Committee Hearing	Present Report at the Military Base to earn a job performance boost and improve your relationship with your boss.	Performance +25	Boss Relationship +25
Space Crisis!	Stay at work until the crisis is averted to earn a large cash bonus.	§4,000	Performance +25
Evening Patrol	Stay late at work to earn a relationship boost with your squad mates.	Co-Worker Relationship +25	
Late Night Latrines	Stay late at work to earn a relationship boost with your squad mates.	Co-Worker Relationship +25	
Aerial Laser Tag	Stay at work to finish the competition, earn a job performance boost, and become the most popular pilot on base!	Performance +20	Boss Relationship +25, Co-Worker Relationship +30
King of the Hill	Stay at work to finish the competition, earn a job performance boost, and become the best pilot on base!	Performance +25	Boss Relationship +25, Co-Worker Relationship +30

MUSIC OPPORTUNITIES

Opportunity	Hint	Reward	Extra Reward
Floating in the Sea	Read Getting Noticed in a Sea of Fans and return to work.	Performance +15	Boss Relationship +20
The Rockiest Road That Is Rock	Read Life on the Hard Rocky Road and return to work.	Performance +15	Boss Relationship +20
Please, No Ego	Read Don't Upstage the Band and return to work.	Performance +20	Boss Relationship +25
Cat Herding to Music	Read Herding Cats: Music Edition and return to work.	Performance +20	Boss Relationship +25
It Shines, It Sparkles	Read Diamonds in the Rough and return to work.	Performance +20	Boss Relationship +25
Keeping the Rhythm	Read It's More than Rhyme Books and return to work.	Performance +25	Boss Relationship +25
It's Synergy!	Read True Symphonic Synergy and return to work.	Performance +25	Boss Relationship +25
First Rule of Rock	Read Developing Good Rock Habits and return to work.	Performance +30	Boss Relationship +20
Becoming a Legend	Read Legends of Rock and return to work.	Performance +30	Boss Relationship +20
The Greatest Symphony Ever	Read Improving Conductivity Between Brass and Woodwinds and return to work.	Performance +30	Boss Relationship +20
Learn That Tune!	Learn the composition in your inventory and return to work to earn some cash and a job performance increase.	Performance +35	§250

MUSIC OPPORTUNITIES, CONTINUED

Opportunity	Hint	Reward	Extra Reward
Filing the Application	Submit Application at City Hall to improve your relationship with your boss and earn a job performance increase.	Boss Relationship +15	Performance +20
On Tour!	Perform three concerts at the Theatre to increase job performance and improve your relationship with your co-workers.	Performance +25	Co-Worker Relationship +20
The Set Up	Help Set Up at the Theatre before time runs out to earn some cash and improve your job performance.	§500	Performance +20
A Skilled Guitarist	Earn a skill level increase with the guitar to improve your job performance.	Performance +25	
Battle of the Bands!	Play Battle of the Bands at the Stadium before time runs out to earn a cash bonus.	§5,000	
The Cinematic Score	Play Symphony at the Theatre before time runs out to earn a cash bonus.	§5,000	
Audio Study	Listen to the stereo until your Sim is enjoying the music to improve job performance and your relationship with co-workers.	Performance +25	Co-Worker Relationship +30
Music Class!	Teach Class at the School before time runs out to earn some cash and a job performance increase.	§500	Performance +20
Stick Around for the Music	Stay late at work to improve your relationship with co-workers and job performance.	Co-Worker Relationship +25	Performance +20

POLITICS OPPORTUNITIES

Opportunity	Hint	Reward	Extra Reward
Wax Away	Read Wax Until There's No More and return to work.	Performance +15	Boss Relationship +20
Hi, I'm Chad	Read Cheating With Chads and return to work.	Performance +15	Boss Relationship +20
Smear It On	Read The Joys of Smear Campaigning and return to work.	Performance +20	Boss Relationship +25
You Really Mean Yes	Read There is No No and return to work.	Performance +20	Boss Relationship +25
Taze Cautiously	Read Taze Gently and return to work.	Performance +20	Boss Relationship +25
Lend Your Ear	Read An Earmark Economy and return to work.	Performance +25	Boss Relationship +25
Pork, the other Legislation	Read Yay, Pork Barrels! and return to work.	Performance +25	Boss Relationship +25
Gerrymandering	Read Gerrymandapalooza and return to work.	Performance +30	Boss Relationship +20
A Free Free Free World	Read A Free Free Free World and return to work.	Performance +30	Boss Relationship +20
Care to Make a Donation?	Meet with Sims and obtain X Campaign Fund donations to receive a raise.	Raise	
Cleaning Out the Phone Book	Become Enemies with [Sim Name] to earn a promotion.	Promotion	
The Bachman-Wood Exam	Discuss Exam at City Hall before time runs out to earn a raise.	Raise	
A Party of Large Wigs	Attend Party at the [set location] before time runs out to earn a cash bonus.	§2,400	
Aiding the Victims	Hold Aid Meeting at City Hall to earn a large cash bonus.	§4,000	
Key Donor	Ask for Donations on [Sim Name] before time runs out for a major campaign contribution!	Raise	
Election Check	Assist Voting Station at the School before time runs out to get a job performance boost.	Performance +25	
Foreign Affairs	Attend Top Secret Meeting at the Military Base before time runs out to earn a cash bonus.	§1,000	
Headline Worthy Event	Throw a Campaign Fundraiser with [Sim Name] invited to earn a job performance increase.	Performance +25	
It's Your Life	Write your Life Story and bring it to work in order to boost to your career.	Performance +25	Raise
Funds for Furniture	Throw a fundraising party using the phone and raise at least §10,000 for a big cash reward.	§6,000	

141

POLITICS OPPORTUNITIES, CONTINUED

Opportunity	Hint	Reward	Extra Reward
Thanks for the Memories	Write your Political Memoirs and bring them to work in order to boost your career performance and earn a raise.	Performance +25	Raise
Chat with the Police	Make [Sim Name] your [set relationship level] to earn a raise.	Raise	
A Friendly Economic Discussion	Make [Sim Name] your [set relationship level] to earn a raise.	Raise	
In the News Tonight	Give Interview at the Journalism Office before time runs out to boost your career.	Performance +25	
The Cutest Photo Shoot	Attend Photo Shoot at the Hospital before time runs out to improve your job performance.	Performance +25	
Speaking Engagement	Give Speech at the School before time runs out to boost your job performance.	Performance +25	
Let's Dine	Dine with [Sim Name] before time runs out to improve your relationship with your boss.	Boss Relationship +20	
Meet and Greet	Meet 4 new Sims to give your career a boost.	Performance +25	
In Shape, In Office	Work Out for [X amount of time] via the method of your choice to earn a raise.	Raise	
Policing the Paper Trail	Deliver Documents at the Police Station before time runs out to earn a raise.	Raise	
The Business of Documentation	Deliver Documents at the Business Office before time runs out to earn a raise.	Raise	
Criminal Collusion	Deliver Documents to the Criminal Hideout before time runs out to earn a raise.	Raise	
A Military Mistake	Deliver Documents to the Military Base before time runs out to earn a raise.	Raise	
Shred-Handed	Destroy the shredded documents in your inventory within the time limit in order to impress your boss.	Boss Relationship +25	
A Rousing Oration	Meet with [Sim Name] and Give Inspirational Speech to receive a job performance boost.	Performance +25	
Rocking for Political Gain	Perform Concert at the Stadium before time runs out to earn a job performance boost.	Performance +20	
Business up Front, Party in Back	Throw a party at your house with [Sim Name] invited to receive a job performance increase.	Performance +20	

PROFESSIONAL SPORTS OPPORTUNITIES

Opportunity	Hint	Reward	Extra Reward
Adonis in the Making	Train until you can't possibly become more muscular, then head back to the Stadium to earn your cash bonus.	§2,400	
Flex and Bend	Train [Sim Name] on the exercise machine for [X amount of time] to earn some cash and improve your relationship.	§350	Relationship w/ Sim +30
Bounce the Crowd	Work as Bouncer at the Theatre before time runs out to earn some cash on the side.	§500	
The Complete Circuit	Work Out using the TV or stereo, and swim for 30 minutes to earn a cash bonus.	§300	
Jog Everywhere	Jog [X amount of time] then return the device for a cash prize.	§550	
Add It Up	Improve your Athletic skill by one level, then return to the Stadium for a cash reward.	§350	
Going Pro	Go to the Stadium and get a job in the Professional Sports career to earn starting cash and performance bonuses.	§250	Performance +25
Bend and Flex	Train [Sim Name] for [X amount of time] to earn some cash and improve your relationship.	§250	Relationship w/ Sim +30
Frequent Fatigue	Work out until Fatigued X times then return to the Stadium to earn a cash prize.	§400	

PROFESSIONAL SPORTS OPPORTUNITIES, CONTINUED

Opportunity	Hint	Reward	Extra Reward
Bursting with Energy	Work Out until you become Pumped to improve your Athletic skill.	Athletic Skill +5	Oddly Powerful Moodlet
Sprint to the Finish!	Work Out using the Quick Burst tone for [X amount of time] to improve your Athletic skill.	Athletic Skill +5	
At the Health Seminar	Lecture at Seminar at the hospital before time runs out to earn some cash.	§250	Relationship w/ Sim +30
Muscle Showdown	Attend Competition at the Stadium before time runs out to improve your Athletic skills and win a cash prize.	§750	Athletic Skill +10
Push It!	Work Out using the Push Self option for [X amount of time] to improve your Athletic skill.	Athletic Skill +8	
No Sweat!	Work Out using the Don't Break a Sweat option for [X amount of time] to improve your Athletic skill.	Athletic Skill +5	

SCIENCE OPPORTUNITIES

Opportunity	Hint	Reward	Extra Reward
Funding the Lab	Deliver Report to City Hall before time runs out to increase your job performance.	Performance +20	
Late Night Science	Stay at work late to improve your relationship with your co-workers.	Co-Worker Relationship +20	
Burning the Late Night Bunsen	Stay at work late to improve your relationship with your co-workers.	Co-Worker Relationship +20	
Extra Appendages Are Fun	Read Living with Mutation and return to work to increase your job performance and your relationship with your boss.	Performance +15	Boss Relationship +20
Hazardous Gizmos	Read Dangerous Device Disposal and return to work to increase your job performance and your relationship with your boss.	Performance +15	Boss Relationship +20
Practical Like a Fox	Read Practical Science: From Boast to Beaker and return to work to increase your job performance and your relationship with your boss.	Performance +20	Boss Relationship +25
Ka-Boom and More	Read Nitrates: They're Not Just for Exploding and return to work to increase your job performance and your relationship with your boss.	Performance +20	Boss Relationship +25
Strange Indeed	Read Strange Correlations of Little Shops and Venues and return to work to increase your job performance and relationship with your boss.	Performance +20	Boss Relationship +25
A Pig Too Far	Read When Pigs Fly: Going Too Far and return to work to increase your job performance and your relationship with your boss.	Performance +25	Boss Relationship +25
What Not to Catch	Read Goldfish, Piranha, and Other Friendly Creatures and return to work to increase your job performance and relationship with your boss.	Performance +25	Boss Relationship +25
Finger Pointing and You	Read Advanced Deniability Procedures and return to work to increase your job performance and your relationship with your boss.	Performance +30	Boss Relationship +20
Do the Robot	Read The Evolution of the Robo-Llama and return to work to increase your job performance and your relationship with your boss.	Performance +30	Boss Relationship +20
Of Fish, Robots, and Robot Things	Give Presentation at City Hall before time runs out to earn a raise.	Raise	
The Best Evaporating Dish Is a Clean One	Wash Dishes in your inventory to increase your job performance.	Performance +20	
Learn a Thing or Two	Conduct Research on your home computer to increase your job performance.	Performance +30	
Fix It!	Repair Thingamajig at the Science Facility to improve your relationship with your co-workers and earn a cash bonus.	Co-Worker Relationship +20	§1,000
Nourishment for Herbivores	Bring X home grown harvestables of Very Nice or better quality to work to earn a cash bonus.	§1,000	

SCIENCE OPPORTUNITIES, CONTINUED

Opportunity	Hint	Reward	Extra Reward
Catch of the Day	Catch X [fish type] and bring them to work with you to earn a raise and job performance increase.	Performance +25	Raise
Global Science Fair	Attend Competition at the School before time runs out to increase your job performance and improve your relationship with your co-workers.	Co-Worker Relationship +25	Performance +25
A Meeting of Minds	Attend Symposium at the [set location] before time runs out to improve your relationship with your boss and co-workers, as well as increase your job performance.	Performance +30	Boss Relationship +25, Co-Worker Relationship +30
One Shall Fall	Stop Dr. Iniquitous at the [set location] before time runs out to earn a cash bonus.	§4,000	

Special Opportunities

The third category of opportunities is not related to a Sim's career or skill set. Any Sim might encounter one of these opportunities, provided they explore Sunset Valley and meet enough people.

SPECIAL OPPORTUNITIES

Opportunity	Hint	Reward	Extra Reward
Music Appreciation Day	Play the Guitar X times at the park to get an Inspired moodlet.	Inspired Moodlet	
Chess Tournament	Win X Chess Games to earn some money and win another chess tourney.	§650	
Community Meet and Greet	Socialize with X Sims to receive the Awesome Party moodlet and become a Socialite.	Awesome Party Moodlet	
Amateur Olympics	Attend Amateur Olympics on the Stadium for a chance to win money, get Pumped, and become an Olympian.	Pumped Moodlet	§1,000
Eating Contest	Enter Eating Contest on the restaurant for a chance to win money and become an Eating Champion.	Stuffed Moodlet	§1,000
Foosball Contest	Win X foosball games to earn money and become a Foosball Champion.	§800	
Neighborhood Grill-A-Thon	Grill X times to improve relationship with Townies and receive a Community Griller Award.	§1,000	
Oh My Ghost!	If someone close to you has recently died, you can bring their ashes to the science lab to restore their ghost.	Playable Ghost Sim	

Relationships and Aging
• • •

Relationships

...s been the mantra of mothers since time began: You are judged by the company you keep. Well, ...thout walking outside the boundaries of your lot and exploring Sunset Valley, you'll never discover ...y such company to be judged by. Socializing with other Sims is an important part of life in Sunset ...lley, and not only because Social is one of your Sims' needs, like Hunger or Hygiene. Developing ...lationships is how you will discover exciting opportunities, meet new friends, and perhaps even ...art the next generation of your family.

...lationships in *The Sims 3* actually unfold not that differently from those in the real world. How you ...eat other Sims is the biggest metric in your overall relationship with them. If you insult another Sim, ...xpect them to get upset in the immediate conversation and for that to have a lasting effect on your ...lationship. Conversely, a constant stream of support or praise will boost the immediate interaction ...d lead to a longer-lasting positive relationship. Developing a successful romance means spotting if ...e other party is receptive to your advances and knowing when to cool your jets.

...nlike *The Sims 2*, the social structure of *The Sims 3* is not navigated with obvious metrics. There ...a touch of mystery in conversations that makes socializing more organic. Instead of running the ...umbers to see if another Sim will be receptive to a specific social interaction (or just known as a ...ocial"), you need to consider the current attitude of the Sim in the conversation, often referred to ... the Target. (Your current Sim is known as the Actor.) That attitude affects the long-term status of ...ur relationships with different Sims.

...efore getting too deep into the intricacies ...f the social system in *The Sims 3*, let's ...etail some basic concepts that will appear ...roughout the remainder of this chapter: ...ort-term context, long-term relationship, ...d commodities. Understanding these three ...ctors is the key to brushing back some of ...e mystery of social interaction with the ...tizens of Sunset Valley.

...ong-Term Relationship (LTR)

...e long-term relationship represents the state ...f the relationship between two Sims, which ...xtends beyond the time during which a ...onversation is taking place. LTR essentially ...escribes the way two Sims view each other ... a given moment. Every Sim outside the ...mily starts out as a Stranger. Once initial ...ontact is made, the LTR moves up to ...cquaintance and can never fall back into ...tranger. However, Acquaintance is the ...roverbial fork in the road. From here, the LTR ...an blossom into friendship or deteriorate ... to rivalry.

The LTR is visually measured by the bar below the portrait of the Sim you are conversing with. If the ...lationship develops in a positive manner, the

right half of the bar fills. Positive relationship status is noted with green. If the relationship is souring, that meter empties back out and can even dip into the left side, which is red. The red bar denotes a negative LTR.

> ### NOTE
> The natural tendency of the LTR is to decay toward zero from either end of the relationship spectrum. Zero puts you back into Acquaintance territory. Decay occurs naturally with each passing day that you do not contact a Sim you have a relationship with.

> ### TIP
> Look in the Relationship panel to easily check out your current LTR with all Sims you have contacted.

How to achieve the different LTRs is explained in the Friendships (and Enemies) section of this chapter, but here is a list of all of the LTRs:

- Stranger
- Acquaintance
- Disliked
- Distant Friend
- Friend
- Good Friend
- Best Friend
- Best Friends Forever (teens only)
- Romantic Interest
- Ex-Spouse
- Ex
- Enemy
- Old Enemies
- Partner
- Fiancee
- Spouse

Short-Term Context (STC)

Short-term contexts are what a Sim thinks about the other Sim in the course of the current conversation, not as an LTR. The STC is displayed in the conversation box in the screen's upper-left as the conversation unfolds. For example, the box may say that "Jenny thinks Sasha is being amusing." STC is affected by the kind of socials used in a conversation. Each social has a commodity

Relationships and Aging

attached to it that directs the course of a conversation. These are all of the STCs:

STCs

- Dull
- Drab
- Insufferably Tedious
- Odd
- Creepy
- Frightening
- Very scary
- Impolite
- Insulting
- Unforgivably Rude
- OK
- Friendly
- Very Friendly
- Amusing
- Funny
- Hilarious
- Flirty
- Seductive
- Hot
- Awkward
- Very Awkward
- Steamed

Not all STCs are symmetrical. One Sim can have a totally different impression of a conversation than the other. The only symmetrical STCs are those associated with the following commodities: friendly, funny, amorous, and steamed. It is very possible that Jenny could think Sasha is being Dull while Sasha does not.

STC also modulates the way socials are accepted. Instead of just hot and cold, STCs and their respective commodities temper reactions. Depending on your LTR and STC, you can see different degrees of reaction to a social. Trying to kiss a Sim on the cheek in the context of the Flirty STC will be a lot more successful than the Friendly STC.

NOTE

The STC of a conversation contributes to the kind of decay an LTR undergoes each day.

Commodity

So, each STC is associated with a commodity? What's a commodity? Think of these as the general categories a social or STC falls under. They are based on specific emotions we all feel, such as awkwardness or love. Use the commodity of a social to inspire and STC, which will in turn effect the overall LTR. Here are the seven commodities:

- Boring
- Creepy
- Insulting
- Friendly
- Funny
- Amorous
- Awkward
- Steamed

As you look at the different STCs and socials in this chapter, check the associated commodities so you can push a conversation in the desired direction.

Decay and Normalizing

Relationships do not operate under inertia. They decay over time if not tended to, even if that time period is as short as 24 hours. This is why regular socializing is so important. Decay is not necessarily a negative slide. While positive relationship can indeed decay into mere Acquaintance, a negative relationship can normalize into the far more desirable Acquaintance. (Apparently Sims don't keep grudges quite like we do.)

Decay can be slowed by something as simple as a phone call.

As mentioned, the STC of a conversation contributes to LTR decay. These commodities dictate the decay. The amount of decay is also determined by the LTR itself. An LTR above zero, which starts heading toward positive territory, will have a different amount of decay from a specific STC/commodity than a negative LTR, which is below zero. No hard math on-screen shows the numerical value of an LTR, but you can sort of eyeball it.

Use this table to understand the way decay occurs as different STCs (with their respective commodities) are used in social encounters

DECAY

STC	Commodity	Normalization from Negative LTR	Decay from Positive LTR
Dull	Boring	1	-2
Drab	Boring	1	-2
Insufferably Tedious	Boring	1	-2
Odd	Creepy	1	-2
Creepy	Creepy	1	-5
Frightening	Creepy	1	-5
Very Scary	Creepy	1	-5
Impolite	Insulting	1	-5
Insulting	Insulting	1	-5
Unforgivably Rude	Insulting	1	-5
OK	Friendly	3	-2
Friendly	Friendly	3	-2
Very Friendly	Friendly	3	-2
Amusing	Funny	3	-2
Funny	Funny	3	-2
Hilarious	Funny	3	-2
Flirty	Amorous	3	-2
Seductive	Amorous	3	-2
Hot	Amorous	3	-2
Awkward	Awkward	1	-5
Very Awkward	Awkward	1	-5
Steamed	Steamed	1	-5

So, here's an example of how this decay works: Jenny and Sasha are Good Friends. If their last encounter was Impolite, then after a few days, the LTR will decay to just Friends. Conversely, if Jenny and Sasha have the Disliked LTR, the relationship will normalize int Acquaintance if the last STC was Friendly.

result in such pleasing moodlets as Flattered or Nicely Decorated, such as if you are invited over to a friend's house that has some great environmental bonuses.

You've seen the general list of LTRs, but now you need to understand how each one is achieved. Because a color bar is used to measure LTR instead of numbers, use the numbers in this table to approximate the amount of the bar above/below the center of the bar needed to achieve the LTR. Some LTRs are achieved by specific socials. Some are achieved by a combination of LTR and a specific social.

NOTE

Decay and normalization are not confined only to friends and pre-marriage Sims. This also applies to familial relationships, such as father or wife. However, the bonds of blood are far deeper than those of friends, so it takes a lot more to adversely affect a familial relationship. Not that it cannot be done. Oh, you can absolutely sour a familial relationship with insulting socials.

riendships (and Enemies)

ow that we've explained the four basics f socialization—LTR, STC, commodity, and ecay—let's look at how relationships bloom nd wither...and what you can do to affect ne course of these relationships. Naturally, ms want friends. Social is a need, after all. ocializing and having friends have a number f different effects on the course of your ims' lives. Developing positive LTRs will:

- **Fulfill wishes:** Some Sims desire to achieve certain LTRs with other Sims, as noted in their wishes. The wish will say which Sim you need to develop the desired LTR with. Some Wishes are more basic, and just desire a certain social, such as just chatting or kissing.

- **Boost Mood:** Social is a need and unless your Sim is a Loner, dipping into negative territory with the Social need will lead to negative moodlets. Negative moodlets pulls down the overall mood, which curbs your chance to earn Lifetime Happiness Points.

- **Promotions:** As seen in the Simology chapter, most of the careers use Relationship with Co-Worker (or a similar idea) as a metric for promotion. You can use tones to meet and chat with co-workers at the job site, but socializing with co-workers outside of work hours can help fast-track promotions.

riendships are a universally positive thing. Having a friends, particularly in an expanded ocial circle, opens you up to a wealth of opportunities for receiving good moodlets. ositive moodlets are the key to earning those oveted Lifetime Rewards. Friendships can

LTR ACHIEVEMENT

LTR	How to Achieve	Visitor Privileges
Stranger	All relationships start here. These two Sims have not yet met, but are aware of each other.	1
Acquaintance	You have interacted with this Sim at least once.	1
Disliked	Relationship level drops to -20 or below.	-1
Distant Friend	If Friends, then relationship level drops below 40 but remains above 20.	1
Friend	Relationship level reaches 40.	2
Good Friend	Relationship level reaches 60.	2
Best Friend	Relationship level reaches 80.	3
Old Friend	Relationship has been above 40 for at least 14 days.	2
Best Friends Forever	Use the BFF social and stay above 60 in the relationship. This is a teen-only LTR.	3
Romantic Interest	Use Confess Attraction or a Kiss social successfully and the relationship must be above zero.	2
Ex Spouse	Use Divorce social.	2
Ex	Use Break Up social.	2
Enemy	Use Declare Nemesis social and relationship is lower than zero.	-1
Old Enemies	Have been Enemies for 14 days.	-1
Partner	Use Propose Going Steady social.	3
Fiancee	Use Propose Marriage social.	4
Spouse	Get married (use Private Wedding social or Get Married at a Wedding Party).	4
Seductive	Amorous	3
Hot	Amorous	3
Awkward	Awkward	1
Very Awkward	Awkward	1
Steamed	Steamed	1

VISITOR PRIVILEGES

Visitor Privileges are things that a Sim can do on another Sim's lot. Some privileges are basic, such as using the toilet to relieve the Bladder need. But as the LTR increases, more interactions become available. The higher the privilege number, the more you/they can do. At just 1, Sims can do basic things like eat food offered to them, clean dishes, and use the bathroom. As that number increases, Sims can start rooting around in the fridge for quick snacks and use the computer. At 4, well, the bedroom comes into play. But more on visitors in a moment...

Achieving these LTRs is done through conversations—and conversations are made up of socials. But there is much more to a conversation/STC than just employing a handful of socials. A Sim's personality is hugely important in determining which socials can be used—and should be used. And it's not only the traits of the Actor that matter. Learning the traits of the Target is also quite important.

Traits and LTRs

An outgoing Sim, such as one with a Good Sense of Humor, is adept at telling jokes. Telling a successful joke slows the daily decay of an LTR and is pretty effective at normalizing relations with an enemy. However, knowing that the Target Sim has No Sense of Humor should moderate whether or not you try to increase friendship by telling jokes. Perhaps talking about books would go further, especially if you discover that the Target Sim is a Bookworm. This makes learning traits an essential part of the socialization game.

Performing trait-related socials is a good way to learn a Target's trait. For example, giving an Amorous Hug to another Sim with the Hopeless Romantic trait reveals that they are indeed a Hopeless Romantic. Being mean to a Target Sim and eliciting a return insult can reveal a Mean-Spirited Sim.

Use our complete list of socials in this chapter to determine which socials are best to use on certain traits—and which socials you can use only if you have a specific trait.

BROWNIE BITES

So, what good is it to have an enemy? Personally, I did not see any real benefit to having enemies in Sunset Valley. In fact, when I developed an enemy or discovered that somebody did not like me, I usually directed some of my daily attention toward fixing that, because having enemies can lead to negative moodlets whenever you are around them. Finding your Sim in an automatic conversation with an enemy will result in the Enemy! moodlet (-10 mood whenever that Sim is around) and risk the Offended/Humiliated moodlets (-15 mood each). Because I wanted to get as many Lifetime Rewards as possible, I generally went out of my way to smooth the waters with Sims and avoid situations that could result in these moodlets.

Romance

All you need is love. Some forgotten pop band sung that and even though the band's name has been scattered to history, the concept still rings true in Sunset Valley.

NOTE

Romance in Sunset Valley is blind to gender. Sims of the same gender can have romantic relationships if directed to do so. The only factors that can prevent two Sims from falling in love and having a romantic relationship are age and blood. Siblings and children/parents cannot have romantic relationships. Sims of wildly different age groups cannot have romantic relationships, either. A teen cannot have a romantic relationship with an adult or elderly Sim. Children and toddlers cannot have romantic relationships with any Sims—not until they reach teen level.

Start the Spark

You cannot immediately engage another Sim in a love affair. You must establish a Friendship first via positive socials with the proper commodities. So, first turn a Stranger into an Acquaintance and then start boosting that Acquaintance into a Friend-related LTR through positive, friendly socials.

Now, established Friendships have the potential to tip into amorous relationships by using socials with the amorous commodity in order to elicit love-related STCs, such as Flirty, Seductive, or Hot. Sounds technical, doesn't it? Well, think about it this way: You wouldn't try just any old line if you really wanted to advance a relationship, would you? No, you' try to steer the conversation toward romance through specific approaches. In *The Sims 3*, these approaches are the socials with the amorous commodity.

Can this friendship be turned into a love affair? With the right amorous socials, it can. Even if they have seen each other eat waffles on the couch in their underwear.

The LTR that determines the difference between a friendship and a love affair is Romantic Interest. To achieve this LTR, you need to have the relationship at least above zero (in the green zone on the bar) and then use the Confess Attraction social or attempt a kiss social.

Rejection

Not every pass will succeed. You need to judge the current LTR appropriately before making your move via an amorous social, such as Confess Attraction or Kiss. Know a little something about the other Sim first. (Whether or not they are married is a good start.) If you try to Kiss or Confess Attraction to a Sim who is not receptive of your amorous social, you get the Awkward STC which is the first rejection of romance. You can recover from this by redirecting the conversation and hopefully having the conversation on a more positive STC, such as Amusing or Friendly. Keep up the rejected passes and you risk moving into Odd or Creepy territory thanks to the creepy commodity. Leaving encounters in STCs with the awkward or creepy commodity will take big hits on your LTR due to the negative decay. It will take real time and effort to reverse course on this.

NOTE

Being rejected does not forever discount the idea of a romantic relationship. It just means you need to do a little more homework (pleasant socials) before trying again.

Building a Romance

You professed attraction to another Sim and they didn't turn you down—excellent. Now

you have the Romantic Interest LTR, which opens up a whole new trajectory for your relationship. How can you build this romance into something more than a little bit of mutual attraction?

Here is where you need to use the list of STCs—particularly the amorous ones. You want the other Sim to find you Flirty, Seductive, and eventually Hot. To keep boosting the relationship and STC, use sequential amorous socials. A simple Compliment Appearance is a good way to get things started, but soon you can move on to Kisses and Amorous Hugs. Keep it up and get that other Sim Hot!

TIP

Here's where the Great Kisser trait comes in handy. The Great Kisser's kisses really boost the STC of interactions that involve lip-locking.

You're in Love (Now What?)

You've loved up on another Sim and now you have a definite love affair going—where do you go from here? Well, you can add some structure to the relationship by using the Propose Going Steady social when the STC is Hot. If the other Sim accepts (and if they are Hot, they will) then you are now Partners.

Partners is not the top of the mountain, though. From here, you can move to Fiancee. To get engaged, use the Propose Marriage social when you are Partners. This social will be accepted and then you can start planning

the eventual wedding if so desired. To get married, either throw a wedding party and then use the Get Married social at the party or just use the Have Private Marriage social on your partner to enjoy a small ceremony.

TIP

For more on parties, including the wedding party, please see the Parties section of this chapter.

The End of the Affair

Not all marriages/partnerships end well. Some of them devolve into bitter endings, either through the natural dissolution of love or the unfortunate actions of one of the Sims in the relationship. How you break up a relationship depends on the current status of the LTR itself. If you are married, you must sink the relationship via negative STCs. Be insulting. Be rude. Be mean. Soon, you will have access to the Divorce social, which ends the marriage. If you are in a Partnership or engaged, you can sink the relationship and then use the Break Up social.

CAUTION

Destroying a relationship will cause great damage to your mood.

Depending on the relationship, a break up can leave a lot of damage in its wake. A Sim who must move out as a result of being divorced is removed from the household and leaves all belongings and children behind.

Moving Out

Sims will move for a number of reasons, such as just wanting to buy a new house. However, when it comes time for a Sim to leave the house under unfortunate circumstances, you can banish a Sim with the Move Out

interaction with the computer or telephone, or use the Ask to Move Out social when the relationship has cratered.

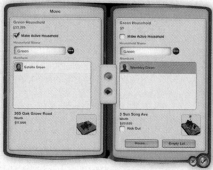

When you ask to move, the Move box appears in the center of the screen and all action pauses. On the left side of the Move box, you see current household, the people in it, and the household value. This household is marked as the active household. The list of Sims in that household appears in the box, too.

To boot a Sim, select them from the list of Sims in a household and press the right arrow button to move them to the right side of the Move box. You have a few options now for terminating the current household arrangement. If you want to mercilessly kick them out, just check the Kick Out option and approve it. The other Sim is sent out the front door. They catch a cab and that's that.

It's time to say goodbye.

However, you can actually choose to either follow the Sim leaving the household or at least set them up with another life. If you choose House or Empty Lot, you select a lot or available house for the departing Sim to live on (as long as it is within their household budget—a departing Sim is given some of the household's money). You can now send that Sim on their way or make the new lot the active household. The Sim(s) in your current

household are left behind to act on their own and you follow the departing Sim as he or she enters the next phase of life.

Jealousy and Betrayal

Sims who are married, engaged, or in partnerships do not have to remain loyal to their commitments. They can flirt with other Sims, or take it a step further and actually cheat on their partners. Any social or interaction with the amorous commodity performed with or on a Sim other than the partner is considered cheating. Cheating requires a little set-up, as you do actually need to raise the LTR with another Sim into at least Friend and then use the Kiss or Confess Attraction social. Once the second Romantic Interest has been initiated, then you are indeed playing a dangerous game.

As long as the Sim being cheated on is not aware of the activity, there is no LTR hit between the cheater and the cheatee. However, should indiscretions be uncovered, jealousy in triggered. The severity of the indiscretion affects the amount of jealousy and what that jealously does to the LTR.

- **Flirting:** A Flirty social will result in a slight relationship hit. This can later be smoothed over.

- **Hugs and Kisses:** If a hug or kiss is discovered, then the relationship takes a bigger hit. The cheatee is saddled with the Betrayed moodlet.

- **Make Out or WooHoo:** Now you just get what you deserve. If such indiscretions are revealed or stumbled upon, the relationship is ripped apart. The LTR takes a huge hit and the cheatee gets the Betrayed moodlet. This level of cheating can spoil an engagement.

Betrayal ripples beyond the cheater and cheatee, too. Other Sims can react to an af in a number of different ways. Cheating can damage the LTR with other Sims:

- If Sim A and Sim B are married, but Sims A is caught cheating with Sim C, the LTR of Sim A to any Sim that both Sims A ar Sim C know will take a hit.

- If a child or toddler witnesses the cheating, the LTR takes a hit.

- If a family member or friend discovers th cheating, they scold the cheater and the the LTR takes a hit.

- If a Sim witnesses cheating, then that Sin can Accuse of Cheating or report the affair back to the cheatee.

Socializing

The building and dismantling of relationship are based on the interactions you have with other Sims. These interactions are called socials. Socials are the building blocks of a conversation that steer STC. Each social has a commodity that has an effect on the STC, which in turn has an effect on the LTR. Selecting the right socials to advance your goals then is very important. We have compiled a complete list of all of the social in the game and detail the limits on each, as well as certain situations in which you would need or want to use a specific socia But before you consult that list, you should understand how to conduct a conversation and understand the situations where you ca be social.

NOTE

Sims will automatically engage in social behavior when left to their own devices and will do so in the spirit of their traits and the current LTR. If one of your Sims starts chatting up a co-worker outside of the office and they have a positive LTR, the Sim is not going to do anything unexpected to damage that LTR.

Social Opportunities

Sunset Valley is one big ball of social opportunities. Some of them fall into your lap—some of them must be sought out and arranged. There are several situations where you can direct the social engagement yourself. (You can meet Sims at work, but you only direct the chance encounters via tone—you do not select actual socials.) Use each of these opportunities to build and bolster LTRs so your Sim can benefit from friendships and relationships. Remember: social Sims are usually happy Sims.

Family

When you create a household through Create a Sim, you can choose to not just fashion a single Sim, but build an entire family to occupy a house. A family does not necessarily need to be blood related. A household can be up to eight Sim roomies living under one roof or any combination of family and friends. You have total control over the social of every Sim inside a family. Naturally, this gives you a bit of an advantage with seeing both sides of a conversation (you can click back and forth between Sims and look at the current STC) so you can direct it to achieve specific goals.

Family members will socialize on their own, but you will get far more benefit out of choosing the socials yourself. For example, if you have a few roomies and you decide you want two of them to take it to the next level, you can direct their socials so that neither of them feels awkward.

TIP

Blood relatives or married Sims have the benefit of being largely positive with each other in their automatic social interactions.

Welcome Wagon

When you first move into Sunset Valley and start to settle, two or three Sims will show up on your doorstep to welcome you to the neighborhood. This is the welcome wagon. Now, you are by no means required to rush outside, socialize, and even invite them inside for a long conversation. However, this is a great chance to make a few acquaintances right away, which will get you on your way to learning about new opportunities. Plus, you never know if somebody in the welcome wagon has the potential to one day be a Romantic Interest. You may meet Mr. Right, right away.

The welcome wagon does not linger terribly long. They will give you a couple hours to step outside and say hello before they dissipate back to their homes. The welcome wagon is typically made up of neighbors right around your lot. If you want to make friends from all over town, well, then you are just going to have to explore the entire town.

Meet and Greet

You do not need to rely on meeting co-workers or the welcome wagon to start making acquaintances. Sunset Valley is full of people you can meet at almost all hours of the day. All you need to do is step outside your front door every once in a while. Sometimes, all you actually need to do is just go outside the front door, because a Sim or two will usually walk by your house a few times a day. If you keep an eye on the front stoop, you may make a new friends with minimal effort.

Just wandering through the city is another way to find Sims and interact with them. When you are out running errands, such as going to the bookstore or the supermarket, don't immediately go back home. Walk around Mirabello Plaza, where you will find a great concentration of Sims. Left-click on one and strike up a conversation. You may occasionally encounter a rude Sim, but for the most part, the folks of Sunset Valley are pretty friendly.

The museum is a good place to find other Sims interested in art. Otherwise, they wouldn't be there!

Sims who play chess are into the Logic skill, so talk to them about logic-related stuff, like stars, after a game.

Use community locations as meeting places, too. Central Park or Maywood Glen are good places to go and find new friends, but so is the gym or the library. In fact, use these community locations to find Sims with similar interests, which will help you develop LTRs easier than just randomly finding somebody to talk to. If you are an athletic Sim and go to the gym, you will immediately have something in common with the Sims there and have

things to talk about, such as Athletic skills. If you like chess, go to Central Park and hang out at the chess boards to find other logic-minded Sims. You may find other anglers at lakes and the beach.

Chat up Sims at community locations to build your database of acquaintances.

Telephone and Computer

So, you met some Sims while you were out and about? An easy way to keep in contact with them in your personal telephone, which is located in your Inventory tab. When you left-click on the telephone, you have a variety of interactions for further relationships (and possibly even making a new one). You can only call Sims you have met—you cannot call strangers. Here are all of the interactions with the telephone that lead to social encounters:

◆ **Chat:** Chatting in the most common action with the telephone. You can both call a Sim or answer a call from another Sim and engage in chit-chat. Chat is a good way to keep up with friends and slow decay.

◆ **Ask on Date:** Ask a Sim you are interested in on a date. If the Sim accepts, the date begins.

◆ **Invite Over/Invite to:** You call a Sim and either invite them to come over to your lot or you invite them to meet you at a community location, such as the beach or park. If you have at least a modest LTR with the Sim you called, it is highly likely they will accept your invitation.

◆ **Call for Services:** Sometimes you need a little outside help. Call for Service connects you to a menu of Service Sim services, such as the Police, Pizza Delivery, or a Baby-sitter. For a full list of the Service Sims and their functions, see the Service Sim section of this chapter.

◆ **Throw Party:** One of the best ways to socialize is to throw a party. There are different types of parties you can throw depending on the desired occasion. Making this call brings up a menu for selecting the type of party, setting the time, setting the dress code, and inviting known Sims.

NOTE

You can also use the telephone to quit a job, retire from a job, change a ringtone, or answer and listen to a potential opportunity.

The computer is another way to keep up with Sims. To chat with Sims you know, left-click on the computer and choose the Chat interaction. From here, you can select with Sim you want to chat online with. Your Sim will sometimes perform this interaction automatically, especially if they are a Computer Whiz. Chatting on the computer helps out with the Fun need and it affects LTR by slowing decay.

Talk to Service Sim Help

Service Sims are Sims who are not friends and neighbors. However, they exist within

Sunset Valley and provide valuable services. The entire list of Service Sims is at the end of this chapter, complete with each Service Sim's function. However, these Sims are not without Social needs. When you call up a Repair Technician to take care of that clogged toilet, for example, you can chat with them directly afterward and make them an acquaintance—or even a friend if you are charismatic enough. Some Service Sims can actually become more than friends. You can have relationships with some Service Sims and even get married.

Parties

Gathering Sims for a party every once in a while is a great way to improve your LTRs or fulfill a party-related wish. As mentioned, to throw a party, you choose the Throw Party interaction from the telephone menu. Once you have the party menu up on-screen, you can designate the invitees, type of party, time of party, and dress code.

There are five types of parties in Sunset Valley:

◆ **House Party:** The house party is just a nice occasion for friends to come together and socialize.

◆ **Wedding:** A wedding party is an occasion for celebrating the impending marriage of two Sims. Sims can either get married at a wedding party or have a private ceremony.

◆ **Funeral:** If a Sim has died, family members can have a wake at a lot to get together and mourn the dead. This is a lot like a house party, but many of the social interactions are based around remembering the deceased, such as Talk Highly About.

◆ **Birthday:** When it is time to make an age transition, throw a birthday party. Birthday parties are like house parties, but with a birthday cake that causes the Sim being honored to age up.

◆ **Campaign Fundraiser:** This party is very similar to a house party, but it is only available to Sims in the Political career. Campaign fundraisers are formal parties where, if successful, Sims do not get LTR boosts, but donate cash to a campaign fund.

The funeral is a good way to send off a Sim with proper respect.

When you choose to throw a party, expect to see your guests start arriving right around the designated time. (Thankfully, you get a warning an hour before the party starts.) Before guests arrive, make sure your house is clean, provide plenty of food, and extend some form of entertainment. Ordering pizza is an easy way to provide food for a party, but you can cook stuff beforehand and have it ready. For entertainment, you can have objects around your house like a guitar, party balloons, or videogame system for guests to play with when not being wowed by your social skills. Fun objects increase the likelihood that a party will be a success.

Will everybody you invited show up? It's possible—that depends on your LTR with the Sims you invited and whether or not any of them have to work. Sims will not come to a party if it takes place during their designated work shift. There is a chance they will show up after work, though. Some Sims will even bring presents. If a Sim brings a present to the party, a note will pop up and tell you what was brought.

Once the party is underway, you need to manage it in order for it to be a success. Make sure that food is out and is plentiful. Make sure those fun objects are where Sims can get to them. And be sure to socialize! Talk to your guests so they feel welcome. Mingle and move around. Be positive.

> ### TIP
> Want that Life of the Party moodlet? Whip that party into a frenzy by using the Wooo! social on at least four party-goers. This moodlet is reserved only for Party Animal Sims.

When the party finally draws down and Sims file out the front door, it's time to find out if the party was a success. If Sims left your party because they thought it was lame, you get no benefit and suffer the Threw a Lame Party moodlet. If the Sims liked your party, you get LTR boosts with all attendees and enjoy the Threw a Great Party moodlet.

Wedding Party

When two Sims are engaged to be married, they can throw a wedding party and invite over all of their friends and acquaintances to witness the special event. The wedding party is set up just like a regular party. You need to have food and fun at the ready. When the wedding party approaches, the two Sims involved enjoy the Wedding Day moodlet boost.

The wedding is a formal occasion, so guests show up in their formal attire. You should socialize at the wedding party as usual, but the focus is definitely living up to the name of the occasion: wedding. Use the Get Married social on your partner to actually get married. This starts the exchange of vows and rings. The audience just eats this part up. When the ceremony is complete, the crowd cheers. The family of the Sim getting married enjoys a moodlet boost, such as Mother of the Bride.

The Art of the Conversation

So, you've approached another Sim, you left-clicked on them, and now you are staring at a menu of different social options. How do you navigate the social structure of a conversation? Well, your options are partially defined by your LTR, current mood, age, and your traits. Categories of socials include things like Friendly, Funny, Mean, Romantic, and Special. Special leads to socials that are encouraged by the Actor having a specific trait, such as Bookworm. Inside the Bookworm menu, there will be options to talk about books or the bookstore.

The menu of available social categories appears around your Sim's head. Left-click on an option to see what socials are available.

Relationships and Aging

Now, select a social from the category to add it to the action queue.

TIP

Socials related to a trait are noted with the symbol of the trait you saw in the Create a Sim tool. Bookworm-related socials, such as Talk About Bookstore, have a small book icon next to them.

NOTE

Social menus have a maximum of 12 options. If there are more than 12 available to a Sim, the friendly socials are the first to get cut from the menu of options.

When you select a social, it is added to your list of activities in the upper-right corner, just as if you were stacking interactions with objects. When a current social ends, the next one automatically begins. But stacking socials is not a wise strategy because you do not want to just babble away about a topic that the other Sim is just not interested in listening to. Use socials and then watch for reactions. A positive social with a positive effect is noted with a chime and a blue symbol of two Sims next to each other. A negative reaction is noted by two red Sims and a minus symbol.

Being Boring

Talking about the same things over and over gets boring to most Sims. The positive effect of a positive social is weakened the more you use it. Repeating a social can also affect the STC. Continuous droning about the same subjects will nudge the STC into Dull, Drab, or Insufferably Tedious territory. If the conversation ends on one of those STCs, the LTR suffers.

The default number of times you can repeat a social without getting boring is two. And if you break apart a conversation, you can use a social more than twice without any STC worries. Some socials can be used more than twice without dullness setting in, such as Chat. Chat has four uses before it is boring in a single conversation. However, it can be "recharged" so that the social can be used six times before it is boring. To recharge a social, you just need to break it up in the conversation. For example, let's say you use Chat four times in a row. The other Sim is not bored, but is about to be if you use it one more time. So, you change course and Talk About Books. After that social runs its course, you have recharged Chat once. Now you can use Chat again without it being boring. However, if you tried to use it again without another recharge, the social would be considered boring.

NOTE

In our chart of socials, two columns that deal with boredom: # of Uses Before Boring and # of Uses If Recharged. Use these numbers to recognize a social that can be used and recharged without adversely affecting STC.

Being Charismatic

The Charisma skill not only unlocks a series of socials, but it can also be developed by using specific socials. Socials that push the STC into

certain areas help develop the Charisma skill, so look at the commodity of socials to see they will help instigate a beneficial STC. Onc you have reached the STC, socials that prop up that STC or that are directly related to the skill will advance the Charisma skill.

CHARISMA

Short Term Context (STC)	Commodity	How Much Charisma?
OK	Friendly	Small
Friendly	Friendly	Medium
Very Friendly	Friendly	High
Amusing	Funny	Small
Funny	Funny	Medium
Hilarious	Funny	High
Flirty	Amorous	Small
Seductive	Amorous	Medium
Hot	Amorous	High

List of Socials

The follow chart details all of the Actor-Targe socials you can perform in a conversation. Use this chart to judge the effect of a social before using it by looking at the commodity and cross-referencing that with which commodities affect which STCs. Here is how the chart is broken down:

- **Social:** Name of social as seen in the conversation menu
- **Commodity:** Commodity associated wit the social
- **Actor/Target Age:** Ages in which the social is applicable
- **Social Available When?:** What prompts the use of the social
- **Required Trait:** Social is only available when Actor has this trait
- **Social Encouraged by Trait?:** Social is potentially more "powerful" due to Actor's trait
- **Social Prevented by Trait?:** Actor's trait prevents them from using this social
- **# of Uses Before Boring:** Number of uses in a conversation before the social is Dull. Default is two. Exceptions are specified.
- **# of Uses if Recharged:** Number of times the social can be used if another social interrupts the re-use of the social

Social	Commodity	Actor Age	Target Age	Social Available When?	Required Trait	Social Encouraged By Trait?	Social Prevented By Trait?	# of Uses Before Boring	# of Uses if Recharged
Accuse of Being a Crybaby	Insulting	T, Y, A, E	T, Y, A, E	Actor knows the Target is a Loser		Mean-Spirited	Good		
Accuse of Being a Workaholic	Insulting	T, Y, A, E	T, Y, A, E	Actor knows the Target is a Workaholic		Family Oriented			
Accuse of Being Boring	Insulting	T, Y, A, E	T, Y, A, E	Actor knows the Target has No Sense of Humor		Mean-Spirited	Good		
Accuse of Being Childish	Insulting	T, Y, A, E	T, Y, A, E	Actor knows the Target is Childish		Dislikes Children, Mean-Spirited	Good		
Accuse of Being Evil	Insulting	T, Y, A, E	T, Y, A, E	Actor knows the Target is Evil		Good			
Accuse of Being Insane	Insulting	T, Y, A, E	T, Y, A, E	Actor knows the Target is Insane		Mean-Spirited	Good		
Accuse of Being Unflirty	Insulting	T, Y, A, E	T, Y, A, E	Actor knows the Target is Unflirty		Flirty	Unflirty		
Accuse of Cheating	Insulting	Y, A, E	Y, A, E	Actor has had Jealousy triggered on Target		Neurotic, Hopeless Romantic		1	1
Accuse of Mean-Spiritedness	Insulting	T, Y, A, E	T, Y, A, E	Actor knows the Target is Mean-Spirited		Good, Friendly			
Admire	Friendly	C, T, Y, A, E	C, T, Y, A, E	Sims are in the Very Friendly STC and are Friends or above or on the romantic relationship		Easily Impressed, Schmoozer, Charismatic			
Amorous Hug	Amorous	T, Y, A, E	T, Y, A, E	Sims are in the Seductive STC or Flirty STC, if not Acquaintances		Hopeless Romantic		1	
Announce Birthday	Friendly	C, T, Y, A, E	C, T, Y, A, E	It is the Actor's birthday		Excitable			
Announce Engagement	Friendly	Y, A, E	C, T, Y, A, E	Actor has become engaged		Family Oriented, Hopeless Romantic, Excitable			
Announce Pregnancy	Friendly	Y, A, E	C, T, Y, A, E	Actor has become pregnant		Family Oriented, Excitable			
Announce Promotion	Friendly	T, Y, A, E	C, T, Y, A, E	Actor has gotten a promotion		Snob, Workaholic, Excitable			
Apologize	Neutral	C, T, Y, A, E	C, T, Y, A, E	Sims are in a negative STC		Friendly, Schmoozer		1	1
Applaud Hard Work	Friendly	T, Y, A, E	T, Y, A, E	Actor knows the Target is a Workaholic		Workaholic, Schmoozer			
Applaud Vegetarianism	Friendly	T, Y, A, E	T, Y, A, E	Actor knows the Target is a Vegetarian		Vegetarian, Schmoozer			
Argue	Insulting	C, T, Y, A, E	C, T, Y, A, E	Actor thinks the Target is being impolite or unforgivably rude or Sims are in Insulting STC		Hot-Headed, Mean-Spirited, Grumpy, Insane		4	
Ask About Antisocial Action	Insulting	T, Y, A, E	T, Y, A, E	Target has performed an antisocial action		Good			
Ask About Bath	Friendly	T, Y, A, E	T, Y, A, E	Actor and Target are in a committed relationship and Target has had a bath					

Relationships and Aging

Social	Commodity	Actor Age	Target Age	Social Available When?	Required Trait	Social Encouraged By Trait?	Social Prevented By Trait?	# of Uses Before Boring	# of Uses if Recharged
Ask About Day	Friendly	C, T, Y, A, E	C, T, Y, A, E	Always available		Friendly, Good, Charismatic, Schmoozer		1	1
Ask About Game	Friendly	T, Y, A, E	T, Y, A, E	Target has played a game					
Ask About Missing Work	Friendly	T, Y, A, E	T, Y, A, E	Target has the Missing Work buff		Workaholic, Neurotic			
Ask About News	Friendly	T, Y, A, E	T, Y, A, E	Target has read the newspaper		Genius			
Ask About Occupation	Friendly	T, Y, A, E	T, Y, A, E	Actor does not know the Target's career		Workaholic, Schmoozer, Ambitious			
Ask About Partner	Amorous	T, Y, A, E	T, Y, A, E	Actor does not know the Target's relationship status		Family Oriented, Flirty, Hopeless Romantic			
Ask About School	Friendly	C, T, Y, A, E	C, T, Y, A, E	Actor learns the Target goes to school		Workaholic, Family Oriented, Ambitious			
Ask About Sleep	Friendly	T, Y, A, E	T, Y, A, E	Target has slept		Heavy Sleeper, Light Sleeper			
Ask About Work	Friendly	C, T, Y, A, E	T, Y, A, E	Always available		Workaholic, Ambitious, Schmoozer			
Ask Are You OK	Friendly	T, Y, A, E	T, Y, A, E	Target has the Too Many People, Horrified, Singed, Lonely, Afraid of the Dark, or Humiliated buff		Good, Friendly	Evil, Mean-Spirited		
Ask for a Promotion	Friendly	T, Y, A, E	T, Y, A, E	Target is Actor's Boss (and it's been 3 days since the Boss was last asked)		Ambitious		1	
Ask for a Raise	Friendly	T, Y, A, E	T, Y, A, E	Target is Actor's Boss (and it's been 5 days since the Boss was last asked)		Ambitious		1	
Ask Good Book	Friendly	T, Y, A, E	T, Y, A, E	Target has read a book		Bookworm			
Ask for Campaign Donation	Friendly	Y, A, E	Y, A, E	Can ask for campaign donations		Schmoozer		1	3
Ask Service Sim to Stay Over	Friendly	C, T, Y, A, E	C, T, Y, A, E	Target is visiting the Actor at home				1	
Ask Service Sim to Stay Over Romantically	Amorous	Y, A, E	Y, A, E	Target is visiting the Actor at home		Flirty		1	1
Ask to Behave	Neutral	T, Y, A, E	C, T, Y, A, E	When in the Very Friendly STC and the Sims have at least 60 LTR		Good			
Ask to Break Up With	Insulting	T, Y, A, E	T, Y, A, E	Wedding Canceled					
Ask to Go Inside	Friendly	C, T, Y, A, E	C, T, Y, A, E	Actor requests Target follow them inside				1	1
Ask to Hang Out	Friendly	C, T, Y, A, E	C, T, Y, A, E	Target is a Service Sim on the job				1	
Ask to Leave	Neutral	T, Y, A, E	C, T, Y, ...	Sim asks Target to leave lot					

Interaction	Type			Requirements				
Ask Everyone to Leave	Neutral	C, T, A, E	C, T, A, E	Sim asks all targets to leave to...		Loser		
Ask to Move In	Friendly	Y, A, E	Y, A, E	Sims are in the Very Friendly STC and are Friends or above or on the romantic relationship			1	3
Ask to Stay Over	Friendly	C, T, Y, A, E	C, T, Y, A, E	Actor is visiting the Target at home			1	
Ask to Stay Over Romantically	Amorous	Y, A, E	Y, A, E	Actor is visiting the Target at home	Flirty		1	1
Ask: Good show?	Friendly	T, Y, A, E	T, Y, A, E	Target has watched TV	Couch Potato	Technophobe		
AskAboutFish	Friendly	T, Y, A, E	T, Y, A, E	Target has fished or Actor is Insane	Angler; Loves the Outdoors, Insane			
Baby Play With	Friendly	T, Y, A, E	T, Y, A, E	Target is a baby	Family Oriented			
Baby Toddler Snuggle	Friendly	T, Y, A, E	T, Y, A, E	Target is a baby	Family Oriented			
Beg for Job Back	Friendly	T, Y, A, E	T, Y, A, E	Target is Actor's Boss and Actor quit work	Workaholic, Loser		1	1
Best Friends Forever	Friendly	T	T	Sims are teens, Best Friends, or Old Friends, and in the Very Friendly STC			1	
Birthday Congratulations	Friendly	C, T, Y, A, E	C, T, Y, A, E	It is the Target's birthday	Family Oriented, Friendly, Schmoozer			
Boast About Athleticism	Friendly	T, Y, A, E	T, Y, A, E	Actor acquired Athletic skill	Athletic, Snob		1	
Boast About Bicycle	Friendly	T, Y, A, E	T, Y, A, E	Actor is a Snob who owns a bicycle	Snob	Snob	1	
Boast About Car	Friendly	T, Y, A, E	T, Y, A, E	Actor is a Snob who owns a car	Snob	Snob	1	
Boast About Computer	Friendly	T, Y, A, E	T, Y, A, E	Actor is a Computer Whiz who improved their computer	Computer Whiz, Snob	Computer Whiz	1	
Boast About Culinary Prowess	Friendly	T, Y, A, E	T, Y, A, E	Actor acquired Cooking skill	Natural Cook, Snob		1	
Boast About Dancing	Friendly	T, Y, A, E	T, Y, A, E	Actor is dancing	Party Animal, Snob		1	
Boast About Finally Winning Something!	Friendly	T, Y, A, E	T, Y, A, E	Actor is a Loser who won	Loser	Loser	1	
Boast About Fishing Feats	Friendly	C, T, Y, A, E	C, T, Y, A, E	Actor acquired Fishing skill	Angler, Snob		1	
Boast About Gardening Glory	Friendly	T, Y, A, E	T, Y, A, E	Actor acquired Gardening skill	Green Thumb, Snob		1	
Boast About Party	Friendly	T, Y, A, E	T, Y, A, E	Actor threw a party	Party Animal, Snob		1	
Boast About Pool	Friendly	T, Y, A, E	T, Y, A, E	Actor is a Snob who has a pool	Snob	Snob	1	
Boast About Reviving Plant	Friendly	T, Y, A, E	T, Y, A, E	Actor revived a plant	Green Thumb, Snob		1	
Bore to Death	Friendly	C, T, Y, A, E	C, T, Y, A, E	Actor has No Sense of Humor or Target thinks the Actor is being very boring	No Sense of Humor		1	
Brag About Being a Doctor	Friendly	Y, A, E	Y, A, E	Actor is in the Medical career	Ambitious, Snob		1	
Break Up	Insulting	T, Y, A, E	T, Y, A, E	Actor and Target are in a committed relationship but not married	Commitment Issues			
Brighten Day	Friendly	T, Y, A, E	T, Y, A, E	Actor is Good	Good	Good		

Social	Commodity	Actor Age	Target Age	Social Available When?	Required Trait	Social Encouraged By Trait?	Social Prevented By Trait?	# of Uses Before Boring	# of Uses if Recharged
Calm Down	Friendly	C, T, Y, E	C, T, Y, A, E	Target has the Betrayed, Can't Stand Art, Offended, Rude Awakening, Rude Guest, or Stuff Taken buff		Good, Friendly, Charismatic	Mean-Spirited, Evil		
Cancel Wedding	Insulting	Y, A, E	Y, A, E	Available on engaged Sim		Commitment Issues			
Charming Introduction	Friendly	T, Y, A, E	T, Y, A, E	Actor has Charisma skill		Charismatic, Schmoozer			
Chat	Friendly	C, T, Y, A, E	C, T, Y, A, E	Always available		Schmoozer, Charismatic		4	6
Cheer Up	Friendly	C, T, Y, E	C, T, Y, A, E	Target has the Heart Broken, Mourning, or Rejected buff		Good, Friendly		3	
Complain About All the People	Friendly	T, Y, A, E	T, Y, A, E	Target had the Too Many People buff or is a Loner	Loner	Loner, Grumpy		1	
Complain About Art	Friendly	T, Y, A, E	T, Y, A, E	Actor Can't Stand Art, knows the Target is Artistic or recently visited an Art Gallery		Can't Stand Art, Grumpy		1	
Complain About Baby	Friendly	T, Y, A, E	T, Y, A, E	Actor has the Crying Baby buff		Dislikes Children, Grumpy	Family Oriented	1	
Complain About Being a Loser	Friendly	T, Y, A, E	T, Y, A, E	Actor is a Loser who lost	Loser	Loser, Grumpy		1	
Complain About Being a Slob	Insulting	T, Y, A, E	T, Y, A, E	Actor knows the Target is a Slob		Neat, Perfectionist, Snob, Grumpy		1	
Complain About Children	Friendly	T, Y, A, E	T, Y, A, E	Actor Dislikes Children	Dislikes Children	Dislikes Children, Grumpy		1	
Complain About Darkness	Friendly	T, Y, A, E	T, Y, A, E	Actor is Scared of the Dark	Coward	Coward, Grumpy		1	
Complain About Exercise	Friendly	T, Y, A, E	T, Y, A, E	Actor recently visited the gym or is a Couch Potato and recently exercised	Couch Potato	Couch Potato, Grumpy		1	
Complain About Foolish Joke	Friendly	T, Y, A, E	T, Y, A, E	Actor has No Sense of Humor and humor was attempted	No Sense of Humor	No Sense of Humor, Grumpy		1	
Complain About Good People	Insulting	T, Y, A, E	T, Y, A, E	Actor knows the Target is Good		Evil, Mean-Spirited, Grumpy	Good	1	
Complain About Inappropriateness	Insulting	T, Y, A, E	T, Y, A, E	Actor knows the Target is Inappropriate		Good, Grumpy	Inappropriate	1	
Complain About Laziness	Insulting	T, Y, A, E	T, Y, A, E	Actor knows the Target is a Couch Potato		Athletic, Grumpy	Couch Potato	1	
Complain About Meat	Friendly	T, Y, A, E	T, Y, A, E	Actor is disgusted by meat	Vegetarian	Vegetarian, Grumpy		1	
Complain About Mess	Friendly	T, Y, A, E	T, Y, A, E	Actor is disgusted by mess	Neat	Neat, Grumpy		1	
Complain About Other	Friendly	T, Y, A, E	T, Y, A, E	Actor is annoyed with a third party		Inappropriate, Mean-Spirited, Grumpy		1	
Complain About Other's Stench	Friendly	C, T, Y, A, E	C, T, Y, A, E	Target has the Stinky buff		Neat, Perfectionist, Snob, Grumpy	Slob	1	
Complain About Being	Friendly	C, T, Y, A, E	C, T, Y	Actor was woken up		Heavy Sleeper, Light		1	

Interaction	Type	Age A	Age B	Age C	Requirement	Req. Trait	Favorable Traits	Opposing Trait	(1)	(3)
Bathtub				A, E			Grumpy			
Complain About Broken Toilet	Friendly	C, T, Y, A, E	C, T, Y, A, E	C, T, Y, A, E	Broken toilet		Neat, Perfectionist, Grumpy		1	
Complain About Dirty Bathtub	Friendly	C, T, Y, A, E	C, T, Y, A, E	C, T, Y, A, E	Dirty bathtub		Neat, Perfectionist, Snob, Grumpy		1	
Complain About Dirty Dishes	Friendly	C, T, Y, A, E	C, T, Y, A, E	C, T, Y, A, E	Dirty dishes		Neat, Perfectionist, Snob, Grumpy		1	
Complain About Dirty Toilet	Friendly	C, T, Y, A, E	C, T, Y, A, E	C, T, Y, A, E	Dirty toilet		Neat, Perfectionist, Snob, Grumpy		1	
Complain About Feeling Sore	Friendly	C, T, Y, A, E	C, T, Y, A, E	C, T, Y, A, E	Actor has the Sore buff		Couch Potato, Grumpy		1	
Complain About Outdoors	Friendly	T, Y, A, E	T, Y, A, E	T, Y, A, E	Actor has the Hates Outdoors trait and is outdoors	Hates the Outdoors	Hates the Outdoors, Grumpy		1	
Complain About Party	Friendly	C, T, Y, A, E	C, T, Y, A, E	C, T, Y, A, E	Actor is preparing for or recently had a party		Loner, Grumpy	Party Animal	1	
Complain About Politicians	Insulting	T, Y, A, E	T, Y, A, E	T, Y, A, E	Actor learns the Target is in the Political career		Insane, Grumpy		1	
Complain About School	Friendly	C, T, Y, A, E	C, T, Y, A, E	C, T, Y, A, E	Actor can complain about school		Couch Potato, Party Animal, Grumpy		1	
Complain About the Police	Insulting	T, Y, A, E	T, Y, A, E	T, Y, A, E	Actor learns the Target is in the Law Enforcement career		Evil, Inappropriate, Grumpy		1	
Complain About TV	Friendly	C, T, Y, A, E	C, T, Y, A, E	C, T, Y, A, E	Actor is Technophobe and the TV is on	Technophobe	Technophobe, Grumpy		1	
Complain About TV Being Turned Off	Friendly	C, T, Y, A, E	C, T, Y, A, E	C, T, Y, A, E	Actor is not Technophobe and the TV was turned off		Couch Potato, Grumpy	Technophobe	1	
Complain About Work	Friendly	T, Y, A, E	T, Y, A, E	T, Y, A, E	Actor has the Fired or Overworked buff, just got home from work, or can complain about work		Grumpy	Workaholic	1	
Compliment	Friendly	C, T, Y, A, E	C, T, Y, A, E	C, T, Y, A, E	Sims are in the Very Friendly STC and are below Friends		Charismatic, Schmoozer, Easily Impressed			3
Compliment Appearance	Amorous	T, Y, A, E	T, Y, A, E	T, Y, A, E	Romance is available and Target's outfit changed or Sims are not in the Seductive or Hot STC		Charismatic, Schmoozer, Easily Impressed, Flirty			3
Compliment Athleticism	Amorous	T, Y, A, E	T, Y, A, E	T, Y, A, E	Target did something athletic		Athletic, Schmoozer, Easily Impressed, Flirty			3
Compliment Braveness	Friendly	T, Y, A, E	T, Y, A, E	T, Y, A, E	Target did something brave		Coward, Schmoozer, Easily Impressed			3
Compliment Cleverness	Friendly	T, Y, A, E	T, Y, A, E	T, Y, A, E	Actor knows the Target is a Genius		Genius, Schmoozer, Easily Impressed			3
Compliment Cooking	Friendly	C, T, Y, A, E	C, T, Y, A, E	C, T, Y, A, E	Target has made food		Natural Cook, Family Oriented, Schmoozer, Easily Impressed			3
Compliment Dancing	Friendly	C, T, Y, A, E	C, T, Y, A, E	C, T, Y, A, E	Target is dancing		Party Animal, Schmoozer, Easily Impressed			3

Relationships and Aging

Social	Commodity	Actor Age	Target Age	Social Available When?	Required Trait	Social Encouraged By Trait?	Social Prevented By Trait?	# of Uses Before Boring	# of Uses if Recharged
Compliment Garden	Friendly	T, Y, A, E	T, Y, A, E	Actor can compliment garden		Green Thumb, Schmoozer, Easily Impressed	Hates the Outdoors		3
Compliment Handiness	Friendly	T, Y, A, E	T, Y, A, E	Target has repaired something		Handy, Schmoozer, Easily Impressed			3
Compliment Home	Friendly	C, T, Y, A, E	C, T, Y, A, E	Actor is visiting the Target at home		Schmoozer, Easily Impressed			3
Compliment Music	Friendly	T, Y, A, E	T, Y, A, E	Target has performed music		Virtuoso, Schmoozer, Easily Impressed			3
Compliment Party	Friendly	C, T, Y, A, E	C, T, Y, A, E	Actor is attending or recently attended a party		Party Animal, Schmoozer, Easily Impressed			3
Compliment Personality	Amorous	T, Y, A, E	T, Y, A, E	Romance is available, Sims are not in the Seductive or Hot STC and don't dislike each other or aren't currently engaged/married		Schmoozer, Easily Impressed, Flirty			3
Confess Cheating	Neutral	T, Y, A, E	T, Y, A, E	Target has had Jealousy triggered on Actor		Good, Family Oriented			
Confess Attraction	Amorous	T, Y, A, E	T, Y, A, E	Romance is available, Sims are not in the Seductive or Hot STC and don't dislike each other or already romantic		Hopeless Romantic, Flirty		1	1
Confess Attraction for Another	Friendly	T, Y, A, E	T, Y, A, E	Actor is attracted to a third party		Hopeless Romantic			
Confess to Being Fired	Friendly	T, Y, A, E	T, Y, A, E	Actor has the Fired buff			Mean-Spirited		
Console	Friendly	C, T, Y, A, E	C, T, Y, A, E	Target is having a bad day, or has the Scared, Heart Broken, Mourning, or Rejected buff		Good, Family Oriented, Friendly			
Coo Over Children	Friendly	T, Y, A, E	C, T, Y, A, E	Actor is Family Oriented	Family Oriented	Family Oriented			
Criticize His Family	Insulting	T, Y, A, E	T, Y, A, E	Actor is Mean-Spirited or Inappropriate or is being Insulting to the Target who is in a committed relationship with them	Mean-Spirited, Inappropriate	Mean-Spirited, Inappropriate		1	
Criticize Lousy Book	Friendly	C, T, Y, A, E	C, T, Y, A, E	Sims are responding to a book		Bookworm, Perfectionist, Snob, Grumpy		1	
Cry on Shoulder	Friendly	T, Y, A, E	T, Y, A, E	Actor has the Heart Broken, Mourning, or Rejected buff		Over Emotional			
Cuddle	Amorous	T, Y, A, E	T, Y, A, E	Can try on Sim		Hopeless Romantic		1	1
Debate Politics	Friendly	T, Y, A, E	T, Y, A, E	Actor or Target is in the Political career		Schmoozer, Charismatic		3	
Declare Nemesis	Steamed	T, Y, A, E	T, Y, A, E	Sims are in the Steamed STC		Evil, Mean-Spirited, Hot-Headed			
Deep Conversation	Friendly	T, Y, A, E	T, Y, A, E	Sims are in the Very Friendly STC and are Good Friends or above or in a committed relationship		Genius		3	4

Interaction	Social Type	Ages 1	Ages 2	Requirement	Trait A	Trait B	#	#
Determine Gender of Baby	Friendly	C, T, Y, A, E	C, T, Y, A, E	Target is pregnant				
Disapprove of Criminals	Insulting	T, Y, A, E	T, Y, A, E	Actor learns the Target is in the Criminal career	Good	Evil		1
Discuss Favorite TV Shows	Friendly	C, T, Y, A, E	C, T, Y, A, E	TV is on	Couch Potato, Charismatic	Technophobe		3
Discuss Fine Cuisine	Friendly	C, T, Y, A, E	C, T, Y, A, E	Respond to the Hunger buff	Natural Cook, Snob			3
Discuss Work	Friendly	T, Y, A, E	T, Y, A, E	Actor is a Workaholic or is talking to a co-worker	Workaholic, Ambitious			
Dismiss	Neutral	T, Y, A, E	T, Y, A, E	Target is a Service Sim on the job				
Dismiss Rudely	Insulting	T, Y, A, E	T, Y, A, E	Target is a Service Sim on the job	Mean-Spirited	Good		
Divorce	Insulting	Y, A, E	Y, A, E	Actor and Target are married	Commitment Issues			
Embrace	Amorous	Y, A, E	Y, A, E	Sims are in the Hot STC or Seductive STC if the Sims are in a romantic relationship or are exes	Hopeless Romantic, Flirty		1	1
End Service	Neutral	T, Y, A, E	T, Y, A, E	Target is a Service Sim on the job and the Sims are Friends or higher	Frugal			
Enthuse About Business	Friendly	T, Y, A, E	T, Y, A, E	Actor learns the Target is in the Business career	Excitable			
Enthuse About Cooking	Friendly	T, Y, A, E	T, Y, A, E	Actor learns the Target is in the Culinary career	Natural Cook, Excitable			
Enthuse About Exercise	Friendly	T, Y, A, E	T, Y, A, E	Actor recently visited the gym or is Athletic and recently exercised or knows the Target is Athletic	Athletic, Excitable	Couch Potato		
Enthuse About Fishing	Friendly	T, Y, A, E	T, Y, A, E	Actor is an Angler or knows the Target is an Angler	Angler, Excitable			
Enthuse About Journalism	Friendly	T, Y, A, E	T, Y, A, E	Actor learns the Target is in the Journalism career	Excitable			
Enthuse About Law Enforcement	Friendly	T, Y, A, E	T, Y, A, E	Actor learns the Target is in the Law Enforcement career	Excitable			
Enthuse About Music	Friendly	T, Y, A, E	T, Y, A, E	Actor is a Virtuoso or learns the Target is in the Music career	Virtuoso, Excitable			
Enthuse About New House	Friendly	C, T, Y, A, E	C, T, Y, A, E	Actor or Target has a new house	Excitable			
Enthuse About Outdoors	Friendly	T, Y, A, E	T, Y, A, E	Actor Loves the Outdoors	Loves the Outdoors, Excitable	Hates the Outdoors		
Enthuse About Party	Friendly	T, Y, A, E	T, Y, A, E	Actor is preparing for a party	Party Animal, Excitable			
Enthuse About Politics	Friendly	T, Y, A, E	T, Y, A, E	Actor learns the Target is in the Political career	Excitable			
Enthuse About Science	Friendly	T, Y, A, E	T, Y, A, E	Actor learns the Target is in the Science career	Excitable			
Enthuse About the Military	Friendly	T, Y, A, E	T, Y, A, E	Actor learns the Target is in the Military career	Excitable			
Enthuse About Wedding	Friendly	T, Y, A, E	T, Y, A, E	Actor is at their wedding party	Hopeless Romantic, Family Oriented, Excitable	Commitment Issues		
Enthuse About Work	Friendly	T, Y, A, E	T, Y, A, E	Actor has gotten home from work	Workaholic, Excitable			

Social	Commodity	Actor Age	Target Age	Social Available When?	Required Trait	Social Encouraged By Trait?	Social Prevented By Trait?	# of Uses Before Boring	# of Uses if Recharged
Express Condolences	Friendly	C, T, Y, A, E	C, T, Y, A, E	Actor is at a Funeral		Good, Friendly			
Express Condolences to Victim	Friendly	C, T, Y, A, E	C, T, Y, A, E	Actor knows Target has been cheated on		Family Oriented, Hopeless Romantic			
Express Embarrassment	Friendly	C, T, Y, A, E	C, T, Y, A, E	Actor has the Embarrassed buff or a conversation has turned Awkward				1	
Express Fear of Graveyards	Friendly	T, Y, A, E	T, Y, A, E	Actor has the Creepy Graveyard buff		Coward, Neurotic	Brave	1	
Express Fear of Swimming	Friendly	T, Y, A, E	T, Y, A, E	Actor is Hydrophobic	Hydrophobic	Hydrophobic		1	
Express Fear of the Dark	Friendly	T, Y, A, E	T, Y, A, E	Actor has the Afraid of the Dark buff		Coward, Neurotic	Brave	1	
Express Fondness	Friendly	T, Y, A, E	T, Y, A, E	Sims are in the Very Friendly STC and are Friends or above or in a romantic relationship		Friendly			
Express Humiliation	Friendly	T, Y, A, E	T, Y, A, E	Actor has the Humiliated buff				1	
Express Need for Exercise	Friendly	T, Y, A, E	T, Y, A, E	Actor is Athletic		Athletic		1	
Express Sympathy for Victim	Neutral	C, T, Y, A, E	C, T, Y, A, E	Actor knows a third party has been cheated on		Family Oriented, Hopeless Romantic			
Family Hug	Friendly	C, T, Y, A, E	C, T, Y, A, E	Actor is Family Oriented		Family Oriented			
Feel Tummy	Friendly	C, T, Y, A, E	T, Y, A, E	Target is pregnant		Family Oriented			1
Fight!	Steamed	T, Y, A, E	T, Y, A, E	Actor has the Betrayed, Can't Stand Art, Offended, Rude Awakening, Rude Guest, or Stuff Taken buff, or Sims are in the Steamed STC		Mean-Spirited, Hot-Headed, Evil	Good		
Fire	Insulting	T, Y, A, E	T, Y, A, E	Target is a Service Sim on the job and the Sims are not Friends or higher		Mean-Spirited			
First Kiss	Amorous	T, Y, A, E	T, Y, A, E	Sims are in the Seductive or Hot context and have not kissed		Great Kisser		1	
Flatter	Friendly	C, T, Y, A, E	C, T, Y, A, E	Actor is a Schmoozer	Schmoozer	Schmoozer			3
Flirt	Amorous	T, Y, A, E	T, Y, A, E	Romance is available		Flirty, Hopeless Romantic	Unflirty		3
Flirty Joke	Amorous	T, Y, A, E	T, Y, A, E	Romance is available but not too hot		Good Sense of Humor, Flirty	Unflirty		3
Fret Over Commitment	Friendly	Y, A, E	Y, A, E	Actor has made a commitment	Commitment Issues	Commitment Issues			
Friendly Hug	Friendly	C, T, Y, A, E	C, T, Y, A, E	Sims are Friends or above		Friendly			
Gaze Into Eyes	Amorous	T, Y, A, E	T, Y, A, E	Sims are in the Seductive STC and Actor is a Hopeless Romantic	Hopeless Romantic	Hopeless Romantic			

Interaction	Type	Ages	Ages	Requirement	Trait	Trait	#	#
Get Married	Amorous	Y, A, E	Y, A, E	Actor is at their wedding party	Hopeless Romantic, Family Oriented			
Give Inspirational Speech	Friendly	T, Y, A, E	T, Y, A, E	Actor can give an inspirational speech	Charismatic			
Give Medical Advice	Friendly	Y, A, E	Y, A, E	Target is pregnant	Genius			
Goodbye	Neutral	C, T, Y, A, E	C, T, Y, A, E	Always available to end conversation				
Goodbye Hug	Friendly	C, T, Y, A, E	C, T, Y, A, E	End conversation with friendly commodity				
Goodbye Kiss	Amorous	T, Y, A, E	T, Y, A, E	End conversation with amorous commodity				
Goodbye Rude	Insulting	C, T, Y, A, E	C, T, Y, A, E	End conversation with insulting commodity	Mean-Spirited	Good		
Goof Around	Funny	C, T, Y, A, E	C, T, Y, A, E	Sims are in the Funny or Hilarious STC	Childish, Good Sense of Humor	No Sense of Humor		
Gossip	Friendly	C, T, Y, A, E	C, T, Y, A, E	Always available	Snob			
Gossip About Other	Friendly	T, Y, A, E	T, Y, A, E	Actor can talk about third party	Mean-Spirited, Snob			
Greet	Friendly	C, T, Y, A, E	C, T, Y, A, E	Always available	Friendly			
Greet Amusing	Funny	T, Y, A, E	T, Y, A, E	Actor has Charisma Level 2–5	Good Sense of Humor, Charismatic			
Greet Flirty	Amorous	T, Y, A, E	T, Y, A, E	Actor has Charisma Level 4–7	Flirty, Charismatic			
Greet Friendly	Friendly	C, T, Y, A, E	C, T, Y, A, E	Always available	Friendly, Charismatic			
Greet Funny	Funny	T, Y, A, E	T, Y, A, E	Actor has Charisma Level 6–7	Good Sense of Humor, Charismatic			
Greet Hilarious	Funny	T, Y, A, E	T, Y, A, E	Actor has Charisma Level 8–10	Good Sense of Humor, Charismatic			
Greet Hot	Amorous	Y, A, E	Y, A, E	Actor has Charisma Level 10	Flirty, Charismatic			
Greet Insulting	Insulting	C, T, Y, A, E	C, T, Y, A, E	Start conversation with insulting commodity	Mean-Spirited	Good		
Greet Seductive	Amorous	Y, A, E	Y, A, E	Actor has Charisma Level 8–9	Flirty, Charismatic			
Guitar Serenade	Amorous	T, Y, A, E	T, Y, A, E	Actor has guitar skill	Charismatic, Flirty		1	1
Have Private Wedding	Amorous	Y, A, E	Y, A, E	Sims are engaged	Family Oriented, Hopeless Romantic		1	1
Hello Rude	Insulting	C, T, Y, A, E	C, T, Y, A, E	Start conversation with insulting commodity	Mean-Spirited	Good		
Hold Hands	Amorous	T, Y, A, E	T, Y, A, E	Romance is available but not too hot	Hopeless Romantic			
Impersonate Celebrity	Funny	C, T, Y, A, E	C, T, Y, A, E	Sims are in the Hilarious STC	Snob, Good Sense of Humor	No Sense of Humor		
Imply Mother is a Llama	Insulting	T, Y, A	T, Y, A, E	Actor is being insulting or unforgivably rude	Inappropriate, Mean-Spirited, Hot-Headed			
I Named A Star After You	Friendly	C, T, Y, A, E	C, T, Y, A, E	Actor named a star after Target	Good		1	

Social	Commodity	Actor Age	Target Age	Social Available When?	Required Trait	Social Encouraged By Trait?	Social Prevented By Trait?	# of Uses Before Boring	# of Uses if Recharged
Insult	Insulting	Y, A, E	T, Y, A, E	Wedding Canceled, Target is being creepy or frightening, or Actor is not being insulting or unforgivably rude		Mean-Spirited	Good		
Insult Bookworms	Insulting	T, Y, A, E	T, Y, A, E	Actor knows Target is a Bookworm		Mean-Spirited	Good		
Insult Home	Insulting	T, Y, A, E	T, Y, A, E	Actor is visiting the Target at home		Mean-Spirited, Inappropriate	Good		
Interview	Friendly	T, Y, A, E	T, Y, A, E	Actor is in the Journalism career					
Invite In	Friendly	C, T, Y, A, E	C, T, Y, A, E	Actor has Sims on front lawn of lot					
Invite Everyone In	Friendly	C, T, Y, A, E	C, T, Y, A, E	Actor has Sims on front lawn of lot					
Invite Over	Friendly	C, T, Y, A, E	C, T, Y, A, E	Actor is not on their home lot				1	
Joke About Children	Funny	T, Y, A, E	T, Y, A, E	Target is the Baby-sitter		Dislikes Children			
Joke About Cooking	Funny	T, Y, A, E	T, Y, A, E	Actor learns the Target is in the Culinary career		Natural Cook, Good Sense of Humor			
Joke About Criminals	Funny	T, Y, A, E	T, Y, A, E	Actor learns the Target is in the Criminal career		Inappropriate, Evil, Good Sense of Humor			
Joke About In-Laws	Funny	Y, A, E	Y, A, E	Sims are engaged or married and are in the Hilarious STC		Good Sense of Humor			
Joke About Old Times	Funny	Y, A, E	Y, A, E	Sims are engaged, married or Good Friends or higher and are in the Hilarious STC		Good Sense of Humor			3
Joke About the Police	Funny	T, Y, A, E	T, Y, A, E	Actor learns the Target is in the Law Enforcement career		Inappropriate, Evil, Good Sense of Humor			
Joke About Work	Funny	T, Y, A, E	T, Y, A, E	Actor is talking to a co-worker		Good Sense of Humor			
Joke That He Can't Cook	Funny	T, Y, A, E	T, Y, A, E	Target has made food		Mean-Spirited, Good Sense of Humor			
Kiss	Amorous	T, Y, A, E	T, Y, A, E	Actor is Inappropriate or Sims have kissed		Inappropriate, Great Kisser		1	
Kiss on Cheek	Amorous	T, Y, A, E	T, Y, A, E	Sims have kissed and STC is not too hot		Hopeless Romantic		1	3
Leap Into Arms	Amorous	Y, A, E	Y, A, E	Sims are in the Hot STC		Hopeless Romantic, Flirty		1	1
Lecture Teen	Steamed	Y, A, E	T, Y, A, E	Target is a teen caught after curfew		Family Oriented			
Let's Just Be Friends	Insulting	T, Y, A, E	T, Y, A, E	Sims are Romantic Interests, Exes, or Ex Spouses					
Listen to Tummy	Friendly	T, Y, A, E	T, Y, A, E	Target is pregnant		Family Oriented			1
Make Fun Of	Insulting	T, Y, A, E	T, Y, A, E	Actor is Inappropriate	Inappropriate	Inappropriate			

Interaction	Type	Age Set 1	Age Set 2	Requirement	Actor Trait	Trait (Great Kisser / Childish, Good Sense of Humor)	Trait (No Sense of Humor)			
Make Out	Amorous	T, Y, A, E	T, Y, A, E	Sims are in the Hot STC or Seductive STC if the Sims are in a committed relationship		Great Kisser		1	1	
Make Silly Face	Funny	C, T, Y, A, E	C, T, Y, A, E	Always available		Childish, Good Sense of Humor	No Sense of Humor		1	1
Massage	Amorous	T, Y, A, E	T, Y, A, E	Actor is responding to the Sore buff or Sims are in the Seductive STC		Flirty			1	1
Mastermind Plot	Friendly	C, T, Y, A, E	C, T, Y, A, E	Actor is Evil	Evil	Evil				
Mock	Insulting	C, T, Y, A, E	C, T, Y, A, E	Target is being odd		Mean-Spirited	Good		1	
Mock Ambition	Insulting	T, Y, A, E	T, Y, A, E	Actor knows the Target is Ambitious		Mean-Spirited	Ambitious, Good		1	
Mock Appearance	Insulting	T, Y, A, E	T, Y, A, E	Target's outfit changed		Inappropriate, Mean-Spirited	Good		1	
Mock Cleverness	Insulting	T, Y, A, E	T, Y, A, E	Actor knows the Target is a Genius		Mean-Spirited	Genius, Good		1	
Mock Dancing	Insulting	T, Y, A, E	T, Y, A, E	Target is dancing		Inappropriate, Mean-Spirited	Good		1	
Mock Grumpiness	Insulting	T, Y, A, E	T, Y, A, E	Actor knows the Target is Grumpy		Mean-Spirited	Grumpy, Good		1	
Mock Hydrophobia	Insulting	T, Y, A, E	T, Y, A, E	Actor knows the Target is Hydrophobic		Inappropriate, Mean-Spirited	Hydrophobic, Good		1	
Mock Misfortune	Insulting	T, Y, A, E	T, Y, A, E	Actor is responding to misfortune		Evil, Inappropriate, Mean-Spirited	Good		1	
Mock Musicians	Insulting	T, Y, A, E	T, Y, A, E	Actor learns the Target is in the Music career		Mean-Spirited	Virtuoso, Good		1	
Mock Party	Insulting	T, Y, A, E	T, Y, A, E	Actor is attending or recently attended a party		Inappropriate, Mean-Spirited	Good		1	
Mock Scientific Pretension	Insulting	T, Y, A, E	T, Y, A, E	Actor learns the Target is in the Science career		Mean-Spirited	Genius, Good		1	
Mock Snobbishness	Insulting	T, Y, A, E	T, Y, A, E	Actor knows the Target is a Snob		Mean-Spirited	Snob, Good		1	
Mock Vegetarianism	Insulting	T, Y, A, E	T, Y, A, E	Actor knows the Target is a Vegetarian		Inappropriate, Mean-Spirited	Vegetarian, Good		1	
Mooch Food	Friendly	C, T, Y, A, E	C, T, Y, A, E	Actor is a Mooch	Mooch	Mooch			1	
Mooch Money (Small)	Friendly	C, T, Y, A, E	C, T, Y, A, E	Actor is a Mooch	Mooch	Mooch			1	
Mooch Money (Large)	Friendly	C, T, Y, A, E	C, T, Y, A, E	Actor is a Mooch	Mooch	Mooch			1	
Patronize	Insulting	T, Y, A, E	C	Target is a Child and Sims are not in the Unforgivably Rude STC		Dislikes Children, Mean-Spirited	Good		1	
Persuade to Change Body Shape	Friendly	C, T, Y, A, E	C, T, Y, A, E	Actor suggests to Target to get healthier						
Petty Jab	Insulting	T, Y, A, E	T, Y, A, E	Sims are in the Insulting or Unforgivably Rude STC		Mean-Spirited	Good		1	
Pick Up Line	Amorous	T, Y, A, E	T, Y, A, E	Sims are Acquaintances and not in the Seductive or Hot STC		Charismatic, Flirty	Unflirty	1	1	3
Play Catch	Friendly	C, T, Y, A, E	C, T, Y, A, E	Actor is Childish		Athletic, Loves the Outdoors, Childish				

Social	Commodity	Actor Age	Target Age	Social Available When?	Required Trait	Social Encouraged By Trait?	Social Prevented By Trait?	# of Uses Before Boring	# of Uses if Recharged
Play Tag	Friendly	C, T, Y, A, E	C, T, Y, A, E	Actor is Childish or Play topic is active		Loves the Outdoors, Childish			
Policeman Talk to Sim	Neutral	Y, A, E	Y, A, E	Actor is a Policeman who needs to talk to the Target					
Policeman Lecture Sim	Insulting	Y, A, E	Y, A, E	Actor is a Policeman who needs to lecture to the Target					
Policeman Express Disappointment	Neutral	Y, A, E	Y, A, E	Actor is a Policeman who needs to express disappointment to the Target					
Policeman Arrest Burglar	Insulting	Y, A, E	Y, A, E	Actor is a Policeman who needs to arrest the Target burglar					
Point Out Flaws	Insulting	T, Y, A, E	T, Y, A, E	Actor is being insulting or unforgivably rude		Perfectionist, Inappropriate, Mean-Spirited	Good	1	
Praise	Friendly	C, T, Y, A, E	C, T, Y, A, E	Target is praiseworthy or Actor is a Schmoozer		Schmoozer, Family Oriented			3
Praise Fantastic Book	Friendly	C, T, Y, A, E	C, T, Y, A, E	Sims are responding to a book		Bookworm, Artistic, Easily Impressed			
Praise Written Book	Friendly	T, Y, A, E	C, T, Y, A, E	Target has written a book		Bookworm, Artistic, Easily Impressed			
Propose Going Steady	Amorous	T, Y, A, E	T, Y, A, E	Sims are Romantic Interests and in the Hot STC		Hopeless Romantic		1	1
Propose Marriage	Amorous	Y, A, E	Y, A, E	Actor is Inappropriate or Insane or Sims are Partners and in the Hot STC		Inappropriate, Family Oriented, Hopeless Romantic		1	1
Propose Truce	Neutral	T, Y, A, E	T, Y, A, E	Sims are Enemies or Old Enemies and are in the Friendly or Very Friendly STC		Good, Friendly			
Question	Friendly	T, Y, A, E	T, Y, A, E	Actor is in the Law Enforcement career		Commitment Issues			
Quit Job	Neutral	T, Y, A, E	T, Y, A, E	Target is Actor's Boss					
Ramble Aimlessly	Friendly	C, T, Y, A, E	C, T, Y, A, E	Actor is being boring		No Sense of Humor		1	
Refuse Entrance	Insulting	Y, A, E	T, Y, A, E	Actor wants to deny entry to Sims		Mean-Spirited	Good		
Regret Commitment	Friendly	T, Y, A, E	T, Y, A, E	Actor needs to turn down invitation		Commitment Issues		1	
Reminisce	Friendly	Y, A, E	Y, A, E	Sims are BFFs, Old Friends, or Spouses and are in the Friendly or Very Friendly STC					
Request Ask for Food	Neutral	C, T, Y, A, E	C, T, Y, A, E	Actor has the Hunger buff or is pregnant					
Request Clean Up	Neutral	C, T, Y, A, E	C, T, Y, A, E	Dirty bathtub, dishes, or toilet		Neat			
Request Do Your Homework	Neutral	C, T, Y, A, E	C, T, Y, A, E	Adult to child		Family Oriented			
Request Feel My Tummy	Friendly	Y, A, E	C, T, Y, A, E	Actor is pregnant		Family Oriented		1	3

Interaction	Mood	Age	Age	Requirement	Actor Trait	Target Trait		
Request Go to Bed	Neutral	C, T, Y, A, E	C, T, Y, A, E	Target has the tired buff	Family Oriented			
Request Go to School	Neutral	C, T, Y, A, E	C, T, Y, A, E	Adult to child	Family Oriented			
Request Practice Your Skills	Neutral	C, T, Y, A, E	C, T, Y, A, E	Adult to child	Family Oriented			
Request Take Out the Trash	Neutral	C, T, Y, A, E	C, T, Y, A, E	Available on Sim when trash is full	Neat			
Return Stolen Object	Friendly	C, T, Y, A, E	C, T, Y, A, E	Available on Sim you stole object from	Kleptomaniac	Good		
Reveal Secret	Friendly	C, T, Y, A, E	C, T, Y, A, E	Sims are Best Friends or BFFs and are in the Friendly or Very Friendly STC			4	
Salute	Friendly	C, T, Y, A, E	C, T, Y, A, E	Greeting for military career				
Say Good Job	Friendly	T, Y, A, E	C, T, Y, A, E	Target has done homework	Family Oriented, Genius			
Say You Look Scared	Friendly	T, Y, A, E	T, Y, A, E	Target has the Creepy Graveyard buff	Good, Friendly			
Say You Look Upset	Friendly	T, Y, A, E	T, Y, A, E	Target has the Upset buff	Good, Friendly			
Set Burglar Free	Friendly	Y, A, E	Y, A, E	Target is a burglar	Evil			
Share Interests	Friendly	C, T, Y, A, E	C, T, Y, A, E	Sims are Acquaintances	Charismatic, Friendly		6	
Share Trivia	Friendly	C, T, Y, A, E	C, T, Y, A, E	Actor has No Sense of Humor	No Sense of Humor		3	3
Share Worries	Friendly	T, Y, A, E	T, Y, A, E	Actor is Neurotic	Neurotic		1	
Shoo	Neutral	C, T, Y, A, E	C, T, Y, A, E	Actor needs to send Sims home				
Sign Autograph	Friendly	C, T, Y, A, E	C, T, Y, A, E	Special interaction from autograph section		Good		
Slap	Steamed	T, Y, A, E	T, Y, A, E	Actor has had Jealousy triggered on Target or Sims are in the Steamed STC	Mean-Spirited, Hot-Headed, Evil	Good		
Smooth Recovery	Neutral	T, Y, A, E	T, Y, A, E	Actor has level 5 Charisma	Charismatic, Schmoozer			
Social Worker Yell At	Insulting	T, Y, A, E	T, Y, A, E	Actor wants to be angry with Social Worker Service Sim				
Speak Highly of Other	Friendly	C, T, Y, A, E	C, T, Y, A, E	Actor is at a Funeral	Good, Friendly			
Speak Madness	Friendly	T, Y, A, E	T, Y, A, E	Actor is Insane or is being creepy or frightening	Insane		1	1
Speak Poorly of Other	Friendly	C, T, Y, A, E	C, T, Y, A, E	Actor is at a Funeral or has had Jealousy triggered on a third party	Mean-Spirited, Inappropriate	Good	1	
Stroke Cheek	Amorous	T, Y, A, E	T, Y, A, E	Sims are in the Hot STC or Seductive STC if the Sims are in a romantic relationship or are exes	Hopeless Romantic		1	
Talk About Burglary	Friendly	T, Y, A, E	T, Y, A, E	Actor can talk about burglary			3	
Talk About Fire	Friendly	C, T, Y, A, E	C, T, Y, A, E	Actor can talk about fire			3	
Talk About Medicine	Friendly	T, Y, A, E	T, Y, A, E	Actor learns the Target is in the Medical career			3	

Relationships and Aging

Social	Commodity	Actor Age	Target Age	Social Available When?	Required Trait	Social Encouraged By Trait?	Social Prevented By Trait?	# of Uses Before Boring	# of Uses if Recharged
Talk About Art	Friendly	T, Y, A, E	T, Y, A, E	Actor is Artistic, knows the Target is Artistic or recently visited an art gallery		Artistic			3
Talk About Books	Friendly	T, Y, A, E	T, Y, A, E	Actor is a Bookworm, knows the Target is a Bookworm or is visiting the library		Bookworm			3
Talk About Celestial Object	Friendly	C, T, Y, A, E	C, T, Y, A, E	Actor has Logic skill					3
Talk About Computers	Friendly	T, Y, A, E	T, Y, A, E	Actor is a Computer Whiz, knows the Target is a Computer Whiz or recently used a computer		Computer Whiz			3
Talk About Conspiracies	Friendly	T, Y, A, E	T, Y, A, E	Actor is Neurotic or Insane		Insane, Neurotic			3
Talk About Cooking	Friendly	T, Y, A, E	T, Y, A, E	Actor or Target has cooked		Natural Cook			3
Talk About Family	Friendly	C, T, Y, A, E	C, T, Y, A, E	Actor is Family Oriented		Family Oriented			3
Talk About Gardening	Friendly	T, Y, A, E	T, Y, A, E	Actor is a Green Thumb, knows the Target is a Green Thumb or acquired Gardening skill		Green Thumb			3
Talk About Great Outdoors	Friendly	C, T, Y, A, E	C, T, Y, A, E	Actor is visiting park, graveyard, or pool, or responding to a park visit		Loves the Outdoors	Hates the Outdoors		3
Talk About Movies	Friendly	C, T, Y, A, E	C, T, Y, A, E	TV is on or Actor is visiting the theatre		Couch Potato			3
Talk About My Possessions	Friendly	T, Y, A, E	T, Y, A, E	Actor is a Snob	Snob	Snob			3
Talk About New Job	Friendly	T, Y, A, E	T, Y, A, E	Actor has a new job		Workaholic, Ambitious			3
Talk About Self	Friendly	T, Y, A, E	T, Y, A, E	Actor is a Snob	Snob	Snob			3
Talk About Sim in Room	Insulting	T, Y, A, E	T, Y, A, E	Actor is Inappropriate	Inappropriate	Inappropriate			
Talk About the Bookstore	Friendly	T, Y, A, E	T, Y, A, E	Actor is visiting a bookstore or responding to a book		Bookworm			3
Talk About Weather	Friendly	T, Y, A, E	T, Y, A, E	Actor is outdoors		Loves the Outdoors			3
Talk to Tummy	Friendly	T, Y, A, E	T, Y, A, E	Target is pregnant		Family Oriented			1
Tell Dirty Joke	Funny	T, Y, A, E	T, Y, A, E	Sims are in the Hilarious STC and are Friends or above or in a romantic relationship		Inappropriate, Flirty, Good Sense of Humor			
Tell Dramatic Story	Friendly	T, Y, A, E	T, Y, A, E	Sims are in the Very Friendly STC or Friendly STC, if Friends or above or in a romantic relationship		Charismatic, Schmoozer			
Tell Funny Story	Funny	C, T, Y, A, E	C, T, Y, A, E	STC is not too funny		Charismatic, Good Sense of Humor			
Tell Ghost Story	Friendly	C, T, Y, A, E	C, T, Y, A, E	Actor is Insane, can tell a ghost story, or is visiting a graveyard		Insane, Childish			
Tell Inside Joke	Funny	C, T, Y, A, E	C, T, Y, A, E	Sims are Good Friends or better		Good Sense of Humor		3	3
Tell Intriguing News Story	Friendly	T, Y, A, E	T, Y, A, E	Actor is in the Journalism career					

Social	Mood	Ages	Ages	Requirements	Trait	Trait	Trait	#	#
Tell Joke	Funny	C, T, Y, A, E	C, T, Y, A, E	Sims are in Dull, Drab, Funny or Hilarious STC		Charismatic, Good Sense of Humor			5
Tell Story	Friendly	C, T, Y, A, E	C, T, Y, A, E	Before Tell Dramatic Story, but not until Friendly if Acquaintances		Charismatic			
Teen Insult	Insulting	T	T, Y, A, E	Always for teen		Mean-Spirited	Good		1
Thank	Friendly	C, T, Y, A, E	C, T, Y, A, E	General thank		Good			1
Thank for Cleaning	Friendly	C, T, Y, A, E	C, T, Y, A, E	Thank for cleaning		Good, Neat			1
Thank for Cooking	Friendly	C, T, Y, A, E	T, Y, A, E	Thank for cooking		Good, Natural Cook			1
Thank for Promotion	Friendly	C, T, Y, A, E	T, Y, A, E	Thank for promotion		Good, Snob, Workaholic			1
Thank for Tutoring	Friendly	C, T, Y, A, E	C, T, Y, A, E	Thank for tutoring		Good, Genius, Workaholic			1
Toddler Chat	Friendly	T, Y, A, E	T, Y, A, E	Target is a toddler		Family Oriented			
Toddler Tickle	Friendly	T, Y, A, E	T, Y, A, E	Target is a toddler		Family Oriented			
Toddler Toss In Air	Friendly	T, Y, A, E	T, Y, A, E	Target is a toddler		Family Oriented			
Trade Kitchen Secrets	Friendly	T, Y, A, E	T, Y, A, E	Actor or Target has cooked, Actor has available recipes to learn and Target has Cooking skill (and it's been 1 day since the Target was last asked)		Natural Cook		1	3
Train Sim	Friendly	T, Y, A, E	T, Y, A, E	Train Sim		Athletic			
Try for Baby	Amorous	Y, A, E	Y, A, E	Sims are romantic and are in the Hot STC		Family Oriented			
Tutor Sim	Friendly	C, T	T, Y, A, E	Actor has Logic skill		Family Oriented		1	0
Tutor Sim in Skill	Friendly	C, T, Y, A, E	C, T, Y, A, E	Actor wants to teach Target skill					
Wedding Congratulations	Friendly	C, T, Y, A, E	C, T, Y, A, E	Target had a wedding		Family Oriented, Friendly, Schmoozer			
Watch This	Friendly	T, Y, A, E	T, Y, A, E	Actor is a Daredevil	Daredevil	Daredevil		3	3
Whine About Broken Computer	Friendly	T, Y, A, E	T, Y, A, E	Computer is broken		Computer Whiz	Technophobe	1	3
Whine About Broken TV	Friendly	T, Y, A, E	T, Y, A, E	TV is broken		Couch Potato	Technophobe	1	
Whine About Plant Dying	Friendly	T, Y, A, E	T, Y, A, E	Plant died		Green Thumb		1	
Whine About Swimming	Friendly	T, Y, A, E	T, Y, A, E	Actor is Hydrophobic or a Couch Potato and has just been swimming	Hydrophobic, Couch Potato	Hydrophobic, Couch Potato		1	
Whisper in Ear	Amorous	Y, A, E	Y, A, E	Sims are in the Hot STC		Flirty, Hopeless Romantic		1	
Wooo!	Friendly	T, Y, A, E	T, Y, A, E	Party happening	Party Animal	Party Animal		1	3
WooHoo	Amorous	Y, A, E	Y, A, E	Sims are romantic and are in the Hot STC					
Worry About Grades	Friendly	Y, A, E	T, Y, A, E	Can worry about grades		Workaholic, Neurotic		1	1
Worry About Money	Friendly	T, Y, A, E	T, Y, A, E	Can worry about money		Frugal, Neurotic		1	
Worry About Relationship	Friendly	T, Y, A, E	T, Y, A, E	Can worry about relationship		Hopeless Romantic, Neurotic		1	

Social	Commodity	Actor Age	Target Age	Social Available When?	Required Trait	Social Encouraged By Trait?	Social Prevented By Trait?	# of Uses Before Boring	# of Uses if Recharged
Worry About Work	Friendly	T, Y, A, E	T, Y, A, E	Can complain about work		Workaholic, Neurotic		1	
Worship	Friendly	C, T, Y, A, E	C, T, Y, A, E	Target is in the Music or Athletic career		Easily Impressed		1	
Yell At	Steamed	T, Y, A, E	T, Y, A, E	Actor has the Betrayed, Can't Stand Art, Offended, Rude Awakening, Rude Guest, or Stuff Taken buff, or Sims are in the Steamed STC		Mean-Spirited, Hot-Headed	Good	5	

Mood-Affecting Socials

Some socials have the power to affect mood. Moodlets inspired by socials are an easy way to lift a Sim's mood and earn Lifetime Happiness Points. These are the socials that result in specific moodlets. Use them within your household to boost mood as often as you can without being boring!

MOODLET SOCIALS

Social	Resulting Moodlet
Insult	Offended
Insult	Humilated
Propose Marriage	Excited
Propose Marriage	Newly Engaged
Compliment	Flattered
Console	Cheered Up
First Kiss	First Kiss
Break Up	Heart Broken
Massage	Removes Aching Back or Sore moodlet
Apologize	Removes Offended or Humiliated moodlet
Joke	Hilarious Conversation
Gossip	Intrigued
Try for Baby	Nauseous, Pregnant, Aching Back
Viewing a Break Up	Heartwrenching Scene
Viewing Cheating	Witnessed Betrayal

Family and Aging

Few bonds in this world are more powerful than family—and family is a strong force inside *The Sims 3*, too. The family unit that lives under one roof is a close unit that is always on the lookout for each other's best interests, both socially and with the tending of moods and needs. But families are not finite things. Families take on many different definitions and are affected by a number of outside factors, like chance, luck, and time.

Time is a constant that cannot be avoided in *The Sims 3*. It is a steady drumbeat in the back of every day, sometimes barely audible above the din of career, socialization, and the little joys of life. Over time, Sims age. The transition between the stages of life, from toddler to child, from adult to elderly. And at the end of the strange, fascinating trip that is life, Sims will die.

There are seven stages of life in *The Sims 3*: baby, toddler, child, teen, young adult, adult, and elder. Each stage has a different number of days that completes an age. At the end of the age, the Sim transitions into the next age. Here are the number of days in each age:

- **Baby:** 2 days
- **Toddler:** 7 days
- **Child:** 7 days
- **Teen:** 14 Days
- **Young Adult:** 21 days
- **Adult:** 21 days
- **Elderly:** 16 days (minimum)

Age Transitions

When a Sim closes in on the transition date, you are given a two-day warning. If the Sim about to age up is younger than a young adult, this transition period is extremely important. When a toddler transitions to a child and a child transitions to a teen, the Sim picks up an additional trait. If the Sim is doing well in life by specific metrics at the point of transition, you get to pick that new trait. If the Sim is struggling, then the trait is either randomly chosen or is chosen from a list of negative traits.

For example, as explained in the Simology chapter, teens in school are graded on their performance and get an A through F mark. An A student at the time of transition gets a selectable trait. Here's another example, a toddler who has been potty trained, taught to walk, and taught to walk before the transition gets a selectable trait. If these Sims were neglected in any way and their performance suffered, the risk is that the trait automatically assigned to the Sim will be negative and cause trouble later in life.

While the transition is natural (it occurs at 7 PM on the designated day), you actually have some control of the exact moment of the aging process. You can advance the transition through the use of a birthday cake. We covered birthday parties earlier in this chapter, but just the presence of a birthday cake on its own is good enough to advance the age.

Just buy a birthday cake from Buy Mode or the supermarket and place it on a flat surface on the lot. Left-click on the cake and choose Blow Out Candles. You then get to choose

which Sim you want to blow out the candles and advance into the next age.

If you have a child or teen who is doing exceptionally well in school, advancing the aging process can be quite beneficial. If a child blows out the candles when they have an A, then you get to choose the trait.

Baby

The most helpless of all Sims, the baby requires a lot of care. Fortunately, this age lasts only a couple days and parents are given the time off from their careers to tend to the baby. Babies are typically carried around by their parents (or adult/elder Sims). While carrying a baby, Sims must limit their interactions to sitting (not in front of a table), using the phone, and any socialization that does not require touching. Babies have fewer needs than other Sims, but the needs they do have are critical. Here is what you need to monitor on a baby:

◆ **Energy:** Babies tend to get tired much faster than other ages. When a baby gets tired, it can fall asleep, as long as it is not in the middle of an activity. Babies typically sleep in a crib, though, so make sure you buy one if your household has a baby in it. It's important to note that babies do not operate on the same night-day sleep cycle as older Sims. Don't count on getting a lot sleep with a baby. When the baby starts crying, you better get up and see what's wrong, even if it's 4 AM.

◆ **Hygiene:** Babies need to relieve themselves like every other Sim, but they do so in their diapers. This makes the baby Smelly, which can cause a negative moodlet on other Sims if the Change Diaper interaction is not selected after the baby alerts you of its stinky predicament. Babies who are not changed soon after they make a number one will cry, which can wake up other Sims in a house.

◆ **Hunger:** Babies need a lot of feeding, but not the kind of food you prepare in the kitchen. Babies need bottles. To feed a baby when it needs it, select the Feed Baby interaction on the baby.

◆ **Social:** Babies need interaction and entertainment, so be sure to regularly play with your new baby.

Play with the baby so it has Fun and you can start building your LTR.

Feed the baby regularly so it doesn't cry from Hunger.

171

Here is the list of baby interactions:

Change Diaper: When a baby smells due to an accident, use this interaction to ward off the stink and restore the baby's Hygiene.

Feed Baby: Baby hungry? Select this interaction to give the baby a bottle and take care of its Hunger needs.

Put to Bed/Crib: When a baby is sleepy, you can put it down in a crib for a nap or even lay it on the floor. Obviously, the crib is a better solution.

Hold: Babies need help getting around and parents love contact with their babies, so use Hold to pick up a baby and cart it around.

Here is the list of baby socials:

Play With: Socialize with your baby! Get right up in its face and make silly noises, much to the baby's entertainment. Unless, of course, the baby needs feeding or change, and then no amount of goofy eyes will help.

Snuggle: Awwww. Snuggle-time! Snuggle up with your baby via this social.

Toddler

Babies age up into toddlers. Toddlers cannot take much better care of themselves than babies, but at least they are somewhat mobile on their own, thanks to the ability to crawl, and they can amuse themselves via toys. Toddlers can be taught how to walk via a special interaction with an teen or older Sim. In fact, teaching a toddler to walk is one of three critical lessons you need to teach a toddler before it ages up into a child. The other necessary lessons are Teach to Talk and Potty Train. Toddlers need attention like babies, so if a toddler starts to fuss, you should definitely pick it up and socialize with it.

Toddlers love toys. You can keep them busy for hours by giving them a few toys to play with, like the baby xylophone.

Toddlers have four needs that must be attended to:

◆ **Energy:** Toddlers need to sleep a little less than babies, but they still get sleepy on a much more regular basis than older Sims.

◆ **Fun:** To keep toddlers in a good mood, you need to either play with them or direct their attention to some toys. You can purchase several toys in Buy Mode from the Kids Room catalog.

◆ **Hunger:** Toddlers need to eat. You can either go the bottle route or feed a toddler in a high chair, which can also be purchased from the Kids Room. To feed a toddler actual food, you need the food processor to puree the meal. Toddlers get the same moodlets from eating food as older Sims.

◆ **Hygiene:** Toddlers use diapers—and fill them with a stink that's even more potent than a baby's. If not potty trained, a toddler will fill its diapers and demand immediate changing. If a toddler has been taught to use the potty, it can use the training potty.

As mentioned, you need to teach the toddler in order for it to properly age up. If you have not taught the toddler all three skills before it ages, you cannot choose the third trait it receives during the transition. To teach the toddler how to walk, talk, and use the potty,

select those interactions/socials by left-clicking on the baby.

Potty Train is a critical skill to impart to a toddler.

Teach to Walk and Teach to Talk are selectable when you left-click on the toddler. The older Sim sits down next to the toddler and starts the lesson. Lesson progress is viewable just like learning a skill in adulthood. A blue bar appears over the toddler's head and fills over the course of the lesson. When the bar fills to the max, the skill has been taught. To handle potty training, you need to buy the small training toilet from Buy Mode. As soon as the toddler has learned any of these skills, that skill vanishes from the interaction menu.

In addition to these important lessons, you can goof off with a toddler by choosing the Tickle or Toss in Air socials on the toddler. The toddler loves to be played with, which has a positive effect on both the player and the playee. Playing gives the toddler a positive moodlet. Toddlers in a good mood learn very fast.

Elder Sims are great teachers for toddlers.

Child

Child Sims have survived being a toddler and are ready to take on a little responsibility of their own: school. Child Sims can socialize and make friends with other children, feed themselves with quick snacks from the fridge,

...d even learn a few of the skills that will ...ve them a leg up on teen and adult life. ...hildren still like to play, so let them have little ...n with toys and games when not working ...homework for school and socializing with ...e family.

...ecause children can leave the house and do ...little exploring, it's important for children to ...ave curfews. Children get curfew warnings ...tting them know it is time to get home ...nless they are staying with a friend at a lot/ ...ouse they were invited to.

...Children can grab snacks from the fridge, but they cannot yet cook full meals.

...heck out the school section in the Simology ...hapter for a full briefing on how to achieve ...uccess in school. A child who gets regular ...ood grades and has an A at the time of the ...ge transition gets to choose the next trait. ...nything less and the trait is either random or ...urposefully negative. However, in addition ...oing to school, children can learn a few ...ills, such as Cooking. The Simology chapter ...so has a complete list of the skills a child ...an learn.

NOTE

Children have access to all non-romantic socials.

...een

...een Sims graduate to high school and ...re impressed with a whole new level of

responsibility. Teen Sims can get part-time jobs to help contribute to the household worth, although doing so leaves them less time to get homework done or be social, both of which are important activities for the teen. Teen Sims must pay attention in school and get homework done so when they graduate to adulthood, they can select the fifth and final trait.

TIP

When Sims reach teen, they get to choose a Lifetime Wish.

Teen Sims share a lot with adult Sims. They can perform most socials at this point, save for marriage and WooHoo. Romance is a big part of the teen experience, as teens want to have relationships and go steady with another teen. (Teens cannot be romantic outside of their age level.) Use the STC, LTR, and social tables in this chapter to help teens navigate the social waters and develop relationships and young love.

School is a great place for teens to make friends. Make sure that they are a little social here. Life cannot be all work.

Teens have a special LTR: Best Friends Forever. This is the teen version of Best Friends. To designate this special friend, use the BFF social on a fellow teen with a high relationship. BFFs long to hang out together. Teens can only have one BFF at a time. If a teen chooses a new BFF, the relationship with the previous BFF takes a significant hit and has an insulting STC.

TIP

Teen Sims can learn all skills, just like adult Sims. This is a good time to figure out what kind of skills you want to nurture and get an early start on them.

Pick a skill and practice it with your teen so the Sim has a jump on that skill in adulthood.

Whereas children must obey curfew, teens can actually flirt with trouble here. In fact, disobeying curfew gives the teen the Out After Curfew! moodlet. Curfew is typically between 11 PM and 6 AM. Curfew violation occurs at 11:01 PM if the teen is not at home or on the lot of a friend who invited them over. (If the teen has the Coward, Good, or Neurotic trait, they automatically try to go home when curfew strikes. You must manually cancel it.) While violating curfew, teens risk getting caught by the police. If the police appear and summon a teen over, the teen must obey. The teen is then taken directly home in the cop car and earns the Caught After Curfew negative moodlet.

Young Adult/Adult

The lives of adult Sims, both young adult and regular adult, are covered quite extensively in the entirety of this guide. Adult Sims have great responsibilities to take care of their charges and maintain a positive household, all while juggling career, skills, and socializations. It's not an easy task. There are thousands of choices to make, from sitting down to write a book to going into the military to looking for butterflies up at SimHenge. But it's the stage and all of its freedoms that makes *The Sims 3* such a wonderful experience.

Elder

Elder Sims are not that different from adult Sims. They learn skills, have careers, like to socialize, and still have Lifetime Wishes.

However, they are nearing the end of the great arc of life. But they still deserve to live this final age with grace and poise. Keep elder Sims active even if they retire from work (and enjoy a nice pension) by continuing to develop skills and relationships. That way, when death finally does knock on your front door, there are zero regrets and the family that the elder Sim leaves behind has a wealth of memories, lessons, and Simoleons.

ADJUSTING LIFESPANS

The previous information is all relevant for a game with normal lifespans of about 90 days. However, you can make adjustments to the lifespan in the Game Options tab. Here, you can set the lifespan to the following settings:

Short: 25 days

Medium: 50 days

Normal: 90 days

Long: 190 days

Epic: 970 days

You can also shut off aging completely via the Enable Aging toggle. If you remove the check mark from this box, your Sims do not age. You can also toggle Enable Story Progression, which turns off life outside your house. Turning it off keeps neighbors and other citizens in their preset roles. They will not socialize, get married, and have families. If you want to freeze the town as it is, turn off this option.

Having a Family

As time marches on, it is important to keep a family going. There are two ways to have a child: pregnancy or adoption.

Adoption

To adopt a baby, all you need to do is pick up the phone and Call Services. Select Adoption Service from the menu and you start the adoption process. As long as there are fewer than eight Sims living on the lot, you can adopt a baby. In just a few hours, the

Social Worker Service Sim shows up at your front door. You are asked what age of youth you want to adopt (baby, toddler, child) and what gender. You then name the baby. After selecting all of these factors, the Social Worker hands over the bundle of joy and you can immediately start playing with it and feeding it.

CAUTION

Be sure to check the traits of your new baby. It only has two, but you don't get to choose either of them. You might be in for a surprise.

TIP

Family members who work get a couple days off when you adopt a baby, just as if the baby arrived through more...natural methods.

NOTE

When the baby first shows up, you are only acquaintances. However, through a little socializing, you and your new baby will become fast friends.

Pregnancy

"When two people love each other very much..." A zillion birds-and-bees talks have started out like this—and now it's going to be a zillion *and one*. In order to get pregnant,

two Sims of the opposite sex must enter a high amorous STC to unlock the Try for Baby social. When this social is selected, the two Sims report directly to the bedroom and jump between the sheets for a little WooHoo. Not every session of WooHoo results in a pregnancy. When Try for Baby is successful, you hear a musical chime directly after WooHoo. Congrats—the female Sim will be pregnant starting the very next day.

Pregnancy lasts just three days in Sunset Valley. The mood of the pregnant Sim is extremely important. Keeping the pregnant Sim happy is a benefit just for general LTR, but if you really work on keeping spirits high, it will have a positive effect on the baby when it is born.

Day One

When your Sim first becomes pregnant, her body shape changes only a little. What makes the pregnancy far more notable on this day is the Nauseous moodlet and the constant need to go to the bathroom, coupled with throwing up in the toilet. The Nauseous moodlet does not occur until eight hours after the start of the pregnancy and will occur intermittently throughout the day.

During the first day of pregnancy, not only will more time be spent in the bathroom, but more time will also be spent with your head inside the fridge. Being pregnant increases Hunger, so be sure to keep the pregnant Sim fed.

Day Two

On the second day of the pregnancy, you can see signs of the baby growing inside the Sim. The pregnant Sim's belly sticks on a little bit and she walks a bit differently to compensate for the extra weight in the front. The Nauseous moodlet is now replaced by the Pregnant moodlet, which is a net positive. We say net positive, because carrying the baby puts strain on the mother's back and initiates the Aching Back moodlet, which is a negative.

A trip to the day spa will take care for that Aching Back moodlet for a little while.

A massage from a husband does the trick, too.

The Aching Back moodlet can be dealt with in two ways. The pregnant Sim's partner can use the Massage social to relieve the moodlet or the pregnant Sim can report to the day spa for a little pampering. Getting a massage at the day spa will remove the Aching Back moodlet, but it will return over the course of the day.

TIP

While pregnant, a Sim gets paid days off! Use this timely wisely.

The second day of pregnancy starts to affect the parents' wishes. The father will have wishes the involve buying toys and Kids Room objects for the baby. The mother will have these wishes, too, but she will also get food-related wishes, such as wanting to eat a grilled cheese sandwich. Fulfill these wishes to keep the mother happy.

TIP

Want to increase everybody's happiness? Use the Feel Tummy and Talk to Tummy social on the mother.

Day Three

The final day of the pregnancy unfolds much like the second day with continued backaches from carrying around the baby and more wishes that involve kids' objects and cravings. However, late in this day, the baby will be born. Look for the The Baby Is Coming moodlet two hours before it is time to give birth. When you get this signal, cancel everything. Clear the action queue. Go to the hospital and use the Have Baby interaction. Any family member who takes the pregnant Sim to the hospital will go inside with her and not come out until the baby has been born.

The baby is almost here! Better make a special room in your house for the little one.

The baby will have a mixture of its parents' physical traits, like hair color, eye color, and skin tone. There is always a slight chance for a physical trait that does not match either parent. Don't take it personally—and don't start looking at the physical make-up of the Mail Carrier.

BABY INFLUENCING

There is a degree of randomness to your baby. The chance for twins and triplets is sort of up to chance. The gender of the baby is sort of up to fate. The traits of the baby are sort of beyond your control.

Why "sort of?"

Because in *The Sims 3*, there are little things you can do during the pregnancy that have a small influence on the development of the unborn child. Here are the things you can affect and how:

Number of Babies: Want twins or triplets? Then watch the kids channel on the TV or listen to the children's music station on the stereo. Doing either activity slightly increases the chance for twins or triplets. Doing both *at the same time* really improves your chances of having twins or triplets.

Gender: Want a boy? Eat three apples during pregnancy to increase the chance of having a little baby boy. If you eat three servings of watermelon, you increase the chances of having a girl.

Traits: Mood is the best way to get the chance to select your baby traits. The happier the mother is, the better. Massage away those backaches. Indulge those food cravings. Pamper her at every chance. If the mother was very happy during the pregnancy, you get to pick both traits for the baby. If she was pretty happy, you get to pick one trait and the other trait is assigned randomly. If she was in an okay mood for the majority of the pregnancy, both traits are assigned randomly. If the mother was a bit unhappy, then one trait is chosen randomly and the second trait is randomly pulled from the pool of negative traits. If the pregnancy is a disaster of sickness, cravings, and backaches, then both traits are negative.

There is one more things you can do to affect the pregnancy and increase

the chances of getting to pick those two traits: read the two pregnancy books from the bookstore. Head down to Divisadero's and buy Totally Preggers: An Expectant Mother's Tale and Baby Incoming: Preparing with Vigilance. Read them both if you can.

Death

There are no taxes in Sunset Valley, but that other great inevitability is a lurking presence: death. Death occurs when a Sim either suffers an unfortunate accident or reaches the end of their natural life and dies through old age. When death occurs, the expired Sim crumples to the ground and the Grim Reaper appears on the lot. With his scythe hovering high in the air, the reaper extends a bony hand toward the deceased. A ghost rises from the remains. The ghost takes the reaper's hand and is sent to the great beyond. The reaper will often leave right away, but occasionally it will hang around for a few moments following the death.

Yes, by all means, Grim Reaper, have a seat? What, no cable in the underworld?

You can converse with the Grim Reaper for a few moments before it vanishes back into the ether.

Those left behind can only mourn and cherish what the deceased left behind. When a partner or spouse dies, the survivor gets the Heart Broken moodlet. Family members or dear friends get the Mourning moodlet.

The arrival of the reaper tends to freak everybody out, too.

When a Sim dies, they leave behind remains. Depending on the death, it could be just a pile of ash or a marker. You can carve an epitaph on a marker, mourn the Sim over a marker, or pick it up and take it to the graveyard to install it there.

> ## Tip
> Unlucky Sims die all the time from things like fire and electrocution, they just don't stay dead. When the Grim Reaper shows up, he just thinks it's amusing and brings the Sim back to life. Quite often, the Grim Reaper shows mercy to the Unlucky Sim and resurrects them on the spot.

Fire is a particularly disturbing death—especially because there is so much time to put the flames out.

There are several ways to die in Sunset Valley: burning, drowning, electrocution, starvation, and old age. Each death changes the physical appearance of the ghost. Death by fire creates a red ghost. Drowning results in a blue ghost. Here are the five ways death becomes you in Sunset Valley and how to avoid it.

Burning

Possible Ages: Child, Teen, Young Adult, Adult, Elder

Source: If a Sim is next to an object or surface that is on fire, they risk catching fire themselves. The On Fire moodlet kicks in with a timer below it. If the fire is not extinguished in time by another Sim or the Sim reaches a water source, the Sim dies. If the Sim makes it to water, the On Fire moodlet becomes the Singed moodlet.

Avoidance: Be cautious around fire. Don't get too close. If your Sim does catch fire, put out the flames right away.

Color of Ghost: Red

Drowning

Possible Ages: Child, Teen, Young Adult, Adult, Elder

Source: Swimming while Fatigued is dangerous. The Fatigued moodlet has a timer beneath it and if the Sim is not out of the pool by the time it reaches zero, he or she drowns.

Avoidance: When Fatigued, a Sim usually tries to get out of the pool. Allow this.

Color of Ghost: Blue

> ## Caution
> Although Sims automatically try to exit a pool when Fatigued, you can keep cancelling the interaction from the action queue or build walls around a pool to prevent them from doing so. Just saying.

Electrocution

Possible Ages: Teen, Young Adult, Adult, Elder

Source: Trying to repair broken electronics without a high enough Handiness skill risks electrocution. So does using an electrical object while standing in a puddle of water.

Avoidance: When a Sims fails to repair an electrical object, they typically get the Singed moodlet as a warning. Take heed of it. If the Sim tries again, they get zapped to the point of death.

Color of Ghost: Yellow

Starvation

Possible Ages: Teen, Young Adult, Adult, Elder

Source: Failure to feed a Sim after a set period initiates the Starving moodlet. There is a timer on the moodlet. If the Sim has not been fed before the timer reaches zero, he or she dies.

Avoidance: Feed the Sim, for goodness sake.

Color of Ghost: Purple

Old Age

Possible Ages: Elder

Source: Reaching the end of the life cycle

Avoidance: None

Color of Ghost: White

TiP

You can extend an age period by nibbling on Ambrosia, but that recipe is available only to Sims with level 10 Cooking skill.

Warding Off Death

There are actually two ways to prevent death from taking a Sim away. One of the special harvestables, the Death Blossom, can be exchanged for another chance at life with the reaper. If the Death Blossom is in a Sim's personal inventory when death occurs, it can be offered in exchange for more time.

Death Blossom

Life Fruit

The other way of keeping death at bay is a steady diet of Life Fruits. Consuming Life Fruits adds extra time to your life span. You can grow both of these plants by reaching the highest levels of the Gardening skill and discovering their seeds.

NOTE

For a complete rundown on the Gardening skill and how to cultivate harvestables such as the Death Blossom and Life Fruit, please see the Simology chapter.

Ghosts

Death is final. Once a Sim has crossed over to the other side, they cannot come back to the realm of the living. But that does not mean they are necessarily gone forever. Deceased Sims have been known to haunt the area around their grave markers. If you install the marker somewhere on your lot, there is a good chance you might see the ghost of a former friend after 11 PM, rattling around the old stomping grounds.

NOTE

Ghosts are friendly—they will not harm anybody on the lot. But they can wake Sims up, disrupting a good night's sleep.

Ghosts can and will interact with objects on the lot, making noise and generally creeping out the living. Different Sims have different reactions to ghosts or haunted objects. Sims with the following traits are actually happy to see a ghost: Brave, Childish, Daredevil, Insane, and Party Animal. Coward and Neurotics Sims have the opposite reaction to a ghost or haunted object. They get the Scared moodlet.

TiP

Want to see a ghost on your lot but nobody has died on it? Send a Kleptomaniac Sim to the graveyard. There is a chance they will steal a grave marker and bring it back. Install the marker somewhere on your lot and there is a chance you will spot a ghost in the near future.

Ghosts also appear at the graveyard at night. If your Sim has a wish to see a ghost, head to the graveyard sometime after midnight but before dawn. Look for rattling objects as a sign of a ghost. You can converse with ghosts in the graveyard, just as with a living Sim. However, they cannot engage in romantic socials, marry Sims, or be asked to move in with the family back on the lot.

TiP

Feed Ambrosia to a ghost and there is a chance it will come back to life.

PLAYABLE GHOST

Remember when we said death was final? Well, that's only 80 percent true. If a loved one died and you have their marker or remains, there is a chance you will get a call from the Landgraab Industries Science Facility. The scientists have developed a way to reverse death! Zoom out to the map and left-click on the science facility. Choose the Restore Ghost option to bring your loved one back from the dead.

Sort of.

It turns out the technology isn't perfect. Your loved one is returned to you, but only as a ghost—a playable ghost. The ghost appears as a selectable Sim with all of the regular interactions and socials, just as when they were alive. Playable ghosts can develop skills, cook food, and attempt to live a regular life in Sunset Valley.

We know what you're thinking—can I be romantic with a playable ghost? The answer is: yes, if it the ghost is of a young adult or adult Sim. You can raise the amorous LTR with a ghost to the point where you can have WooHoo and even Try for Baby. If the interaction conceives a child, there is a chance it will be a ghost baby. You can actually start an entire ghost family this way.

Service Sims

Service Sims are Sims that exist in Sunset Valley, but do not necessarily live in the neighborhood. You will not see these Sims in the park, for example. These Service Sims exist to provide essential services for you and your Sims. Service Sims can be reached via your telephone or will appear automatically when something on your lot needs to be tended to, such as a fire or robbery.

Your Sims can socialize and interact with most of the Service Sims. Some of the Service Sims can even be turned into more than just acquaintances, such as the Firefighter. If you play the social game just right, you can actually fall in love with some of these Service Sims and even marry them.

> ### CAUTION
> If you want to develop an LTR with an Service Sim, firing them is a negative STC. That's no way to start a friendship.

Baby-sitter

Age: Teen

Cost of Service: §75

Can Be Social: Yes

Can Be Married: No

If you need to leave your lot and you have children, you should always call the Baby-sitter. The Baby-sitter will take care of your kids while you are away, making sure they are fed and picked up after. (Baby-sitters are not Maids, though, so don't expect them to clean up too much.) If you leave your lot for too long without hiring a Baby-sitter and your children are neglected, you risk a visit from the Social Worker Service Sim.

Burglar

Age: Young Adult, Adult, Elder

Can Be Social: Yes

Can Be Married: Yes

There is a chance, while you are asleep at night, that a Burglar will creep into your house and steal at least one of your objects. If you have an alarm, it will shriek, stopping the Burglar in his tracks as the police arrive to take care of business.

If you catch the Burglar and your Sim is Brave, you can fight the intruder. If you win the fight (depends on Athletic skill), you get the Winner! moodlet and all of your stolen belongings are put back where they were. If the police show up, the officer and the Burglar will scuffle around the room. If the officer wins the brawl, the objects are returned. Here is where you can start a relationship with a Burglar. Left-click on the captured Burglar and set him free. Now the Burglar is an acquaintance and can be socialized with like other Sims.

> ### NOTE
> If one of your Sims and the Burglar move in together and boost an LTR to the point of having kids, there is a chance that your child will inherit a Sneaking trait from the burglar.

Cleaning Service

Age: Young Adult, Adult, Elder

Cost of Service: §125/day

Can Be Social: Yes

Can Be Married: Yes

If your lot is a mess and you just don't have the time to clean it, you can phone up a cleaning service and they will send a Maid right over. The Maid will begin picking up and scrubbing surfaces. You can socialize with the Maid while she is on your lot. After the Maid finishes cleaning, you can Ask to Hang Out and explore where this could go...

> **NOTE**
>
> If you have a child with a Maid, there is a good chance the baby will have the Clean trait and not make messes.

Firefighter

Age: Young Adult, Adult

Cost of Service: §500 fine if there is no fire on lot

Can Be Social: Yes

Can Be Married: Yes

If a fire breaks out on your lot and you have an alarm, the fire department is immediately called into service. A Firefighter arrives within minutes. Otherwise, you need to call the fire department so a Firefighter is dispatched to deal with the inferno. Once the Firefighter puts out the fire on your lot, you have a few moments to socialize before he or she leaves. Use this time to Ask to Hang Out or Chat with the Firefighter. Maybe later on the two of you can start a fire of a different kind...?

> **NOTE**
>
> Firefighters' kids can get one of two traits, Immune to Fire or Pyromania (Sim can set things on fire).

Mail Carrier

Age: Young Adult, Adult, Elder

Can Be Social: Yes

Can Be Married: Yes

The Mail Carrier arrives on your lot to deliver bills, mail, and packages (cut gems, ingots, etc.). For a few moments after placing items in your mailbox, the Mail Carrier will linger. Use this opportunity to step out and start talking to the Mail Carrier.

Newspaper Delivery

Age: Child, Teen

Can Be Social: Yes

Can Be Married: No

Every morning, the Newspaper Delivery Kid will show up and drop a paper right in front of your door. Like the Mail Carrier, the Delivery Kid will linger for a few moments, giving you a chance to socialize with Ask to Hang Out and Chat. This is a good way for kids in a new house to make a friend.

Pizza Delivery

Age: Young Adult, Adult, Elder

Cost of Service: §30

Can Be Social: Yes

Can Be Married: Yes

Sometimes, Sims want to eat at home but not cook. What to do? Call for pizza! Within a few minutes, the Pizza Delivery Sim appears on the front stoop with a piping hot pie. You take the pizza off the delivery Sim's hands and pay for it. The pizza can then be placed on any flat surface and treated like a food object with interactions like Have a Slice or Put Away Leftovers. Eating a delivered pizza gives Sims the Amazing Meal moodlet.

Like other Service Sims, the Delivery Sim hangs out for a couple moments after the transaction is complete. Here, you can Ask to Hang Out or Chat with the Service Sim.

Police

Age: Young Adult, Adult

Cost of Service: §500 fine if no burglar is on the lot

Can Be Social: Yes

Can Be Married: Yes

The police will show up whenever the alarm goes off in your house due to the arrival of a Burglar or if you call the police because you spotted the Burglar on your own. The Police Officer will fight the Burglar if he or she makes it in time before the Burglar leaves the lot.

If the Police Officer apprehends the Burglar, your stolen objects are returned.

Following the apprehension (or attempt at apprehension), the Police Officer stays on the lot for a few moments. Socialize with the officer to make a new acquaintance. Perhaps it will lead to something positively arresting?

Repair Technician

Age: Young Adult, Adult, Elder

Cost of Service: §50

Can Be Social: Yes

Can Be Married: Yes

When an object on your lots breaks, such as the computer or toilet, you can either try to fix it yourself or call a Repair Technician. Within a few minutes, the technician shows up and repairs the object with a 99 percent success rate. (That other one percent? Death by electrocution.) After finishing the job, the Repair Technician will linger and is available for socializing.

Repo Man

Age: Young Adult, Adult

Can Be Social: Yes

Can Be Married: Yes

If you fail to pay your bills on time, the Repo Man is dispatched to your lot to take back enough objects to meet the owed amount. While the Repo Man is on your lot, he goes from room to room, sucking up objects with a special repo gun. When the Repo Man has repossessed enough objects to meet his required quota, he will leave. Before the Repo Man takes off, you can socialize with him—although you aren't exactly off to a great start.

> ### NOTE
> If you do not have enough objects to repo, the Repo Man will just take the money from your account.

> ### TIP
> The Repo Man will not repossess essential objects, like the toilet.

Social Worker

Age: Young Adult, Adult

Can Be Social: Yes

Can Be Married: Yes

There are two occasions where you will see the Social Worker. One is quite a joyful experience—she is dropping off the new baby you just adopted. The other? You neglected a baby, toddler, or child for too long. The Social Worker arrives and takes the child away—but not until she has sufficiently berated you for your poor parenting.

If the Social Worker is taking a child, then there is no positive interaction of any kind. After dropping off an adopted baby, though, you can chat up the Social Worker and make a new acquaintance.

Tour of Sunset Valley

• • •

City Life

Sunset Valley is a pleasant little place to call home, which is why so many families have settled down in its quiet neighborhoods. The streets are lined with Sims who love, laugh, and play. Shops offer goods and services to make life a little better. And the job scene is positively robust, as Sims can land a promotion-packed career just by waltzing through the front door of various locations, such as the stadium or police station.

Of course, this microcosm of life is not without its quirks and intrigue. Not every career track is on the up-and-up. Not every couple sitting around a meal table is all smiles. And the prices at the day spa prove that some economic disparity bubbles under the surface of Sunset Valley.

To be an effective, prosperous citizen of Sunset Valley, you need to know all about the town around you. Learn exactly where you need to go for classes to better your Sims. Know the inventory of the local bookshop so when you need to catch up on your reading, you spend less time browsing and more time learning. (Or goofing off with a trashy romance novel.)

Places of Employment

Many of the places you check into to land a career also offer special events or classes. The areas around these facilities are interesting to explore, too, because you can run into new Sims and interact with them as well as find cool objects to collect such as seeds and butterflies. (More on that in a little bit.) In fact, with careers being such an important part of many Sims' lives, there's no better place to start the grand tour of Sunset Valley.

NOTE

When opportunities arise, many of these locations will get new interactions specific to the corresponding opportunity, such as attending an athletic event or donating something to science.

Llama Memorial Stadium

Interactions

◆ Join Professional Sports Career

◆ Attend Athletic Class (§400)

◆ Attend Game (§60)

◆ Attend Concert

Rah-rah-rah! Go team! The Llama Memorial Stadium is home to Sunset Valley's pro teams and a mecca for sporting fans. It's also an excellent place to go if you want to get in better shape, because this is the only place in Sunset Valley that offers a basic fitness class. Once the Athletic skill is acquired here, it can be developed and maintained both at home with exercise equipment or at the 28 Hour Wellness Gym.

The Llama Memorial Stadium is also a great place to let off a little steam while watching a game or attending a concert. If you spot your Sims getting a little stressed or strained, pile into the family truckster and head up to the stadium for a little entertainment.

Fort Gnome Military Base

Interactions

◆ Join Military Career

◆ Attend Handiness Class (§400)

◆ Tour Base

Report for duty at Fort Gnome, the Sunset Valley military base. The main reason for visiting the base is to join the ranks of Sunset Valley's bravest, but any Sim tired of paying repair technicians to fix appliances that constantly go kaput should also enroll in the Handiness class. For a paltry §400, your Sims will get started in the fine art of tinkering, which can be a real money-saver once the skill has been developed. The military base is more than happy to accept visitors, too. Just sign up for a tour to see Fort Gnome up close. Well, not too close. Parochial security prevents personnel from showing citizens everything on the grounds. Wait, what's in that strange hangar out back? Move along... nothing to see here.

NOTE

When you undertake the Military career, you unlock special interactions for the base to impress friends and dates: Show Sim the Jet and Show Sim the Spaceship.

Police Department

Interactions

◆ Join Law Enforcement Career

The Police Department isn't much of a tourist-friendly place. In fact, the only thing to do at this location is join the Law Enforcement career track and then report back if you indeed accept the badge. However, should you become a law officer in Sunset Valley, there are a couple exciting interactions you can do with another location

in town...such as that creepy old warehouse surrounded by trees. It looks like a front for unsavory activities.

Little Corsican Bistro

Interactions

◆ Join Culinary Career

◆ Attend Cooking Class (§400)

◆ Eat Here (prices vary)

◆ Get Drinks (prices vary)

◆ Eat Outside (prices vary)

The Little Corsican Bistro is one of two eateries in Sunset Valley where Culinary careers can be launched. If your Sim has the gift of cooking, then this is a great place to make a living. But even if you don't saunter through the front doors with a Natural Cook trait to your resume, the cooking classes here are sure to help develop this skill.

NOTE

You automatically change into your formal wear if you choose to wine and/or dine at the Little Corsican Bistro. Swank!

Hogan's Deep-Fried Diner

Interactions

◆ Join Culinary Career

◆ Become a Partner (§6,000)

◆ Attend Cooking Class (§400)

◆ Eat Here (prices vary)

◆ Get Drinks (prices vary)

Hogan's Deep-Fried Diner is another place to build a career or take a cooking class. It's a bit less heady than the bistro, but the cooking classes here are by no means inferior. Either one will get novice cooks started on a lengthy (and satisfying) skill development process.

You can also take friends and dates to the diner. If you're just starting out or are a bit short, the diner is a great destination because it's much more affordable than the bistro. Of course, the difference in food quality will not provide as substantial a moodlet. But still, it's a fun place to eat and worth stopping into from time to time, even if your cooking skill is well developed and you can make extraordinary dishes at home.

INVESTING

If you have the money, you can invest in a number of businesses around Sunset Valley. You can invest money in the bistro, bookstore, business tower, day spa, diner, supermarket, warehouse, hospital, science facility, stadium, and theatre. After making your initial investment, you get a cut of the profits every week. Some weeks will be better than others. When you save up even more, you can outright buy the business and keep all of the profits to yourself. Here are the investments required for each business (investment/ownership):

◆ Bistro: §12,500/§25,000

◆ Bookstore: §7,000/§20,000

◆ Corporate Tower: §18,000/§40,000

◆ Day Spa: §15,000/§35,000

◆ Diner: §6,000/§18,000

◆ Supermarket: §7,000/§20,000

◆ Warehouse: §15,000/§35,000

◆ Hospital: §30,000/§75,000

◆ Science Facility: §40,000

◆ Stadium: §35,000/§80,000

◆ Theatre: §18,000/§40,000

Wilsonoff Community Theater

Interactions

◆ Join Music Career

◆ Attend Guitar Class (§400)

◆ Tour Theater

◆ See Movie (§40)

The Community Theater is the destination for Sims with a penchant for music. Whether it is to launch a Music career that will eventually take you to super-stardom (maybe you can throw a concert at that stadium?) or just a place to start noodling around on the five-string, the theater is definitely one of the first places musicians should stop at in Sunset Valley.

The theater also doubles as a movie house. Here, you can take in a flick and enjoy a great entertainment boost that lasts for hours. This is a relatively inexpensive way to get a mood boost. You can also tour the theater to blow off a little steam. However, if your Sims have no artsy genes, the tour will only leave them bored.

Sacred Spleen Memorial Hospital

Interactions

◆ Join Medical Career

The Sacred Spleen Memorial Hospital is where Sims who desire Medical careers go ply their trade. This is not a place to tour and play, as there are no other options for citizen Sims at the hospital. Occasionally though, there will be opportunities that take Sims to

acred Spleen. But for the most part, few ims will darken this place's doorstep, which s actually a fairly positive thing if you think bout it.

Doo Peas Corporate Towers

Interactions

- Join Business Career
- Join Journalism Career
- Attend Writing Class (§400)

he Doo Peas Corporate Towers are where wo careers can be launched: Business nd Journalism. While it seems like those wo careers might be at odds with each, oday's multinational communication negacorporations have fused these two professions closer than ever. Whether you want to be a boardroom titan or a star news nchor one day, step through the lobby oors at some point to start a fresh career.

his is also where Sims go to take writing lasses that advance understanding of the seful skill. If your Sim has designs on being a amous author, taking a writing class is a great vay to get a handle on the ins-and-outs of imlish before going to home to refine the art. Once the skill has been partially developed, ou're ready to start writing your first novel.

City Hall

Interactions

- Join Political Career
- Attend Charisma Class (§400)
- Tour City Hall

It's not surprising that the place politicians come to be heard to is the same place that teaches a course on charisma, the most valuable commodity in politics. Here, Sims can learn the finer nuances of smooth talk, which unlocks new socials capable of improving relationship-building, including the extremely useful Smooth Recovery social for conversations that are of the edge of being deep sixed by a faux pas.

Sims can also tour City Hall, which is interesting to Sims who have shown an aptitude for charisma or politics. Watch those bubbles in conversations so you know when you're dealing with somebody who fancies this sort of thing.

Outstanding Citizen Warehouse Corp.

Interactions

- Join Criminal Career
- Raid Warehouse (Special Agents only)

There is nothing suspicious about this warehouse. It's only tucked in the midst of a copse of trees, and slivers of light can be seen between its boarded-up windows at night. And a name like Outstanding Citizen Warehouse? That's just good advertising! (Actually, it's not. The crime boss in charge of working the criminal element of Sunset Valley just has a dry sense of humor and an appreciation for forced irony.) Sims who want to work the shadier side of the street apply here for their marching orders.

> **TIP**
>
> Once a Sim initiates a life of crime, burglars no longer threaten his or her house.

> **TIP**
>
> The yard behind the warehouse is home to a number of bugs and harvestable plants.

Landgraab Industries Science Facility

Interactions

- Join Science career
- Attend Gardening Class (§400)
- Attend Logic Class (§400)
- Tour Science Lab
- Donate Insects to Science

High on the hills overlooking Sunset Valley, scientists spend day and night toiling over the building blocks of the universe, hoping to unlocks the secrets that fill the gaps between that which is known and that which we cannot answer. Or it's just a bunch of goofballs turning screwdrivers in things to look busy while planning their costumes for the next con. Either way, Sims with a set of brains should head up to the gleaming dome on the hill to enroll in the Science career.

As for Sims with a green thumb, well, head up that same hill, too. This is where you take the gardening class that acquaints you with the basics of planting and growing seeds into harvestables. Sims who want to expand their horizons should check out the logic class, which starts another skill track that can lead to chess victories and celestial spotting via the telescope. Sims can also tour the science lab, but unless they already have at least a slight interest in the sciences, they may be bored by the excursion.

Finally, if Sims have started collecting insects around Sunset Valley, they can bring them up to the Landgraab Industries Science Facility to donate them to science. And by donate, we mean collect a nice little purse of Simoleons for turning in some rare bugs.

Shopping and Commerce

Sunset Valley's economic ecosystem requires places to spend hard-earned Simoleons to remain healthy. In addition to the restaurants in the previous section, there are three places to trade money for goods and services. Spending Simoleons at these locations not only helps with skills and needs, but also with inspiring moodlets that boost overall mood and keep those Lifetime Happiness Points rolling in on a regular basis.

Divisadero Budget Books

Interactions

◆ Shop for Books (prices vary)

◆ Get Part-Time Job

Inventory

BOOKSTORE INVENTORY – GENERAL

Title	Genre	Price
Point Farmer	Autobiography	§25
The Warlock of Palladia	Fantasy	§35
Where's Bella?	Children's	§40
The Adventues of Raymundo	Children's	§50
Murder in Pleasantview	Mystery	§65
A Magnetic Attraction	Trashy	§80
Commitment Issues	Drama	§130
Stragedy and Other Messterpieces	Humor	§135
Zombies? Zombies!	Sci-Fi	§180
Totally Preggers: An Expectant Mother's Tale	Non-Fiction	§200
Abstract with Turkey	Fiction	§210
Unicorns for Audrey	Fantasy	§210
Exit at Powell	Satire	§230
Gpod	Sci-Fi	§250
Baby Incoming: Preparing with Vigilance	Non-Fiction	§300
The Economy	Political Memoir	§310
How to Spin Plates	Non-Fiction	§360
Game of Thorns	Mystery	§405
The Crumplebottom Legacy	Historical	§480
I'm Still Cool	Humor	§535
Thunking	Fiction	§580
Llama Rights	Historical	§610
Special Snowflake	Romance	§705
On the Margins	Satire	§780
The Point of Pointilism	Non-Fiction	§875
No Expecting Much	Vaudeville	§940
The Noble History of Socks	Biography	§1,000

BOOKSTORE INVENTORY – SKILL

Title	Skill	Level Required	Price
Logic Vol. 1: Knights vs. Bishops	Logic	0	§50
Cooking Vol. 1: Too Much Salt!	Cooking	0	§50
Handiness Vol. 1: Unplug It First!	Handiness	0	§50
Charisma Vol. 1: Fixing the Friend Problem	Charisma	0	§350
Gardening Vol. 1: The Watercan Chronicles	Gardening	0	§350
Charisma Vol. 2: Talking to Anyone	Charisma	3	§500
Gardening Vol. 2: Odor Free Fertilizer	Gardening	3	§500
Cooking Vol. 2: Why You Need Baking Soda	Booking	3	§500
Logic Vol. 2: To Xor or Not to Xor	Logic	3	§500
Handiness Vol. 2: Turn Off the Water	Handiness	3	§500
Charisma Vol. 3: Becoming Irresistable	Charisma	6	§750
Handiness Vol. 3: Puddles and Electricity Don't Mix	Handiness	6	§750
Gardening Vol. 3: Gardening to Riches	Gardening	6	§750
Cooking Vol. 3: Yummy and Delicious	Cooking	6	§750
Logic Vol. 3: 3.14159265	Logic	6	§750

BOOKSTORE INVENTORY – SHEET MUSIC

Item	Level Required	Price
Yes Ma'am, I Do	5	§100
Flamenco Fever	6	§250
A Perfect Moment	7	§425
Improvise Here and Now	8	§600
Dream Escape	9	§1,400

BOOKSTORE INVENTORY – CHILDHOOD DEVELOPMENT

Title	Price
Jimmy Sprocket and the Squishy Stone	§50
Bluish Eggswith a Side of Pastrami	§50
Counting for Those Who Cannot	§50
Finger Painting 101	§50
Handprints of the Masters	§125
Jimmy Sprocket and the Chalice of Lichens	§125
Squares Are Not Triangles	§125
Frank I'm Not	§125
Oh the Destinations You'll Briefly Visit	§210
Don't Stay Within the Lines	§210
Jimmy Sprocket and the Escape from "Fun" Land	§210
Being Smart for Fun and Profit	§210

BOOKSTORE INVENTORY – FISHING

Title	Level Required	Price
The Wee Swimmers: Reeling Anchovy and Minnow	1	§100
The Whiskered Deep: Catfish and You	1	§200
Gilled Tragedy: Trout and Clownfish Baiting Techniques	3	§300
All That Glitters Is Goldfish	4	§400
Predators of the Deep: Piranha, Shark, and Swordfish Tips	4	§600
Sushi Swimmers: How to Catch Tuna, Salmon, and Blowfish	4	§700
Heavenly Delicacies: Hooking Angelfish and Lobster	6	§1,000
Binary Fishing and Analog Bait for Robot Fish	6	§1,600
Fishing for the Dead: Deathfish and Vampire Fish on the Line	7	§2,500

BOOKSTORE INVENTORY – RECIPES

Recipe Name	Level Required	Price
Ratatouille	1	§25
Fish and Chips	3	§50
Cookies	3	§100
Fruit Parfait	4	§200
Cheesesteak	5	§300
Cobbler	6	§450
Eggs Machiavellian	7	§5,890
Tri-Tip Steak	8	§650
Stuffed Turkey	9	§800
Baked Angel Food Cake	10	§1,000
Ambrosia	10	§12,000

Divisadero's Budget Books should be a regular stop for all Sims, not just bookworms. This bookstore sells a variety of books that fulfill a number of goals and provide great degrees of pleasure. The bookstore contains skill developing manuals that help with the growth of Cooking, Logic, Fishing, and other talents. The shop also sells recipes that expand the repertoire of cooking Sims, sheet music for Sims who love to play the guitar, and more.

The bookstore also sells more than just volumes for edifying the masses. Novels provide the means to unwind after a stressful day at work. Numerous genres are represented, from romance and drama. And kids also benefit from the supply of children's books on hand.

Teenagers in school and Sims with pursuits that aren't exactly compatible with a full-time job can also seek a part-time gig at Divisdero. For just a few hours a day, Sims can pull in some cash to keep the fridge stocked with food and books and the shelf.

> **TiP**
>
> If one of your Sims has a career as a celebrated novelist, you may see his or her books showing up on the shelves here at Divisadero.

EverFresh Delights Supermarket

Interactions

- Shop for Groceries
- Get Part-Time Job
- Attend Fishing Class (§400)
- Sell Harvestables
- Sell Fish

Inventory

SUPERMARKET INVENTORY – PRODUCE

Item	Price
Tomato	§3
Lettuce	§3
Apple	§5
Grapes	§5
Onion	§8
Potato	§8
Lime	§11
Watermelon	§11
Bell Pepper	§15
Garlic	§18

SUPERMARKET INVENTORY – HOME

Item	Price
Birthday Cake	§30
Duckworth of Billington	§40
Mood-Lite Candle	§65
Bubble Bath	§100

SUPERMARKET INVENTORY – FISH

Item	Price
Anchovy	§5
Catfish	§6
Goldfish	§6
Rainbow Trout	§9
Tuna	§11
Salmon	§14
Black Goldfish	§16
Swordfish	§17
Lobster	§25

SUPERMARKET INVENTORY – MEAT AND CHEESE

Item	Price
Links	§8
Cheese	§8
Egg	§11
Patty	§24
Roast	§30
Steak	§30

Need to get some produce or meat for recipes or to use as bait when fishing? Then make a stop at the EverFresh Delights Supermarket. Here, Sims can shop for groceries and some housewares (like a rubber duckie). Commerce goes both ways at the grocery store, though. Sims who grow fruits and vegetables can sell these at EverFresh for profit. And Sims who like to put a hook in the water—after taking the fishing class here, of course—can also sell their haul to the shopkeeper for cash.

The EverFresh Delights Supermarket is another place Sims can go for a part-time job in the evenings after school. There are no full-time jobs available at this location.

Sharma Day Spa

Interactions

- Get Part-Time Job as a Spa Specialist
- Get Part-Time Job as a Receptionist
- Get Massage: Quick Shiatsu Massage (§50)
- Get Massage: Relaxing Swedish Massage (§250)
- Get Massage: Deep Tissue (§500)
- Get Facial: Mini-Facial (§50)
- Get Facial: Mud Facial (§200)
- Get Facial: Seaweed Facial (§500)
- Body Treatments: Steam Bath (§250)
- Body Treatments: Salt Scrub (§750)
- Body Treatments: Volcanic Clay Bath (§1,500)
- Salon: Manicure (§25)
- Salon: Pedicure (§50)
- Salon: Pedicure/Soak: (§100)
- Packages: Great Escape (§1,00)
- Packages: Relaxing Rendezvous (§3,000)
- Packages: Soothing Salvation (§7,500)

Sims like to be pampered and no place in Sunset Valley powders 'em up better than the Sharma Day Spa. At this day spa, Sims can come in for a variety of personal treatments, from massage to manicures. Prices for these services range from §50 to §1,500, but you get what you pay for. The more expensive the service, the longer the effects last after the Sim leaves. Moodlets from the day spa include benefits like Smooth Skin and Completely At Ease. These moodlets can last for days, too, giving you real bang for your buck.

he day spa offers two different part-time bs. Sims can grab a few hours a day behind e receptionist's desk or slather healing mud n the well-to-do as a spa specialist. The pay n't spectacular, but the hours are perfect for ms with other pursuits.

ommunity Spots

unset Valley provides a number of services community locations that allow Sims to ursue activities that they perhaps cannot ford at home. Most benefits from these ommunity spots such as the gym and library n be had at home, but visiting these spots ves Sims access to the same goods and ar without the object outlay.

here is another benefit to visiting these ommunity spots, too: meeting Sims. These cations can get pretty busy, giving you mple opportunities to socialize and meet w people. If your Sim thirsts for contact d conversation, then definitely use these ots to play the meet-and-greet game. rhaps the love of your Sim's life is admiring statue in the museum or waiting for a weight achine at the gym?

8 Hour Wellness Gym

teractions

Swim

Work Out

Pump Iron

The 28 Hour Wellness Gym is an excellent place to get in shape. This facility contains several pieces of gym equipment, such as weight machines and treadmills that you can use without paying a single Simoleon. For example, Sims can work on their Athletic skill without dropping §1,500 on a weight machine. There is no limit to how long you can use the machines or how often, and the same goes for the pool downstairs.

The gym is almost always busy. And when you visit the gym, you know what the Sims there are interested in: fitness. When you strike up a conversation, you can usually talk about working up a sweat and find immediate common ground.

Wade in the pool for some exercise. Sims love to swim.

Papyrus Memorial Library

Interactions

- Read
- Play With
- Brush Teeth
- Wash Hands

Reading is a right, not a privilege. However, owning books falls into the latter. If your home library is a little slim, check out the library to read books for free and at your leisure for as long as you like. There are many, many shelves to browse, as well as objects to look at, such as a globe. Children will love the play room inside the library, too, which is stocked with toys to goof around with.

Reading books in the library is a good way to relieve some stress.

Like the gym, the library is usually packed with people. Folks wandering the library are likely into reading, so focus your first socials on reading to establish an easy connection. From there, spin out into other topics. Love has been known to blossom over books, so perhaps a soul mate will be found among the shelves?

Check out that globe and educate yourself.

NOTE

The shelves of the library are stocked with plenty of books, but you will not find any recipes or sheet music here. Those must be purchased at the bookstore.

The library has bathrooms, so you don't have to leave to go.

TIP

The museum, library, and cemetery are great places to earn the Educated moodlet.

Sunset Institute of Modern Art

Interactions

◆ View

The Sunset Institute of Modern Art is the city's cultural center, where Sims go to get in touch with their inner Picasso. At this community spot, Sims can view priceless works of art for absolutely free and get the benefits of basking in their presence. Frazzled Sims find it's a good place for leisure, too. There is not as much to actually do here as the gym or library, but this is another good place to find Sims with similar pursuits.

Art is in the eye of the beholder. What is this fellow beholding?

The Sunset Institute of Modern Art is a great place to meet people.

CAUTION

Don't send a Sim with the Can't Stand Art trait to the museum. It will just result in a negative moodlet.

Community School for the Gifted

Interactions

◆ Attend Painting Class (§400)

The Community School for the Gifted is where children go during the day to fill their brains with the knowledge needed to be productive adults. Getting good grades here can lead to a wonderful adult life full of engagement. Adults, however, don't have much to do here other than attend a painting class and start their personal art careers.

Cemetery

Interactions

◆ Get Part-Time Job
◆ Mourn
◆ View
◆ Tour Mausoleum
◆ Explore Catacombs

Sims who have gone before are buried at the cemetery. The chief purpose of this community spot is to mourn the dead, but there are plenty of other interactions availab among the tombstones and grave markers. There are statues to admire, such as the grim reaper stationed near the entrance. The cemetery is almost overrun by trees, so an outdoorsy Sim will get great pleasure from being around those. The grounds need fairly regular up-keep, so consider taking a part-time job at the cemetery working the lot and keeping things tidy.

The central feature of the cemetery, though, is the mausoleum. This imposing structure houses more of the dead. Touring the mausoleum can be educational for some Sims. The option to explore the catacombs below the graveyard is a source of excitement for Sims made of sterner stuff, to

NOTE

If a Service Sim your Sim knows dies, you can find their marker at the graveyard and bring it back to your lot. Their ghost will always be with you then.

What's New

Creating a Sim

Creating a House

A Day in the Life

Simology

Relationships and Aging

Tour of Sunset Valley

Design Corner

Object Catalog

Community

CAUTION

Watch out if you decide to explore the catacombs beneath the cemetery. Sims without the Brave trait risk getting spooked. The Horrified moodlet slashes overall mood for hours.

Barely escaping the catacombs with your life leaves a mark. Hit the showers and get the stench of death off you.

Do you dare visit the cemetery at night? You may spot a ghost, which scares some Sims. Other Sims, though, actually wish to see one.

Pools

Not every Sim can afford a pool in the backyard, so they can use any of the three public pools in Sunset Valley. One of those three pools is at the 28 Hour Wellness Gym. The other two are open-air pools that cater to different crowds.

Le Petit Shark Pool Center

Interactions

◆ Swim

Family-oriented Sims should take their brood to the Le Petit Shark Pool Center where they can swim and play under the sun to their hearts' content. This huge pool is usually packed with people, making it a good social spot. Single Sims, though, should be warned: most of the other adults at this pool are in relationships with spouses.

Lofty Cerulean Blue Pool

Interactions

◆ Swim

This pool is more suited for social Sims who are just as interested in being seen as getting wet. The Lofty Cerulean Pool attracts a slightly older crowd, making it a great place to seek out new friends—and partners.

Parks

There are three parks in Sunset Valley. The parks are excellent social grounds for meeting new Sims or hooking up with acquaintances. Parks are nice for just getting outdoors (certain Sims get a charge just by being at a park) and having a pleasant little picnic, but these locations also have special facilities such as chess boards and grills you can use for free.

Central Park

Interactions

◆ View   ◆ Fish

◆ Sit   ◆ Practice Chess/Play Chess

Central Park is the main park in downtown Sunset Valley. On any given day, Central Park is positively bustling with life. Sims are everywhere, just enjoying the mild weather by having picnics or sitting by the huge fountain. In addition to enjoying nature, Sims can also practice or play chess at outdoor sets around the park tol help develop the Logic skill.

Use the chess boards to increase your Logic skill.

Sims who want to fish can also use the pond at Central Park to try out their lines. This is actually a great beginner's spot to fish, when you are still experimenting with bait and just want to get a nibble or two to satisfy a wish. There are also a handful of fruit trees in Central Park. Pick limes and apples from the fruit trees and then plant them on your lot to start your very own orchard.

Central Park has bathrooms so Sims do not need to report to home base to relieve themselves.

Practice fishing at the pond in Central Park.

Tour of Sunset Valley

Maywood Glen

Interactions

◆ View
◆ Sit
◆ Practice Chess/Play Chess

Maywood Glen is a smaller park set closer to the mountains. It lacks a body of water for fishing, but contains many more trees, which really please outdoorsy Sims. Maywood Glen is often busy with picnics and Sims on strolls, making it a good place to socialize. Like Central Park, there are chess sets for practice and play—great for building up the Logic skill without having to invest in a set for the house.

Play at the chess tables in Maywood Glen to increase your Logic skill.

Old Pier Beach

Interactions

◆ Sit
◆ Practice Chess/ Play Chess
◆ Have Drink
◆ Make Drink
◆ Serve Meal

The Old Pier Beach is an excellent place for Sims to go sun themselves while soaking up the conversation of other beachgoers. There are plenty of seats to lounge in while unwinding after a busy shift or a lengthy writing session in front of the computer. There is a chess set at the beach, too, for practicing the ancient game.

The beach is also notable for its food features. There is a juice bar on the lower part of the beach, near the sand. Sims can jump behind the bar and serve up fresh drinks for others Sims—a superb ice breaker. There are two grills just above the bar where Sims can cook meals for free. Not only is this a good way to meet other Sims by serving up some eats, but the Cooking skill can be practiced here on the cheap. And with all the benefits of getting some sun while doing so!

Fishing Spots

Fishing is a great way to relax, plus you can earn some money on the side. Reeling in a big catch and selling it to the supermarket is a fun way to line your pockets with Simoleons. Several fishing spots in Sunset Valley are loaded with fish. The pond in Central Park has already been noted. Here are the other fishing spots in Sunset Valley, which are located far and wide.

Recurve Strand

Sunnyside Strand

Crystal Springs

Summer Hill Springs

Stoney Falls

Pinochle Pond

Now, are all fishing spots equal? No. But a lot also depends on what kind of bait you e and the degree of your Fishing skill. For a l explanation of how to catch fish, please 'er to the Fishing skill section in the Simology apter. However, here is where to look for ecific fish and what kind of bait is best for tching them:

TIP

The Robot Fish can only be caught at the pond at the Landgraab Industries Science Facility. The Vampire Fish can only be caught at the pond in the graveyard.

The best time to go fishing is between 4AM and 6AM. This is when the best and biggest fish are biting!

ı rare occasions, you will reel in something ıer than a fish from the waters of Sunset ley. Litterbugs in Sunset Valley have carded belongings in the lakes and ponds, t at least their refuse is another Sim's asure. When you do manage to reel in a ite, there is a good chance it will contain a uable item, such as Bubble Bath or Death wer. If you're really lucky, the crate will have ıagic gnome inside of it!

BOXES

ate Item	Chance of Finding
ıptop	3%
ıbber Ducky	20%
ıitar	10%
ıbble Bath	16%
oodLite Candle	16%
rthday Cake	16%
ame Fruit	3%
eath Flower	3%
oney Tree Seed	5%
ysterious Mr. Gnome	6%

aces to Go Collecting

rking hard isn't the only way to make a ıg in Sunset Valley. Actually, you can pull in retty solid income without punching a time ck. There are many, many valuable things collect in Sunset Valley in addition to the ınty pulled out of the water or from your sonal garden. You can collect butterflies and beetles to sell to the Science Facility (or keep for yourself). Precious gems and metals can be located and refined into brilliant treasures. Space rocks hurtling down from the heavens have smashed into the ground all around Sunset Valley, too. Seek out these collectibles to both make money and beautify your lot.

BROWNIE BITES

Wait, a magic gnome? Of all the different things you can collect in Sunset Valley, the most entertaining are the magic gnomes. These little fellows look very similar to the regular yard gnomes you can pick up in Buy Mode (the main difference is that they have stars), but like their name suggests, they are magical. In fact, they are Mysterious Mr. Gnomes!

When you discover a Mysterious Mr. Gnome, put him in your house or somewhere on your lot. Immediately, you get a nice environmental bump. But the real magic of these little gnomes doesn't kick in until between the hours of 3AM and 6AM. While you are sleeping, these little gnomes like to get into mischief. When you are not looking, these gnomes move around. Sometimes they just move into new positions, like lounging next to your pool or in the shade of a tree. However, some of the gnomes like to cause trouble, like turning on the TV or stereo in the middle of the night, waking up Sims.

NOTE

You do not need any special equipment to collect any of these things. All you need to do is left-click on the collectible and choose the Collect interaction. Your Sim will take care of the rest!

TIP

Collectibles respawn after anywhere between one and three days, so keep checking back in all of the spots we point out to see what you will discover next.

SimHenge is a wonderful place to look for collectibles like butterflies, meteorites, and gems.

Insects

There are two types of insects to collect in Sunset Valley: butterflies and beetles. These insects can be sold to the Science Facility for a few Simoleons (although, the rarest butterflies are really worth some dough) or kept on your lot in terrariums. It's fun to have a collection of pretty bugs around the homestead, so consider your lot environment before going straight for the cash. Having an attractive butterfly in a terrarium could be the difference between an okay room and one that gives your Sim the Nicely Decorated moodlet upon walking into the immediate area.

Butterflies

Beautiful butterflies love to flutter about in special areas of Sunset Valley. Use this map to find the exact spots to look for certain types of butterflies. Now, if the map says you will find a variety of butterflies in a specific spot, it's likely you will only discover one or two from the list. When you collect a butterfly, your Sim closes in on a single insect from the bunch and gently takes it in his hands. Then, the rest of the butterflies vanish until the next day. Once collected, the butterfly goes into your personal inventory. You can now either take it to the Science Facility and collect your bounty or take it home and place it in a terrarium.

BUTTERFLIES

Butterfly	Rarity	Base Value
Moth	Common	5
Monarch	Common	10
Zephyr Metalmark	Common	25
Red Admiral	Common	35
Mission Blue	Uncommon	50
Green Swallowtail	Uncommon	90
Royal Purple Butterfly	Uncommon	150
Silver-Spotted Skipper	Rare	325
Zebra Butterfly	Rare	650
Rainbow Butterfly	Extraordinarily Rare	1,080

The Rainbow Butterfly is the rarest of the butterflies. It's worth a lot of Simoleons, but it also really beautifies a room on your lot. Consider taking this treasure home instead of selling it!

Butterflies Spawned

1 Moth

2 Monarch

3 Monarch, Red Admiral, Mission Blue

4 Monarch, Zephyr Metalmark, Green Swallowtail

5 Zephyr Metalmark, Red Admiral, Green Swallowtail, Royal Purple Butterfly

6 Zephyr Metalmark, Mission Blue, Silver-Spotted Skipper

7 Red Admiral, Mission Blue, Green Swallowtail, Royal Purple Butterfly, Silver-Spotted Skipper, Zebra Butterfly

8 Zephyr Metalmark, Red Admiral, Royal Purple Butterfly, Silver-Spotted Skipper, Zebra Butterfly, Rainbow Butterfly

9 Moth, Monarch, Zephyr Metalmark, Red Admiral, Mission Blue, Green Swallowtail, Royal Purple Butterfly, Silver-Spotted Skipper, Zebra Butterfly, Rainbow Butterfly

10 Silver-Spotted Skipper

11 Zebra Butterfly

12 Rainbow Butterfly

Beetles

the ground moving? Or is there something live down there? You may have to squint, but there are tiny bugs and beetles squirming around the ground that can be picked up and collected just like butterflies. Beetles are another excellent source of income, but they can also be kept on a lot to boost the environmental bonus of a room.

BEETLES

Beetle	Rarity	Base Value
Ladybug	Common	10
Cockroach	Common	1
Japanese	Common	15
Water	Common	30
Light	Uncommon	40
Rhino	Uncommon	90
Stag	Uncommon	175
Spotted	Rare	400
Trilobite	Rare	750
Rainbow	Extraordinarily Rare	1,400

When you drag a beetle out of your personal inventory and place it in your house, it is automatically stored in a terrarium.

Beetles Spawned

1. Cockroach
2. Ladybug
3. Japanese Beetle
4. Water Beetle
5. Light Beetle
6. Rhino Beetle
7. Japanese Beetle, Stag Beetle
8. Ladybug, Spotted Beetle
9. Water Beetle, Trilobite
10. Light Beetle, Rainbow Beetle
11. Cockroach, Ladybug, Japanese Beetle, Water Beetle, Rhino Beetle, Stag Beetle, Spotted Beetle, Trilobite, Rainbow Beetle

Gems, Metals, and Rocks

Precious metals and sparkling gems are yours for the taking—but first you have to find them. And once they are in your personal inventory, you must send them away to have a professional process them. Once they're processed, you can either sell metals and gems for profit or place them on your lot for environmental bonuses.

To have ore or rocks processed, you must send them off via your mailbox. (Left-click on the ore or rock in your personal inventory to send it off.) It costs Simoleons to get them processed. The cost of smelting ore into an ingot is §50 flat. The cost of getting a gem cut depends on the kind of cut you desire. The full list of cuts and cut costs is listed in the gem section of this chapter.

NOTE

To sell a treasure like a gem or precious metal, just use the Sledgehammer Tool in Buy Mode. Left-click on the treasure to get rid of it and add the Simoleons to your account. Be mindful, though. You cannot buy back a gem or meteorite once it has been sold.

Gems

Keep an eye open for rocks on the ground—there are treasures inside them. When you swipe a rock from the ground, you are immediately told what you have found. Here are the best places to locate valuable gems:

GEMS

Gem	Min. Weight	Max. Weight	Value of Min. Weight	Value of Max. Weight
Aqua	1	105	9	21
Smoky	1	105	15	25
Emerald	1	105	20	30
Ruby	1	105	25	35
Yellow	1	105	35	60
Tanzanite	1	105	65	95
Diamond	1	105	100	200
Rainbow	1	105	450	700
Special	1	105	150	350
Pink	1	105	1,200	1,650

Having a gem cut increases its value, but this comes at a cost. You must pay to have a gem cut, which occurs when you send it away via the mailbox out front of your lot. Now, when you first start collecting gems, there is only one cut available: Emerald. The next available cut is Oval, but to unlock this cut, you need to send off four previously collected gems to be cut by the professional jeweller. After that fourth cut, you get a note saying the Oval cut is now available. So, while it does cost to get these gems cut, the more you do it, better cuts you get—and the more money you can make from selling. The best cut is the Heart cut, which multiplies the value of the gem five-fold.

There are three ways to display a gem on your lot: on the ground, on a pillow, and on a pedestal. Left-click on the gem when it is on your lot to select your preferred display.

Gems Spawned

1. Aqua
2. Aqua, Emerald, Yellow, Diamond
3. Smoky, Ruby, Yellow, Tanzanite
4. Aqua, Smoky, Diamond, Rainbow
5. Emerald, Ruby, Yellow, Tanzanite, Rainbow
6. Yellow, Tanzanite, Diamond, Special
7. Ruby, Tanzanite, Diamond, Pink

GEM CUTS

Gem Cut	Available After # Cuts	Value Multiplier	Cost of Cut
Emerald	0	1.25	10
Oval	4	1.5	20
Pear	8	1.75	35
Plumbbob	16	2	50
Marquis	30	2.3	75
Crystalball	45	2.6	100
Brilliant	60	3.5	250
Heart		5	1,000

NOTE

The Heart Cut is available after finding all gem types.

Metals

There are five different kinds of precious metals you can pull off the ground in Sunset Valley: iron, silver, gold, palladium, and plutonium. However, when you pick them up, they are still in ore form. These metals must be smelted to make them valuable—and pretty. To turn ore into ingots, just send them away via an interaction with your lot's mailbox. When the ingot comes back, the value has improved by up to 75 percent. That's quite a boost for the §40 smelting fee.

METALS

Metal Ore	Min. Weight	Max. Weight	Value of Min. Weight	Value of Max. Weight
Iron	1	52	7	20
Silver	1	52	25	35
Gold	1	52	40	120
Palladium	80	300	300	500
Plutonium	0.1	5	1,000	1,800

Here is a map showing where to look for the different metals around Sunset Valley:

Metals Spawned

1	Iron	3	Gold	5	Palladium
2	Silver	4	Iron, Silver, Gold	6	Plutonium

NOTE

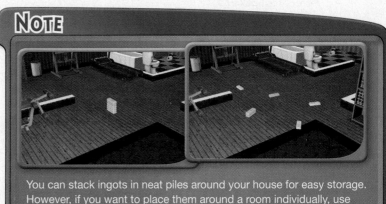

You can stack ingots in neat piles around your house for easy storage. However, if you want to place them around a room individually, use Alt to drop the ingot free of the snap-to-grid.

Meteorites

Space rocks streak through the atmosphere over Sunset Valley all of the time. Some of them actually crash down and can be recovered by Sims. There are three sizes: small, large, and huge. Use this map to find places to look for meteorites v Sunset Valley:

Huge meteorites are as big as a couch!

Like gems and metals, meteorites can be worth quite a bit of money once analyzed. But unlike those other treasures, there is a degree of risk when you analyze a meteorite to find out exactly what it is. Sometimes the raw value of a meteorite is greater than its worth once it has been identified. For example, if analysis reveals your meteorite is Ordinary Chondrite, the meteorite is now or worth half of its previous value.

Meteorites Spawned

1 Small Space Rock
2 Large Space Rock
3 Small Space Rock, Large Space Rock
4 Small Space Rock, Large Space Rock, Huge Space Rock

METEORITES

Meteorite	Min. Weight	Max. Weight	Value of Min. Weight	Value of Max. Weight
Small	1	65	10	30
Large	100	1,050	50	200
Huge	50,000	1,001,000	2,000	4,500

After analyzing it, there is no way to reverse the process, so you might be stuck with a less valuable space rock. Here is a list of all of the possible results of analysis and the value multipliers of such discoveries:

METEORITES VALUES

Meteorite	Value Multiplier
Acapulcoite	0.7
Angrite	1
Ataxite	1.5
Aubrite	1.4
Brachinite	1.2
Carbonaceous Chondrite	5
Chassignite	1.2
Diogenite	0.9
Enstatite Chondrite	6
Eucrite	0.8
Hexahedrite	1.6
Howardite	0.7
Kamasite	1.75
Lodranite	0.8
Lunar	1.3
Mesosiderite	10
Nakhlite	1.1
Octahedrite	1.8
Ordinary Chondrite	0.5
Pallasite	4
Rumurutite	3
Shergottite	1
Unusual Bellacite	1.6
Unusual Custerous Gossticite	1.9
Unusual Dukeadite	2.2
Unusual Holmberic	1.8
Unusual Llamatite	2
Unusual Mazzadrayte	2.1
Unusual Pearsonite	2.1
Unusual Rodiekceous	2
Unusual Sporecite	1.7
Ureilite	0.9
Winonaite	1.3

NOTE

There is a slight chance that after sending away a meteorite, you will receive a Mysterious Mr. Gnome in the mail.

TIP

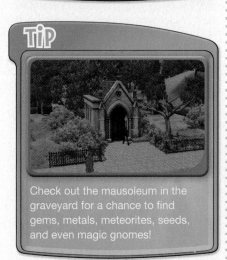

Check out the mausoleum in the graveyard for a chance to find gems, metals, meteorites, seeds, and even magic gnomes!

REARRANGE TOWN

Of course, you can rearrange Sunset Valley any way that you like via the Edit Town options from the Save/ Options menu. You can push houses to new locations and move community locations such as the gym and library around. This is a very powerful tool that can not only make Sunset Valley truly your own creation, but also make life easier for your Sims, particularly if you are moving in with a clear plan of action. If your Sim is going to be in the Law Enforcement career and regularly enjoy the benefits of the day spa, why not move those locations closer to your house? You can also turn private lots into community lots where all Sims can gather for fun and frivolity.

When in Edit Town, click on a lot to open a menu of options, such as turning a private lot into a community lot or bulldozing a lot so you can use it for something other than its original purpose.

Within Buy Mode, you can add trees and objects to lots, both private and community.

Move lots around Sunset Valley to completely reconfigure the town to your liking.

Design Corner

Truly Custom Content

Earlier this year, Electronic Arts invited some of the world's best *The Sims* players out to its Redwood City headquarters to participate in a special week-long event called Creators' Camp. At this event, these designers sat down and pored over Build Mode, Buy Mode, and Create a Style to erect elaborate lots, Sims, Machinima, furniture sets, and more. They were created to not only show off the power of the Create a Style tools, but to inspire players to really dig in and try new things when building their ideal lots in Sunset Valley.

We've had a chance to look at many of these lots. The artistry is astounding. With a little mouse-clicking and a lot of imagination, these designers created real estate that we wish we could own in the real world. Until that magic lottery ticket comes in, though, we'll have to be satisfied with the virtual paradises of Design Corner.

We picked five of the lots created at Creators' Camp to share with you. In addition to just showing off these incredible creations, we'll also show you how some sections of the houses were made. Hopefully, you will be just as inspired to fashion your own amazing lots and turn Sunset Valley into a metropolis buzzing not only with exciting Sims, but also houses that make you wish Sunset Valley existed on both sides of the screen.

Winsome Farmhouse

Created by: Parsimoniuskate

This lovely rustic home, parked in the idyll of cherry trees and lily-pad lined ponds, is pleasing to the eye—especially if you are fond of pink. The farmhouse in painted in similar tones and hues to the ever-blossoming cherry trees that surround the lot and cast leisurely shade on its grounds. Not all of the

farmhouse is living space, mind you. The upper stories of the farmhouse are actually empty, designed to give it imposing height over the trees and recall days of grander homes. (The days prior to the creation of garish McMansions, of course.)

Let's look at some of the most bracing features of the Winsome Farmhouse and see both how they were created and what they contribute to the character of the lot.

The First Floor

The first floor of the house has the most square footage, which is necessary for building multi-story homes with Build Mode. You cannot ignore basic laws of weight distribution. The ground floor has a nice great room just inside the front door, giving the household plenty of space for socializing. A lovely living room set would look nice in here, but the view demand less clutter so it can be truly enjoyed. As you move deeper into the house, you have spaces for a dining table and breakfast nook. There is easy access to the bathroom, which is just big enough for the essential functions. Next to the stairs is a nice small room that would be perfect for a home office.

Notice how everything matches in the kitchen. The Chillgood fridge normally comes in white, but with Create a Style, you can grab a color off the walls or counters and splash it on any object. Now the fridge matches the style of the room. There is ample counter space in this kitchen for multiple Sims. You want to avoid bottlenecks in your houses, and this kitchen does that.

Note that the downstairs bathroom also matche the kitchen. Use the drag-and-drop patterns in Create a Style to easily make objects match. In the bathroom, for example, the metals on the toilet, sink, and bathtub are all the same brassy color.

What's New | Creating a Sim | Creating a House | A Day in the Life | Simology | Relationships and Aging | Tour of Sunset Valley | **Design Corner** | Object Catalog | Community

Once you have settled on colors and patterns for a window, use the Eyedropper tool to replicate it without having to dig back into Create a Style for each one.

The Second Floor

The second floor of the house matches the general appearance of the first floor, but the two bedrooms offer slightly different decor so the entire house doesn't blend together. The huge balcony overlooking the grounds in a nice touch. If you have a Sim who likes to paint, setting up an easel out there would be nice, especially once they reach level 5 and can paint still-life scenes picked out by you. The small bathroom upstairs lacks a bath or shower, so it can be smaller and give extra room to the social area at the top of the stairs.

A cool thing about the Winsome Farmhouse is that it challenges where objects can be placed. The fence around the stairs is pulled from the fence category in Build Mode, but there is no hard and fast rule that it needs to be outside. In fact, the lattice at the top of the fence adds to the rustic atmosphere of this

quaint farmhouse. However, leaving the fence white is a good choice because despite what you may think, there is such a thing as *too much pink*.

The Gables

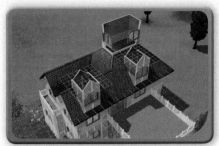

A striking feature of the Winsome Farmhouse is the gables. Creating gables actually isn't that difficult. It just takes a little patience to lay out your plan and then construct it.

After laying out the second floor, create a ceiling just above it. Then, use the Wall tool to make small "rooms." These will not be connected to any other room. There will be no doors.

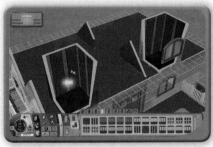

However, because there will be windows, it's important to paint the inside of these small rooms that make the artful gables.

After making these rooms, go up one floor and place down a section of roof. Don't use auto-roof, because you want control over the height and positioning.

The Grounds

The grounds are just as critical to the beauty of the Winsome Farmhouse as the gabled house itself. The incredible amount of plant life on the grounds really makes the house

stand out. On this lot, the pink theme extends from the house to the cherry trees that highlight the grounds. There are shrubs everywhere, too, and the use of the terrain patterns lets you transform regular grass into pleasing patches of small flowers without spending Simoleons on vegetation.

To give the lot "texture," use different sizes of trees. There are two sizes of cherry trees, for example. Mixing them together ensures that the top view of your lot isn't all the same.

Mix up the trees, too. The cherry trees are beautiful, but adding a voluminous willow gives the grounds additional character.

Brambles, azaleas, and other flowers give the lot additional texture at a ground level.

199

Don't forget that both the garbage can and mailbox can be dressed up with Create a Style. The Winsome Farmhouse's pink theme carries over to the trash, which is nicely sectioned off from the grounds in a small fenced area decorated with flowers.

Sinking a pond with the Water tool is a good way to also add depth to your creations. Smooth it out for a professional look.

Le Grand Palace

Created by: Lightside

This sprawling, regal estate uses almost every square inch of the immense lot to heighten its sense of opulence. Features that make this lot such a standout include the central pond, the wing-shaped design of the house itself, and the creative garden labyrinth in the back. That's a perfect place for children to play. Le Grand Palace is loaded with living space, which makes it great lot for a large household or a Sim who constantly throws parties for the whole town.

The House

Let's look at some of the tricks employed to create the manor's dynamic appearance.

Note the shape of the outer walls. The indentations every 10 or so feet give the exterior of the house real texture. These small alcoves gather shadows and give the exterior some character. However, these alcoves are not entirely practical for room shapes. Look at how the designer left some empty space and created an extra interior wall to smooth the inside of the manor wings. The outside is allowed some of those alcoves, but the interior wall is smoothed off. Because this interior wall prevents the exterior windows from looking in on a nicely decorated room, painting the interior wall is critical for appearances.

Let's bring it down one more floor. Here, you can see just how powerful the Wall tool is. Try to think of it as more than just the means of closing off a room. It is a way to create interesting living space shapes. Check out the exterior of the entire lot. Those small "towers" that line the lot and anchor the fence line were created with just the Wall tool. Plaster the exterior with a cement or stucco texture and you have a nice small tower.

Create different shapes in the towers and then link them with fences to fashion a dynamic "wall" for the exterior of your lot.

The Labyrinth

The hedge maze is one of those cool ideas that you have to see somebody else create to think of it yourself. Again, this is a testament to the versatility of Build Mode. You get all of these pieces that seem to have specific uses, but to get the most out of them, you need to free yourself of preconceptions. Those hedges don't have to line driveways or property—they can create a cool labyrinth. This kind of thing gets your lot noticed on The Exchange.

This labyrinth was made with the High Shrubber from the fence collection. To make the maze, just pull small pieces along to make a path. Maximize the space you designate for your labyrinth by starting from the outside and working in.

The Pool

The pool is another remarkable feature on this lot. It defies the common idea of a swimming pool by creating fun shapes in the water. You are not stuck with just a rectangle. Think bigger and more elaborate, like this designer did. Create a pool with unique islands in the center so your Sims have an interesting space to explore. Don't just leave those islands empty. Place a cherry tree in the center of the pool. You don't have to worry about roots bursting through the sides of your pool.

The Pond

The pond that decorates the courtyard looks expensive but is relatively cheap to make. The three cattails that mark the pond are just §10 each, but they give the pond needed texture. After placing the three cattails in the pond at different intervals, start sinking it with the Water Tool. The square brush works best.

You can sink the pond and then use the terrain leveller to create the dimensions of the pond itself. Once you have done that, you can section off the pond with short shrubbery from the fence category.

The House Interior

Much of the house interior is left blank. Consider the rooms your canvas and imagine what you would fill a mansion with. The central area where the two wings meet is very regal. The sitting room upstairs has lots of seating. The lighting is essential to complete the look of the room, as it cannot be too modern. Old's Kool candle fixtures on the wall are a nice touch.

Use art that matches your theme. The Prince of Pickleburp is practically made for an estate like this.

TIP

Don't neglect your Sims' painted creations. You can get great environmental bonuses from your Sim's personal paintings.

FoxGlen Manor

Created by: Sterling DT

The FoxGlen Manor is a very nice statehouse build on elevated grounds and surrounded by various trees. Using trees as natural fencing instead of walls is a nice way to blend a house with the natural surroundings. Many of the neighborhoods in lower Sunset Valley do not offer the space necessary for a manor like this, so such a lot is better suited for the vistas overlooking the town.

The Grounds

By turning on Build Mode and pulling back, you can see how the lot was textured to build a sort of "pedestal" for the manor. Raising the land to create a multi-tiered lot like this is very easy with the Terrain tools. Use the Raise Terrain tool to pull the land up. Then soften the rough edge with the Smoothing tool so you create natural-looking steps instead of a harsh landscape.

Decorate the various steps with flower and small trees. To highlight these trees at night, drill lights into the soil at the bases of the trees.

The front of the house features a nice walk-up. Sims will walk up raised ground on their own, but the stairs add refinement. To stretch stairs over the incline, just anchor them at the top level and "pull" the stairs in the direction you want them to drop.

201

If you create elaborate grounds, use large windows (Ye Olde Window is pictured here) so you can see the splendor from inside the house.

Exterior balconies overlooking the grounds are another good feature. This Sim may want a chair out here to sit and read. That would help get a Beautiful Vista moodlet. This balcony would also be a great place to paint.

The Kitchen

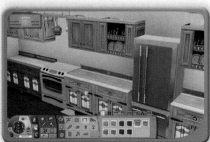

The kitchen in FoxGlen manor is large and loaded with nice equipment. Interestingly, the counters and cabinets are not all exact matches. Mixing elements keeps an environment from looking too similar. It's inviting to the eye because you are trying to see which elements are slightly different without being too intrusive on each other.

TIP
This kitchen boosts the environment bonus by using objects like the hanging pot rack.

This kitchen is very attractive, but it does not splurge on objects. You do not need to buy top of the line all of the time, especially if you are not developing a particular skill. This kitchen is huge and pleasing to look at, but does not go crazy with small appliances, disposals, or dishwashers. It keeps an elementary look so the designer could spend Simoleons elsewhere, such as on those impressive exterior grounds.

Fireplaces

No large manor is complete without a fireplace. Fireplaces add warmth to your Sims' lives (the Cozy Fire moodlet is a easy pleaser), but they also add a central point in a house for you to build out from. From this Fireplace 2.0—complete with the ability to change the color of the flames—you build out into a sitting room where Sims will enjoy lounging with a book. A skill book, perhaps?

See how having a focal point like a fireplace anchors a room? Now you have a "starting point" for building out, which helps with creating symmetry.

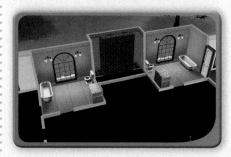

Fireplace chimneys automatically stretch to the roof of a house, no matter if it's two

stories or seven. This constant anchor gives you a reference point when constructing an upper floor above the main level. Here, you can see how two bathrooms look appealing when built symmetrically on each side of the chimney. If desired, you can wall off a chimney without any worry of a fire hazard.

The Cherry Tree Houses

Created by: Lightside

Not every lot must contain a single building. Explore the idea of multiple units on a single lot, as you see in this design sample. Here, you have what are essentially three condo buildings on the same lot. Each building mirrors the other two, giving the lot a great deal of symmetry. These buildings are empty, so the interior tour will not necessarily jump off the page because of intriguing object placement. But the shapes and assembly of the rooms show how you can get a lot of building without needing a major footprint.

The Buildings

If you want a story with different Sims who are not related by family or marriage, creating a lot like this is an good place to start. Strip away the rooftops and you see two upper rooms that would be perfect for a small bathroom and bedroom. Because each unit has limited space, you can save some money on objects. You could even dedicate one of these buildings to skills and communal activities. Maybe the top floor of the third condo has the computer and a telescope.

What's New | Creating a Sim | Creating a House | A Day in the Life | Simology | Relationships and Aging | Tour of Sunset Valley | **Design Corner** | Object Catalog | Community

The bottom level demonstrates how the small footprint doesn't necessarily sacrifice living space. The upstairs is dedicated to bathroom and sleeping, while the downstairs has a nice entry that doubles as a living room and a side area for a kitchen. Returning to the communal idea, you could break down the walls between two of these rooms to create a large kitchen for everyone to use.

The Courtyard

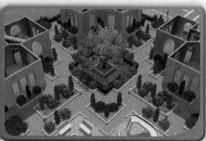

Check out the detail and symmetry in this courtyard. It's natural to take chaos and put it in order, which is why a symmetrical courtyard like this is so inviting. The equal proportions on the shrubs is nice. However, the most grabbing feature is the central pond with the large cherry tree in the middle. The low shrubbery that surrounds the pond is a nice touch, and notice the flowerbeds built from shrubs. The shrub border extends onto the concrete, giving the pond an added element of composition, rather than just serving as a containment field for the pond.

The island in the center of the pond with the tree has a nice border on it. It's built out of the small Stream of Consciousness fence.

Each piece of the fence has a post. However, if you stretch it all the way along a border, you only get two posts: one at the start and the other at the end. To create multiple posts as seen here, stretch the fence along one segment at a time. Let off the left mouse button and the fence piece drops into place with the post at the end of it.

The Playground

If you place your Sims in multiple smaller units on a single lot, you need a place for them to get together and relax. Children will love a playground, seen here constructed out of a swing set and slide. Grown-ups enjoy sitting around the fire pit, getting the Cozy Fire moodlet and roasting meats or marshmallows to sate hunger.

> ### TIP
>
> When creating lots, think about where your Sims will spend time together. Being social is an important part of the Sim experience, so building specific places where it is natural for Sims to socialize is important for getting the most out of the game.

Use [Alt] while placing objects so you can adjust their placement in smaller increments than 45-degree rotational clicks.

Drag the colors from one object to the next in Create a Style to match up all of the outdoor pieces.

Richmond Manor

Created by: Estatica

The Richmond Manor sidesteps the McMansion look by appearing on a thoughtful lot that includes the always desirable feature of a moat. Sure, this moat does not go all the way around the house, but such a prominent feature affects your first impression. The house itself is a smart collection of rooms that organically feed into each other. Inside the manor, the areas make sense in the context of each other.

The Moat

After creating the base of the house, sinking a moat is actually pretty simple with the Water tool. Hold down the left mouse button and simply trace the main line of the moat, and then go back over it, sinking the earth where desired and watching it fill back up with water. After completing a pass or two, switch to the Smoothing tool and sand down any rough edges. When you have nice, smooth declines into the water, you can start on the bridge.

Design Corner

To create a patio or deck that extends out from the base of the house and goes partially over the water, you must create supports. Use the Wall tool here to create 1x1 squares on the ground. Paint those walls with brick so they look like stone pillars inside of interior walls and then go up one level to place your patio/landing on top of it.

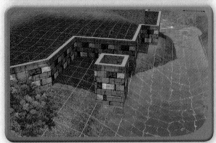

The patio needs a feature. An outdoor chess table is the perfect fit. It provides both Fun and Logic development.

Use the terrain textures to create rock paths around the grounds. There is no charge for this tool, so make good use of it like this designer did.

House Interior

The inside of the Richmond Manor is smartly detailed with very little wasted space. Note the clean line from the front door to the door leading on to the back patio with the chess set. Off this main drag is the staircase, which provides a natural division for the ground floor.

The kitchen is just off the main entrance. The kitchen incorporates an informal dining area in addition to the main dining table in the larger section of the ground floor. This small dining area is constructed of cheaper objects because it is off from the main entrance. Sims entering get the benefit of Nicely Decorated when they come in the front door. They don't need an expensive dining nook to maintain a good mood.

The study is tucked almost beneath the stairs as a way to place a solitary activity like using the computer away from more community-oriented living spaces.

The upstairs in the manor is nicely sectioned, too. The stairs lead up to a simple, tastefully decorated landing. Off this main landing is a sitting area for gathering with friends. Two bedrooms flow off the landing, each

with a small bathroom that uses a space-saving shower.

The table in one of the guest bedroom is decorated with accent items like Stack o' Mags and a Beauty Box. These simple, inexpensive objects bump the room's environment rating.

BROWNIE BITES

Use these lots as inspiration for your own creations. You don't need to mirror the features you see here—although I wouldn't blame you if you built a moat on every lot you make. Moats are just cool.

Thinking about the houses you have seen in the real world seems like a natural jumping off point when designing your own lots, but it can also limit your imagination. Don't anchor yourself to the practical. In real life, you could never plant a tree on an island in a pool, because the roots would eventually poke through the walls and ruin the pool. But such things are not concerns in Build Mode. Let that free you to think about the real definition of a "dream house."

Object Catalog

With the exception of your Sims' appearance, your home is the ultimate personal expression in *The Sims 3*. You may only start out with a little money, but once you settle into your new life and your family begins bringing in steady paychecks, you can really indulge that interior decorator that exists inside all of us. Will every room be a masterpiece? No, but your evolving home will eventually be paradise to you—and that's really all you can ask for.

This full catalog of objects inside *The Sims 3* lists everything you can purchase and customize for your homes. From stoves to cones, every item is detailed here with all relevant prices and properties, such as effects on skills or the well-being of your Sims. We've also assembled a few rooms to fire up your imagination so you can see how objects are sorted. Of course, you are not limited to putting sinks in bathrooms and couches in living rooms. This is your dream house. If you dream of having a bathtub in the kitchen, then so be it. It's just a click away.

NOTE

Some objects in these rooms have been customized with different patterns and colors than the default settings. You should experiment, too, and come up with your own incredible home decor ideas.

CAUTION

All objects you can buy in this catalog depreciate the moment you click out of Buy Mode. The first day's worth of depreciation is 10 percent. Each day thereafter strips another 10 percent of value from the object. The full depreciated value of the object, though, bottoms out at 40 percent of its original value. It can never be worth less than that unless the object is broken or severely damaged in a fire.

Ingredients, fish, harvestables, walls, floors, fences, and doors do not depreciate in value.

USING THIS CATALOG

Each object has a price and the potential for additional values. Some objects meet needs, like Bladder and Hunger. Other objects contribute to skill development, such as Logic or Cooking. When an object has properties that fall into these categories, it is noted in the table. The numerical value is listed under the heading of the need or skill. The higher the number, the more the object satisfies that need or helps with that skill's development.

Additional columns in these tables rate the object's environmental rating, group activity, and comfort. The more objects with a good environmental rating that are in a room, the better Decorated moodlet your Sims will enjoy. Group activity (marked with an X when present) indicates that multiple Sims can either use the object or the object is designed to bring Sims together for entertainment. Finally, the comfort rating (rated in +'s) notes how comfortable an object is, which can result in a nice Comfy moodlet.

Living Room

The living room is the central nervous system of your household. Sims do most of their socializing here. You can set up your living room in a variety of ways. You can feed directly into it from the front door or bury it deeper in your house. You are also not limited to making just one distinct living room. Try creating specialized or themed rooms such as a parlor for entertaining guests or a media room for a good night of vegging in front of the telly.

Social Setting

Immediately welcome your guests into your home by fashioning a warm social area right inside the front door. Inviting chairs positioned so everybody faces each other are perfect for getting a good conversation going—which might do wonders for your social

life, especially if you are new in town. Just be sure you have something on-hand to fill any potential silences. A nice stereo is sure to fill those awkward conversational potholes.

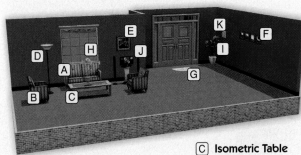

[A] **The Prim and Proper**
§400
Comfort

[B] **The Avant**
§375
Environment: 2, Comfort

[C] **Isometric Table**
§265
Environment: 1

[D] **Blushing Torchiere**
§120

[E] **Village No. 7**
§250
Environment: 5

[F] **Photo Series: Hipster Edition**
§440
Environment: 6

[G] **Poor Man's Half-Round Rug**
§30

[H] **Blossoming Sunflower Vase**
§70
Environment: 1

[I] **Philodendron**
§95
Environment: 1

[J] **85g Audio Explosion from Landgraab Industries**
§1,800
Fun: 3, + Athletic, Group Activity, Music

[K] **Thief-Tech's Gotcha! Burglar Alarm**
§250

Object Catalog

SOFAS & LOVESEATS

Object	Price	Daily Depreciation	Fully Deprec. Value	Environment	Hygiene	Hunger	Bladder	Energy	Fun	Logic	Charisma	Cooking	Athletic	Painting	Guitar	Handiness	Gardening	Writing	Fishing	Stress Relief	Group Activity	Comfort
The Cuddler Loveseat	225	22.5	90																			1
Big Sky County Couch	335	33.5	134																			1
Power of Loveseat	350	35	140																			2
The Prim and Proper	400	40	160																			2
Super Sunshine Happy Sofa	450	45	180																			2
The Plutonic Loveseat	695	69.5	278																			2
El Sol Sofa by Gunter	750	75	300	2																		2
The Matchmaker	795	79.5	318	2																		3
Sofa LE	895	89.5	358																			2
Catharti-Couch	900	90	360																			2
Patata del Sofa	915	91.5	366																			2
The Suitable Sofa	925	92.5	370																			2
Sofa Souffle	985	98.5	394	3																		3
Sofa Sonata	1,100	110	440	3																		2
The Dromedary	1,200	120	480	3																		3

NOTE

When creating a house, you must have these objects: bed, toilet, and refrigerator. These are essential for basic needs.

LIVING ROOM CHAIRS

	Object	Price	Daily Depreciation	Fully Deprec. Value	Environment	Hygiene	Hunger	Bladder	Energy	Fun	Logic	Charisma	Cooking	Athletic	Painting	Guitar	Handiness	Gardening	Writing	Fishing	Stress Relief	Group Activity	Comfort
	The Savannah	115	11.5	46																			1
	Lazy Lounger	225	22.5	90																			2
	The Avant	375	37.5	150	2																		2
	Swank Living Room Chair	450	45	180	2																		2
	Passable Mission Chair	660	66	264	2																		3
	The Olafian	695	69.5	278	2																		3
	Bracken Living Room Chair	900	90	360	2																		3
	Pete's Living Room Chair	1,000	100	400	2																		3

ALARMS

	Object	Price	Daily Depreciation	Fully Deprec. Value	Environment	Hygiene	Hunger	Bladder	Energy	Fun	Logic	Charisma	Cooking	Athletic	Painting	Guitar	Handiness	Gardening	Writing	Fishing	Stress Relief	Group Activity	Comfort
	Panic Rouser Fire Alarm	100	10	40																			
	Thief-Tech's Gotcha! Burglar Alarm	250	25	100																			

Media Room

Before bedding down for the evening, why not retire to the media room to catch up on your favorite television series or movie. Kids can definitely keep themselves out of trouble in here with the videogame console hooked up to the television.

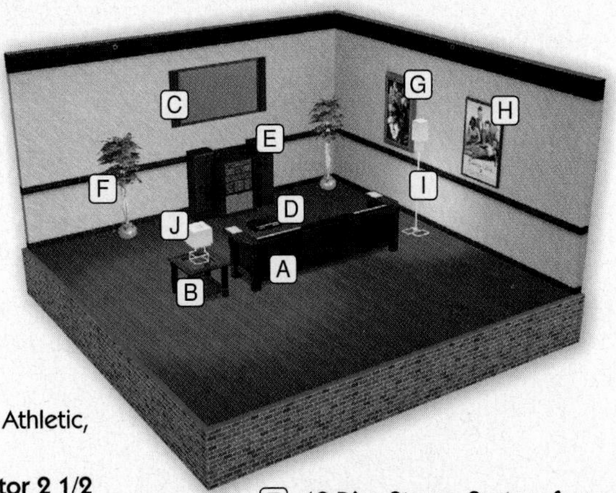

A **El Sol Sofa by Gunter**
§750
Environment: 2,
Comfort

B **Roman Coffee Table**
§185
Environment: 1

C **WallVuu Standard TV**
$8,000
Fun: 8, + Cooking, + Athletic,
Group Activity

D **Maxoid Game Simulator 2 1/2**
§750
Fun: 7

E **18 Disc Stereo System from Albacore Audio**
§475
Fun: 3, + Athletic, Group Activity, Music

F **Ficus Tree Shrub**
§230
Environment: 2

G **Obscure Film Poster**
§415
Environment: 2

H **Detention Hall Poster**
§30
Environment: 2

I **Golden Glow Floor Lamp**
§415
Environment: 2

J **Baronian Table Lamp**
§300
Environment: 2

TVS

Object	Price	Daily Depreciation	Fully Deprec. Value	Environment	Hygiene	Hunger	Bladder	Energy	Fun	Logic	Charisma	Cooking	Athletic	Painting	Guitar	Handiness	Gardening	Writing	Fishing	Stress Relief	Group Activity	Comfort
Old Timey Tele	200	20	80						3				x								x	
Channel Trowler 27" Deluxe TV	500	50	200						4			x	x								x	
UberVision Panoramic from Landgraab Industries	1,200	120	480						5				x				x	x				
36" HiFi Plasmondo TV from Landgraab Industries	3,500	350	1400						6			x	x				x	x				
WallVuu Standard TV	8,000	800	3200						8													

VIDEO GAMES

Object	Price	Daily Depreciation	Fully Deprec. Value	Environment	Hygiene	Hunger	Bladder	Energy	Fun	Logic	Charisma	Cooking	Athletic	Painting	Guitar	Handiness	Gardening	Writing	Fishing	Stress Relief	Group Activity	Comfort
Maxoid Game Simulator 2 1/2	750	75	300						7													
SimLife Googles	9500	950	3800						10													

The Parlor

Distinguished company will enjoy retreating to your inner parlor for a stimulating evening of drinks and deep conversation. Nestled inside the rich wood accents and deep reds, sophicated people can talk about sophisticated things such as politics and business. Just make sure your friends use coasters. Because coasters are pretty high society.

[A] **The Dromedary**
§1,200
Environment: 3, Comfort

[B] **Bracken Living Room Chair**
§900
Environment: 2, Comfort

[C] **Decaf Coffee Table**
§325
Environment: 1

[D] **Bunker Hill Floor Light**
§300
Environment: 2

[E] **Old's Kool Lighting**
§165
Environment: 1

[F] **Ficus Tree Shrub**
§230
Environment: 2

[G] **RocketRug from Randy Homson**
§140

[H] **Class E Juice Bar**
(from the Dining Room catalog)
§640
Fun: 6, Environment: 1

COFFEE TABLES

Object	Price	Daily Depreciation	Fully Deprec. Value	Environment	Hygiene	Hunger	Bladder	Energy	Fun	Logic	Charisma	Cooking	Athletic	Painting	Guitar	Handiness	Gardening	Writing	Fishing	Stress Relief	Group Activity	Comfort
Two-Ton Table	90	9	36																			
Old Timer's Coffee Table	125	12.5	50																			
The Mission Coffee Table by Lulu Designs	150	15	60																			
Roman Coffee Table	185	18.5	74	1																		
The Larger Mission Coffee Table by Lulu Designs	245	24.5	98	1																		
Isometric Table	265	26.5	106	1																		
Case Closed Coffee Table	285	28.5	114	2																		
Literal Coffee Table	300	30	120	1																		
Decaf Coffee Table	325	32.5	130	1																		

AUDIO

Object	Price	Daily Depreciation	Fully Deprec. Value	Environment	Hygiene	Hunger	Bladder	Energy	Fun	Logic	Charisma	Cooking	Athletic	Painting	Guitar	Handiness	Gardening	Writing	Fishing	Stress Relief	Group Activity	Comfort
Audio Lite by LoFi Audio	150	15	60						3				x								x	
18 Disc Stereo System from Albacore Audio	475	47.5	190						3				x								x	
85g Audio Explosion from Landgraab Industries	1800	180	720						3				x								x	

The Singleton

Living alone has its benefits—you need less room, and that equates into real estate savings. Less room means less stuff to clean, too. Try combining room functions into the same space, such as this living room/study hybrid. With a bookcase and computer within reach of your TV chair, the only risk is over-stimulation.

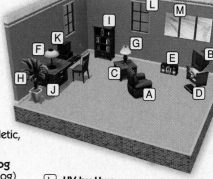

[A] **Lazy Lounger**
§225
Comfort

[B] **Channel Trowler 27" Deluxe TV**
§500
Fun: 4, + Cooking, + Athletic, Group Activity

[C] **Two-Ton Table**
§90

[D] **Maxoid Game Simulator 2 1/2**
§750
Fun: 7

[E] **Audio Lite by LoFi Audio**
§150
Fun: 3, + Athletic, Group Activity

[F] **Lodge Lamp**
§75

[G] **Lamp Revere**
§65

[H] **Philodendron**
§95
Environment: 1

[I] **Shelves del Libro** (from Study catalog)
§350
Fun: 3, + Cooking, + Athletic, + Handiness

[J] **Desk Moderne from Gorog Designs** (from Study catalog)
§325
Environment: 1

[K] **Easy Machine from Fred's PC Hut** (from Study catalog)
§800
Fun: 3

[L] **UV by Uwe**
§50

[M] **Smooth Jam in Three Parts**
§1,100
Environment: 7

RUGS

Object	Price	Daily Depreciation	Fully Deprec. Value	Environment	Hygiene	Hunger	Bladder	Energy	Fun	Logic	Charisma	Cooking	Athletic	Painting	Guitar	Handiness	Gardening	Writing	Fishing	Stress Relief	Group Activity	Comfort
Poor Man's Half-Round Rug	30	3	12	2																		
The Saxony	35	3.5	14	2																		
L7 Rug	50	5	20	2																		
Modern Oval Rug	50	5	20	2																		
Welcome, Matt	65	6.5	26	2																		
Aristocratic First Oval Rug	80	8	32	3																		
Purrrfect Rug	95	9.5	38	3																		
Flying Carpet	100	10	40	3																		
RocketRug from Randy Homson	140	14	56	3																		
Marathon Carpet Runner	165	16.5	66	4																		
Dated, Faded Floral Rug	315	31.5	126	4																		
Chandelier Rug	400	40	160	4																		

NOTE

Don't forget, you can also add fireplaces to living rooms for a hearty hearth that the entire household will enjoy.

What's New | Creating a Sim | Creating a House | A Day in the Life | Simology | Relationships and Aging | Tour of Sunset Valley | Design Corner | Object Catalog | Community

Kitchen

Since no Sim can properly function in society without a full stomach, the kitchen is another critical part of the house. Stock the kitchen with the things necessary to create at least simple meals, such as a stove, sink, and refrigerator. Counter space is also important, as your Sim will need someplace to prepare meals more complex than a bowl of cereal.

Posh Kitchen

Top of the line appliances highlight this cavernous kitchen. Sims skilled in the art of cooking will have a fine time developing their latest dishes in this kitchen. Note the absence of a microwave, though. Zapped meals? How gauche.

A **The Fresher Refrigerator**
§1,800
Hunger: 8, Environment: 1

B **Festus 44**
§1,000
Hunger: 9, + Cooking

C **Real Flat Counter**
§800
Environment: 2

D **Volcanor Sulphorous Sink**
§415
Hygiene: 4, Environment: 1

E **Real Flat Overhead Cabinet**
§310
Environment: 2

F **Far Out Wall Sconce**
§95

G **Crazy Grady's Trash Compactor**
§400

H **Panic Rouser Fire Alarm**
§100

I **Excellent Anson Hot Beverage Maker**
§1,100
Energy: 3

J **Immobile Phone**
§50

REFRIDGERATORS

Object	Price	Daily Depreciation	Fully Deprec. Value	Environment	Hygiene	Hunger	Bladder	Energy	Fun	Logic	Charisma	Cooking	Athletic	Painting	Guitar	Handiness	Gardening	Writing	Fishing	Stress Relief	Group Activity	Comfort
Chillgood Fridge	375	37.5	150			5																
2-Door Galore Refrigerator	650	65	260			6																
Icebox Drawer	1200	120	480			7																
The Fresher Refrigerator	1800	180	720	1		8																

STOVES

Object	Price	Daily Depreciation	Fully Deprec. Value	Environment	Hygiene	Hunger	Bladder	Energy	Fun	Logic	Charisma	Cooking	Athletic	Painting	Guitar	Handiness	Gardening	Writing	Fishing	Stress Relief	Group Activity	Comfort
SimmerChar Dual-State Stove	400	40	160			4						x										
Cowpoke Stove	550	55	220			5						x										
Tri-Forge Stove	800	80	320			7						x										
Festus 44	1000	100	400			9						x										

Object Catalog

SINKS

	Object	Price	Daily Depreciation	Fully Deprec. Value	Environment	Hygiene	Hunger	Bladder	Energy	Fun	Logic	Charisma	Cooking	Athletic	Painting	Guitar	Handiness	Gardening	Writing	Fishing	Stress Relief	Group Activity	Comfort
	Plain Basin	120	12	48	2																		
	Squatter's Sink	150	15	60	2																		
	Pepper Pot Sink	215	21.5	86	3																		
	The Unsinkable Sink	240	24	96	3																		
	Rinky Dinky Kitchen Sinky	290	29	116	3																		
	Volcanor Sulphorous Sink	315	31.5	126	4																		
	Fontainebleu Fountain Sink	390	39	156	2	4																	
	Sink in Despair	500	50	200	3	5																	

Modest Kitchen

Sometimes, simple is best—and this is one simple kitchen. Stocked with only the essentials for preparing simple meals, this kitchen is perfect for the beginner homeowner who isn't interested in keeping up with the Joneses. After all, once you start that contest, you never know where it could end.

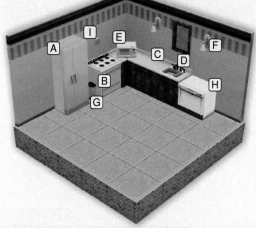

[A] **Chillgood Fridge**
§375
Hunger: 5

[B] **SimmerChar Dual-State Stove**
§400
Hunger: 4, + Cooking

[C] **Counter Culture Counter**
§215
Environment: 1

[D] **Rinky Dinky Kitchen Sinky**
§290
Hygiene: 3

[E] **Steak & Prank Microwave**
§240

[F] **Werffelhousen Sconce**
§75

[G] **Mirage Garbage**
§50

[H] **Swish Dishwasher**
§300

[I] **Panic Rouser Fire Alarm**
§100

COUNTERS

	Object	Price	Daily Depreciation	Fully Deprec. Value	Environment	Hygiene	Hunger	Bladder	Energy	Fun	Logic	Charisma	Cooking	Athletic	Painting	Guitar	Handiness	Gardening	Writing	Fishing	Stress Relief	Group Activity	Comfort
	Country Fried Counter	140	14	56																			
	Country Fried Counter Island	145	14.5	58																			
	Counter Culture Counter	215	21.5	86	1																		

COUNTERS, CONTINUED

Object	Price	Daily Depreciation	Fully Deprec. Value	Environment	Hygiene	Hunger	Bladder	Energy	Fun	Logic	Charisma	Cooking	Athletic	Painting	Guitar	Handiness	Gardening	Writing	Fishing	Stress Relief	Group Activity	Comfort
Counter Culture Counter Island	220	22	88	1																		
The Impossible Mission Counter	475	47.5	190	1																		
The Impossible Mission Counter Island	480	48	192	1																		
The Immemorial Counter	625	62.5	250	2																		
Immemorial Counter Island	630	63	252	2																		
Real Flat Counter	800	80	320	2																		
Real Flat Counter Island	805	80.5	322	2																		

CABINETS

Object	Price	Daily Depreciation	Fully Deprec. Value	Environment	Hygiene	Hunger	Bladder	Energy	Fun	Logic	Charisma	Cooking	Athletic	Painting	Guitar	Handiness	Gardening	Writing	Fishing	Stress Relief	Group Activity	Comfort
Country Fried Overhead Cabinet	100	10	40	1																		
Country Fried Overhead China	105	10.5	42	1																		
Counter Culture Overhead Cabinet	130	13	52	1																		
Counter Culture Overhead Cabinet (Double-Sided)	135	13.5	54	1																		
Hanging Pot Rack	150	15	60	1																		
Immemorial Overhead Cabinet	165	16.5	66	1																		
Immemorial Overhead Cabinet (Double-Sided)	170	17	68	1																		
The Impossible Mission Overhead Cabinet	230	23	92	1																		
The Impossible Mission Overhead Cabinet (Double-Sided)	235	23.5	94	1																		

Object Catalog

CABINETS, CONTINUED

Object	Price	Daily Depreciation	Fully Deprec. Value	Environment	Hygiene	Hunger	Bladder	Energy	Fun	Logic	Charisma	Cooking	Athletic	Painting	Guitar	Handiness	Gardening	Writing	Fishing	Stress Relief	Group Activity	Comfort
Real Flat Overhead Cabinet	310	31	124	2																		
Real Flat Overhead Cabinet (Double-Sided)	315	31.5	126	2																		

DISPOSALS

Object	Price	Daily Depreciation	Fully Deprec. Value	Environment	Hygiene	Hunger	Bladder	Energy	Fun	Logic	Charisma	Cooking	Athletic	Painting	Guitar	Handiness	Gardening	Writing	Fishing	Stress Relief	Group Activity	Comfort
Open Arms and Feelings Trashcan	25	2.5	10																			
Mirage Garbage	50	5	20																			
Crazy Grady's Trash Compactor	400	40	160																			

Family-Style

Growing households need a larger kitchen that can accommodate at least two people preparing a meal. This family kitchen is complete with a wraparound counter that offers additional space for food prep. Note the dishwasher under the counter, which is achieved by installing it after the counter is in place.

[A] **2-Door Galore**
§650
Hunger: 6

[B] **Tri-Forge Stove**
§800
Hunger: 7, + Cooking

[C] **Impossible Mission Counter**
§475
Environment: 1

[D] **Rinky Dinky Kitchen Sinky**
§290
Hygiene: 3

[E] **Impossible Mission Overhead Cabinet**
§230
Environment: 1

[F] **Hanging Pot Rack**
§150
Environment: 1

[G] **Primo Deluxe Dishwasher**
§700
Environment: 2

[H] **Nanowaver**
§300
+ Cooking

[I] **998 Table Top Topia Phon**
§35

[J] **Core Precesso 235X**
§280
+ Cooking

[K] **Super-Absorbent Super Towels**
§20
Environment: 1

SMALL APPLIANCES

Object	Price	Daily Depreciation	Fully Deprec. Value	Environment	Hygiene	Hunger	Bladder	Energy	Fun	Logic	Charisma	Cooking	Athletic	Painting	Guitar	Handiness	Gardening	Writing	Fishing	Stress Relief	Group Activity	Comfort
Steak & Prank Microwave	240	24	96									x										
Ingredient Eviscerator 235X	280	28	112									x										

214

SMALL APPLIANCES, CONTINUED

Object	Price	Daily Depreciation	Fully Deprec. Value	Environment	Hygiene	Hunger	Bladder	Energy	Fun	Logic	Charisma	Cooking	Athletic	Painting	Guitar	Handiness	Gardening	Writing	Fishing	Stress Relief	Group Activity	Comfort
The Nanowaver	300	30	120									x										
Excellent Anson Hot Beverage Maker	1100	110	440					3														

DISHWASHERS

Object	Price	Daily Depreciation	Fully Deprec. Value	Environment	Hygiene	Hunger	Bladder	Energy	Fun	Logic	Charisma	Cooking	Athletic	Painting	Guitar	Handiness	Gardening	Writing	Fishing	Stress Relief	Group Activity	Comfort
Swish Dishwasher	300	30	120																			
Primo Delux Dishwasher	700	70	280	2																		

Dining Room

The dining room is another place in the household for Sims to gather and gab over a good meal. Dining rooms are essential for Sims who like to host parties. Single Sims may not see much point in creating one of these rooms when first moving in. Soup can be enjoyed on the couch in front of the television, after all. But once you have a little extra in the bank, install at least a modest dining table and some chairs. It will do wonders for a growing family to spend meal times together.

Simple Dining

Maybe it's just you in that house—or a young couple just starting out. You need a place where you can sit and enjoy a bowl of cereal in the morning before rushing out the door to work. A small, simple dining area is a great place to shovel it down in the AM and relax over a hot meal in the PM.

A Table-Licious
§60

B Exquisite Bistro Chair
§40

C Cortinas Festivas!
§50
Environment: 2

D Small Ivy
§5
Environment: 2

E Stack o'Mags
§7
Environment: 1

F Philodendron
Environment: 1

DINING TABLES

Object	Price	Daily Depreciation	Fully Deprec. Value	Environment	Hygiene	Hunger	Bladder	Energy	Fun	Logic	Charisma	Cooking	Athletic	Painting	Guitar	Handiness	Gardening	Writing	Fishing	Stress Relief	Group Activity	Comfort
Table-Licious	60	6	24																			
Knack Outdoor Tables	85	8.5	34																			

DINING TABLES, CONTINUED

Object	Price	Daily Depreciation	Fully Deprec. Value	Environment	Hygiene	Hunger	Bladder	Energy	Fun	Logic	Charisma	Cooking	Athletic	Painting	Guitar	Handiness	Gardening	Writing	Fishing	Stress Relief	Group Activity	Comfort
Table de Bistro by Bourgeois Creations	195	19.5	78																			
Another Era Dining Table	200	20	80																			
Sunup Breakfast Table	225	22.5	90	1																		
Rendezvous Picnic Table	235	23.5	94																			
Style Town Dining Table	250	25	100	1																		
The Upscale Dining Table	285	28.5	114	1																		
Great Eats' Recycled Consumables Buffet Table	300	30	120			4																
Phobic Dining Table	450	45	180	2																		
Missionaire Dining Table	650	65	260	2																		
Xtra Long Dining Table	900	90	360	2																		

DINING CHAIRS

Object	Price	Daily Depreciation	Fully Deprec. Value	Environment	Hygiene	Hunger	Bladder	Energy	Fun	Logic	Charisma	Cooking	Athletic	Painting	Guitar	Handiness	Gardening	Writing	Fishing	Stress Relief	Group Activity	Comfort
The Exquisite Bistro Chair by Bourgeois Creations	40	4	16																			1
Simmer Down Chair	75	7.5	30																			1
Rafkin's Dining Chair	80	8	32																			1
Mount of Comfort Dining Chair	90	9	36																			1
The Cozinator 450	100	10	40																			1
Final Contribution Dining Chair from Mike's Garage	115	11.5	46																			1
The Elsinore	120	12	48																			2

DINING CHAIRS, CONTINUED

Object	Price	Daily Depreciation	Fully Deprec. Value	Environment	Hygiene	Hunger	Bladder	Energy	Fun	Logic	Charisma	Cooking	Athletic	Painting	Guitar	Handiness	Gardening	Writing	Fishing	Stress Relief	Group Activity	Comfort
 Sit-Up Straight Dining Chair	150	15	60																			2
 Yankee Doodle Dining Chair	225	22.5	90																			2
 The Muga Sitzer	325	32.5	130	2																		2
 Old Sam's Dining Chair	900	90	360	2																		3
 UV by Uwe	50	5	20																			1
 Wellness Dining Chair	165	16.5	66																			2
 Overworked Office Chair	195	19.5	78																			2

Dinner Is Served

"...eeves, we will take our meal in the red room." ...his regal dining hall seats many distinguished ...uests on evenings where you throw your ...oors open to the neighborhood or invite over ...olleagues who require a little impressing.

A **Xtra Long Dining Table**
§900
Environment: 2

B **Old Sam's Dining Chair**
§900
Environment: 2

C **Curtains de Mish**
§285
Environment: 3

D **Chandelier Rug**
§400

E **Medusa Victim**
§1,650
Environment: 5

F **Old's Kool Lighting**
§165
Environment: 1

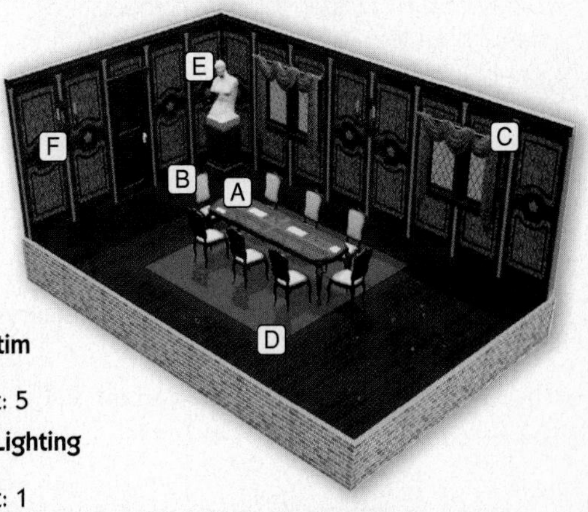

BARS

Object	Price	Daily Depreciation	Fully Deprec. Value	Environment	Hygiene	Hunger	Bladder	Energy	Fun	Logic	Charisma	Cooking	Athletic	Painting	Guitar	Handiness	Gardening	Writing	Fishing	Stress Relief	Group Activity	Comfort
 Class E Juice Bar	640	64	256	1					6													
 Juice Station	725	72.5	290	1					6													
 Bar de Mish	975	97.5	390	1					6													
Family Time Bar	1500	150	600	1					6													

Object Catalog

BARSTOOLS

Object	Price	Daily Depreciation	Fully Deprec. Value	Environment	Hygiene	Hunger	Bladder	Energy	Fun	Logic	Charisma	Cooking	Athletic	Painting	Guitar	Handiness	Gardening	Writing	Fishing	Stress Relief	Group Activity	Comfort
Parlor Perch Barstool	185	18.5	74																			1
Sturdy Stool	215	21.5	86																			2
Barstool de Mish	285	28.5	114																			2
Bab's Towering Barstool	435	43.5	174																			2
Old Sam's Barstool	520	52	208																			2

Grandma's Nook

Noshing is celebrated in this homey breakfast nook. You may be hard-pressed to see your food among the swirl of patterns and textures on the table and walls, though. However, a simple nook like this recalls the good times of days gone by, when you could slow down and enjoy the paper while eating a farmer's breakfast. Nowadays, it's just rush, rush, rush...

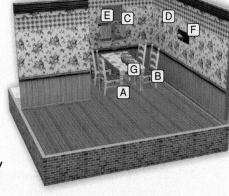

[A] **Sunup Breakfast Table**
§225
Environment: 1

[B] **The Cozinator**
§100

[C] **Vickleberry Country Curtain**
§95
Environment: 2

[D] **Grandma Wholesome's Folk Art Thingy**
$50
Environment: 2

[E] **Blossoming Sunflower Vase**
$70
Environment: 1

[F] **Wall-Mounted Fish**
$85
Environment: 1

[G] **Crocks O' Stuff**
$45
Environment: 1

CURTAINS & BLINDS

Object	Price	Daily Depreciation	Fully Deprec. Value	Environment	Hygiene	Hunger	Bladder	Energy	Fun	Logic	Charisma	Cooking	Athletic	Painting	Guitar	Handiness	Gardening	Writing	Fishing	Stress Relief	Group Activity	Comfort
Cortinas Festivas!	50	5	20	2																		
Traditional Curtains	68	6.8	27.2	2																		
Eyes Aside Curtains by Fancy Drapes	80	8	32	2																		
Vickleberry County Curtains	95	9.5	38	2																		
Tangle-Free Blinds	105	10.5	42	2																		

CURTAINS & BLINDS, CONTINUED

Object	Price	Daily Depreciation	Fully Deprec. Value	Environment	Hygiene	Hunger	Bladder	Energy	Fun	Logic	Charisma	Cooking	Athletic	Painting	Guitar	Handiness	Gardening	Writing	Fishing	Stress Relief	Group Activity	Comfort
Shout Out Shutters	130	13	52	2																		
Lofty Curtains	155	15.5	62	3																		
Shy Shutters	160	16	64	3																		
Cute Lil' Curtain	170	17	68	3																		
Simple Shade	185	18.5	74	3																		
Flattery Curtains	195	19.5	78	3																		
Antique Curtains by Respectable Rags	215	21.5	86	3																		
Hygieni-Curtains	230	23	92	3																		
Static Blinds	260	26	104	3																		
Curtains de Mish	285	28.5	114	3																		
Three Bean Bay Curtain	315	31.5	126	3																		
Wide, Lofty Curtains	325	32.5	130	3																		
The Window Protector	400	40	160	3																		

MISC. DECOR

Object	Price	Daily Depreciation	Fully Deprec. Value	Environment	Hygiene	Hunger	Bladder	Energy	Fun	Logic	Charisma	Cooking	Athletic	Painting	Guitar	Handiness	Gardening	Writing	Fishing	Stress Relief	Group Activity	Comfort
Wish-You Tissues	4	0.4	1.6	1																		
Stack o'Mags	7	0.7	2.8	1																		
Plain Pad & Pen Set	12	1.2	4.8	1																		
Beauty Box	15	1.5	6	1																		

MISC. DECOR, CONTINUED

Object	Price	Daily Depreciation	Fully Deprec. Value	Environment	Hygiene	Hunger	Bladder	Energy	Fun	Logic	Charisma	Cooking	Athletic	Painting	Guitar	Handiness	Gardening	Writing	Fishing	Stress Relief	Group Activity	Comfort
Rooster Utensil Holder	18	1.8	7.2	1																		
Super-Absorbent Super Towels	20	2	8	1																		
Decorative Fire Tools	25	2.5	10	1																		
Stink Mask Perfume	35	3.5	14	1																		
Crocks O' Stuff	45	4.5	18	1																		
Life Preserver	55	5.5	22	1																		
His/Hers Trophy Shelf	62	6.2	24.8	1																		
Magazine Restraint System	65	6.5	26	1																		
Mood-Lite Candle	65	6.5	26	1																		
The MediCabi	75	7.5	30	1																		
The Shrinkomatic Fishbowl	80	8	32																			
Main Attraction Puzzle Shelf	85	8.5	34	1																		
Wall-Mounted Fish	85	8.5	34	1																		
Already Retro CD Display Shelving	120	12	48	1																		
Mission Partition	180	18	72	4																		
Globe Sculpture	195	19.5	78	4																		
Bathroom Junk Holder	225	22.5	90	4																		
Peekaboo! Partition	410	41	164	5																		
Cow Plant	475	47.5	190	6																		
Sun Disk	1500	150	600	7																		

MISC. DECOR, CONTINUED

Object	Price	Daily Depreciation	Fully Deprec. Value	Environment	Hygiene	Hunger	Bladder	Energy	Fun	Logic	Charisma	Cooking	Athletic	Painting	Guitar	Handiness	Gardening	Writing	Fishing	Stress Relief	Group Activity	Comfort
 Medusa Victim	1650	165	660	7																		
Nearly-Perfect Pedestal	2000	200	800	5																		
 Immoderate Water Fountain	2150	215	860	8																		
 Ambiguity Itself	12225	1222.5	4890	10																		

Bedroom

Every night, you must lay your head down to sleep...lest you start losing basic motor skills. Sleep is very important for a Sim, whether it's a full night of rejuvenating slumber or a stolen nap. To get the right kind of sleep so you don't make tragic mistakes at your job or cannot even function in a conversation, you must have a bedroom complete with at least a bed. If you want to keep your job, an alarm clock isn't such a bad purchase either.

Let Us Retire

Co-habitating Sims will appreciate a bedroom with a little extra space. This mid-sized bedroom features everything you need for a pleasing night of sweet slumber as well as getting ready for the following day. The extra outlay on decor goes a long way toward boosting the environmental effects of the room, something that's important for keeping up a good mood in both the evening and the morning.

[A] **Sleep-Slave Double Bed**
§3,500
Energy: 9, Stress Relief: 3,
Environment: 3

[B] **Meta Table**
§195
Environment: 1

[C] **Smooth Slides Luxury Dresser**
§725
Environment: 2

[D] **The Reflectinator**
§350
Fun: 3, Environment: 4,
+ Charisma

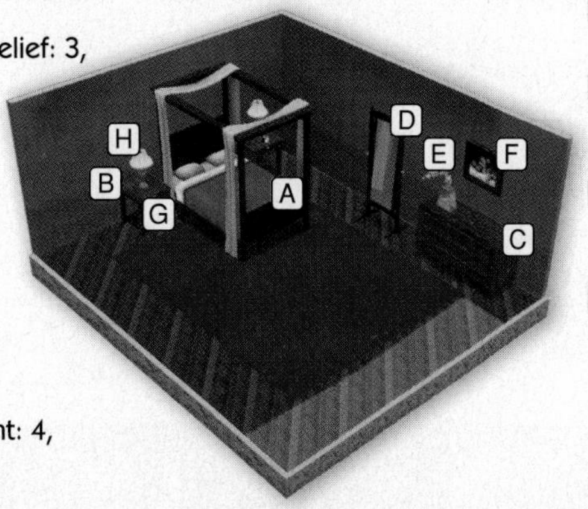

[E] **Modern Orchid**
§435

[F] **Still-Life Harvest**
§930
Environment: 6

[G] **No Snooze! Alarm Clock**
§60

[H] **Lamp Revere**
§65
Beds

BEDS

Object	Price	Daily Depreciation	Fully Deprec. Value	Environment	Hygiene	Hunger	Bladder	Energy	Fun	Logic	Charisma	Cooking	Athletic	Painting	Guitar	Handiness	Gardening	Writing	Fishing	Stress Relief	Group Activity	Comfort
 The Single Post Bed from McKraken Industries	300	30	120					4												3		
 Small Brass Bed	425	42.5	170					4												3		
 B.R.A.S.S. Double Bed	450	45	180					4												3		
 The Slumber Saddle of Sleepnir by Dulac Industries	560	56	224					4												3		
 The Four Post Bed from McKraken Industries	650	65	260					4												3		

Object Catalog

BEDS, CONTINUED

Object	Price	Daily Depreciation	Fully Deprec. Value	Environment	Hygiene	Hunger	Bladder	Energy	Fun	Logic	Charisma	Cooking	Athletic	Painting	Guitar	Handiness	Gardening	Writing	Fishing	Stress Relief	Group Activity	Comfort
The Emoti-Cot	700	70	280					4												3		
The Lullaby Bed	950	95	380	2				5												3		
The Legendary Bedscalibur by Dulac Industries	1100	110	440					5												3		
Single Sophisticate Bed	1450	145	580	4				8												3		
Double Sleep Raft	1500	150	600	2				6												3		
LuxurLove Sleepset from Lothario Designs	2200	220	880	2				8												3		
The Lexington	2800	280	1120	3				8												3		
Sleep-Slave Double Bed	3500	350	1400	4				10												3		

DRESSERS

Object	Price	Daily Depreciation	Fully Deprec. Value	Environment	Hygiene	Hunger	Bladder	Energy	Fun	Logic	Charisma	Cooking	Athletic	Painting	Guitar	Handiness	Gardening	Writing	Fishing	Stress Relief	Group Activity	Comfort
The Evrityme Dresser	450	45	180																			
Werkbunnst Stonewood Dresser	515	51.5	206																			
Homestead Dresser from McKraken Industries	600	60	240	2																		
Drawers of Dismissal Dresser	650	65	260	2																		
Smooth Slides Luxury Dresser	725	72.5	290	2																		
DeForester Dresser by William DeForester	850	85	340	2																		

he Devilish Suitor

hat time is it? It's business time. This boudoir where the suitor (or suitor-ette?) goes hen the lights are down low. The mirrored alls are perfect for just soaking in personal lendor. And nothing says sexy quite like bra print. That's a scientific fact. At least, it or zebras.

LuxurLove Sleepset
§2,200
Energy: 8, Stress Relief: 3, Environment: 2

[B] **LuLu's Artisan End Table**
§75

[C] **Golden Glow Floor Lamp**
§415
Environment: 2

[D] **Photon-Master 3000, Tabletop Edition**
§325
Environment: 2

[E] **Looking Glass Supreme**
§500/panel
Fun: 3, Environment: 4, + Charisma

[F] **Purrrfect Rug** (from Living Room)
§95

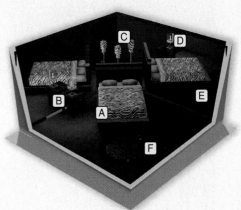

END TABLES

Object	Price	Daily Depreciation	Fully Deprec. Value	Environment	Hygiene	Hunger	Bladder	Energy	Fun	Logic	Charisma	Cooking	Athletic	Painting	Guitar	Handiness	Gardening	Writing	Fishing	Stress Relief	Group Activity	Comfort
Syntactic End Table	45	4.5	18																			
Trails End Table	50	5	20																			
LuLu's Artisan End Table	75	7.5	30																			
Double-Delux End Table	125	12.5	50																			
Virtual End Table	165	16.5	66	1																		
Meta Table	195	19.5	78	1																		
Tabla Del Extremo	245	24.5	98	1																		
Chaible	255	25.5	102	1																		
Gibson Butter Table from Gibson Dairy and Furnishings	285	28.5	114	1																		
Royal Francois End Table from XIV Antiquities	315	31.5	126	2																		

MIRRORS

Object	Price	Daily Depreciation	Fully Deprec. Value	Environment	Hygiene	Hunger	Bladder	Energy	Fun	Logic	Charisma	Cooking	Athletic	Painting	Guitar	Handiness	Gardening	Writing	Fishing	Stress Relief	Group Activity	Comfort
Mirror of Variance	50	5	20	2					3		x											
The Reflektor	80	8	32	2					3		x											
The Outhouse Mirror	100	10	40	2					3		x											
Functional Eloquence Mirror	175	17.5	70	2					3		x											
Feel Good Mirror	200	20	80	3					3		x											
Stock Mirror	250	25	100	3					3		x											
Reflection V	275	27.5	110	3					3		x											
Hi-Def Mirror	300	30	120	3					3		x											
Rustic Glass	320	32	128	4					3		x											
The Reflectinator	350	35	140	4					3		x											
Clearer Mirror	400	40	160	4					3		x											
Looking Glass Supreme	500	50	200	4					3		x											
Fabulous, Darling Mirror	950	95	380	3					3		x											

The Starter

You just moved into town and haven't quite landed a stellar job yet. Your bed only needs room for one, too. There's no need to spend big or to have an exquisite bedroom right now. Instead, keep it simple with this starter bedroom stocked only with the essentials.

[A] **Small Brass Bed**
§425
Energy: 4, Stress Relief: 3

[B] **Syntactic End Table**
§45

[C] **Evrityme Dresser**
§450

[D] **Bloomington Lamp**
§50

[E] **Quick Tick Wall Clock**
§40

[F] **Small Ivy**
§5
Environment: 2

[G] **Mirror of Variance**
§50
Fun: 3, Environment: 2, + Charisma

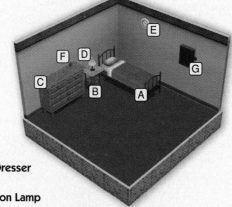

CLOCKS

Object	Price	Daily Depreciation	Fully Deprec. Value	Environment	Hygiene	Hunger	Bladder	Energy	Fun	Logic	Charisma	Cooking	Athletic	Painting	Guitar	Handiness	Gardening	Writing	Fishing	Stress Relief	Group Activity	Comfort
Quick Tick Wall Clock	40	4	16																			
No Snooze! Alarm Clock	60	6	24																			
4258g Alarm Clock from Landgraab Industries	150	15	60																			

The Pretty Princess

For the girl who says, "There's no such thing as too much pink." This bedroom looks like the inside of a unicorn's dream, complete with pink trim on practically everything. Not that there's anything wrong with matching pink dressers and beds. And night stands. And carpet. And wallpaper...

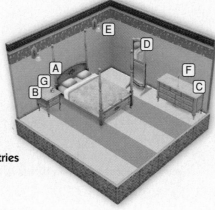

A **Four Post Bed from McKraken Industries**
§650
Energy: 4, Stress Relief: 3

B **Trails End table**
§50

C **Homestead Dresser from McKraken Industries**
§600
Environment: 2

D **Rustic Glass**
§320
Fun: 3, Environment: 4, + Charisma

E **Werffelhousen Sconce**
§75

F **Narcisscus Vase**
§40
Environment: 1

G **No Snooze! Alarm Clock**
§60

Bathroom

Few rooms are more essential than the bathroom, primarily because hygiene is so important to life and well-being. Without a place to scrub down or lift the lid, Sims will quickly succumb to sickness or pass out. Despite the almost singular purpose of the bathroom, there are many ways to construct and decorate one. Don't feel like you have to go super-fancy right away, but over time, keep building onto this essential room so that Sims enjoy stepping inside of it to take care of business.

Rustic

The rustic bathroom, complete with wood floor and clawed bathtub, is a simple place to get ready for the day and relieve unwanted pressure. Just make sure to add some electric lights so your Sims can see their way to the toilet. Bucking history might prevent a nightmare "accident" or two.

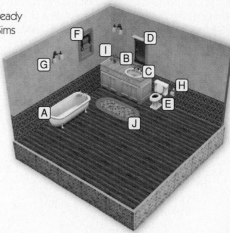

A **Schmidt's Clawed Tub**
§1,000
Hygiene: 5, Stress Relief: 6

B **Country Fried Counter**
§140

C **Pepper Pot Sink**
§215
Hygiene: 4

D **The Outhouse Mirror**
§100
Fun: 3, Environment: 2, + Charisma

E **Bargain John**
§250
Bladder: 10

F **Cortinas Festivas!**
§50
Environment: 2

G **Light Freshener**
§65

H **Three-Ply Tushy Tissue**
§2
Environment: 1

I **Cow Plant**
§28
Environment: 1

J **Aristocratic First Oval Rug**
§80

TUBS

Object	Price	Daily Depreciation	Fully Deprec. Value	Environment	Hygiene	Hunger	Bladder	Energy	Fun	Logic	Charisma	Cooking	Athletic	Painting	Guitar	Handiness	Gardening	Writing	Fishing	Stress Relief	Group Activity	Comfort
JustaTub	500	50	200	3																4		
Schmidt's Clawed Tub	1000	100	400	5																6		
Bath Today from Plumbrite	1400	140	560	6																7		
Shower of Power	1600	160	640	1	9															9		
Tub Nouveau	2100	210	840	4	7															9		

SHOWERS

Object	Price	Daily Depreciation	Fully Deprec. Value	Environment	Hygiene	Hunger	Bladder	Energy	Fun	Logic	Charisma	Cooking	Athletic	Painting	Guitar	Handiness	Gardening	Writing	Fishing	Stress Relief	Group Activity	Comfort
Simple Shower	425	42.5	170	7																		
Exhilarating X-Foliator Shower	925	92.5	370	9																		
Shower of Power	1600	160	640	1	9															9		

Multi-Use Bath

With multiple places to wash in this bathroom, a household can get ready to greet the day together. This bathroom features simple, direct furnishings that are essential for maximizing hygiene so social engagements and work performance are not affected by, well, *stink*.

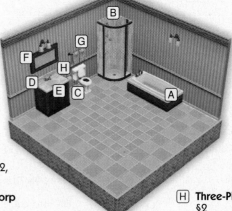

[A] **Bath Today from Plumbrite**
§1,400
Hygiene: 6, Stress Relief: 7

[B] **Exhilarating X-Foliator Shower**
§925
Hygiene: 9

[C] **Bargain John**
§250
Bladder: 10

[D] **Counter Culture Counter**
§215
Environment: 1

[E] **Squatter's Sink**
§150
Hygiene: 2

[F] **The Reflektor**
§80
Fun: 3, Environment: 2,
+ Charisma

[G] **The Rack by DecorCorp**
§35
Environment: 1

[H] **Three-Ply Tushy Tissue**
§2
Environment: 1

ACCENTS

Object	Price	Daily Depreciation	Fully Deprec. Value	Environment	Hygiene	Hunger	Bladder	Energy	Fun	Logic	Charisma	Cooking	Athletic	Painting	Guitar	Handiness	Gardening	Writing	Fishing	Stress Relief	Group Activity	Comfort
Three-Ply Tushy Tissue from Plumbrite	2	0.2	0.8	1																		
NeveRust Towel Ring	30	3	12	1																		
The Rack by DecorCorp	35	3.5	14	1																		

TOILETS

Object	Price	Daily Depreciation	Fully Deprec. Value	Environment	Hygiene	Hunger	Bladder	Energy	Fun	Logic	Charisma	Cooking	Athletic	Painting	Guitar	Handiness	Gardening	Writing	Fishing	Stress Relief	Group Activity	Comfort
First Step Potty Chair	70	7	28																			
Bargain John	250	25	100				10															
Odor-Free Toilet	575	57.5	230				10															
The Thru-Flush Toilet	800	80	320				10															
The Porcelain Throne	1800	180	720	2			10															

Classy Bathroom

ack-and-white still spells swank. This upscale bathroom features the latest in hygiene echnology, such as the Shower of Power and the Porcelain Throne. With these objects, Sims will be able to emerge from the bathroom squeaky clean and devoid of any discomfort.

[A] **Shower of Power**
§1,300
Hygiene: 9, Stress Relief: 9, Environment: 1

[B] **Porcelain Throne**
§1,800
Bladder: 10, Environment: 2

[C] **Fontainbleu Fountain Sink**
§500
Hygiene: 5, Environment: 3

[D] **High-Def Mirror**
§300
Fun: 3, Environment: 3, + Charisma

[E] **Real Flat Counter**
§800
Environment: 2

[F] **Far Out Wall Sconce**
§95

[G] **Three-Ply Tushy Tissue**
§2
Environment: 1

[H] **Mood-Lite Candle**
§65
Environment: 1

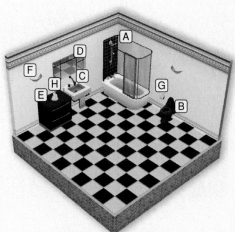

Object Catalog

Study

Where do Sims go to learn and sometimes laugh? The study. While not an essential room—the furniture and objects in the office can be placed in other rooms—the study serves as a good place for industrious Sims to fine-tune skills such as Cooking and Handiness via books. And writers need a computer to work on their bad books so they can eventually create a good one. Not everybody pens *Crime and Punishment* on their first try, you know.

Basic Study

When you're first starting out, there isn't much need for an extreme home office—just a place to check online postings, play the occasional computer game, and stack books that help develop necessary skills. Once the money starts rolling in, the study can be upgraded with extras that increase the environment rating.

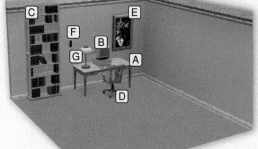

A   **Drawltop Worksurface**
§150

B   **Easy Machine from Ed's PC Hut**
§800
Fun: 3

C   **21st Century Library Bookshelf**
§325
Fun: 3, + Cooking, +
Handiness, + Logic

D   **Wellness Dining Chair**
§165

E   **Obscure Film Poster**
§160
Environment: 4

F   **Immobile Phone**
§50

G   **Lodge Lamp**
§75

BOOKSHELVES

Object	Price	Daily Depreciation	Fully Deprec. Value	Environment	Hygiene	Hunger	Bladder	Energy	Fun	Logic	Charisma	Cooking	Athletic	Painting	Guitar	Handiness	Gardening	Writing	Fishing	Stress Relief	Group Activity	Comfort
Classically Tasteful Literature Shelving	175	17.5	70						2	x		x				x						
Back2SChool Bookshelf	250	25	100						2	x		x				x						
21st Century Library Bookshelf	325	32.5	130						3	x		x				x						
Shelves de Libro	350	35	140						3	x		x				x						
The Book Corral	430	43	172	1					3	x		x				x						
Bookshelf Revisited	545	54.5	218	1					3	x		x				x						
Penningway Bookshelf	650	65	260	1					4	x		x				x						
The Constitutional Bookshelf	750	75	300	2					5	x		x				x						
Sturdy Shelf	895	89.5	358	2					5	x		x				x						

COMPUTERS

Object	Price	Daily Depreciation	Fully DepreC. Value	Environment	Hygiene	Hunger	Bladder	Energy	Fun	Logic	Charisma	Cooking	Athletic	Painting	Guitar	Handiness	Gardening	Writing	Fishing	Stress Relief	Group Activity	Comfort
Easy Machine from Fred's PC Hut	800	80	320						3													
oTron 200 Thinking Computer from Landgraab Industries	3000	300	1200						3													
XS 4258p Laptop from Landgraab Industries	4000	400	1600						7													

The Refinement Room

Here, grand novels are written. With a window overlooking the serene outdoors, the serious (and highly successful) author sits and composes yet another 700-page masterpiece about the human condition, the ties that bind, and the mortal coil. That is, if they can peel their eyes off the painting that set them back an entire royalty check.

[A] Desk Historia from XIV Antiquities
§900

[B] oTron 200 Thinking Computer
§3,000
Fun: 7

[C] The Elsinore
§120

[D] Constitutional Bookshelf
§750
Fun: 5, Environment: 2, + Cooking, + Handiness, + Logic

[E] Puck's Soliloquy
§7,300
Environment: 10

DESKS

Object	Price	Daily Depreciation	Fully Deprec. Value	Environment	Hygiene	Hunger	Bladder	Energy	Fun	Logic	Charisma	Cooking	Athletic	Painting	Guitar	Handiness	Gardening	Writing	Fishing	Stress Relief	Group Activity	Comfort
Drawltop Worksurface	150	15	60																			
Workspace de Mish	300	30	120																			
Desk Moderne from Gorog Designs	325	32.5	130	1																		
The Rollin' Secretary from McKraken Industries	450	45	180																			
Desk Historia from XIV Antiquities	900	90	360	1																		

TiP

Nothing says refinement quite like a well-placed column or arch, so be sure to check those out and tastefully add them to your distinguished study.

Artiste!

A starving artist only needs four walls and a few oils. Once a career is born, though, that stark lifestyle must be traded in for auspicious oddity. This studio is set up to foster absolute creativity through ridiculous pretension. The easel can be easily replaced by a guitar for the tortured songwriter who can only scribe songs about unrequited love by flickering candlelight.

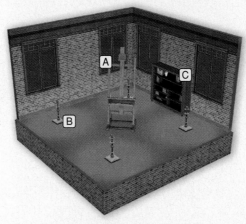

[A] **Artsy Easel**
§300
Fun: 2, + Painting

[B] **Bawdy Candle**
§65

[C] **Classically Tasteful Literature Shelving**
§175
Fun: 2, + Cooking, + Handiness, + Logic

INDOOR ACTIVITIES

	Object	Price	Daily Depreciation	Fully Deprec. Value	Environment	Hygiene	Hunger	Bladder	Energy	Fun	Logic	Charisma	Cooking	Athletic	Painting	Guitar	Handiness	Gardening	Writing	Fishing	Stress Relief	Group Activity	Comfort
	Shut-in Treadmill	900	90	360										x							5		
	The Exercise Queen	1500	150	600										x							5		
	Mad Llama Foosball Table	6250	625	2500						9												x	

HOBBIES & SKILLS

	Object	Price	Daily Depreciation	Fully Deprec. Value	Environment	Hygiene	Hunger	Bladder	Energy	Fun	Logic	Charisma	Cooking	Athletic	Painting	Guitar	Handiness	Gardening	Writing	Fishing	Stress Relief	Group Activity	Comfort
	Artsy Easel	300	30	120						2					x								
	Epic 10th Anniversary Chess Set	450	45	180						4	x												
	Astral Playground Telescope	600	60	240						2	x												
	Sonaflux Guitar	600	60	240						2						x							

Kids' Room

The little ones need a space to call their own—someplace they can play and goof off out of the way of busy Sims rushing to work or practicing skills needed to fulfill Lifetime Wishes. The Kids' Room catalog is full of toys and kid-centric objects, like a colorful xylophone and turtle-shaped playtable. With objects like these, kids will be stimulated as they grow.

Little Boy's Room

Soft flooring and colorful wallpaper turn this room into a boy's paradise. Rocketships and trains adorn the walls—promises of the adventures to come in the future. Be sure to decorate childrens' rooms with toys special kids' décor so they truly have a unique space that says, 'a child lives here.'

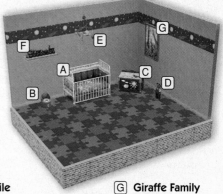

A | Kinder Kontainer
§275
Energy: 4

B | First Step Potty Chair
§70

C | Roy Rock's Toy Box
§75
Fun: 5

D | Wugglesworth Schnuggles Bear
§50

E | Space Mobile
§70
Environment: 1

F | Elevated Train Set
§185
Environment: 2

G | Giraffe Family Portrait
§80
Environment: 4

TOYS

Object	Price	Daily Depreciation	Fully Deprec. Value	Environment	Hygiene	Hunger	Bladder	Energy	Fun	Logic	Charisma	Cooking	Athletic	Painting	Guitar	Handiness	Gardening	Writing	Fishing	Stress Relief	Group Activity	Comfort
Baby Brainiac Peg Toy Box	30	3	12						5													
Rip Co. Xylophone	40	4	16						5													
Wugglesworth Schnuggles Bear	50	5	20						6													
Infinitoy Imagination Station	55	5.5	22						5													
Toy Pirate Chest	60	6	24						5													
Roy Rock's Toy Box	75	7.5	30						5													
Rip Co. Little Baker Oven	100	10	40						3													
Genesis Building Blocks	200	20	80						4													
Sunnybrook Home Dollhouse	650	65	260						7													

Object Catalog

Twin Girls' Room

Twin girls can be a handful, so give them their very own room where they can talk, giggle, and go just a little boy-crazy. Maximize space with smaller twin beds, slid up against walls. And be sure to hang a few posters of popular singers and artists that are all the rage with the tween set. You may not think a Diva Doll Poster looks all that hot, but consider the world through the eyes of a 13-year-old, and then make with the hanging.

[A] **The Single Post Bed from McKraken Industries**
§300
Energy: 4, Stress Relief: 3

[B] **Sunnybrook Home Dollhouse**
§650
Fun: 6

[C] **Flora's Funky Floor Lamp**
§225

[D] **Real Pretty Butterflies**
§265
Environment: 2

[E] **Diva Doll Poster**
§55
Environment: 2

[F] **Edgy, Edgy Bill**
§25
Environment: 2

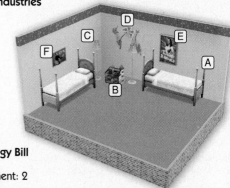

KIDS FURNITURE

Object	Price	Daily Depreciation	Fully Deprec. Value	Environment	Hygiene	Hunger	Bladder	Energy	Fun	Logic	Charisma	Cooking	Athletic	Painting	Guitar	Handiness	Gardening	Writing	Fishing	Stress Relief	Group Activity	Comfort
Yummer's High Chair	60	6	24																			
Kinder Kontainer	275	27.5	110					4														
Rock-a-Baby Crib	425	42.5	170					5														

Shared Room

Sometimes, space is at a premium and children must double (or triple) up in bedrooms. This basic bedroom is for a pair of kids at different ages, but despite the years between them, they can peacefully co-exist—as long as they have just enough room so they aren't living on top of each other. That's when the "hands to self" lecture turns into a daily occurrence.

[A] **Rock-a-Baby Crib**
§425
Environment: 6

[B] **Small Brass Bed**
§425
Energy: 4, Stress Relief: 3

[C] **Blushing Torchiere**
§120

[D] **Baby Brainiac Peg Toy Box**
§30
Fun: 5

[E] **Toy Pirate Chest**
§600
Fun: 5

[F] **Rip Co. Xylophone**
§40
Fun: 5

[G] **Genesis Building Blocks**
§200
Fun: 4

[H] **Infinitoy Imagination Station**
§55
Fun: 5

[I] **My Little House**
§110
Environment: 4

[J] **Anabolic Cham**
§9
Environment: 2

KIDS DECOR

Object	Price	Daily Depreciation	Fully Deprec. Value	Environment	Hygiene	Hunger	Bladder	Energy	Fun	Logic	Charisma	Cooking	Athletic	Painting	Guitar	Handiness	Gardening	Writing	Fishing	Stress Relief	Group Activity	Comfort
Space Mobile	70	7	28	1																		
Elevated Train Set	185	18.5	74	2																		
Real Pretty Butterflies	265	26.5	106	2																		

Multi-Room Objects

No object is limited to just one specific room. If you really want a sink in the living room, that's your perogative—with just a few clicks, your Sims will lather their hands in front of the television. However, there are several categories of objects that appear in multiple room lists, such as painting and plants. These universal objects add environment bonuses to many rooms and serve to make your houses look more lived-in.

PAINTINGS & POSTERS

Object	Price	Daily Depreciation	Fully Deprec. Value	Environment	Hygiene	Hunger	Bladder	Energy	Fun	Logic	Charisma	Cooking	Athletic	Painting	Guitar	Handiness	Gardening	Writing	Fishing	Stress Relief	Group Activity	Comfort
Anabolic Champ	9	0.9	3.6	2																		
Bethany and Miranda	15	1.5	6	2																		
Edgy, Edgy Bill	25	2.5	10	2																		
Forest-Fresh Corkboard	25	2.5	10	1																		
Detention Hall Poster	30	3	12	7																		
Heinrich Stubbman and the Gypsies	45	4.5	18	2																		
Diva Doll Poster	55	5.5	22	2																		
Giraffe Family Portrait	80	8	32	3																		
Dancing Bunny	100	10	40	3																		
My Little House	110	11	44	4																		
Obscure Film Poster	160	16	64	4																		
Speedinator Marketing Poster	175	17.5	70	4																		
Village No. 7	250	25	100	5																		
Fishing Scene	300	30	120	5																		
Photo Series: Hipster Edition	400	40	160	6																		
Bouquet in Repose	500	50	200	6																		

Object Catalog

PAINTINGS & POSTERS, CONTINUED

Object	Price	Daily Depreciation	Fully Deprec. Value	Environment	Hygiene	Hunger	Bladder	Energy	Fun	Logic	Charisma	Cooking	Athletic	Painting	Guitar	Handiness	Gardening	Writing	Fishing	Stress Relief	Group Activity	Comfort
Saturday Morning Fun Kids!	620	62	248	6																		
Insouciance No. 12	750	75	300	6																		
McBob Landscape	800	80	320	6																		
Still-Life Harvest	930	93	372	6																		
Smooth Jam in Three Parts	1100	110	440	7																		
Capital City Skyline	2300	230	920	7																		
Mission at Noon, Lance Ng	3900	390	1560	8																		
Puck's Soliloquy	7300	730	2920	10																		

PHONES

Object	Price	Daily Depreciation	Fully Deprec. Value	Environment	Hygiene	Hunger	Bladder	Energy	Fun	Logic	Charisma	Cooking	Athletic	Painting	Guitar	Handiness	Gardening	Writing	Fishing	Stress Relief	Group Activity	Comfort
998 Table Top Topia Phone	35	3.5	14																			
Immobile Phone	50	5	20																			

LIGHTS

Object	Price	Daily Depreciation	Fully Deprec. Value	Environment	Hygiene	Hunger	Bladder	Energy	Fun	Logic	Charisma	Cooking	Athletic	Painting	Guitar	Handiness	Gardening	Writing	Fishing	Stress Relief	Group Activity	Comfort
Light Freshner	65	6.5	26																			
Werffelhousen Sconce	75	7.5	30																			
Wall-eyed Wall Lamp	80	8	32																			
Far Out Wall Sconce	95	9.5	38																			

LIGHTS, CONTINUED

Object	Price	Daily Depreciation	Fully Deprec. Value	Environment	Hygiene	Hunger	Bladder	Energy	Fun	Logic	Charisma	Cooking	Athletic	Painting	Guitar	Handiness	Gardening	Writing	Fishing	Stress Relief	Group Activity	Comfort
Funshine Wall Lamp	115	11.5	46																			
Modern Sconce	125	12.5	50																			
The Candle Cradler	125	12.5	50																			
"The Snake Lamp"	130	13	52																			
Feisty Fiesta Wall Lantern	145	14.5	58	1																		
Photophile Wall Light	150	15	60	1																		
Old's Kool Lighting	165	16.5	66	1																		
Bawdy Candle	65	6.5	26																			
Blushing Torchiere	120	12	48																			
Omnidirection Lightcaster	165	16.5	66	1																		
Flora's Funky Floor Lamp	225	22.5	90																			
Bunker Hill Floor Lights	300	30	120	2																		
Delux Lux	365	36.5	146	2																		
Moderne-Torchiere Floor Lamp	385	38.5	154	2																		
Goldon Glow Floor Lamp	415	41.5	166	2																		
Lodge Lights	45	4.5	18																			
Lucid Light	95	9.5	38	1																		
The Swinging Light	115	11.5	46																			
Luz del Sol	180	18	72	1																		
Greaves' Ceiling Lights	225	22.5	90																			

LIGHTS, CONTINUED

Object		Price	Daily Depreciation	Fully Deprec. Value	Environment	Hygiene	Hunger	Bladder	Energy	Fun	Logic	Charisma	Cooking	Athletic	Painting	Guitar	Handiness	Gardening	Writing	Fishing	Stress Relief	Group Activity	Comfort
	The Revita-Lite	350	35	140	2																		
	Sawed-off Lightcaster	45	4.5	18																			
	The Bloomington Lamp	50	5	20																			
	Lamp Revere	65	6.5	26																			
	Hurricane Candle	70	7	28																			
	Lodge Lamp	75	7.5	30																			
	Homespun Table Lamp	85	8.5	34																			
	Luz Lenta	285	28.5	114	2																		
	The Baronian Table Lamp	300	30	120	2																		
	The Photon-Master 3000 Tabletop Edition	325	32.5	130	2																		

PLANTS

Object		Price	Daily Depreciation	Fully Deprec. Value	Environment	Object		Price	Daily Depreciation	Fully Deprec. Value	Environment	Object		Price	Daily Depreciation	Fully Deprec. Value	Environment
	Small Ivy	5	0.5	2	2		Ring-O-Posies Commercial Planter	42	4.2	16.8	2		The Perma-Palm	70	7	28	1
	Hanging Fern	15	1.5	6	2		Fern	45	4.5	18	2		Orchid Vase	90	9	36	1
	Fern Keeper Deluxe!	25	2.5	10	1		Calla Lillies	48	4.8	19.2	2		Philodendron	95	9.5	38	1
	Sphere of Ivy	35	3.5	14	2		Hanging Basket	50	5	20	2		Tigervine Plant	135	13.5	54	2
	Narcissus Vase	40	4	16	1		Mixed Flowers Planter by BowerFlox	65	6.5	26	2		Ficus Tree Shrub	230	23	92	2
	Potted Perennials	40	4	16	2		Blossoming Sunflower Vase	70	7	28	1		The Modern Orchid	435	43.5	174	5

Outdoors and Landscaping

Deck

The majority of your decorating attention is bound to be spent indoors, but don't ignore the exterior of your house. A bright deck or a compelling garden will surely increase the happiness and health of your household as well as draw the attention of neighbors. What better way to increase your social circle than having the house on the block everybody wants to visit? You are not limited strictly to a simple deck, although that might be the easiest thing to build after your initial move. Be sure to experiment with trees, rocks, and flowers sooner rather than later. As the old saying goes: You can bury a lot of troubles digging in the dirt.

Household Get-Together

The contemporary deck is a good way to get the household outdoors and relaxing on their days off, something that is essential for maintaining a healthy mood. Setting up a little barbecue next to the pool makes your house the focus of the block, as neighbors will turn up the charm for a chance to enjoy a little sun, a little water, and a lot of free grub.

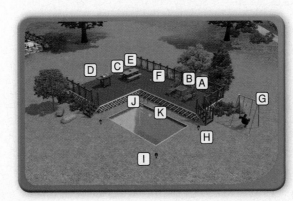

A Contempo Outdoor Living Lounge
§200

B Knack Outdoor Table
§85

C Rendezvous Picnic Table
§235

D Barbe-Cute
§600
Hunger: 4, Group Activity

E Fuzzy Logic Picnic Basket
§150
Hunger: 4, Group Activity

F Foot-and-hand-ball
§85
Fun: 6, + Athletic

G Sky Screamer Swings
§400
Fun: 3, Group Activity

H Step Lights
§75

I The Aftergloe II
§35

J Aquatic Ascent Ladder
§315

K Sea Underwater Pool Lights from Landgraab Industries
§35

OUTDOOR COOKING

Object	Price	Daily Depreciation	Fully Deprec. Value	Environment	Hygiene	Hunger	Bladder	Energy	Fun	Logic	Charisma	Cooking	Athletic	Painting	Guitar	Handiness	Gardening	Writing	Fishing	Stress Relief	Group Activity	Comfort
Birthday Inferno Birthday Cake	30	3	12			2																
Fuzzy-Logic Picnic Basket	150	15	60			4															x	
Portable Fire Pit	295	29.5	118			2			4												x	
Carnivore XL	300	30	120			2						x										
Barbe-Cute	600	60	240			4						x										
Deluxe Agile Grill	1200	120	480			5						x										

OUTDOOR SEATING

Object	Price	Daily Depreciation	Fully Deprec. Value	Environment	Hygiene	Hunger	Bladder	Energy	Fun	Logic	Charisma	Cooking	Athletic	Painting	Guitar	Handiness	Gardening	Writing	Fishing	Stress Relief	Group Activity	Comfort
Community Bench	85	8.5	34																			
Comtempto Outdoor Living Lounge	200	20	80																			1
The Breckenridge	325	32.5	130																			2
Herkimer Loveseat	400	40	160																			2
The Dawdler Lounge Chair	515	51.5	206	2																		2
Sticky Bench	650	65	260																			2
Tomorrow Lounger	750	75	300	2																		2

OUTDOOR ACTIVITIESS

Object	Price	Daily Depreciation	Fully Deprec. Value	Environment	Hygiene	Hunger	Bladder	Energy	Fun	Logic	Charisma	Cooking	Athletic	Painting	Guitar	Handiness	Gardening	Writing	Fishing	Stress Relief	Group Activity	Comfort
Baseball	65	6.5	26						5				x									
Foot-and-hand-ball	85	8.5	34						6				x									
Schuper Schprinkler from Schprinkler Tech	90	9	36						5													
The Waxbottom Slide	335	33.5	134						8													
Outdoor Chess Table	350	35	140						4	x												
Skyscreamer Swings	400	40	160						3												x	
The Juungal Jungle Gym	550	55	220						8													

POOL ITEMS

Object	Price	Daily Depreciation	Fully Deprec. Value	Environment	Hygiene	Hunger	Bladder	Energy	Fun	Logic	Charisma	Cooking	Athletic	Painting	Guitar	Handiness	Gardening	Writing	Fiishing	Stress Releof	Group Activity	Comfort
Pool Rules Sign	13	1.3	5	1																		
Sea Underwater Pool Lights from Landgraab Industries	35	3.5	14																			
Mesmerizing Mosaic	212	21.2	85																			
Aquatic Ascent Ladder	315	31.5	126																			

Private Getaway

Adventurous design should not be limited to four walls. The greatest room of all is that which exists under the broad sky, so construct a garden where you can truly escape from the hustle and bustle of city life. Majestic trees are wonderful sentinels for your outdoor getaway, surrounding a secret garden that you can share with those you love or retreat to by yourself just to unwind and remember exactly what's important in this world.

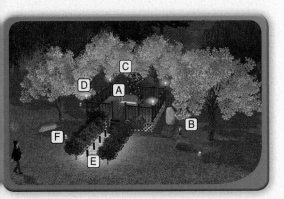

[A] **Herkimer Loveseat**
§400

[B] **Sleeping Gnome McNulty**
§35
Fun: 2, Environment: 1

[C] **Obelisk Vine**
§145
Environment: 2

[D] **Burb-Light**
§45

[E] **Stoic Bollard**
§100

[F] **Limelights**
§30

OUTDOOR LIGHTS

Object	Price	Daily Depreciation	Fully Deprec. Value	Environment	Hygiene	Hunger	Bladder	Energy	Fun	Logic	Charisma	Cooking	Athletic	Painting	Guitar	Handiness	Gardening	Writing	Fiishing	Stress Releof	Group Activity	Comfort
Limelights	30	3	12																			
Patio Party Lamp	30	3	12																			
The Aftergloe II	35	3.5	14																			
The Little Lamp That Could	35	3.5	14																			
Volcano Table Torch	35	3.5	14																			

Object Catalog

OUTDOOR LIGHTS, CONTINUED

Object	Price	Daily Depreciation	Fully Deprec. Value	Environment	Hygiene	Hunger	Bladder	Energy	Fun	Logic	Charisma	Cooking	Athletic	Painting	Guitar	Handiness	Gardening	Writing	Fishing	Stress Relief	Group Activity	Comfort
Cobblestone Fence Light	40	4	16																			
Burb-Light	45	4.5	18																			
Mason Lamp	50	5	20																			
Path Glow Garden Lighting	50	5	20																			
Simple Porch Light	70	7	28																			
Step Lights	75	7.5	30																			
Stoic Bollard	100	10	40																			
Pele's Postlight from Nothing Atoll	125	12.5	50																			
Ankle-Height Light by GamGleam Industries	175	17.5	70																			
Apology Streetlight	200	20	80																			
Clean-Wave Streetlight	245	24.5	98	2																		
Seramorson Streetlamp	335	33.5	134	2																		
The Streetbrite	340	34	136	2																		
Hard Knocks Streetlight	500	50	200	2																		
The Champ	565	56.5	226																			
Multifunction Searchlight Device	4,500	450	1800	1																		

LAWN ORNAMENTS

Object	Price	Daily Depreciation	Fully Deprec. Value	Environment	Hygiene	Hunger	Bladder	Energy	Fun	Logic	Charisma	Cooking	Athletic	Painting	Guitar	Handiness	Gardening	Writing	Fishing	Stress Relief	Group Activity	Comfort
Shocking Pink Flamingo - 2nd Edition	5	0.5	2	1					2													

PRIMA OFFICIAL GAME GUIDE

LAWN ORNAMENTS, CONTINUED

Object	Price	Daily Depreciation	Fully Deprec. Value	Environment	Hygiene	Hunger	Bladder	Energy	Fun	Logic	Charisma	Cooking	Athletic	Painting	Guitar	Handiness	Gardening	Writing	Fishing	Stress Relief	Group Activity	Comfort
Party Balloons	15	1.5	6	1																		
Sleeping Gnome McMulty	35	3.5	14	1					2													
Square Hay Bale	4	0.4	1.6																			
Round Hay Bale	65	6.5	26																			
Obelisk Vine	145	14.5	58	2																		
Fire Hydrant	150	15	60																			
Beach Sign	201	20.1	80.4																			
Traditional Sign	223	22.3	89.2																			
Modern Sign	242	24.2	96.8																			
Mission Sign	270	27	108																			
Country Sign	318	31.8	127.2																			
Contemporary Sign	322	32.2	128.8																			
Stacked Hay Bales	350	35	140																			
Cemetery Sign	365	36.5	146																			
Commercial Dumpster	659	65.9	263.6																			
Town Clock	1200	120	480																			
Farm Windmill	2130	213	852																			
Outdoor School Bell	2500	250	1000																			
Military Guard Tower	6475	647.5	2590																			
The Plaza Gusher	50000	5000	20000	9																		

LAWN ORNAMENTS, CONTINUED

Object	Price	Daily Depreciation	Fully Deprec. Value	Environment	Hygiene	Hunger	Bladder	Energy	Fun	Logic	Charisma	Cooking	Athletic	Painting	Guitar	Handiness	Gardening	Writing	Fishing	Stress Relief	Group Activity	Comfort
Landgraab Industries Science Facility Fountain	60000	6000	24000	10																		
F-Class Hunter-Killer	75000	7500	30000	10																		

TRANSPORTATION

Object	Price	Daily Depreciation	Fully Deprec. Value	Speed	Object	Price	Daily Depreciation	Fully Deprec. Value	Speed
Vertistation Bike Rack	35	3.5	14		Wornado Triage	4500	450	1800	4
Car-Spot Parking Space	150	15	60		4-Everything Van	6100	610	2440	4
Bi-Trike for Kids	250	25	100	1	Yomoshoto Evasion	9800	980	3920	5
NostalgiCycle	250	25	100	2	Tofunda Wagon	19600	1960	7840	5
Closure Garage Door	600	60	240		VFN Kompensator	36000	3600	14400	6
Sloppy Jalopy	950	95	380	3	Bwan Speedster YL	85000	8500	34000	8
Big Lemon	1200	120	480	3	Margaret Vaguester	105000	10500	42000	10
Vorn P328	3700	370	1480	4					

Plants and Rocks

here are several categories of outdoor decor for your gardens and lawns, including trees and rocks. These are wonderful building blocks for unique corners of the world where your Sims can grab a few moments of much needed solitude or silence. The costs of building a garden are often far outweighed by the benefits of natural beauty on the soul, so be sure to add some green to your yard as soon as possible.

TREES

Object	Price	Daily Depreciation	Fully Deprec. Value	Object	Price	Daily Depreciation	Fully Deprec. Value	Object	Price	Daily Depreciation	Fully Deprec. Value
Small Bamboo Tree	65	6.5	26	Small Fir Tree	180	18	72	Fan Leaf Palm Tree	275	27.5	110
Small Aspen Tree	95	9.5	38	Spruce Tree	190	19	76	Tall Cypress Tree	300	30	120
Buckhorn Tree	100	10	40	Black Gum Tree	200	20	80	Small Western Cypress Tree	315	31.5	126
Bamboo Tree	115	11.5	46	Tall Fir Tree	210	21	84	Oak Tree	320	32	128
Aspen Tree	125	12.5	50	Small Juniper Tree	245	24.5	98	Purple Tree	325	32.5	130
Small Pear Tree	130	13	52	Cherry Tree	250	25	100	Classic Palm Tree	335	33.5	134
Small Spruce Tree	140	14	56	Small Purple Tree	260	26	104	Large Western Cypress Tree	340	34	136
Small Black Gum Tree	150	15	60	Small Cypress Tree	265	26.5	106	Willlow Tree	350	35	140
Small Cherry Tree	155	15.5	62	Large Juniper Tree	270	27	108	Creepy Tree	400	40	160
Pear Tree	165	16.5	66								

SHRUBS

Object	Price	Daily Depreciation	Fully Deprec. Value	Object	Price	Daily Depreciation	Fully Deprec. Value	Object	Price	Daily Depreciation	Fully Deprec. Value
Brambles	5	0.5	2	Coleus	15	1.5	6	Round Hedge	70	7	28
Waterlillies	8	0.8	3.2	Boston Fern	35	3.5	14	Evergreen	80	8	32
Cattail	9	0.9	3.6	Buckhorn	40	4	16	Hedge	85	8.5	34
Pampas Grass	12	1.2	4.8	Boxwood	50	5	20	Topiary Plant	95	9.5	38
Cattails	10	1	4	Banana Leaf	60	6	24				

FLOWERS

	Object	Price	Daily Depreciation	Fully Deprec. Value		Object	Price	Daily Depreciation	Fully Deprec. Value		Object	Price	Daily Depreciation	Fully Deprec. Value
	Hydrangea	1	0.1	0.4		Lithodoroa w/ Rounded Corners	10	1	4		Marigold	16	1.6	6.4
	Dandelions	2	0.2	0.8		Moss Rose	10	1	4		Solo Sunflower	17	1.7	6.8
	Popular Pansies	8	0.8	3.2		Moss Rose w/ Diagonal Corners	10	1	4		Sunflowers	19	1.9	7.6
	Clover	10	1	4		Moss Rose w/ Rounded Corners	10	1	4		Heather	20	2	8
	Clover w/Diagonal Corners	10	1	4		Phlox	10	1	4		Azaleas	22	2.2	8.8
	Clover w/Rounded Corners	10	1	4		Phlox w/Diagonal Corners	10	1	4		Classic Daisies	23	2.3	9.2
	Daisies of our Lives	10	1	4		Phlox w/Rounded Corners	10	1	4		Laizy Daises	24	2.4	9.6
	Ice Plant	10	1	4		Plot of Daisies w/ Diagonal Corners	10	1	4		Vivid Roses	25	2.5	10
	Ice Plant w/ Diagonal Corners	10	1	4		Plot of Daisies w/ Rounded Corners	10	1	4		Pink Roses	35	3.5	14
	Ice Plant w/ Rounded Corners	10	1	4		Perennial Pansies	11	1.1	4.4		Wild Rosey Roses	40	4	16
	Lithodoroa	10	1	4		Agapanthus	12	1.2	4.8		Semi Roses	42	4.2	16.8
	Lithodoroa w/ Diagonal Corners	10	1	4		Dianthus	14	1.4	5.6		Rosey Roses	45	4.5	18

ROCKS

	Object	Price	Daily Depreciation	Fully Deprec. Value		Object	Price	Daily Depreciation	Fully Deprec. Value
	Landscaping Rock - Small Round	5	0.5	2		Landscaping Rock - Square	18	1.8	7.2
	Landscaping Rock - Horizontal	6	0.6	2.4		Landscaping Rock - Vertical	30	3	12
	Landscaping Rock - Medium Round	15	1.5	6		Ancient Rock	35	3.5	14

Community Objects

There are a handful of objects that exist at community locations, like the graveyard and parks. These objects have limited interactions, such as just being able to view the Grim Reaper statue at the graveyard. However, you can adjust the color of streetlight to truly customize the town to your liking. With just a few clicks of the mouse, you can line the streets with a rainbow of colors.

Object	Interactions
Flagpole	None
Picnic Table	Sit
Public Lightning	Turn On/Turn Off, Change Color
Public Statue	View
Public Trashcan	Rummage

BREAKABLE OBJECTS

Some objects just break down over time or with multiple uses. If an electrical, mechanical, or plumbing object breaks, you can either summon a repair technician to fix the object for §50 or attempt to fix the object yourself. The higher the Handiness skill of the Sim trying to repair the object, the greater chance it will succeed.

When an object breaks for the first time, the chance of it breaking again increases. The more it breaks, the more likely it is to break again. At a certain point, the object may completely break down and need to be replaced. If an object breaks beyond repair or is destroyed in a fire, you get a slight insurance payment to help offset the cost of replacing the object.

Occasionally, objects will spill water on the floor around it. To sop up the water, choose the Mop interaction on the puddle. Mopping up a puddle right away is important, especially if you are going to be tinkering with an electrical object nearby.

Some objects can be upgraded so they do not break or catch fire. See the Handiness skill section in the Simology chapter to learn more about upgrading objects so they don't break, don't catch fire, and even clean themselves when not in use.

Object Interactions

you have played The Sims games before, ou know that most objects can be used nd abused) by Sims—in fact, that's usually e point of putting an object on your lot. should serve a function. Some objects ave no function beyond boosting a room's nvironmental score and giving Sims the ecorated or Nicely Decorated moodlets. ther objects have interactions that provide arning or entertainment or satisfy a need. hese objects and their interactions are etailed in this section of the object catalog.

 see what interactions are available n an object, just left-click on it. A radial enu appears. Click on an interaction to dd it to the action queue in the screen's pper-left corner. (If you ever need to ancel an interaction, just click on it in the ction queue.)

NOTE

Objects here are designated by category. If a specific object in that category has a unique interaction, it will be called out separately.

Alarm Clock

he alarm clocks are useful for getting specific ims out of bed at designated times. You can ways set a Sim to sleep until they are fully ested, but an alarm is good for making sure a im never oversleeps for work or school.

- **Set/Unset Alarm Clock:** Multiple Sims can set a special alarm that only works on them. However, if that Sim is not in the room when the alarm goes off, the alarm wakes up everybody else in the room, disturbing their sleep.

Bar

Bars are great party objects. Sims can use them to make refreshments for either just themselves or a crowd, as the interaction Make Drink can be modified to make multiple beverages.

- **Make Drink(s):** Use this interaction to make drinks at the bar for the Sim and other Sims in the room. Other Sims can interact with drinks made at the bar and consume them to satisfy Hunger.

Baseball/Football

Baseballs and footballs are outdoor activities great for entertaining Sims. Athletic Sims and Sims who Love the Outdoors will get the most enjoyment out of throwing around the ol' pigskin or a baseball.

- **Play Catch:** To use this interaction, there must be another Sim nearby. The two Sims then toss the ball back and forth, having fun. This activity also increases LTR.

TIP

Developing the Athletic skill? Play with the baseball or football to increase that skill by a little bit for every hour you play.

Bathtubs

There are several bathtubs you can choose from, but this general rule applies: the more expensive the bathtub, the greater the chance of it breaking and the less time it takes to take a bath. (This last part is particularly useful because as you get busier in life, you can save a lot of time with quicker baths and showers.) Bathtubs remove the Grungy and Smelly moodlets.

TIP

Buy the rubber duckie from the supermarket and place it on the tub so every time you bathe, you get the Duck Time moodlet. It's an easy way to boost your mood every day!

- **Take Bath/Take Bubble Bath:** This is the most common interaction with the bathtub. This fills the tub with water and directs your Sim to bathe. Normally, the Sim bathes until he or she is clean, but you can cancel the action early. If you buy bubble bath from the supermarket, you can modify the bath into a bubble bath. Take Bubble Bath will give your Sim the Tranquil moodlet.

- **Clean Bathtub:** When the bath is dirty, you should clean it with this interaction. Sims don't like dirty surroundings (in fact, it's a negative moodlet), so keep the tub clean.

- **Repair Tub:** If the tub is broken, your Sim can attempt to repair it instead of calling a repair technician. The chance of this succeeding increases with a higher Handiness skill.

- **Upgrade:** There are two upgrades for the bathtub—Self-Cleaning and Unbreakable. This interaction initiates the upgrade process. If interrupted, it can be resumed later.

TIP

You must place the bubble bath from your personal inventory on to the tub in order to open the Take Bubble Bath interaction.

Bed

The bed is a critical part of each house. Sims need a bed so they can sleep for an extended period and charge their Energy need. If a Sim does not sleep, they become exhausted and can eventually pass out.

> **CAUTION**
>
> A cheap bed sometimes gives you the negative Bad Night's Sleep moodlet.

- **Sleep:** All Sims need to sleep. Use this interaction to get the Sim in bed for an extended period of time. This will negative moodlets like Tired, Sleepy, and Exhausted if you sleep for longer than a few hours. Drag the action in the queue to the right to direct the Sim to Sleep Until Rested.

- **Nap:** Napping is a great way to rest up without spending too much time. A nap can result in the Had a Nice Nap as well as dispel negative moodlets like Sleepy, Tired, and Exhausted. If the Sim is Buzzed, they cannot take a nap.

- **Relax:** This interaction directs a Sim to the bed. They lay on top of the cover and just unwind with a book or watch a nearby TV. If another Sim is relaxing on the same bed, they can chat. Relaxing is a good way to lower stress.

- **Daydream:** While Sims are on the bed relaxing, they can daydream. This interaction lets the Sim really unwind with daydreams of Sims they know and places they have been. Ambitious Sims like to daydream more than other Sims.

- **Make Bed:** This interaction directs the Sim to make the bed. An unmade bed lowers the environmental rating of a room.

- **Cuddle:** If two Sims are on the bed and have an amorous LTR, this interaction gets them to snuggle up close. In this interaction, a number of romantic socials are available, such as kiss, make out, and WooHoo.

Bicycle

Bicycles are cheap ways to get around town—and younger Sims love them. To put a bike on your lot, you must make sure to have a Bike Rack, too. There are two types of bicycle: Bi-Trike for Kids and NostalgiCycle. The Bi-Trike can only be used by child Sims.

Birthday Cake

When it comes time to transition between ages, a birthday cake is the way to celebrate. The birthday cake can also be used to force an age transition—but it only works one way. You can either buy a cake at the supermarket or in Buy Mode (look in the Outdoor tab). Sims can eat cake as well as use it to age-up.

- **Blow Out Candles:** This is the interaction that facilitates the age transition. After selecting this interaction, you must then choose when Sim in the family is going to age-up.

- **Grab a Plate:** Tell other Sims to partake of the cake with this interaction. Cake satisfies hunger.

- **Clean Up:** Cakes can spoil just like any other food, so be sure to clean up a cake after the party is over. This interaction places the cake in the trash.

Book

Books are one of the most cherished and most useful objects in *The Sims 3*. Books provide great entertainment for Sims, giving them Fun. Books are a good way for some Sims to relieve stress. The higher the quality of the book, the more Fun it provides. If you direct a Sim to read a skill book, they will also learn the skill associated with the book while reading.

> **TIP**
>
> Bookworms read faster than other Sims.
>
> The first time you read a Masterpiece-rated book in any genre, you get the Read a Masterpiece moodlet.

- **Read Book:** This interaction directs a Sim to sit down and read a book. Sometimes, Sims will flip through a book while standing.

- **Get Book:** This interaction grabs a book from a bookshelf.

- **Put Away Book:** This interaction shelves a book on the nearest bookshelf.

Bookshelf

Bookshelves are convenient places to store all of your household books so they do not clutter up your rooms—or your personal inventory.

- **Open Bookshelf:** To see what books are on a shelf, use this interaction.

- **Read/Read Something:** To read a book from the bookshelf, select this interaction. You can either be specific with the Read interaction or more general with the Read Something interaction.

- **Put Away Books:** This interaction puts all books not on the shelf away. This is a good way to get all books out of your personal inventory and clear up clutter.

Buffet Table

Need to serve multiple Sims at the same time. Buying the buffet table from the Outdoor Cooking collection is an instant solution to your outdoor eating needs. Food can be placed inside the buffet and then Sims can take it as they want or need it. When food has not been placed inside the buffet table, the table is considered "unserved."

- **Serve:** This interaction places food inside the buffet table so other Sims can easily grab a plate.

- **Grab a Plate:** With multiple food types, the Grab a Plate interaction is modified to include the different types of food in the buffet table. This interaction feeds a Sim, reducing hunger.

- **Clean Up:** When the party is over and the guests go home, clean up the table so food doesn't go rotten and stink up the place. This returns the buffet table to its unserved state.

> **TIP**
>
> If high quality food was placed inside the buffet table, Sims who eat of it will get one of the different Meal moodlets.

> **NOTE**
>
> The picnic basket is just like a portable buffet table. It has the same interactions.

Burglar Alarm

The burglar alarm does not have any interactions. Instead, it sits on the wall and protects your house against theft. When a burglar creeps inside your house and enters a room with the alarm, the alarm sounds and not only wakes any sleeping Sim on the

...ot, but it also triggers an automatic call to the police. A police officer will be at the lot within a minute or two.

Candles

Candles provide both illumination and environmental boosts for a room. You can place a candle on any flat surface.

- **Light Candle:** Sim instantly lights the candle, providing light.

- **Extinguish Candle:** Sims puts out the candle.

> **TIP**
>
> Candles cannot set your lot on fire, so don't worry if you accidentally forget to blow them out before leaving home.

Car

- There are several automobiles you can purchase in Buy Mode. The more expensive the vehicle, the faster it goes. However, to place a car on your lot, you need to also buy a parking space bar and designate a parking spot for the vehicle.

> **NOTE**
>
> Vehicles are expensive luxury items, but they are fun to customize with different paint jobs.

> **TIP**
>
> If you advance in the Law Enforcement career, you get your very own police cruiser.

- **Go to:** Use this interaction to designate a particular spot in town you want the Sim to drive to.

- **Go Shopping:** Use this interaction to set up a shopping trip.

- **Go to Community Lot:** Send the Sim off to a known community lot, like the library or museum.

Chair: Lounge

There are indoor and outdoor lounge chairs that do not have the same properties as a regular chair or seat. The lounge chair is in a permanently reclined position and offers a high amount of comfort.

- **Relax:** Relaxing in a lounge chair reduces stress.

- **Nap:** Napping in a lounge chair is like napping in bed. It reduces stress, and if you get enough of a snooze, you earn the Had a Nice Nap moodlet.

Chess Table

- The chess table is an excellent way to improve your Sims' Logic skill. The more a Sim plays chess, the better they get at the game. Playing chess with other Sims is a good way to socialize and raise LTRs.

- **Challenge Sim to a Game:** This interaction directs your Sim and a designated Sim to an open chess table. While playing, your Sim increases the Logic skill. When the game is over, both Sims stand up and leave the table. If you won, the game is logged in the Logic Skill Journal.

- **Play Chess With:** Play Chess is a good way just to enjoy a leisurely game with a nearby Sim. While playing, the Sim increases his or her Logic skill. You can also adjust this interaction in the action queue to play until the skill level improves.

- **Practice Chess:** This is a single Sim interaction with the chess table. The Sim sits down and pores over the pieces, improving Logic skill. This interaction can be adjusted in the action queue to play until the skill level improves.

- **Watch Chess:** Watching other Sims play chess provides Fun.

Computer

The computer is one of the most important objects in the house because it has so many functions. The computer is a communication tool, it can be used to move, it is used to have fun and relax, and it is applicable to certain skills. Having a computer on your lot is a good investment. The better the computer, the less of a chance it has to break and the more Fun it provides when playing games. The more expensive computers also help do homework faster.

- **Chat:** Chatting on the computer is fun and it improves LTRs with other Sims.

- **Check for Responses:** If your Sims left a forum post, you can check for a response with this interaction. This can result in different moodlets, depending on the answer.

- **Find Coupons:** Frugal Sims can use the computer to seek out deals around town.

- **Find Job:** Every day, five new career options become available via the computer. Use this interaction to see who's hiring.

- **Hack:** Computer Whiz Sims can hack away on the computer to earn a little extra money on the side.

> **TIP**
>
> The more you hack, the better you get at it. Hacking is a hidden skill.

- **Join/Leave Book Club:** Use this interaction to sign up for a book club that delivers new books every week. You can also cancel the service.

- **Make Inappropriate Forum Post:** Inappropriate Sims can exercise this trait online and leave nasty posts in message boards.

- **Move Out:** When it comes time to move or kick a Sim out of the house, use this interaction to bring up the Moving interface.

- **Overclock:** Computer Whiz Sims can attempt to overclock the computer. If successful, they get an upgrade.

- **Play Chess:** Logic-minded Sims can play chess against the computer to improve the skill.

- **Play Computer Games:** Sitting down and playing computer game is a good way to have easy, harmless fun. (Games are harmless, right?)

- **Repair Computer:** If the computer breaks, the Sim can attempt to repair it. Handy Sims have a better chance at actually fixing the machine.

- **Resolve Work Issues:** Workaholic Sims get this interaction for checking in on the office while away from work. This increases work performance.

- **Run Forensic Analysis:** Level 10 Law Enforcement Sims in the Forensics track can use this interaction to make money from home.

- **Solve the Unsolvable:** Genius Sims can attempt to run some hardcore formulas at home to make extra cash.

- **Upgrade:** Handiness skill Sims can upgrade with either Improve Graphics

Object Catalog

(makes playing games more fun) or Make Unbreakable (computer no longer breaks).

- **Work from Home:** Workaholic Sims can work from home to improve work performance, but it will add stress and decrease Fun.

- **Write Report/Review:** Sims in the Journalism career use this interaction to write reports and reviews for work.

- **Refine Writing Skill:** Practice the Writing skill with this interaction without actually working on a novel.

- **Write Novel:** Use this interaction to start a novel. You are asked which genre from a list of known genres, determined by skill level, and then for a book title. Whenever the Sim comes back to the computer, they can Continue Writing... or Scrap Novel to start over with a new book.

Crib

The crib is where babies and toddlers sleep to get the most energy refreshed. Babies happily remain in cribs until they get hungry or lonely and cry for attention.

- **Hold:** Use this interaction to pick a baby or toddler out of the crib.

- **Put in Crib:** Place a baby or toddler into the crib.

> **NOTE**
>
> Cribs can never catch fire if a baby or toddler is inside of it.

Dishwasher

When Sims have a dishwasher in their kitchen, they automatically use it when directed to clean up plates and dishes. The dishwasher is faster than washing dishes by hand in the sink. Cheap dishwashers are loud and prone to breaking.

- **Repair Dishwasher:** If the dishwasher breaks, you can try to fix it. The higher the Handiness skill of the Sim repairing it, the better the chances of actually making the repairs.

- **Upgrade:** There are two upgrades that can be performed on the dishwasher— Make Silent and Make Unbreakable. These upgrades silence the dishwasher and keep it from breaking down.

Dollhouse

Kids love playing with a dollhouse in their room, but the dollhouse has a few extra interactions for Sims with a certain *disposition*.

- **Play:** This interaction sits the Sim down in front of the dollhouse to play with it and increase fun.

- **Join:** Join lets other Sims sit with a toddler or child already playing with the dollhouse and share in the fun.

- **Smash:** Mean-Spirited Sims can actually smash a child's dollhouse. If this action is seen by an adult, the adult will scold the young Sim who smashed the dollhouse.

- **Dispose:** Use this to clean up a broken dollhouse.

Door

Almost every house must have at least one door on it. Sims automatically move through doors when directed inside or outside. However, you can designate one door on your house as the "front door," which all other Sims will use to enter the house. Left-click on the door and choose the Set as Front Door interaction. If you want to designate a different door, just Unset Front Door on the previous front door and pick a different one on the house.

Dresser

Some dressers are nice enough to improve the environment of a room, but all of them let Sims interact with their clothing collections.

- **Change Outfit:** This directs the Sim to change into one of their other outfits.

- **Create Outfit:** This interaction takes the Sim into Create a Sim where a new outfit can be picked out to replace older duds.

Easel

The easel is how Sims improve the Painting skill. When Sims interact with the easel, they slowly raise their Painting skill. There are different interactions the Sim can perform with the easel depending on their Painting skill, as well as different sizes of canvases to paint. However, there are two main painting interactions:

- **Paint:** When a Sim is above level 3, they get the Paint interaction.

- **Practice Paint:** Sims below level 4 in the Painting skill can only choose Practice Paint from the interaction menu.

Food Processor

The food processor is a useful small appliance that speeds your cooking process if you have a recipe that requires chopping, mixing, or doing anything with the cutting board. Your Sim will instead take the food from the fridge and go directly to the food processor. Once the food processor is done, the cooking process continues normally.

- **Have/Serve:** Left-clicking on the food processor brings up the Have/Serve interaction, but it leads only to recipes that would use the food processor.

Fire

Fire is a dangerous thing. If an object catches fire, such as a fireplace or a stove, it has the potential to spread to surrounding surfaces and objects. It can also catch Sims on fire, too, and that has the potential to kill them. If a fire breaks out, you must take care of as soon as possible.

- **Extinguish:** Use this interaction to put out the flames. Your Sim automatically pulls out a fire extinguishers and starts hosing down the flames, putting it out in a moment or two.

Fire Alarm

Like the burglar alarm, the fire does not have any interactions. It hangs on the wall in any room, ready to alert you of fire. If a fire occurs in the same room as the fire alarm, the alarm sounds. Any sleeping Sim on the lot is immediately woken. A firefighter is also dispatched to the house to take care of the flames if no Sim is on the lot to extinguish the flames themselves.

Fire Pit

The outdoor fire pit is a good place for multiple Sims to gather, warm themselves, and be social.

- **Light Fire:** This interaction lights the fire pit. This is required to do any of the other interactions.

- **Sit at Fire:** This interaction sits your Sim down at the fire where they can be social and have Fun.

- **Warm Self:** Warm Self gives Sims the Cozy Fire moodlet.

- **Poke Fire:** Poking the fire keeps it going and gives the Sim a little bit of Fun.

- **Roast:** If Sims have food items in their personal inventory, they can roast them over the fire and fill some Hunger.

Roast Marshmallow: If the Sim has no food items in personal inventory, then Roast Marshmallow is the default interaction. Also satisfies some Hunger.

Fireplace

The fireplace is a central point of the household where multiple Sims can gather to warm themselves and socialize.

Light Fire: This interaction lights the fireplace. This is required to do any of the other interactions.

Warm Self: Warm Self gives Sims the Cozy Fire moodlet.

Poke Fire: Poking the fire keeps it going and gives the Sim a little bit of Fun.

Put Out Fireplace: Extinguish the flames before leaving the house!

Change Fire Color: High-end fireplaces and upgraded cheap fireplaces can be directed to change flame color.

Upgrade: There are multiple fireplace upgrades for tinkering Sim to try out— Auto-Light, Fireproof, and Fire Colors.

With a nice fireplace, you can change the color of the flames to your personal tastes? Like purple? You got it!

Fish Bowl

Have a cool collection of fish thanks to your advanced fishing skill? Buy fish bowls and place them around the house to show off your wet little friends. Fish add to the environment of a room.

Dispose: Get rid of a dead fish with this interaction.

Feed: Feed the fish in the bowl.

Stock/Restock: Sims can order a fish to place in the bowl directly from the Sim's personal inventory.

Scoop Out Fish: This places a fish in a bowl back into a Sim's inventory.

Flamingo

The flamingo is a yard ornament that is just fun to have around. It improves the environment of an area.

Kick: Evil and Mean-Spirited Sims can kick over flamingos. If the Sim is on a neighbor's lot and is seen abusing the pink, plastic feathered friend, they lose LTR.

Stand Up: Stand a kicked flamingo back up so it can again contribute to the environment of a room/area.

Food

Food is any prepared recipe or dish that comes from the kitchen, is stored in the fridge, or is delivered to the lot by pizza delivery. Food satisfies Hunger and, if the food is high quality, gives Sims good Meal-related moodlets.

Serve: Prepare a recipe for the family on the lot. After cooking, the food will remain on the counter until put away.

Clean Up: Clean up food on the counter so it does not spoil. Throwing away perfectly good food gives a negative moodlet.

Put Away Leftovers: Store unfinished portions in the fridge for later consumption.

> **NOTE**
>
> For more about food interaction, see the Cooking skill section of the Simology chapter.

Foosball Table

The foosball table is a fun object that can relieve stress and improve LTRs with Sims who play together, because they socialize while playing. Unlike chess, foosball games are not tracked.

Play Foosball: Step right up to the foosball table and start fiddling with the knobs. Right away, Fun is satisfied. Other Sims nearby will automatically join in.

Join Foosball: If other Sims are playing foosball, use this interaction to join in.

Fridge

The fridge is a crucial object for your house -- like a toilet or a bed, it is not complete without one. The fridge is where you store

all of your ingredients for cooking so you can just left-click on it and select a recipe to prepare.

> **TiP**
>
> The higher quality your fridge, the less of a chance your leftovers will taste bad, thus giving you the Tastes Like Fridge negative moodlet.

Have/Serve: This interaction leads to a list of possible recipes. If the recipe requires ingredients not in the fridge, the price of making the dish is listed next to it. The funds are automatically deducted when choosing the recipe to have or serve. Serving a recipe creates a larger set of portions. This takes longer, but results in leftovers which can be eaten later.

Have Quick Meal: Grab a quick meal for free from the fridge. These meals do not boost cooking skills, but do sate hunger.

Eat Leftovers: Eat a serving of leftover dishes in the fridge.

Clean Out Bad Food: After a few days, leftovers go bad. The fridge starts to stink, which makes Sims Disgusted to be around it. Use this interaction to take the food to the trash.

Garden Gnome/Magic Gnome

The garden gnomes are nice little sculptures that add an environmental benefit to any room/area they are in. The Mysterious Mr. Gnome version of the garden gnome has some cool magic tricks it pulls when nobody is looking.

Kick Gnome: Pushing the gnome over with your foot eliminates its environmental bonus.

Stand Up: To restore the gnome, use this interaction.

View: Just bask in the gnome's glow.

Grill

Whether you are using the grill at home or at a community lot like the beach, the grill is great place to gather up friends and have a communal meal. Sims make grill-ready foods on them, like hot dogs and hamburgers.

Grill/Serve: This interaction directs a Sim to the grill and has them start whipping up some grilled delicacies for other Sims to enjoy.

Guitar

- **Play:** This is the common interaction with the guitar and is a good way to start the Guitar skill development cycle. When you get good, the music that comes out of the guitar is quite pleasant and cheers up Sims in the immediate area.

- **Perform:** This interaction lets you pick a specific composition to play.

- **Serenade:** This is a romantic interaction for wooing a would-be partner.

- **Play for Tips:** When a Sim takes a guitar off the lot, they can play for tips. Passing Sims may kick in a few Simoleons depending on the skill of the player.

Harvestable

Harvestables are fruits and vegetables grown from the Gardening skill or bought from the supermarket. Most harvestables are food and can be used to cook recipes. The higher quality the harvestable, the better the dish.

- **Eat:** Eat the harvestable.

- **Pick Up:** Pick up a harvestable from a surface or the ground.

- **Plant:** You can plant any harvestable in the ground to grow it. Once planted, you can water, weed, and care for it with tricks picked up by developing the gardening skill. For more on how to grow harvestables, please see the Gardening skill section of the Simology chapter.

High Chair

The high chair is a special seat for toddlers. Toddlers are happy to sit in the high chair. While a toddler is in a high chair, it cannot catch fire.

- **Put in Chair:** Place a baby in the high chair so it can be fed.

- **Serve Food:** Use this interaction on a baby in a high chair to give it pureed food from the food processor.

- **Give Bottle:** No food processor? No worries. Give the baby a bottle to sate its hunger.

- **Clean:** Babies are messy. Clean the high chair after it has been used.

Hot Beverage Maker

The hot beverage maker is a kitchen object that can only be placed on the counter. The machine makes caffeinated beverages.

- **Serve Hot Beverage:** Use this interaction to create up to six hot drinks for Sims from the machine.

- **Drink Hot Beverage:** Use this interaction to create a single-serving hot drink from the machine. The drink is caffeinated, so it gives Sims the Buzzed moodlet.

CAUTION

Don't drink from the hot beverage maker if you plan on taking a nap anytime soon.

Lights

Sims need light sources in every room so they can see what they are doing. Whether you place a ceiling lamp on the ceiling or a regular lamp on a table, you need to make sure rooms have plenty of light. There are several interactions for lights:

- **Auto-Light:** Set lights in your house to turn on automatically as night approaches.

- **Turn On/Turn Off:** Manually turn on lights in your house. You can choose just the selected light, all lights in a single room, or all lights in a house.

- **Set Color:** Spice up your house by changing the color of the bulb in the light. There are several colors to choose from.

- **Set Intensity:** Change the intensity of the light from dim to normal to bright.

Mailbox

Every household lot has a mailbox out front. Use the mailbox to send and receive mail, including gems and metals that you send away for processing. Don't forget to check the mailbox for bills and pay them regularly.

- **Get Mail:** Get mail sends a Sim to the mailbox to collect whatever the mail carrier brought that day.

- **Pay Bills:** Pay bills to keep the repo man at bay.

- **Donate:** Good Sims can donate to charities and get the Charitable moodlet. Evil Sims can give money to nasty causes and enjoy the Evil moodlet.

Microwave

Like the food processor, the microwave is an optional piece of kitchen equipment that increases the speed of cooking a meal. However, using the microwave does decrease the quality of the food. Having the

microwave adds the frozen meal to the quick meal menu at the fridge.

- **Have/Serve:** Use this interaction on the microwave to make dishes and recipes that can be sped up by using the microwave.

- **Upgrade:** Upgrade the microwave with Faster Cooking to make the object work even faster.

Mirror

The mirror is a common household object with multiple uses, such as working on the Charisma skill. Some mirrors add environmental bonuses to rooms and give the Sim a bit of Fun.

- **Change Appearance:** Use this interaction to change the Sim's outfit.

- **Check Self Out:** Snob Sims love this interaction, but all Sims get a little fun out of checking themselves out.

- **Gussy Up:** Sims who love to check themselves out will walk up to the mirror and start posing. They get the I Am Beautiful moodlet.

- **Play with Mirror:** Young Sims love to play in front of mirrors. They have a lot of fun doing so.

- **Practice Speech:** This interaction practices public speaking and increases the Charisma skill.

Newspaper

Unless directed otherwise, the Newspaper Delivery Service Sim delivers a newspaper every morning. Newspapers can stack up and be a real eyesore, so don't let them accumulate outside the house. Over time, old newspapers darken and look gross. Fresh papers are always bright.

- **Read Newspaper:** Sims will pick up the paper and find a place to sit, if possible. They scan the paper for news and events including discount skill classes.

- **Find Job:** Use this interaction to spot a job listing in the paper. Several job openings are displayed. You can select any of them -- or none if you so choose. Different jobs are offered every day.

- **Clip Coupon:** Frugal Sims can spot deals in the paper for the shops in town.

- **Recycle:** Use this interaction to direct your Sim to place the newspaper in the trash.

hone

he phone which you can buy and install in
our house behaves exactly like the cellphone
your personal inventory. From the phone,
ou can call for services, chat with friends and
cquaintances, start the moving process, and
range a party.

ool

ols are wonderful things to have on your
t, but you can also get the same benefits by
siting one of the community pools in town.
wimming in the pool increases the Athletic
ill, but does lead to the Fatigued moodlet if
u swim for a very long time. Sims no longer
ed a ladder to get in and out of the pool.
hey can get out anywhere if directed.

- **Swim:** This is the basic interaction for a
pool. This directs the Sim to change into a
swimsuit and get in the water.

- **Extinguish Self:** If a Sim is on fire and
near a pool, they can dive in and put out
the flames.

otty Chair

he potty chair is a special toilet for toddlers.
rown Sims can teach a toddler how to use
e bathroom by interacting with the potty
hair. This is an important interaction to teach
necessary skill before the toddler ages up
o child.

- **Potty Train:** Teach the toddler how to use
the potty.

- **Empty:** Empty a used potty chair so it
doesn't smell and disgust other Sims.

- **Use:** Once trained, toddlers can use this
interaction to go to the bathroom all on
their own.

eat

ere are a variety of seats you can buy and
stall on your lot, such as barstools, dining
airs, couches, sofas, loveseats, and desk
airs. Each chair has its own comfort rating,
hich in turn can give Sims a Comfy moodlet.
ms instinctively use seats when eating
reading.

- **Sit:** Direct a Sim to sit down in a chair,
sofa, or some sort of seat.

- **Cuddle:** Two Sims can cuddle up on a
loveseat.

- **Nap:** Sims can take naps on couches and
loveseats and enjoy the same benefits as
napping on a bed or lounge chair.

- **Chat:** Sims can sit down on a sofa or
couch and chat with other Sims also
sitting on the couch.

Seeds

Many harvestables start out as seeds, which
can be planted in the ground and taken care
of until they sprout into bushes and trees that
give off fruit and flowers.

- **Pick Up:** Use this command to pick up a
found seed.

- **Plant/Plant Many:** Use this interaction
to place seeds into the ground in and
around your lot.

> **NOTE**
>
> To learn more about planting seeds
> and gardening, see the Gardening
> skill section of the Simology
> chapter.

Shower

Showers satisfy Hygiene requirements faster
than baths and depending on the quality
of the shower, give a variety of moodlets.
Showers also remove negative Hygiene
moodlets, like Grungy and Smelly. Cheap
showers occasionally give the Cold Shower
moodlet, while expensive showers result in
Exhilarating Shower.

- **Take Shower:** Use this interaction to take
a shower. Sometimes, you receive the
Squeaky Clean moodlet.

- **Clean:** When a shower is dirty, clean it
out.

- **Repair Shower:** If the shower is broken,
you can attempt to repair it instead of
calling a repair technician to take care of it.

- **Put Out Self in Shower:** If a Sim is on fire,
use this interaction to extinguish the flames
in the shower.

- **Upgrade:** Handy Sims can upgrade this
shower so it is Unbreakable or Self-
Cleaning.

> **NOTE**
>
> The Shower Tub combo combines
> the best of the shower and
> bathtub. Sims can take both
> showers and baths and enjoy all
> the different benefits/moodlets.

Sink

Sinks function quite as you might expect.
These objects are good for taking care of
Hygiene needs. In the kitchen, sinks are used
to wash dishes. In the bathroom, they are
used to wash up and brush teeth.

- **Brush Teeth:** This interaction makes Sims
brush their teeth, which in turn gives the
Minty Breath moodlet.

- **Wash Hands:** After using the toilet,
your Sim should use the Wash Hands
interaction to regains some lost Hygiene.

- **Clean:** Dirty sinks need to be cleaned
regularly or else they become disgusting.

- **Repair:** Broken sinks squirt water
everywhere and can lead to puddles.
If a Handy Sim is on the lot, they can
repair the sink. Otherwise, phone a
repair technician.

- **Upgrade:** Handy Sims can upgrade sinks
so they do not break.

Sprinkler

The sprinkler is a great object for gardeners
as this cuts down on the amount of time
needed to water harvestables. Sprinklers have
a large watering radius, which you can see in
Buy Mode when moving it on to your lot.

- **Turn On/Off:** Turn on the sprinkler to start
watering plants. Within a few seconds, the
harvestables are at their maximum needed
water level.

- **Play With:** Sims like to play in the sprinkler.
Use this interaction to direct fun-loving
Sims to the sprinkler so they dance and
play. This satisfies Fun needs.

- **Upgrade:** The sprinkler can be upgraded
to Auto-Water, which takes care of
plants every day without any need for
further interaction.

Stereo

The stereo is a fun object that offers
entertainment to Sims within listening distance,
especially if the stereo is tuned to a station
playing the same kind of music that is the
Sim's favorite. Sims around a stereo get the
Enjoying Music moodlet. If the music favorite
is a match, that moodlet gives a greater mood
boost. The stereo is also used to work on the
Athletic skill via workouts.

- **Turn On/Off:** This interaction turns the
stereo on and off.

- **Change Station:** Use this interaction
to change the station on the stereo.

The stereo stations match the different kinds of music Sims can pick as favorites in Create a Sim.

- **Change Volume:** Adjust the volume of the stereo in case others are sleeping.

- **Workout:** Start working out with the stereo to boost the Athletic skill.

- **Dance:** Dancing to the music coming out of a stereo meets the Fun need. Sims can dance with each other, which improves the current STC.

- **Repair:** If the stereo breaks, a Sim can try to fix it.

- **Upgrade:** There are three stereo upgrades—Make Unbreakable, Soup Up Speakers, and Wire House with Speakers. Make Unbreakable guarantees the stereo will not break down anymore. The Soup Up Speakers increases the Enjoying Music moodlet. Wire House with Speakers lets every room in the house listen to music from a stereo. This can amplify the range of the Enjoying Music moodlet. (It can also wake up sleeping Sims if you aren't mindful.)

Stove

The stove is a critical component of the kitchen if you plan on cooking meals. Without it, making food is almost impossible. The stove is key to boosting the Cooking skill. As the Sim cooks over the stove, the blue skill meter fills. Cheap stoves have a tendency to burn food and catch on fire. The nicer the stove, the better the food, the quicker the food cooks, and the fewer times you need to worry about fire damage.

- **Have/Serve:** This interaction starts cooking a selected recipe.

- **Clean:** Stoves get dirty, so clean them regularly to make sure you serve only the best food.

- **Upgrade:** There are a few upgrades for the stove. The Self-Cleaning upgrade eliminates the need to ever clean the stove again. Improve Cooking Quality is a good way to help a cheap stove make food like an expensive one. Fireproof a stove so it never catches your kitchen on fire.

Swing Set

The swing set is a fun outdoor activity for Sims of all ages. Sims who swing together

get a nice LTR bump for having fun with each other. Sims who Love the Outdoors also get a boost just out of being outside and playing on the swings.

- **Push:** This interaction directs a Sim to push another Sim on the swing and get them started. While pushing another Sim, both have Fun and get an LTR bump.

- **Swing:** A Sim can play on the swings alone to get a little Fun.

Telescope

The telescope is a key object for logical Sims. This object is a little expensive, but worth it for its ability to help develop the Logic skill and bring in money through the Search Galaxy interaction.

- **Look Through/Stargaze:** During the day, Sims look through the telescope. At night, they stargaze. Sims have fun with these activities and get a small Logic skill boost while doing so.

- **Search Galaxy:** Once a Sim reaches Logic skill level 3, they can start searching the galaxy for celestial bodies and make extra cash. Searching the galaxy also raises the skill.

Terrarium

When you bring an insect home (butterfly, beetle) and drag them from your personal inventory to a surface, they are automatically placed inside a terrarium. Here, the bug lives until you decide to release it, if ever. Terrariums increase the environmental rating of a room, too. The rarer the bug, the more it adds to a room.

- **Watch:** Enjoy watching the bug in the terrarium -- it's relaxing.

- **Give Name:** Name your bugs.

- **Release:** Set the bug free.

Toilet

- **Use:** To relieve the Bladder need, use the toilet. The Sim sits down and takes care of business without any further assistance.

- **Flush:** Once the Sim has finished going to the toilet, flush. Please. Sometimes, flushes result in clogged toilets and puddles.

- **Clean:** When the toilet gets dirty—which is often, especially on cheap toilets—Sims must clean it. Otherwise, they get Disgusted when they see it.

- **Unclog:** When a toilet gets clogged up, Sims can try to unclog it on their own. Handy Sim have a better shot at success.

- **Upgrade:** Make Self-Cleaning fixes up a toilet so Sims no longer have to clean it. Make Uncloggable eliminates the need to ever have to repair the toilet again.

Tombstone/Marker/Urn

When Sims die and the grim reaper takes them away, they leave behind a grave marker or urn for their remains. Sims can carve an epitaph on it or mourn over it. Sims can also pick up the marker and keep it with them or take it to another lot (such the graveyard).

- **Engrave:** Chisel a nice epitaph to a Sim who now sees the shadows behind the skies.

- **Pick Up:** Pick up the marker and place it personal inventory.

- **Mourn:** Weep and wail over the death o a loved one.

Toys

Children and toddlers have a variety of toys they can play with to keep busy and satisfy Fun. The stuffed bear can be carried around for Fun or remove the Lonely moodlet. If Sim sleep with the bear, they get the Cuddle Time moodlet. The toy xylophone is fun to play with. Baking with the toy oven actually gives kids a head-start on the Cooking skill. Cakes cooked in the toy oven give the Good Meal moodlet. Up to four Children can play with the activity table.

Trash

Trash bags are real eye sores and they can lead to negative moodlets. Be sure to get rid of trash bags by dragging them into trashcan either inside your house or to the trashcan near the curb outside.

Trashcans and Compactors

Every household lot has a trashcan outside o the house. Sims in the Journalism career can sift through the trash to get the necessary dir to write a report. There are interior trashcans and compactors for taking care of garbage inside the house.

- **Empty:** When the interior trashcan gets smelly, empty it into the trashcan outside

- **Rummage:** Want to check out your neighbors' trash? Use the rummage interaction on another lot's trashcan to do through it. Who knows what you might find?

- **Repair Compactor:** If you have a compactor and it breaks, use this

interaction to attempt a repair. Handy Sims have a greater chance of success.

◆ **Upgrade:** Handy Sims can upgrade the interior trash compactor so it can take more trash before needing to be emptied. They can also upgrade it to Unbreakable.

Treadmill

The treadmill is one of two pieces of exercise equipment you can install on your lot, but it is also available at the gym for free. Working out on the treadmill lowers your Hygiene, so make sure you have time for a shower after using it.

◆ **Work Out:** Directs the Sims to the treadmill. While on the treadmill, you can set the tone for the actual workout. Any moodlets related to the kind of exercise are earned, such as Fatigued, Sore, and Pumped.

◆ **Train:** If the Sim has the ability to train another Sim in Athletics (level 6), use this interaction to train a Sim on the treadmill.

TV

The television is, as they say, a necessary evil. With the exception of the Technophobe, Sims love to watch TV. They enjoy vegging out with their favorite shows, flipping channels to find something that tickles their fancy. There are a few education channels on the TV that increase skills, such as Cooking and Gardening. But a number of different traits are also well served by the TV, depending on whether or not it has a lot of channels. Cheap TVs only have a few channels. Expensive TVs have all of the possible channels. Here is the channel break down by the level of television:

1: Romantic Rendezvous: Over-Emotional and Hopeless Romantic Sims get a boost out of this channel.

1: KidZ Zone: Children love to watch this station—as do Childish adult Sims.

1: Action World: Excitable, Daredevil, and Party Animal Sims like this channel.

1: Sports Universe: Athletic Sims like this station.

2: Got Garden?: Green-Thumb, Vegetarian, and Loves the Outdoors Sims like this channel. It also boosts the Gardening skill.

2: Cookin' Cable: The Cooking skill is boosted by this channel. Natural Cook and Couch Potato Sims like this channel, too.

2: Terror TV: Neurotic, Coward, and Over-Emotional Sims actually get Scared by this channel.

3: Fishing Fracas: The Fishing skill is boosted by this channel. Angler Sims and Loves the Outdoors Sims enjoy this channel.

4: Super Shopping: This is the top channel you can get on TV. It provides a lot of fun.

Here are the TV interactions:

◆ **Turn On/Off:** This interaction turns the TV on and off. Turning the TV off when somebody else is watching it is considered rude.

◆ **Watch TV:** Plop down in front of the TV and just start watching.

◆ **Change Channel:** Pick a channel from the selection your TV gets.

◆ **Workout with TV:** Watch an workout show and exercise along with it to boost your Athletic skill.

◆ **Repair TV:** If the TV breaks, you can try to fix it. If you don't have a high Handiness skill, you may fail and get a nasty shock.

◆ **Sabotage:** Technophobe Sims can purposefully break a TV.

◆ **Upgrade:** The Make Unbreakable upgrade prevents the TV from breaking. The Boost Channels upgrade raises the TV up to the next tier of channels. This only works once per TV. You cannot take the cheapest TV all the way up to HD.

> ## Tip
> Watching the top TVs in high-def gives the Pristine Picture moodlet.

Videogame System

Videogames are a great way to blow off steam and escape from the hustle of the real world. (Hey, we don't have to tell you that, right?) Videogames are not cheap, but they offer a lot of Fun. Videogame systems must be placed near a TV to be useful.

◆ **Play Videogames:** This is a fun interaction that satisfies a Sim's need for leisure.

◆ **Adventure:** This interaction works on the goggles system. There are three kinds of VR adventures to take: action, fantasy, and sci-fi.

You actually play along with your Sim on the adventure, guiding them through choices that appear on-screen.

Window

Houses need windows to let in natural light and just look attractive. There is just one interaction Sims can have with windows.

◆ **Look In Window:** Teens and older can use this interaction to walk up to a neighbor's house and peer through the windows. This lets you see inside the house. If the owner of that house spots you peeking, they shoo you away and your LTR takes a hit.

Workout Bench

The workout bench is a weight system that increases strength training. This piece of equipment can be bought in Buy Mode and found at the local gym.

◆ **Work Out:** Directs the Sims to the exercise bench. While on the bench, you can set the tone for the actual workout. Any moodlets related to the kind of exercise are earned, such as Fatigued, Sore, and Pumped.

◆ **Train:** If the Sim has the ability to train another Sim in Athletics (level 6), use this interaction to train a Sim on the workout bench.

Sharing with the World

The Sims 3 features a robust online experience for taking your Sims well beyond the city limits of Sunset Valley. From The Game Launcher that starts to game to *The Sims 3* site where you can build your own profile pages and share movies of your Sims, *The Sims 3* is loaded with easy-to-use toolsets.

The Game Launcher

When you start up *The Sims 3*, you open a launcher. The left side of The Game Launcher features a giant "Play" button that begins the game. However, below the button is a collection of additional buttons that turn The Game Launcher into much more than a way to start the game. The default view of The Game Launcher is Welcome, which shows you what's new in the world of *The Sims 3*.

From The Game Launcher screen, you can store and upload all content shared from the game, including screenshots, videos, patterns, clothing and accessory styles, wall and floor styles, object styles, Sims households, and lots.

From the Welcome screen, you can see new objects and clothing that are being offered in The Store (which uses virtual SimPoints) and The Exchange, which is where other players upload their creations to share with the rest of *The Sims 3* community. News about the game is noted on the Welcome screen, too.

The Downloads button launches the Downloads screen, which is where objects and items you select from The Store and The Exchange appear. Here, you can easily install all downloaded content into your game. Just check the box next to the item you want installed into your game and click the Install button.

Community

• • •

> ### NOTE
> You will need to exit your game if you try to install while *The Sims 3* is running.

> ### NOTE
> You must be a registered user to upload and download items for *The Sims 3*.

The Uploads button takes you to a springboard for uploading your custom content to The Exchange. From The Game Launcher screen, you can share screenshots and video taken with the Camera tool. (More on this in a moment.) Custom patterns and decorated objects can also be uploaded to The Exchange here, too. These uploaded items are featured on your My Page and My Studio.

Wait, what's a My Page?

My Page

Each registered user gets their very own My Page site, which is their online profile for connecting and sharing with other *The Sims 3* players. You can customize your My Page with an avatar created and shared from Create a Sim, post blog entries detailing your experiences inside the game (or just air some thoughts), and share screens and video with other community members.

> ### TIP
> The My Page has a friends list for keeping tabs on your favorite *The Sims 3* players.

The My Studio column on the left side of your My Page is where content you have uploaded appears so you can keep track of it and manage it for sharing. Lots, Sims, and a of your uploaded content appear over here so other players can click on them and then go straight to The Exchange where they can download your shared stuff.

> ### NOTE
> Content in My Studio can be shared with popular social networks like Facebook, MySpace, and more.

Your profile page also shows which items you have tagged as favorites in The Exchange. This lets other players see the kind of stuff you are interested in and what you might have downloaded and installed into your game.

The Exchange and The Store

The Exchange is where content created by other *The Sims 3* players is shared. On this page, you can scroll through highlighted objects, Sims, and lots. You can also can dig deeper into The Exchange and  follow an object listing into a My Page and se what other content the player has to offer. The categories of content that can be shared in The Exchange include:

◆ Objects   ◆ Clothing
◆ Sims   ◆ Hair Color
◆ Lots   ◆ Accessories
◆ Households   ◆ Patterns

he Exchange keeps a running tab on the
ost popular downloads in each category
nd features them in the center of the
age. To the right of the Top Downloads
re related items from The Store, which is
nother destination for content that can be
ownloaded into your game.

SHARING YOUR CONTENT

In order to share content
with *The Sims 3*
community, you need to
create something first.
Inside one of the Create tools, such as
Create a Sim, you have the option to
customize a pattern or style and then
save it as a style. To view only custom
content, click the "*" button. Here,
you only see saved or downloaded
custom hairstyles. To prepare content
for upload inside *The Sims 3*, simply
click the ✱ button. Enter a name and
description that will appear on The
Exchange. It's a great idea to provide
keywords or other important
information in the description. Now it
is stored in The Game Launcher so
you can easily upload it to The
Exchange and your My Studio.

Your saved custom content appears
in the interface with a folder icon.
Custom content downloaded from
The Exchange appears with a "*"
icon. Official downloaded content
appears with a plumbob icon.

he Store
where
fficial
ontent is
ollected
d offered
The Sims
players for
ownload
d installation into your game. The Store
orks a bit differently from The Exchange.
any of the categories of content are
e same, but to download content from
e Store requires SimPoints, which are a
tual currency.

NOTE

For more details on SimPoints,
please see the documentation that
came with your copy of *The Sims 3*
or the *store.thesims3.com* website.

Movies & More

In addition
to sharing
content
created
in Create
a Sim and
Create
a Style
(as well
as your Sims, households, walls and floors,
objects, and entire lots), you can also share
the screenshots and videos you take inside
the game. To take a screenshot of the current
activity, just press ⓒ. The camera flashes
and the screenshot is saved to The Game
Launcher. (Taking a screenshot strips out the
user interface by default. You can adjust these
settings and other media settings from the
game Options panel.) To take a video clip
inside the game, press ⓥ. Immediately, the
camera starts recording the on-screen action.
You can set whether or not you want the have
the UI on-screen in the Options tab. To stop
recording, press ⓥ again. Like screenshots,
your video is saved to the Uploads tab of
The Game Launcher.

TIP

For best results, keep your clips to
5–10 seconds.

While recording a video, press Tab to
unlock the camera and enjoy greater
freedom to set up amazing shots.

Once you have finished recording your video
clips and taken your screens, upload them
to your My Studio via The Game Launcher.
Now, log back on to *The Sims 3* site via your
web browser and check out the Movies &
More tab. This tab contains a movie studio
for editing those clips into a movie, adding
special transitions such as wipe and dissolve,
slapping captions on top of the action,
and finishing it off with a soundtrack. (The
soundtrack comes from clips in the Movies &
More tool. You cannot use your own music.)

To create a mashup video, just drag the saved
clips and screens into an on-screen viewer to
preview the clip and set it up in the timeline

of your
movie. Drag
transitions
between
the clips
to instantly
preview
them. The
Text tool lets

you add subtitles to scenes and even further
explain the action or just add a snarky running
commentary on the plight of the Sims in the
video. You can even place filters over the
clips to make them look like old-timey flicks or
cast entire scenes in favored hue.

Once
you have
assembled
the video,
it's simple
to save and
share with
community,
or publish it
privately so

TIP

In cameraman mode,
you can zoom in and
around landscapes
and Sims to get artful
close-ups or broad
establishing shots.

only you can see it. Saved movies can be
further edited by going to your My Studio,
selecting the movie and clicking the Edit link.
The Video tool is one of the most exciting
new features in *The Sims 3*. We cannot wait
to see what you all come up with—and, who
knows? Perhaps we'll put up a few videos of
our own, too!

SHARING VIDEOS ONLINE

You're ready to share your
masterpieces with the world. But be
aware of file size limitations before you
shoot your epic. *The Sims 3* Exchange
supports a maximum file size of 1 GB
per video clip. If you record at the
"Medium" size (640 x 480) and "High"
quality, you should be able to record
approximately 20 minutes of footage
and still be within the 1 GB limit. If you
have changed the in-game capture
settings to record uncompressed
video, the resulting files can exceed
the 1 GB limit quickly.

This is important for players using Mac
OS X: Videos recorded in *The Sims 3*
use the VP6 codec. Apple users can
view their videos with a plug-in like
Perian available at
http://www.apple.com/downloads.

Custom Vine Pattern*

Apply the exclusive Fluid Vines pattern to any item—from outfits to weight machines to cars and more—or choose to customize your pattern even further in Create a Style!

Here's how to get your EXCLUSIVE Style Pattern:

1. Install your The Sims 3 game first!

2. Register your game with The Sims 3 Community if you haven't already. Go to **www.thesims3.com/register** or click the "Sign Up Now" button in the Game Launcher.

3. To download your exclusive item, Go to **www.thesims3.com/vinespattern** and just follow the onscreen instructions.

Now you're ready to customize everything with your new style pattern!

To download this code, please go to the following link and enter in your Fluid Vines code listed below.

URL: **www.thesims3.com/vinepattern**
Downloadable Code:
Fluid Vines: 75GNR32P

* Requires The Sims 3 game software. Downloadable code expires December 31, 2009. Code redemption requires EA Online Account and online game registration with serial code enclosed with The Sims 3. EA Online Terms & Conditions can be found at www.ea.com. You must be 13+ to register for an EA Online Account. MAC users must update to the latest version of The Sims 3 launcher to access online services and/or features. Offer may not be substituted, transferred, exchanged, sold or redeemed for cash or other goods or services. Valid only in the U.S. and Canada. May not be combined with any other offer, gift card, rebate or discount coupon. Void where prohibited, taxed or restricted by law.